Francis A. Drexel
LIBRARY

Books For College Libraries
Third Edition

Core Collection

A

PHILOSOPHICAL AND POLITICAL

HISTORY

OF THE

SETTLEMENTS AND TRADE

OF THE

EUROPEANS

IN THE

EAST AND WEST INDIES.

———

REVISED, AUGMENTED, AND PUBLISHED,

IN TEN VOLUMES,

BY THE ABBE RAYNAL.

———

NEWLY TRANSLATED FROM THE FRENCH,

BY J. O. JUSTAMOND, F. R. S.

WITH A

New Set of Maps adapted to the Work, and a copious Index.

IN SIX VOLUMES.

VOL. V.

SECOND EDITION.

NEGRO UNIVERSITIES PRESS
NEW YORK

Originally published in 1798
by J. Mundell & Co., London

Reprinted 1969 by
Negro Universities Press
A DIVISION OF GREENWOOD PUBLISHING CORP.
NEW YORK

Library of Congress Catalogue Card Number 69-18996

SBN 8371-1555-8

CONTENTS

VOL. V.

BOOK XIV.

Page.

SETTLEMENT of the English in the American Islands, — 1

The state of England when she began to form settlements in
the American islands, - - 2
Causes which hastened the population of the British islands, 3
By what men the British islands were peopled, - 10
Under what form of government the British islands were esta-
blished. - - - 11
Means employed by the mother-country to secure to itself all
the productions of the islands, - - 14
Diminution of the advantages which England derived from
its islands. Cause of it, - - 16
The English form a settlement at Barbadoes. Great prosperi-
ty of this island, - - - 17
Conspiracy formed by the slaves in Barbadoes, - 18
Present state of Barbadoes, - 19
Is Barbadoes capable of making a good defence, - 21
Events that have happened at Antigua. Productions and ex-
pences of that island. The importance of it to Great Britain, 22
State of the settlement formed by the English at Montserrat, 25
Ancient manners, and present state of the island of Nevis, 26
St. Christopher's, which is at first divided between the English
and French, at last belongs entirely to Great Britain, 27
What St. Christopher's became under the British government, 28
Wretched catastrophes that have happened at St. Christopher's, 29
Particularities concerning Barbuda, - - 32
The colony of Anguilla is very wretched, and its fate cannot
be changed, - - - 33
Tortola is the only one of the Virgin Islands which the En-
glish have cultivated. The government censured, - 34
Description of Jamaica, - - - 34
The Spaniards discover Jamaica, and settle there some time
after, - - - 36
Jamaica is conquered by the English. Events that have hap-
pened in the island since they have become masters of it, 38
Cultures established in Jamaica, - - 45

                                                              Page.
Prefent ftate of Jamaica, confidered in every point of view,   49
Means which Jamaica hath to preferve herfelf from invafion,   53
Advantages of Jamaica for war,   -   -   61
Its difadvantages for navigation,   -   62
Revolutions which have happened in the Lucaya iflands. State
    of thefe iflands,   -   -   -   63
Poverty of the Bermudas. Character of the inhabitants,   65
Granada was firft occupied by the French. What the firft co-
    lonifts did there,   -   -   -   68
Events which have happened at Granada fince it is fallen un-
    der the Britifh government,   -   -   71
Cultures of Granada, and of the Granadines,   -   73
The ifland of Tobago, which was the caufe of great difputes
    between the Dutch and the French, becomes a Britifh pof-
    feffion,   -   -   -   -   74
Plan for clearing the American iflands,   -   78
Misfortunes which the Englifh have fuffered at Tobago, for
    having deviated from the maxims which we have juft laid
    down,   -   -   -   -   80
Hiftory of the favages of St. Vincent,   -   ib.
The arrival of the French at St. Vincent raifes difputes be-
    tween the red and black Caribs,   -   82
St. Vincent falls into the hands of the Englifh. State of the
    ifland under their dominion,   -   -   85
Great Britain takes poffeffion of Dominica,   -   88
Difturbances between the Englifh of Dominica and the French
    of the neighbouring iflands,   -   -   90
In what confifts the importance of Dominica,   -   92
Laws peculiar to Dominica,   -   -   93
Plan conceived by the Britifh miniftry, to render flourifhing
    the three iflands which were formerly neutral,   - 95
Obftacles which have prevented the profperity of the neutral
    iflands,   -   -   -   -   98
Prefent ftate of the Englifh iflands,   -   - 99
Summary of the riches that Europe draws from the Ameri-
    can iflands,   -   -   -   106
The beft mode to be adopted for increafing the productions
    of the American Archipelago,   -   -   107
What will be the fate of the American iflands hereafter, 109

BOOK XV.

Settlements of the French in North America. Upon what Ba-
    fis was founded the Hope of their Profperity. Confequence
    of the Settlements,   -   -   -   113

Reafons which prevented the French for a long time from
    purfuing the plan of forming fettlements in the New World, ib.

Page.

Errors and misfortunes which rendered memorable the firſt
    expeditions of the French in the New Hemiſphere,   115
The French turn their views towards Canada,   -   120
Government, cuſtoms, virtues, vices, and wars, of the ſavages
    that inhabited Canada,   -   -   122
The French imprudently take a part in the wars of the ſa-
    vages,   -   -   -   151
The French ſettlement makes no progreſs. The cauſe of
    this,   -   -   -   154
The French are rouſed from their inactivity. Means by which
    this change was effected,   -   -   157
The furs are the foundation of the connections between the
    French and the Indians,   -   -   163
Figure of the beavers. Their diſpoſition and form of govern-
    ment,   -   -   -   167
In what places, and in what manner, the fur trade was car-
    ried on,   -   -   -   177
France is compelled to cede part of the provinces that were
    united to Canada,   -   -   184

BOOK XVI.

*A new Order of things is eſtabliſhed in the French Colonies in
    North America. Reſult of theſe Arrangements,*   -   186

The French, to recover their former loſſes, people and for-
    tify Cape-Breton; and eſtabliſh conſiderable fiſheries there, 187
Settlement of the French in the iſland of St. John. Tendency
    of this undertaking,   -   -   194
Diſcovery of the Miſſiſſippi by the French,   -   196
The French ſettle in the country that is watered by the Miſ-
    ſiſſippi, and call it Louiſiana,   -   -   200
Louiſiana becomes very famous in the time of Law's ſyſtem.
    Reaſon of this,   -   -   -   201
Extent, ſoil, and climate of Louiſiana,   -   -   207
General character of the ſavages of Louiſiana, and of the Nat-
    chez in particular,   -   -   -   211
Settlements formed by the French in Louiſiana,   -   217
France might have derived great advantages from Louiſiana.
    Faults that have impeded this ſucceſs,   -   223
The French miniſtry cede Louiſiana to Spain. Had they a
    right to do it,   -   -   -   -   233
Conduct of the Spaniards at Louiſiana,   -   239
State of Canada at the peace of Utrecht,   -   241
Population of Canada, and diſtribution of its inhabitants,   242
Manners of the French Canadians,   -   247
Form of government eſtabliſhed in Canada. Impediments
    which cultivation, induſtry, and fiſhing, experienced from
    it,   -   -   -   249

Taxes levied in Canada. Expences of the ministry in that country. Manner in which they were paid. To what excess they were carried, and how they were got rid of, 253

Advantages which France might have derived from Canada, 255

Difficulties which France had to overcome, in order to derive advantages from Canada, 260

Origin of the wars between the English and the French in Canada, 262

Conquest of Cape-Breton by the English, 263

The English attack Canada. They at first experience great misfortunes there. Causes of them, 267

Taking of Quebec by the English. The conquest of this capital brings on in time the surrender of the whole colony, 272

Hath the acquisition of Canada been advantageous or prejudicial to England, 276

BOOK XVII.

English Colonies settled at Hudson's Bay, Canada, the Island of St. John, Newfoundland, Nova-Scotia, New-England, New-York, and New-Jersey, 278

First expeditions of the English in North America, ib.

The continent of America is peopled in consequence of the religious wars that disturb England, 282

Parallel between the Old and the New World, 289

Comparison between civilized people and savages, 297

The state in which the English found North America, and what they have done there, 302

Climate of Hudson's Bay, and customs of its inhabitants. Trade carried on there, 303

Whether there be a passage from Hudson's Bay to the East Indies, 310

Hath the passage from Hudson's Bay to the East Indies been properly searched for, 315

State of Canada since it hath been under the dominion of Great Britain, 317

What is become of the islands of St. John, of Magdalen, and of Cape Breton, since they have been subject to the British government, 323

Description of the island of Newfoundland, 325

At what period, and in what manner, the English and French have settled at Newfoundland, ib.

It is the cod fish alone which renders Newfoundland of importance. Present state of this fishery, divided into wandering and stationary fishery, 329

Sketch of Nova Scotia. The French settle there. Their conduct in this settlement, 344

Page.

France is compelled to cede Nova Scotia to England,   347

Manners of the French who remained subject to the English government in Nova Scotia,   - -   348

Present state of Nova Scotia,   - -   353

Foundation of New England,   - -   355

Form of government established at New England,   -   357

Fanaticism occasions great calamities in New England,   358

Extent, natural history, fisheries, population, cultures, manufactures, and exportations of New England,   -   366

The Dutch found the colony of New Belgia, afterwards called New York,   - - -   374

At what period, and in what manner, the English make themselves masters of New Belgia,   - -   375

The colony is ceded to the Duke of York. Principles upon which he founded its administration,   -   377

King William gives a government to this colony. Events previous to this new arrangement,   -   379

Soil, population, and commerce of the colony,   -   381

Ancient and modern manners of New York,   -   383

Revolutions which have happened in New Jersey,   -   384

Present state of New Jersey, and what it may become,   386

A

PHILOSOPHICAL AND POLITICAL

HISTORY

OF THE

SETTLEMENTS AND TRADE

OF THE

EUROPEANS

IN THE

EAST AND WEST INDIES.

BOOK XIV.

Settlement of the English in the American Islands.

A NEW order of things now opens itself to our
view. England is, in modern hiftory, the country of
great political phenomena. It is there that we have
feen liberty the moft violently combating with defpotifm, fometimes trampled under its feet, at other times
victorious in its turn. It is there that its triumph has
been completed; which every thing, even the fanaticifm of religion, hath concurred in bringing about.
There it is, that one king, juridically brought to the
fcaffold, and another depofed, with his whole race, by
the decree of the nation, have given a great leffon to
the earth. There it is, that in the midft of civil commotions, and in the intervals of momentary tranquillity, we have feen the exact and deep fciences carried
to their greateft perfection; we have feen the minds
of men accuftomed to reafon, to reflect, and to turn
their attention particularly to government. It is there,

B O O K in a word, that, after long and violent ftruggles, that
XIV. conftitution hath been formed, which, if it be not perfect, and free from all inconveniencies, is, at leaft, the
moft happily fuited to the fituation of the country;
the moft favourable to its trade; the beft calculated
to unfold genius, eloquence, and all the powers of the
human mind; the only conftitution, perhaps, fince
man hath lived in a focial ftate, where the laws have
fecured to him his dignity, his perfonal liberty, and his
freedom of thought; where, in a word, they have
made him a citizen, that is to fay, a conftituent and
integral part of the conftitution of the ftate and of the
nation.

The ftate   England had not yet difplayed to the world this
of England great fcene, when her fettlements in the Archipelago
when fhe
began to of America were firft begun. Her agriculture was
form fettle- not extended either to flax or hemp. The attempts
ments in
the Ameri- that had been made to raife mulberry-trees, and breed
can iflands. filk-worms, had been unfuccefsful. The labours of
the hufbandman were wholly engaged in the growing
of corn, which, notwithftanding the turn of the nation for rural employments, was feldom fufficient for
home confumption, and many of their granaries were
ftored from the fields bordering on the Baltic.

Induftry was ftill lefs advanced than agriculture. It
was confined to woollen manufactures. Thefe had
been increafed fince the exportation of unwrought
wool had been prohibited; but thefe iflanders, who,
feemed to work only for themfelves, were ignorant of
the method of fpreading thofe elegant ornaments upon
their ftuffs, which tafte contrived, to promote the fale
and confumption of them. They fent their cloths
over to Holland, where the Dutch gave them their
colouring and glofs; from whence they circulated all
over Europe, and were even brought back to England.

Navigation fcarce employed, at that time, ten thoufand failors. Thefe were in the fervice of exclufive
companies, which had engroffed every branch of trade,
not excepting that of woollen cloth, which alone con-

ftituted a tenth part of the commercial riches of the B O O K
nation. Thefe, therefore, were centered in the hands XIV.
of three or four hundred perfons, who agreed, for
their own advantage, to fix the price of goods, both at
going out and coming into the kingdom. The privileges of thefe monopolizers were exercifed in the capital, where the court fold the provinces. London
alone had fix times the number of fhips that all the
other ports of England had.

The public revenue neither was nor could be very
confiderable. It was farmed out ; a ruinous method,
which has preceded the eftablifhment of the finance in
all ftates, but has only been continued under arbitrary
governments. The expences were proportionable to
the low ftate of the treafury. The fleet was fmall,
and the fhips fo weak, that in times of neceffity the
merchantmen were turned into men of war. A hundred and fixty thoufand militia, which was the whole
military ftrength of the nation, were armed in time of
war. There were no ftanding forces in time of peace,
and the king himfelf had no guards.

With fuch confined powers at home, the nation
fhould not have ventured to extend itfelf in fettlements
abroad. Notwithftanding this, fome colonies were
eftablifhed, which laid a folid foundation of profperity.
The origin of thefe fettlements was owing to certain
events, the caufes of which may be traced very far
back.

Whoever is acquainted with the hiftory and progrefs Caufes
of the Englifh government, knows that the regal au- which haft-
thority was for a long time balanced only by a fmall population
number of great proprietors of land called Barons. of the Bri-
They perpetually oppreffed the people, the greater tifh iflands.
part of whom were degraded by flavery; and they
were conftantly ftruggling againft the power of the
crown, with more or lefs fuccefs, according to the character of the leading men, and the chance of circumftances. Thefe political diffenfions occafioned much
bloodfhed.

The kingdom was exhaufted by inteftine wars, which

4

BOOK
XIV.
had lafted two hundred years, when Henry VII. affumed the reins of government on the decifion of a
battle in which the nation, divided into two camps,
had fought to give itfelf a mafter. That able prince
availed himfelf of the ftate of depreffion into which a
feries of calamities had funk his fubjects, to extend the
regal authority, the limits of which, the anarchy of
the feudal government, though continually encroaching upon them, had never been able to fix. He was
affifted in this undertaking by the faction which had
placed the crown upon his head, and which, being the
weakeft, could not hope to maintain itfelf in the principal employments to which thofe who were engaged
in it had been raifed, unlefs they fupported the ambition of their leader. This plan was ftrengthened, by
permitting the nobility, for the firft time, to alienate
their lands. This dangerous indulgence, joined to a
tafte for luxury, which then began to prevail in Europe, brought on a great revolution in the fortunes of
individuals. The immenfe fiefs of the barons were
gradually diffipated, and the eftates of the commoners
increafed.

The rights belonging to the feveral eftates being divided with the property of them, it became fo much
the more difficult to unite the will and the power of
many againft the authority of one. The monarchs
took advantage of this period, fo favourable to their
ambition, to govern without controul. The decayed
nobility were in fear of a power which they had reinforced with all their loffes. The commons thought
themfelves fufficiently honoured by the privilege of
impofing all the national taxes. The people, in fome
degree eafed of their yoke, by this flight alteration in
the conftitution, and whofe circle of ideas is always
confined to bufinefs or labour, became tired of fedi-
tions, from the defolation and miferies which were the
confequence and the punifhment of them. So that,
while the nation was employed in fearch of that fovereign authority which had been loft in the confufion of
civil wars, its views were fixed upon the monarch

alone.   The majesty of the throne, the whole lustre of
which was centered in him, seemed to be the source
of that authority, of which it should only be the visible
sign and permanent instrument.

Such was the situation of England, when James I.
was called thither from Scotland, as being sole heir to
the two kingdoms, which, by his accession, were united under one head.   A turbulent nobility, imparting
their fury to their barbarous vassals, had kindled the
fire of sedition in those northern mountains which divided the island into two distinct states.   The monarch
had, from his earliest years, been as averse from limited authority, as the people were from despotism and
absolute monarchy, which then prevailed all over Europe ; and, as the new king was equal to other sovereigns, it was natural that he should be ambitious of
the same power.   His predecessors had enjoyed it,
even in England, for a century past.   But he was not
aware that they owed it to their own political abilities, or to favourable circumstances.   This religious
prince, who believed he held all from God and nothing from men, fancied that strength of reason, wis-
dom, and council, was centered in himself, and seemed to arrogate to himself that infallibility of which the
pope had been deprived by the reformation, the tenets of which he adopted, though he disliked them.
These false principles, which tended to change government into a mystery of religion, the more odious,
as it equally influences the opinions, wills, and actions
of men, were so rooted in his mind, together with all
the other prejudices of a bad education, that he did
not even think of supporting them with any of the
human aids of prudence or force.

Nothing could be more repugnant to the general
disposition of the people than this system.   All was in
commotion both at home and abroad.   The discovery
of America had hastened the advancement of Europe.
Navigation extended round the whole globe.   The
mutual intercourse of nations would soon have removed prejudices, and opened the door to industry

B O O K and knowledge. The mechanical and liberal arts
XIV. were extended, and were advancing to perfection by
the luxury that prevailed. Literature acquired the
ornaments of tafte ; and the fciences gained that degree of folidity which fprings from a fpirit of calculation and commerce. The circle of politics was extended. This univerfal ferment exalted the ideas of
men. The feveral bodies which compofed the mon-
ftrous coloffus of Gothic government, roufed from that
lethargic ftate of ignorance in which they had been
funk for many ages, foon began to exert themfelves
on all fides, and to form enterprifes. On the continent, where mercenary troops had been adopted, under pretence of maintaining difcipline, moft princes
acquired an unlimited authority, oppreffing their fubjects either by force or intrigue. In England, the
love of liberty, fo natural to every feeling or thinking
man, excited in the people by the authors of religious
innovations, and awakened in the minds of men, enlightened by becoming converfant with the great writers of antiquity, who derived from their democratic
government that fublimity of reafon and fentiment by
which they are diftinguifhed ; this love of liberty kindled in every generous breaft the utmoft abhorrence
for unlimited authority. The afcendant which Elizabeth found means to acquire and to preferve, by an
uninterrupted profperity of forty years, withheld this
impatience, or turned it to enterprifes that were bene-
ficial to the ftate. But no fooner did another branch
afcend the throne, and the fceptre devolved to a monarch, who, by the very violence of his pretenfions,
was not much to be dreaded, than the nation afferted
its rights, and entertained the ambitious thoughts of
governing itfelf.

It was at this period that warm difputes arofe between the court and the parliament. Both powers
feemed to be making trial of their ftrength by continual oppofition. The prince pretended, that an entire
paffive obedience was due to him ; and that national
affemblies were only the ornaments, not the bafis, of

the conftitution. The citizens loudly exclaimed a- gainft thefe principles, always weak when they come to be difcuffed ; and maintained, that the people were an effential part of government, as well as the monarch, and, perhaps, in a higher degree. The one is the matter, the other the form. Now, the form may, and muft change, for the prefervation of the matter. The fupreme law is the welfare of the people, not that of the prince ; the king may die, the monarchy may be at an end, and fociety fubfift without either monarch or throne. In this manner the Englifh reafoned at the dawn of liberty. They quarrelled, they oppofed, and threatened each other. James died in the midft of thefe debates, leaving his fon to difcufs his rights, with the refolution of extending them.

The experience of all ages has fhown, that the ftate of tranquillity which follows the eftablifhment of abfolute power, occafions a coolnefs in the minds of the people, damps their courage, cramps their genius, and throws a whole nation into an univerfal lethargy. But let us explain the fucceffive progreffion of this mifery; and let the people be acquainted with the profound ftate of annihilation into which they are funk, or with which they are menaced.

As foon as the great object, which men only view with fear and trembling, hath been raifed up in the midft of the nation, the fubjects are divided into two claffes. One of them keeps at a diftance, from fear; the other approaches this object, from ambition ; and the latter flatters itfelf with fecurity, from the confcioufnefs of its meannefs. It forms, between the defpot and the reft of the nation, an order of fubaltern tyrants, not lefs fufpicious, and more cruel, than their mafter. One hears nothing from them but thefe words : The king hath faid it ; it is the king's pleafure ; I have feen the king ; I have fupped with the king ; it is the king's intention. Thefe words are always liftened to with aftonifhment ; and they are foon confidered as the orders of the fovereign. Should there be any energy remaining, it is among the military,

BOOK whofe fenfe of their own importance only ferves to
XIV. make them more infolent. What part doth the prieft
act in this conjuncture? If he be in favour, he com-
pletes the flavifhnefs and degeneracy of the people by
his example and by his difcourfes : if he be neglected,
he grows out of humour, becomes factious, and feeks
out fome fanatic, who will facrifice himfelf to his
views. In all parts where there are no fixed laws, no
juftice, no unalterable forms, no real property, the influence of the magiftrate is little or nothing ; he waits
only for a fignal to become whatever one may choofe.
The great nobleman cringes before the prince, and the
people cringe before the great nobleman. The natural dignity of man is eclipfed ; and he hath not the
leaft idea of his rights. Around the defpot, his agents
and his favourites, the fubjects are crufhed under foot,
with the fame inadvertence that we crufh the infects
which fwarm among the duft of our fields. The morals are become corrupt. There comes a time when
the moft inordinate vexations, and the moft unheard-
of outrages, lofe their atrocious character, and no longer excite horror. Any one who fhould pronounce the
names of virtue, of patriotifm, and of equity, would
only be confidered as a man of too much warmth ; an
expreffion which always implies an abject indulgence
of crimes by which we profit. The body of the nation becomes diffolute and fuperftitious; for defpotifm
cannot be eftablifhed without the interference of fuperftition, nor be maintained without its fupport; and
fervitude leads on to debauchery, which affords fome
relief to the mind, and is never fuppreffed. Men of
information, if there be any of them remaining, have
their views ; they pay their court to the great, and
profefs the religion of policy. Tyranny, leading on
in its train a number of fpies and informers, thefe are
confequently to be found in all ftates, not excepting
the moft diftinguifhed of them. The leaft indifcretion
affuming the hue of high treafon, enemies are very
dangerous, and friends become fufpicious. Men think
little, fay nothing, and are afraid of reafoning : they

are even alarmed at their own ideas. The philofopher keeps his thoughts to himfelf, as the rich man conceals his treafure. The man who leads the beft life is the moft unknown. Miftruft and terror form the bafis of the general manners. The citizens live feparate from each other; and the whole nation becomes melancho-ly, pufillanimous, ftupid, and filent. Such is the feries, fuch the fatal fymptoms, or the fcale of mifery, by which every nation may learn the degree of its own wretchednefs.

If, in lieu of the preceding phenomena, we imagine others that are directly contrary, they will indicate that motion of legiflative bodies which tends to liber-ty. It is diforderly, it is rapid, it is violent. It is a fever, more or lefs ardent, but always attended with convulfions. Every thing announces fedition and mur-ders. Every thing makes the people tremble, left a general diffolution fhould take place; and if they be not deftined to experience this laft evil, it is in blood that their felicity muft revive.

England experienced this in the beginning of the reign of Charles I.; who, though not fo great a pedant as his father, was equally fond of authority. The di-vifion which had begun between the king and the par-liament, fpread itfelf throughout the nation. The higheft clafs of the nobility, and the fecond, which was the richeft, afraid of being confounded with the vulgar, engaged on the fide of the king, from whom they derived that borrowed luftre, which they return-ed him by a voluntary and venal bondage. As they ftill poffeffed moft of the confiderable land eftates, they engaged almoft all the country people in their party; who naturally love the king, becaufe they think he muft love them. London, and all the great towns, in-fpired by municipal government with the republican fpirit, declared for the parliament, and drew along with them the trading part of the nation, who, valu-ing themfelves as much as the merchants in Holland, afpired to the fame freedom as that democracy.

Thefe divifions brought on the fharpeft, the moft

B O O K bloody, and the moſt obſtinate civil war ever recorded
XIV.   in hiſtory.   Never did the Engliſh ſpirit ſhow itſelf in
ſo dreadful a manner.   Every day exhibited freſh
ſcenes of violence, which ſeemed to have been already
carried to the higheſt exceſs; and theſe again were
outdone by others, ſtill more atrocious.   It ſeemed as
if the nation was juſt upon the brink of deſtruction,
and that every Briton had ſworn to bury himſelf under
the ruins of his country.

By what   In this general tumult, the moſt moderate ſought for
men the   a peaceable retreat in the American iſlands, which the
Britiſh
iſlands were Engliſh had lately ſeized upon.   The tranquillity they
peopled.   found there, induced others to follow them.   While
the ſedition was ſpreading in the mother-country, the
colonies grew up and were peopled.   The patriots who
had fled from faction were ſoon after joined by the
royaliſts, who were oppreſſed by the republican party,
which had at laſt prevailed.

Both theſe were followed by thoſe reſtleſs and ſpirit-
ed men, whoſe ſtrong paſſions inſpire them with great
deſires and vaſt projects; who deſpiſe dangers, hazards,
and fatigues, and wiſh to ſee no other end to them but
death or fortune; who know of no medium between
affluence and want; equally calculated to overturn or
to ſerve their country, to lay it waſte or to enrich it.

The iſlands were alſo the refuge of merchants who
had been unfortunate in trade, or were reduced by
their creditors to a ſtate of indigence and idleneſs.   Unable as they were to fulfil their engagements, this very
misfortune paved the way to their proſperity.   After
a few years they returned with affluence into their own
country, and met with the higheſt reſpect in thoſe very
places from whence they had been baniſhed with ignominy and contempt.

This reſource was ſtill more neceſſary for young
people, who in the firſt tranſports of youth had been
drawn into exceſſes of debauchery and licentiouſneſs.
If they had not quitted their country, ſhame and diſgrace, which never fail to depreſs the mind, would have
prevented them from recovering either regularity of

manners or public efteem.   But, in another country, where the experience they had of vice might prove a leffon of wifdom, and where they had no occafion to attempt to remove any unfavourable impreffions, they found, after their misfortunes, a harbour in which they refted with fafety.   Their induftry made amends for their paft follies ; and men who had left Europe like vagabonds, and who had difgraced it, returned honeft men, and ufeful members of fociety.

All thefe feveral colonifts had at their difpofal, for the clearing and tilling of their lands, the moft profligate fet of men of the three kingdoms, who had deferved death for capital crimes ; but who, from motives of humanity and good policy, were fuffered to live and to work for the benefit of the ftate.   Thefe malefactors, who were tranfported for a term of years, which they were to fpend in flavery, became induftrious, and acquired manners, which placed them once more in the way of fortune.   There were fome of thofe, who, when reftored to fociety by the freedom they had gained, became planters, heads of families, and the owners of the beft plantations ; a proof how much it is for the intereft of a civilized fociety to admit this lenity in the penal laws, fo conformable to human nature, which is frail, but capable of fenfibility, and of turning from evil to good.

The mother-country, however, was too much taken up with its own domeftic diffenfions, to think of giving laws to the iflands under its dominion ; and the colonifts were not fufficiently enlightened to draw up fuch a fyftem of legiflation as was fit for an infant fociety. While the civil war was rectifying the government in England, the colonies, juft emerging from a ftate of infancy, formed their own conftitution upon the model of the mother-country.   In each of thefe feparate fettlements, a chief reprefents the king ; a council, the peers ; and the deputies of the feveral diftricts, the commons.   The general affembly enacts laws, regulates taxes, and judges of the adminiftration.   The executive part belongs to the governor ; who alfo oc-

Under what form of government the British iflands were eftablifhed.

BOOK XIV. casionally determines upon causes which have not been tried before, but in conjunction with the council, and by the majority of votes. But as the members of this body derive their rank from him, it is seldom that they thwart his designs.

Great Britain, to reconcile her own interests with the freedom of her colonies, took care that no laws should be enacted there which were inconsistent with their own. She hath required that her delegates should take an oath, that, in the places subject to their authority, they would never allow, upon any pretence whatever, any deviation from the regulations established for the prosperity of her trade. This tie of an oath hath been contrived, because, as the islands themselves regulate and pay the greater part of the salaries of their chiefs, it was to be apprehended that some of these commanders might endeavour to excite liberality by their indulgence. Another check hath been put to corruption. It is necessary that the stipend granted to the governor, should extend to the whole duration of his administration ; and that it should be the object of the first bill passed on his arrival. These precautions have however appeared insufficient to some persons of a despotic turn of mind. Accordingly, it hath been their opinion, to proscribe a custom, which in some measure made those who issue orders dependent upon men who were subordinate to them; but the parliament have always refused to make this alteration. Justly dreading that spirit of rapaciousness which induces men to cross the seas, they have always kept up a custom which they think proper to check the spirit of cupidity and tyranny. It is with the same view that they have decreed against those governors who should violate the laws of the colonies, the same penalties as are inflicted in England on those who trespass upon the national constitution.

The parliament have likewise empowered the islands, to have in the mother-country deputies appointed to take care of their interests. Their principal duty is to obtain the confirmation of the statutes passed in the colonies. These acts are executed provifionally; but they do not pafs into a law till they have been approved of by the fovereign. This fanction once obtained, they can only be revoked by an affembly of the colony itfelf, or by the parliament; which exercifes fupreme authority over the whole empire. The bufinefs of the agents of the iflands at London, is the fame as that of the reprefentatives of the people in the Britifh fenate. Unhappy will it be for the ftate, if ever it fhould difregard the clamours of the reprefentatives, whoever they may be. The counties in England would rife; the colonies would fhake off their allegiance in America; the treafures of both worlds would be loft to the mother-country, and the whole empire would fall into confufion.

The fources of public felicity have not yet been corrupted by this improper fpirit. The fettlements formed in the Weft Indies have been always attached to their own country by the ties of blood, and by thofe of neceffity. Their planters have been conftantly looking up to their mother-country, who is ever attentive to their prefervation and their improvement. One might fay, that as the eagle, who never lofes fight of the neft where fhe fofters her young, London feems to look down upon her colonies, and to fee them grow up and profper under her tender care. Her numberlefs veffels, covering an extent of two thoufand leagues with their proud fails, form, as it were, a bridge over the ocean; by which they keep up an uninterrupted communication between both worlds. With good laws, which maintain what fhe has once eftablifhed, fhe preferves her poffeffions abroad without a ftanding army, which is always an oppreffive and ruinous burden. Two very fmall corps, fixed at Antigua and Jamaica, are fufficient for a nation which thinks, with reafon, that maritime forces, well maintained, kept in continual employment, and always directed towards the public good, are the true fortifications of thefe ufeful fettlements.

By thefe beneficent regulations, dictated by humanity and found policy, the Englifh iflands foon grew happy, though not rich. Their culture was confined to tobacco, cotton, ginger, and indigo. Some of the enterprifing colonifts imported fugar canes from Brazil, and they multiplied prodigioufly, but to no great purpofe. They were ignorant of the art of managing this valuable plant, and drew from it fuch indifferent fugar, that it was either rejected in Europe, or fold at the loweft price. A feries of voyages to Fernambucca taught them how to make ufe of the treafure they had carried off; and the Portuguefe, who till then had engroffed all the fugar trade, found, in 1650, in an ally, whofe induftry they thought precarious, a rival who was one day to fupplant them.

Means employed by the mother-country to fecure to itfelf all the productions of the iflands.

The mother-country, however, had but a very fmall fhare in the profperity of her colonies. They themfelves fent their own commodities directly to all parts of the world, where they thought they would be difpofed of to moft advantage ; and indifcriminately admitted fhips of all nations into their ports. This unlimited freedom muft of courfe throw almoft all their trade into the hands of that nation which, in confequence of the low intereft their money bears, the largenefs of their ftock, the number of their fhips, and the reafonablenefs of their duties of import and export, could afford to make the beft terms, to buy at the deareft, and fell at the cheapeft rate. Thefe people were the Dutch. They united all the advantages of a fuperior army ; which, being ever mafter of the field, is free in all its operations. They foon feized upon the profits of fo many productions, which they had neither planted nor gathered. Ten of their fhips were feen in the Britifh iflands to one Englifh veffel.

The nation had paid little attention to this evil during the difturbances of the civil wars ; but as foon as thefe troubles were compofed, and the ftate reftored to tranquillity by the very violence of its commotions, it began to turn its views towards its foreign poffeffions. It perceived that thofe fubjects, who had as it were taken refuge in America, would be loft to the ftate, if foreign powers, which confumed the fruits of the induftry of the colonies, were not excluded. The deliberate and weighty difcuffion of this point brought on the famous navigation act in 1651, which excluded all foreign fhips from entering the harbours of the Englifh iflands, and confequently obliged their produce to be exported directly to the countries under the dominion of England. The government, though aware of the inconveniencies of fuch an exclufion, was not alarmed at it, but confidered the empire only as a tree, the fap of which muft be turned back to the trunk, when it flows too freely to fome of the branches.

However, this reftraining law was not then enforced in its utmoft rigour. Perhaps the fhips belonging to the mother-country were not fufficiently numerous to carry off all the productions of the iflands; perhaps, apprehenfions might prevail, that the colonifts might be exafperated by fuddenly depriving their coafts of a competition which increafed the price of their commodities. Perhaps, the plantations ftill required fome fupport, in order to bring their cultures to that degree of perfection that was expected. However this may be, it is certain, that the act of navigation was not rigoroufly put in execution till 1660. At this period, the Englifh fugars had been fubftituted to thofe of Portugal, in all the northern parts of Europe. It is to be fuppofed, that they would equally have fupplanted them to the fouth, had not the obligation impofed upon all the navigators to ftop at the Britifh ports before they paffed the Straits of Gibraltar, put an infurmountable obftacle to this trade. It is true, that in order to attain this fuperiority over the only nation that was in poffeffion of this commodity, the Englifh had been obliged greatly to lower the price of it; but their plentiful crops made them ample amends for this neceffary facrifice. If other nations were encouraged by their fuccefs to raife plantations, at leaft for their own confumption, the Englifh opened other markets, which fupplied the place of the former. The only misfortune they experienced in a long feries of years,

B O O K
XIV.

B O O K was, the feeing many of their cargoes taken by French
XIV. privateers, and fold at a low price. The planter fuftained by this a double inconvenience, that of lofing
part of his fugars, and being obliged to fell the remainder below their value.

Diminution   Notwithftanding thefe tranfient piracies, which al-
of the ad-   ways ceafed in time of peace, the plantations ftill con-
vantages
which Eng-   tinued to increafe in the Englifh iflands. All the pro-
land deriv-   ductions peculiar to America were more carefully ated from its
iflands.   tended to; but the wealthy proprietors attached them-
Caufe of it. felves more particularly to the culture of fugar, the
fale of which was conftantly increafing throughout all
Europe. This profperity exifted for the fpace of half
a century, when attentive men perceived that the exportations decreafed. It was then almoft generally believed that the colonies were exhaufted; even the national fenate adopted this idea, not confidering that if
the foil no longer had that degree of fertility peculiar
to lands newly cleared, it ftill retained that fhare of
fruitfulnefs which the earth feldom lofes, unlefs its
fubftance be altered by the calamities or by the irregularities of nature. The truth was foon afcertained,
and the Englifh were obliged to acknowledge, that
the foreign marts were infenfibly fhut againft Great
Britain, and would foon be opened only to France.
This kingdom, which, from its natural advantages, and
from the active genius of its inhabitants, fhould be
foremoft in every undertaking, is fo reftrained by
the nature of its government, that it is the laft in becoming acquainted with its own interefts. The French
firft procured their fugars from the Englifh. They
afterwards made fome for their own confumption, then
for fale, till reftraints of every kind obliged them to
confine themfelves merely to what they wanted. It
was not till 1716, that their iflands began again to fupply other nations. The fuperiority of their foil, the
advantage of frefh lands, the frugality of their planters, who were yet poor, all confpired to enable them
to fell the production at a lower price than their competitors. It was moreover of a better quality; ac-

cordingly, as it increafed, that which was formerly in
fo great requeft, was rejected in all the markets.   Towards the year 1740, the fugar of the French plantations became fufficient for general confumption, and
at this period the Englifh were reduced to cultivate
no more than what they wanted for their own ufe.
The quantity they made was ftill very trifling at the
beginning of the century, but the ufe of tea, and the
habit of other indulgences, foon increafed prodigioufly the confumption of this article.

Barbadoes was one of the Britifh poffeffions which
furnifhed moft of this commodity.   This ifland, which
is fituated to windward of all the reft, appeared to
have never been inhabited even by favages, when, in
1627, fome Englifh families went to fettle there, but
without any interference of government.   It was not
till two years after, that a regular colony was eftablifhed there, at the expence, and by the care of the earl
of Carlifle, who, on the tragical death of Charles I.
was deprived of a property which had been too imprudently granted him by that weak prince.   It was
found covered with fuch large and hard trees, that uncommon refolution and patience were required to fell
them and root them up.   The ground was foon cleared of this encumbrance, or ftripped of this ornament:
for it is doubtful whether nature does not decorate her
work better than man, who alters every thing for himfelf alone.   Some patriots, tired of feeing the blood of
their countrymen fpilt, went and peopled this foreign
land.   While the other colonies were rather ravaged
than cultivated by thofe vagabonds who had been
driven from their native country by poverty or licentioufnefs, Barbadoes daily received new inhabitants,
who brought along with them not only their ftock of
money, but a turn for labour, courage, activity, and
ambition; thofe vices and virtues which are the effect
of civil wars.

By thefe means, an ifland, which is no more than
feven leagues in length, from two to five in breadth,
and eighteen in circumference, attained, in lefs than

B O O K
XIV.

The En-
glifh form
a fettle-
ment at
Barbadoes.
Great pro-
fperity of
this ifland.

B O O K forty years, to a population of more than a hundred
XIV.   thoufand fouls, and to a trade that employed four
         hundred fhips, of 150 tons burden each. Never had
the earth beheld fuch a number of planters collected
in fo fmall a compafs, or fo many rich productions
raifed in fo fhort a time. The labours, directed by
Europeans, were performed by flaves purchafed in
Africa, or even ftolen in America. This new fpecies
of barbarity was but a ruinous kind of prop for a new
edifice, and very nearly occafioned the fubverfion of
it.

Confpira-   Some Englifhmen, who had landed on the coafts of
cy formed
by the   the continent to get flaves, were difcovered by the Ca-
flaves in ribs, who were the objects of their fearch. Thefe fa-
Barbadoes vages fell upon them, and put them all to death or to
flight. A young man, who had been long purfued,
ran into a wood ; where an Indian woman meeting
him, faved his life, concealed and fed him, and fome
time after conducted him to the fea-fide. His companions were lying at anchor there, waiting for the
men they miffed, and fent the boat to fetch him. His
deliverer infifted on following him on board the fhip.
They were no fooner landed at Barbadoes, but the
monfter fold her who had faved his life, and had beftowed her heart, as well as her perfon upon him. To
vindicate the honour of the Englifh nation, one of
their poets has recorded this fhocking inftance of avarice and perfidy, to be abhorred by pofterity : it has
been told in feveral languages, and held out to the
deteftation of all foreign nations.

The Indians, who were not bold enough to under-
take to revenge themfelves, imparted their refentment
to the Negroes, who had ftronger motives, impoffible,
for hating the Englifh. The flaves unanimoufly vowed the death of their tyrants. This confpiracy was
carried on with fuch fecrecy, that, the day before it
was to have been carried into execution, the colony
had not the leaft fufpicion of it. But, as if generofity
was always to be the virtue of the wretched, one of
the leaders of the plot informed his mafter of it. Let-

ters were immediately difpatched to all the plan- B O O K
tations, and came in time to prevent the impend- XIV.
ing deftruction. The following night the flaves were
feized in their huts ; the moft guilty were executed
at break of day ; and this act of feverity reduced the
reft to obedience.

They have never revolted fince, and yet the colony Prefent
hath declined confiderably from its former profperity. ftate of
It ftill reckons ten thoufand white people, and fifty Barbadoes.
thoufand Negroes ; but the crops are not anfwerable
to the population. In the moft favourable feafons,
they do not amount to more than twenty millions
weight of fugar, and are very often below ten millions;
and yet to obtain this trifling produce, expences are
required much more confiderable than were neceffary
for double the produce in the beginning.

The foil of the colony, which is no more than a
rock of calcareous ftone, covered with very little earth,
is entirely exhaufted. It is neceffary to make a deep
opening in it every year, and to fill up with manure
the holes which have been made. The moft ordinary
of thefe manures is the Varec, a fea-weed which is
periodically thrown upon the coaft by the fea-tide.
The fugar-canes are planted in this fea-weed. The
natural foil is of little more ufe in the growth of them,
than the chefts in which the orange trees are put in
Europe.

The fugar which is produced by thefe cultures,
hath generally fo little confiftence, that it cannot be
exported in its raw ftate, but muft previoufly be earth-
ed ; a method which is not followed in the other Englifh fettlements, although it be not prohibited there,
as feveral writers have advanced. One great proof
of its bad quality is, that it is fooner reduced to molaffes than any where elfe. The droughts, which are
fo frequent at Barbadoes fince the country hath been
entirely laid open, ferve to complete the misfortunes
of the inhabitants of this ifland, which was formerly
in fo flourifhing a ftate.

 ‚Accordingly, though the taxes do not amount annually to more than 136,291 livres [5678 l. 15 s. 10d.], paid by a trifling pol-tax upon the Negroes and by fome other impofts, the colonifts are reduced to a ftate of mediocrity which approaches to indigence. This fituation prevents them from leaving the care of their plantations to agents, in order to go and inhabit milder climates. It even renders them inhuman towards their flaves, whom they treat with a degree of cruelty unknown in the other colonies.

Barbadoes was very lately the only trading poffeffion belonging to the Englifh in the Windward iflands. The fhips coming from Africa ufed generally to put in there. They delivered their whole cargo to one fingle purchafer, and at a fettled price, without diftinction of either age or fex in the bargain. Thefe Negroes, thus bought in the wholefale way by the merchants, were fold in retail in the ifland itfelf, or in the other Englifh fettlements, and the refufe of them was either clandeftinely or openly introduced in the colonies of the other nations. This great trade hath confiderably decreafed. Hence moft of the other Britifh iflands have chofen to receive their flaves directly from Guinea, and have fubmitted to the eftablifhed cuftom of paying for them with bills of exchange at ninety days fight. This credit, which was infufficient, hath fince been extended to a twelvemonth, and it hath frequently been neceffary to prolong it even beyond that term.

Before this revolution, a confiderable quantity of fpecie was in circulation at Barbadoes. The little coin which is at prefent ftill found there, is Spanifh ; it is confidered as merchandife, and is only taken by weight. The navy which is appropriated to this fettlement confifts of a few veffels, which are neceffary for its feveral correfpondences, and of about forty floops, employed in the fifhery of the flying-fifh.

Barbadoes is generally even, and every where fufceptible of cultivation, except in a very fmall number of hollow ways. It is only at the centre that the territory rifes imperceptibly, and forms a kind of mountain, covered up to its fummit with plantations equally convenient and agreeable, becaufe they were all efta-blifhed in times of great opulence. The ifland is not watered with rivers, but fprings of water fit for drink-ing are rather common in it; and it is interfected from one end to another by very fine roads. Thefe all terminate at Bridgetown; a town badly fituated but well built, where the commodities deftined for exportation are embarked, although it be only a road open to feveral winds.

B O O K XIV.

The colony, divided into eleven parifhes, doth not afford one poft where an enemy once landed could be ftopped; and the landing, which is not poffible in feveral parts of the coaft, is very practicable in others, notwithftanding the redoubts and batteries planted to prevent it Military men think, that the fureft way of fucceeding in an attack, would be to make it be-tween the capital and the town of Hole-town.

Is Barba-does capa-ble of mak-ing a good defence?

This enterprife would require more confiderable forces than might be imagined, confidering that Bar-badoes hath no regular troops. It is filled with plant-ers of fmall ftature, brave and active, accuftomed to military exercifes, and who probably would make fcarce lefs refiftance than a mercenary army. The ar-mament deftined for this conqueft fhould be difpatch-ed from Europe; if it were formed at Martinico, or at any other fettlement fituated to leeward, the Englifh fquadrons which would be in thofe latitudes, might block up the port where the expedition was prepar-ing, or might arrive at Barbadoes, time enough to di-fturb the operations of the befiegers.

This ifland is to the windward of all the others, and yet no great advantage can be reaped from its pofi-tion, confidered in a military light. It hath only fuch harbours as are fit to receive veffels that come to trade there; and though it be lefs expofed to ftorms and to hurricanes than the neighbouring latitudes, it doth not offer at any time a fecure afylum to men of war, and ftill lefs during the laft fix months of the year, when the fea is more tempeftuous. The mother-country

hath therefore formed no naval eftablifhment upon it.
The national fquadrons are never ftationed there ; and
if any of them fometimes appear, it is only for a little
while. Thus it was, that, in 1761 and in 1762, during the fine weather in the months of January and
February, the fleets deftined for the conqueft of Martinico and of the Havannah were affembled there.

Events that
have hap-
pened at
Antigua.
Production
and ex-
pences of
that ifland.
The im-
portance of
it to Great
Britain.
Antigua, which hath a circular form, and is about
twenty miles long, was found totally uninhabited by
thofe few Frenchmen who fled thither in 1628, upon
being driven from St. Chriftopher's by the Spaniards.
The want of fprings, which doubtlefs was the reafon
why no favages had fettled there, induced thefe fugitives to return, as foon as they could regain their former habitations. Some Englifhmen, more enterprifing than either the French or the Caribs, flattered
themfelves that they fhould overcome this great obftacle, by collecting the rain-water in cifterns; and
they therefore fettled there. The year in which this
fettlement was begun is not exactly known ; but it appears that in January 1640 there were about thirty
families on the ifland.

The number was not much increafed, when lord
Willoughby, to whom king Charles II. had granted
the property of Antigua, fent over a confiderable
number of inhabitants at his own expence in 1666.
It is probable they would never have enriched themfelves by the culture of tobacco, indigo, and ginger,
the only commodities they dealt in, had not colonel
Codrington introduced into the ifland, which was then
reftored to the dominion of the ftate, a fource of
wealth, in the year 1680, by the culture of fugar.
This being at firft black, harfh, and coarfe, was rejected in England, and could only be difpofed of in
Holland, and in the Hans towns, where it fold at a
much lower price than that of the other colonies.
By the moft affiduous labour, art got the better of
nature, and brought this fugar to as great a perfection, and to fell for as high a price, as any other.
Every one was then defirous of extending this cul-

ture. In 1741 it employed three thousand five hundred and thirty-eight white men, and twenty-seven thousand four hundred and eighteen Negroes. Since that period, the number of free men hath been much diminished, and that of the slaves is considerably increased. Their united labours produce eighteen or twenty millions weight of raw sugar, and a proportionate quantity of rum. This income is considerably less in those seasons, which occur too frequently, when the colony is afflicted with drought; and for this reason it is very much indebted.

All the tribunals are established at St. John's, situated to the West of the island. The greatest part of the trade hath been likewise concentrated in that town. Unfortunately, its port is closed up by a bar, upon which there is no more than twelve feet of water. If the depth of water should still decrease, the navigators will take in their cargoes to the north of the colony, in the road of Parham, which is much preferable to the one they now frequent, but which is infinitely less convenient for the collecting of the commodities.

Motives of great importance should excite England to prevent, by all possible means, the decline of so valuable a settlement. It is the only bulwark of the numerous and small islands which that country possesses in these latitudes. They all depend upon Antigua, and upon the English Harbour, an excellent port, where the naval forces designed for their protection, anchor, and where the squadrons find collected in arsenals, and in well-stocked magazines, the articles necessary to carry on their operations. The maintenance of the small fortifications which surround the two principal harbours; part of the pay of six hundred men, intrusted with their defence; the costs occasioned by the artillery; all these expences are defrayed by the colony, and absorb two thirds of the 272,502 livres [11,357l. 11s. 8d.] which it is obliged to require annually from its inhabitants.

This is too great a burden. In order to diminish

BOOK
XIV.

the weight of it, the affembly of the ifland thought of laying a tax upon thofe proprietors who fhould refide in Europe : but the mother-country annulled a regulation which was evidently injurious to the liberty of individuals. The colony then ordered, that the planters fhould for the future have only one white man, or two white women, to every fet of thirty Negroes. This law, which was adopted by feveral other iflands, is not much attended to, becaufe it is lefs expenfive to tranfgrefs it, than to maintain free men, whofe attendance cannot be compelled. The penalties, therefore, which are regulated for punifhing the tranfgreffion of this law, are become one of the greateft refources of the public treafury of that fettlement.

Its legiflative body hath fometimes difplayed a remarkable fhare of courage. The Englifh iflands have no coin which belöngs properly to themfelves : that which is circulated there is all foreign. The mother-country thought it neceffary to fettle the value of it in the beginning of the century. This arrangement was judged to be contrary to the intereft of the colony, who themfelves fettled it upon a higher footing. It was natural to imagine, that parliament would annul an act fo repugnant to their authority. The lawyers agreed, if that event fhould take place, never to lend their affiftance to any of thofe who fhould have refufed to accept the coin at the price fixed by the affembly.

Another occurrence exhibited, in a ftill ftronger light, the kind of fpirit which prevailed at Antigua. The governor, colonel Park, fetting equally at defiance the laws of morality and decency, was unreftrained and intemperate in all his proceedings. The colony demanded, and obtained, his recal. As he did not feem difpofed to depart, feveral of the moft confiderable inhabitants went to expoftulate with him, in the ftrongeft terms, upon this kind of difobedience. They were repulfed with brutality by his guards. The people took up arms, and the tyrant was attacked in his own houfe, and maffacred. His body was then thrown naked into the ſtreet, and mutilated by thoſe whoſe bed he had diſhonoured. The mother-country, more moved by the ſacred rights of nature than jealous of her own authority, overlooked an act which her vigilance ought to have prevented, but which ſhe was too equitable to revenge. It is only the part of tyranny to excite a rebellion, and then to quench it in the blood of the oppreſſed. Machiaveliſm, which teaches princes the art of being feared and deteſted, directs them to ſtifle the victims whoſe cries grow importunate. Humanity preſcribes to kings, juſtice in legiſlation, mildneſs in government, lenity to prevent inſurrections, and mercy to pardon them. Religion enjoins obedience to the people ; but God, above all things, requires equity in princes. If they violate it, innumerable witneſſes will riſe up againſt a ſingle man at the final judgment.

The council of Antigua doth not extend its juriſdiction over the neighbouring iſlands, which have all their particular aſſemblies : but the governor of Antigua is alſo governor of the other iſlands, except Barbadoes, which, on account of its poſition and importance, hath deſerved particular diſtinction. This governor-general muſt pay an annual viſit to the places under his authority ; and he uſually begins his tour by Montſerrat.

This iſland, diſcovered in 1493 by Columbus, and occupied in 1632 by the Engliſh, is only eight or nine leagues in circumference. The ſavages, who lived peaceably in it, were expelled, according to cuſtom, by the uſurpers. This act of injuſtice was not at firſt followed with any very fortunate circumſtances. The progreſs of the new ſettlement was for a long time ſo ſlow, that ſix and fifty years after its foundation it ſcarce contained ſeven hundred inhabitants. It was not till towards the end of the century, that the population, both in white men and Negroes, became as numerous as it could be in ſo confined a poſſeſſion. Sugar-canes were then ſubſtituted to commodities of little value, which had occaſioned their planters to languiſh in a ſtate of miſery. War and the elements over-

State of the ſettlement formed by the Engliſh at Montſerrat.

B O O K threw, at feveral intervals, the beft founded expecta-
XIV. tions, and obliged the colonifts to contract debts which
are not yet paid off. At the prefent period, the activity of a thoufand free perfons, and the labours of
eight thoufand flaves, produce five or fix millions
weight of raw fugar, upon plains of little extent, or in
valleys which are fertilized by the waters falling from
the mountains. One of the difadvantages of this ifland,
the public expences of which do not exceed annually
49,887 livres [2078l. 12s. 6d.], is, that it has not one
fingle harbour where the lading and unlading can eafily be made. The fhips would even be in danger upon thefe coafts, if the mafters did not take care, when
they fee a ftorm approaching, to put out to fea, or to
take fhelter in fome neighbouring harbour. Nevis is
expofed to the fame inconvenience.

Ancient   The moft generally received opinion is, that the
manners
and prefent Englifh fettled on this ifland in 1628. It is properly
ftate of the nothing more than a very high mountain, of an eafy
ifland of
Nevis.   afcent, and crowned with tall trees. The plantations
lie all round, and, beginning at the fea-fide, are continued almoft to the top of the mountain; but the
higher they ftand, the lefs fertile they are, becaufe the
foil grows more ftony. This ifland is watered by many ftreams, which would be fo many fources of plenty, if they did not, in ftormy weather, fwell into torrents, wafh away the lands, and deftroy the treafures
they have produced.

The colony of Nevis was a model of virtue, order,
and piety. Thefe exemplary manners have been owing to the paternal care of the firft governor. This
incomparable man infpired all the inhabitants, by his
own example, with a love of labour, a reafonable economy, and innocent recreations. The perfon who
commanded, and thofe who obeyed, were all actuated
by the fame principle of the ftricteft equity. So rapid
was the progrefs of this fingular fettlement, that, if we
may credit all the accounts of thofe times, it foon contained 10,000 white people and 20,000 blacks. Ad-
mitting even that fuch a population, upon a territory

of two leagues in length and one in breadth, fhould B O O K
be exaggerated, ftill it will fhow the amazing but in- XIV.
fallible effect of virtue, in promoting the profperity of
a well-regulated fociety.

But even virtue itfelf will not fecure either individuals or focieties from the calamities of nature, or from
the injuries of fortune. In 1689 a dreadful mortality
fwept away half this happy colony. It was ravaged
in 1706 by a French fquadron, which carried off three
or four thoufand flaves. The next year the ruin of
this ifland was completed, by the moft violent hurricane ever recorded. Since this feries of difafters, it
has recovered a little. It contains fix hundred free
men and five thoufand flaves, the taxes upon whom
do not exceed 45,000 livres [1875l.], and who fend to
England three or four millions weight of raw fugar,
the whole of which is fhipped under the walls of the
agreeable city called Charleftown. Perhaps thofe who
repine moft at the deftruction of the Americans and
the flavery of the Africans, would receive fome confo-
lation if the Europeans were every where as humane
as the Englifh have been in this ifland of Nevis, and
if all the iflands in America were as well cultivated in
proportion ; but nature and fociety afford few inftances of fuch miraculous profperity.

Saint Chriftopher's was the nurfery of all the En- St. Chrifto-
glifh and French colonies in America. Both nations pher's,
which is at
arrived there on the fame day, in 1625. They fhared firft divid-
the ifland between them, figned a perpetual neutrality, ed between
the Englifh
and entered into a mutual engagement to affift each and French,
other againft their common enemy the Spaniard, who at laft belongs en-
for a century paft had invaded or difturbed the two tirely to
hemifpheres. Unfortunately, by an inconfiderate kind Great Britain.
of convention, hunting, fifhing, the woods, the harbours, and the falt-pits, had all been left in common.
This arrangement mixed too many perfons together,
who could not be agreeable to each other, and jealoufy foon divided thofe whom a temporary intereft
had united. This fatal paffion created daily quarrels,
fkirmifhes, and devaftations ; but thefe were only do-

B O O K meſtic animoſities, in which the reſpective governments
XIV. took no part. Concerns of greater importance having,
in 1666, kindled between the two mother-countries a
war, which continued almoſt uninterruptedly during
the remainder of the century, their ſubjects in St.
Chriſtopher's fought with a degree of obſtinacy that
was not to be found elſewhere. Sometimes conquerors and ſometimes conquered, they alternately drove
each other from their plantations. This long conteſt,
in which both parties alternately had the advantage,
was terminated by the total expulſion of the French
in 1702 ; and the peace of Utrecht cut off all their
hopes of ever returning thither.

This was no great ſacrifice for a people who had
never ſeriouſly attended to the care of cultivating
productions upon their domain. Their population
amounted but to 667 white people, of all ages and
both ſexes, 29 free blacks, and 659 ſlaves. All their
herds conſiſted only of 265 head of horned cattle, and
157 horſes. They cultivated nothing but a little cotton and indigo, and had but one ſingle ſugar plantation.

What St.
Chriſto-
pher's be-
came under
the Britiſh
govern-
ment.

Though the Engliſh had for a long time made a
greater advantage of this iſland, yet they did not immediately reap all the benefit they might have done
from having the ſole poſſeſſion of it. This conqueſt
was for a long time a prey to rapacious governors,
who ſold the lands for their own profit, or gave them
away to their creatures, though they could only war-
rant the duration of the ſale, or grant, during the term
of their adminiſtration. The parliament of England
at length remedied this evil, by ordering, that all lands
ſhould be put up to auction, and the purchaſe money
paid into the public coffers. After this prudent regulation, the new plantations were as well cultivated as
the old ones.

The iſland, which is in general narrow, but very
unequally ſo, may have an extent of thirty-ſix leagues
ſquare. Mountains, thick ſet and barren, though covered with verdure, and which occupy one third of

the territory, interfect it almoft throughout its whole length. From the foot of thefe mountains iffue an infinite number of fprings, which, unfortunately, are for the moft part dried up in the dry feafons. Scattered over the plain we meet with a number of agreeable, neat, and convenient habitations, which are ornamented with avenues, fountains, and groves. The tafte for rural life, which the Englifh have retained more than any other civilized nation in Europe, prevails in the higheft degree at St. Chriftopher's. They never had the leaft occafion to form themfelves into fmall focieties, in order to pafs away the time ; and, if the French had not left there a fmall town, where their manners are preferved, they would ftill be unacquainted with that kind of focial life which is productive of more altercations than pleafures ; which is kept up by gallantry, and terminates in debauchery ; which begins with convivial joys, and ends in the quarrels of gaming. Inftead of this image of union, which is in fact only a beginning of difcord, the reprefentatives of the proprietors, who are almoft all of them fettled in Europe, the number of which amounts to eighteen hundred, live upon the plantations ; from whence they gather, by the labour of twenty-four or twenty-five thoufand flaves, eighteen millions weight of raw fugar, which is the fineft in the New World. This produce enables the colony to provide with eafe for the public expences, which do not annually exceed 68,145 livres 10 fols [2839l. 7s. 11d.].

It was at St. Chriftopher's, that in 1756 was exhibited a fcene worthy of being recounted. Wretched cataftrophes that have happened at St. Chriftopher's

A Negro had, from his childhood, partook of the amufements of his young mafter. This familiarity, which is commonly fo dangerous, extended the ideas of the flave, without altering his character. Quazy foon deferved to be chofen overfeer over the labours and over the plantations ; and he difplayed in that important poft an uncommon fhare of underftanding and an indefatigable zeal. His conduct and his talents increafed his favour, which appeared to be unalterably fixed, when this director, hitherto fo much beloved and fo much diftinguifhed, was fufpected of having infringed the eftablifhed laws of the police, and publicly threatened with an humiliating punifhment.

A flave who hath for a long time efcaped chaftifement, inflicted too readily and too frequently upon his equals, is infinitely jealous of that diftinction. Quazy, who dreaded fhame more than the grave, and who did not flatter himfelf with being able to aver* the fentence pronounced againft him by his entreaties, went out in the midft of the night, in order to obtain a powerful mediation. His mafter unfortunately perceived him, and attempted to ftop him. They grappled with each other; and thefe two dexterous and vigorous champions wreftled for fome time with varied fuccefs. At length the flave threw down his inflexible mafter, and kept him in that difagreeable fituation; when, putting a dagger to his breaft, he addreffed him in the following terms :

" Mafter, I have been brought up with you. Your
" pleafures have been mine. My heart hath never
" known any other interefts than yours. I am inno-
" cent of the trifling offence of which I am accufed;
" but had I even been guilty of it, you ought to have
" forgiven me. All my fenfes are roufed with indig-
" nation at the recollection of the affront which you
" are preparing for me; and thus it is that I will avoid
" it." On faying thefe words, he cut his own throat, and fell down dead, without curfing the tyrant, whom he covered with his blood.

In the fame ifland, love and friendfhip have been fignalized by a tragic event, which hath never been paralleled either in fable or in hiftory.

Two Negroes, both young, handfome, robuft, courageous, and born with a foul of an uncommon caft, had been fond of each other from their infancy. Partners in the fame labours, they were united by their fufferings; which, in feeling minds, form a ftronger attachment than pleafures. If they were not happy,

they comforted each other at leaft in their mifery. B O O K
Love, which generally obliterates the remembrance of   XIV.
all misfortunes, ferved only to make theirs complete.
A Negro girl, who was likewife a flave, and whofe
eyes fparkled, no doubt, with greater vivacity and fire
from the contraft of her dark complexion, excited an
equal flame in the hearts of thefe two friends.   The
girl, who was more capable of infpiring than of feeling a ftrong paffion, would readily have accepted either; but neither of them would deprive his friend of
her, or yield her up to him.   Time ferved only to increafe the torments they fuffered, without affecting
their friendfhip or their love.   Oftentimes did tears of
anguifh ftream from their eyes, in the midft of the de-
monftrations of friendfhip they gave each other, at the
fight of the too beloved object that threw them into
defpair.   They fometimes fwore that they would love
her no more, and that they would rather part with life
than forfeit their friendfhip.   The whole plantation
was moved at the fight of thefe conflicts.   The love
of the two friends for the beautiful Negro girl was the
topic of every converfation.

One day they followed her into a wood; there each
embraced her, clafped her a thoufand times to his heart,
fwore all the oaths of attachment, and called her every
tender name that love could fuggeft; when, fuddenly,
without fpeaking or looking at each other, they both
plunged a dagger into her breaft.   She expired, and
they mingled their tears and groans with her laft
breath.   They roared aloud, and made the wood re-
found with their violent outcries.   A flave came running to their affiftance, and faw them at a diftance
ftifling the victim of their extraordinary paffion with
their kiffes.   He called out to fome others, who foon
came up, and found thefe two friends embracing each
other upon the body of this unhappy girl, and bathed
in her blood, while they themfelves were expiring in
the ftreams that flowed from their own wounds.

Thefe lovers and thefe friends were flaves.   Is it in
fo degrading a ftation that we fee fuch actions as muft

aftonifh the whole world? If there can be a man who is not ftruck with horror and compaffion at the greatnefs of this ferocious love, Nature muft have formed him, not for the flavery of the Negroes, but for the tyranny of their mafters. Such a man muft have lived without commiferating others, and will die without comfort ; he muft never have fhed a tear, and none will ever be fhed for him.

Particularities concerning Barbuda.
Barbuda, which belongs entirely to the Codrington family, and the circumference of which is fix or feven leagues, hath dangerous coafts. This is perhaps the moft even of all the American iflands. The trees which cover it are weak, and not very high, becaufe there are never more than fix or feven inches of earth upon a layer of lime-ftone. Nature hath placed great plenty of turtles here ; and caprice hath occafioned the fending thither of deer, and feveral kinds of game; chance hath filled the woods with pintados, and other fowls, efcaped from the veffels after fome fhipwreck. Upon this foil are fed oxen, horfes, and mules, for the labours of the neighbouring fettlements. No other culture is known there, except that of the kind of corn which is neceffary for the feeding of the numerous herds, in thofe feafons when the pafture fails. Its population is reduced to three hundred and fifty flaves, and to the fmall number of free men who are appointed to overlook them. This private property pays no tribute to the nation, though it be fubject to the tribunals of Antigua. The air here is very pure and very wholefome. Formerly, the fickly people of the other Englifh iflands went to breathe it, in order to ftop the progrefs of their difeafes, or to recover their ftrength. This cuftom hath ceafed, fince fome of them have indulged themfelves in parties of deftructive chafe.

Muft men then be fuffered to perifh, in order that animals fhould be preferved? How is it poffible that fo atrocious a cuftom, which draws down the imprecation of almoft all Europe upon the fovereigns and upon the lords of our countries, fhould be fuffered, and fhould even be eftablifhed, beyond the feas? I have

asked this question, and I have been answered, that the B O O K
island belonged to the Codringtons; and that they had ___XIV.___
a right to dispose of their property at their pleasure.
I now ask, Whether this right of property, which is
undoubtedly sacred, hath not its limits? Whether this
right, in a variety of circumstances, be not sacrificed to
public good? Whether the man who is in possession of
a fountain, can refuse water to him who is dying with
thirst? Whether any of the Codrington family would
partake of one of those precious pintados, that had cost
his countryman or his fellow-creature his life? Whether the man who should be convicted of having suffered a sick person to die at his door, would be suffi-
ciently punished by the general execration? And whether he would not deserve to be dragged before the
tribunals of justice as an assassin? Possessor of Barbuda,
thou art the assassin of all those whom thou dost deprive of the salubrity of the air, which would have preserved them; and if this circumstance should not drive
thee to despair upon thy death-bed, it is because thine
heart will bid defiance to the divine justice! Hasten,
therefore, to recal that shameless representative, who,
in his concern for a seraglio of Mulatto women, in
whom, it is said, all his delights are centered, rigorously
pursues the execution of your barbarous prohibition.

Anguilla is seven or eight leagues in length, and is The colony
very unequal in its breadth, which never exceeds two of Anguilla
leagues. Neither mountains, nor woods, nor rivers, is very
wretched,
are found upon it, and its soil is nothing more than and its fate
chalk. cannot be
changed.
Some wandering Englishmen settled upon this porous
and friable rock towards the year 1650. After an obstinate labour, they at length succeeded in obtaining
from this kind of turf a little cotton, a small quantity
of millet-seed, and some potatoes. Six veins of vege-
tating earth, which were in process of time discovered,
received sugar canes, which, in the best harvest, yield
no more than fifty thousand weight of sugar, and sometimes only five or six thousand. Whatever else comes
out of the colony hath been introduced into it clan-

B O O K deſtinely from Santa Cruz, where the inhabitants of
XIV. Anguilla have formed ſeveral plantations.

In ſeaſons of drought, which are but too frequent,
the iſland hath no other reſource but in a lake, the ſalt
of which is ſold to the people of New England ; and
in the ſale of ſheep and goats, which thrive better in
this dry climate, and upon theſe arid plains, than in the
reſt of America.

Anguilla reckons no more than two hundreed free
inhabitants, and five hundred ſlaves. Neverthelefs, it
hath an aſſembly of its own, and even a chief, who is
always choſen by the inhabitants, and confirmed by the
governor of Antigua. A foreigner who ſhould be ſent
to govern this feeble ſettlement, would infallibly be
driven away by men who have preferved ſomething of
the independent manners, and of the rather ſavage
character of their anceſtors.

The coaſt of this iſland affords but two harbours ;
and even in theſe very ſmall veſſels only can anchor.
They are both defended by four pieces of cannon,
which, for half a century paſt, have been entirely unfit for ſervice.

Tortola is   The Virgin Iſlands are a group of about ſixty ſmall
the only   iſlands, moſt of them mountainous, dry, and arid, where
one of the
Virgin   the Spaniards of Porto-Rico were for a long time alone
Iſlands   employed in catching turtle, which were very plenty
which the
Engliſh   there. The Dutch had juſt begun a ſmall ſettlement
have culti- at Tortola, one of the beſt of theſe iſlands, and that
vated. The
govern-   which hath the ſafeſt harbour, when, in 1666, they
ment cen- were driven from it by the Engliſh ; who ſoon after
ſured.   diſperſed themſelves over the neighbouring ſmall iſlands
and rocks. There they lived, during near a century,
like ſavages, employed ſolely in the culture of cotton.
It was not till after the peace of 1748 that their induſtry was turned towards ſugar, of which they have
ſince regularly ſent to the mother-country four or five
millions weight.

Before this period, there had not been any regular
form of government, nor any public worſhip, at Tortola.
Both the one and the other have been very recently

eftablifhed; and what perhaps was more difficult to
bring about, the inhabitants have been prevailed upon
to pay the treafury four and a half per cent. on the
going out of their productions. A prudent adminiftration would have folicited a bill to fecure the feveral
properties, all, or almoft all, of which have been tranf-
mitted in an irregular manner; and if they were juridically attacked, there are few colonifts who might not
be legally ruined.

Here then is an inftance, at Tortola, of the government being very eager to draw money from the colonifts, and caring very little about fecuring their felicity, although it would have coft them only a little benevolence, without any kind of facrifice. Is it poffible
to fay to men in a more impudent manner, " You are
" nothing to us; you have only to continue ftill to pay
" us; and when you fhall no longer be able to do it,
" you may perifh, you may die; we care very little
" about the matter? The concern we take in your
" fate is in proportion to the fums you fupply us with."
Such inhuman fentiments are never uttered in any
place; but ftill this is the way in which people think
and act in all parts. Subjects are every where treated
as we do the mines, which we ceafe to attend to when
they yield no more ore. It is every where forgotten,
that, with a fmall fhare of juftice and protection, they
would become an inexhauftible fund. Empires in all
parts think themfelves eternal, and thofe who govern
them conduct themfelves as if they had not one day to
laft. The fame danger that threatens Tortola, does
not extend itfelf to Jamaica.

This ifland, which lies to leeward of the other Englifh iflands, and which geographers have ranked among
the greater Antilles, may be forty-three or forty-four
leagues in length, and fixteen or feventeen in its greateft breadth. It is interfected with feveral ridges of
high, craggy mountains, where dreadful rocks are
heaped one upon another. Their barrennefs does not
prevent their being covered all over with a prodigious
quantity of trees of different kinds, that ftrike their

BOOK XIV.

Defcription of Jamaica.

B O O K roots through the clefts of the rocks, and attract the
   XIV.   moisture that is depofited there by ftorms and frequent
          fogs. This perpetual verdure, kept up and embellifh-
ed by a multitude of plentiful cafcades, makes a conftant fpring all the year round, and exhibits the moft
enchanting profpect in nature. But thefe waters,
which fall from the barren fummits, and fertilize the
plains below, are brackifh and unwholefome. The
climate is ftill more dangerous. Of all the American
iflands, Jamaica is the moft deftructive. Men perifh
there very rapidly ; and although the lands have been
cleared for two centuries paft, yet there are ftill fome
very fruitful diftricts, even near the capital, where a
free man would not pafs the night, unlefs in a cafe of
extreme neceffity.

The Spa-   Columbus difcovered this great ifland in 1494, but
niards dif-   made no fettlement there. Eight years after, he was
cover Ja-
maica, and thrown upon it by a ftorm. Having loft his fhips, and
fettle there being unable to get away, he implored the humanity
fome time
after.   of the favages, who gave him all the affiftance that natural pity fuggefts. But thefe people, who cultivated
no more land than what was juft fufficient to fupply
their own wants, foon grew tired of fupporting ftrangers, to the manifeft rifk of ftarving themfelves, and
infenfibly withdrew from their neighbourhood. The
Spaniards, who had already indifpofed the Indians
againft them by repeated acts of violence, grew outrageous, and proceeded fo far as to take up arms againft
a humane and equitable chief, becaufe he difapproved
of their ferocity. Columbus availed himfelf of one of
thofe natural phenomena, ·in which a man of genius
may fometimes find a refource, which he may be excufed for having recourfe to in a cafe of urgent neceffity.

From the knowledge he had acquired in aftronomy,
he knew there would foon be an eclipfe of the moon.
He took advantage of this circumftance, and fummon-
ed all the Caciques in the neighbourhood to come and
hear fomething that nearly concerned them, and was
effential to their prefervation. He then pronounced

with emphafis, as if he were infpired : *To punifh you for* B O O K *the cruelty with which you fuffer my companions and me* XIV. *to perifh, the God whom I worfhip is going to ftrike you with his moft terrible judgments. This very evening you will fee the moon turn red, then grow dark, and withhold her light from you. This will be only a prelude to your calamities, if you obftinately perfift in refufing to give us food.*

The admiral had fcarce done fpeaking, when his prophecies were fulfilled. The favages were terrified beyond meafure; they thought they were all loft; they begged for mercy, and promifed to do any thing that fhould be defired. They were then told, that heaven, moved with their repentance, was appeafed, and that nature was going to refume her wonted courfe. From that moment, provifions were fent in from all quarters; and Columbus was never in want of any during the time he remained there.

It was Don Diego, the fon of this extraordinary man, who fixed the Spaniards at Jamaica. In 1509, he fent thither feventy robbers from St. Domingo, under the command of John d'Efquimel; and others foon followed. It feemed as if they all went over to this peaceable ifland, for no other purpofe than to fhed human blood. Thofe barbarians never fheathed their fword while there was one inhabitant left to preferve the memory of a numerous, mild, plain, and hofpitable people. It was happy for the earth that thefe murderers were not to fupply their place. They had no inclination to multiply in an ifland where no gold was to be found. Their cruelty did not anfwer the purpofe of their avarice ; and the earth, which they had drenched with blood, feemed to refufe her affiftance to fecond the barbarous efforts they had made to fix there. Every fettlement raifed upon the afhes of the natives grew unfuccefsful, when labour and defpair had completed the deftruction of a few favages who had efcaped the fury of the firft conquefts. That of St. Jago de la Vega was the only one that fupported itfelf. The inhabitants of that town, plunged in idlenefs, the

B O O K ufual confequence of tyranny after devaftation, were
  XIV. content with living upon the produce of fome few
plantations, and the overplus they fold to the fhips that
paffed by their coafts. The whole population of the
colony centered in the little fpot that fed this race of
deftroyers, confifted of 1500 flaves, commanded by as
many tyrants, when the Englifh came and attacked the
town, took it, and fettled there in 1655.

Jamaica is
conquered
by the En-
glifh.
Events that
have hap-
pened in the
ifland fince
they have
become ma-
fters of it.
The Englifh brought the fatal fources of difcord
along with them. At firft the new colony was only
inhabited by three thoufand of that fanatical militia,
which had fought and conquered under the ftandards
of the republican party. Thefe were foon followed
by a multitude of royalifts, who were in hopes of finding reft and peace in America, or comfort after their
defeat. The divifions which had prevailed for fo long
a time, and with fo much violence, between the two
parties in Europe, followed them beyond the feas.
This was fufficient to have renewed in America the
fcenes of horror and bloodfhed which had fo often
been acted in England, had not Penn and Venables,
the conquerors of Jamaica, given the command of the
ifland to the moft prudent man among them, who
happened to be the oldeft officer. This was Dudley,
who, although he had fubmitted to the authority of a
conquering fellow-citizen, had not yet loft any of his
attachment to the Stuarts. Twice did Cromwell, who
had difcovered his fecret fentiments, appoint fome of
his own party in his ftead, and Dudley was as often
reftored to his office by the death of his opponents.

The confpiracies that were forming againft him were
difcovered and fruftrated. He never fuffered the fmalleft breach of difcipline to go unpunifhed; and always
kept the balance even between the faction his heart
detefted, and the party he was attached to. He excited induftry; and encouraged it by his attention,
his advice, and his example. His authority was enforced by his difinterefted behaviour. He never could
be prevailed upon to accept of a falary, being content to live upon the produce of his own plantations.

In private life, he was plain and familiar; in office, an intrepid warrior, a fteady and ftrict commander, and a wife politician. His manner of governing was altogether military, becaufe he was obliged to reftrain or to regulate an infant colony, wholly compofed of foldiers; and to prevent and repulfe any invafion from the Spaniards, who might attempt to recover what they had loft.

But when Charles II. was called to the crown, by the nation that had deprived his father of it, a form of civil government was eftablifhed at Jamaica, mo-delled, like thofe of the other iflands, upon that of the mother-country. It was not, however, till the year 1682, that the code of laws was drawn up, which to this day preferves the colony in all its vigour. Three of thefe wife ftatutes merit the attention of our political readers.

The defign of the firft is to excite the citizens to the defence of their country, without prejudice to their private fortunes; which might otherwife divert them from attending to it. It enacts, that whatever mif-chief is done by the enemy, fhall be immediately made good by the ftate; or at the expence of all the fub-jects, if the money found in the treafury fhould prove infufficient.

Another law concerns the means of increafing po-pulation. It enacts, that every fhip-captain who brings a man into the colony, who is unable to pay for his paffage, fhall receive a general gratuity of 22 livres 10 fols [18s. 9d.]. The particular gratuity is 168 livres 15 fols [about 7l.] for every perfon brought from Eng-land or Scotland; 135 livres [5l. 11s. 6d.] for every perfon brought from Ireland; 78 livres 15 fols [about 3l. 5s. 7d.] for every perfon brought from the conti-nent of America; and 45 livres [1l. 17s. 6d.] for every perfon brought from the other iflands.

The third law tends to the encouragement of agri-culture. When a proprietor of land is unable to pay either the intereft or capital of the money he has bor-rowed, his plantation is fold at a price fixed by twelve

B O O K planters. The value of the plantation, whatever it
  XIV.   may be, frees the debtor entirely from any further ob-
ligation ; but if it fhould exceed his debt, the overplus muft be returned to him. This regulation, though
it may be thought partial, yet it hath the merit of
abating the rigour of the landlord's and merchant's
law-fuits againft the planter. It is to the advantage
of the foil, and of mankind in general. The creditor
is feldom a fufferer by it, becaufe he is upon his guard;
and the debtor is more obliged to be vigilant and honeft, if he means to find credit. Confidence then becomes the bafis of all agreements ; and confidence is
only to be gained by the practice of virtue.

Time hath produced other regulations. It was perceived that the Jews, fettled in great numbers in Jamaica, made a jeft of deceiving the tribunals of juftice. A magiftrate imagined that this evil might arife
from the circumftance of the Bible, which was prefented to them, being in Englifh. It was determined
that they fhould take their oath in future upon the
Hebrew text ; and after this precaution, perjuries became infinitely lefs frequent.

In 1761, it was decided, that every man who was
not a white man could not inherit more than 13,629
livres 3 fols 4 deniers [about 567l. 17s. 7½d.]. This
ftatute was difpleafing to feveral members of the Affembly, who were incenfed at the circumftance of depriving affectionate fathers of the fatisfaction of leaving a fortune, purchafed by long labours, to their beloved pofterity, becaufe they were not of the fame
colour. Difputes arofe, and the parliament of England took part in them. One of the moft celebrated
orators in the Houfe of Commons declared openly
againft the Negroes. His opinion was, that they were
a fet of vile beings, of a fpecies different from ours.
The teftimony of Montefquieu was the ftrongeft of his
arguments, and he read with confidence the ironical
chapter of laws upon flavery. None of his hearers
fufpected the real views of fo judicious a writer, and
his authority influenced the whole Britifh fenate.

The whole Britifh fenate! The whole legiflative B o o k
body, affembled to difcufs the interefts of the nation,   XIV.
and to determine gravely upon a motion, which, from
its injuftice and unreafonablenefs, deferved only to be
rejected with contempt! And wherefore fhould it not
have been determined that the Blacks fhould be entirely difinherited? If their colour gave a fanction to
deprive them of a portion of their fathers fortunes,
why not equally to deprive them of the whole? Opinions fo palpably abfurd, fhould have been combated
by ridicule, and not by arguments : and if even, contrary to all probability, this had been the fentiment of
Montefquieu, of what avail would his authority have
been? The Englifh fhould at leaft have made themfelves certain of the true meaning of the author.

The bill was going to be extended to the Indians,
when one man, lefs blinded than the reft, obferved,
that it would be a horrible piece of injuftice to confound the ancient proprietors of the ifland with the
Africans ; and that, moreover, there were not above
five or fix families of the former remaining.

The colony had already acquired fome degree of
fame before thefe laws had been made. Some adventurers, as well from hatred and national jealoufy, as
from a reftlefs difpofition and want of fortune, attacked the Spanifh fhips. Thefe pirates were feconded by
Cromwell's foldiers, who, retaining nothing after his
death, except that public averfion which their former
fucceffes had drawn upon them, went into America in
queft of promotion, which they could never expect in
Europe. Thefe were joined by a multitude of Englifhmen of both parties, accuftomed to blood by the
civil wars which had ruined them. Thefe men, eager
for rapine and carnage, plundered the feas, and ravaged the coafts of America. Jamaica was the place
where the fpoils of Mexico and Peru were always
brought by the Englifh, and frequently by foreigners.
They found in this ifland more eafe, a better reception, protection, and freedom, than any where elfe,

B O O K whether for landing, or for spending, as they chose,
XIV. the spoils arising from their plunder. Here extrava-
gance and debauchery soon plunged them again into
indigence. This only incitement to their sanguinary
industry made them hasten to commit fresh depredations. Thus the colony reaped the benefit of their
perpetual vicissitudes of fortune, and enriched itself by
the vices which were both the source and the ruin of
their wealth.

When this destructive race became extinct, by reason of the frequency of the murders they committed,
the funds they had left behind, and which, indeed,
had been taken from usurpers still more unjust and
cruel than themselves, proved a fresh source of opulence, by facilitating the means of opening a clandes-
tine trade with the Spanish settlements. This vein of
riches, which had been opened about the year 1672,
gradually increased, and with great rapidity, towards
the end of the century. Some Portuguese, with a capital of three millions [125,000l.], of which the sovereign had advanced two thirds, engaged, in 1696, to
furnish the subjects of the court of Madrid with five
thousand blacks, each of the five years that their treaty was to last. This Company drew a great many of
those slaves from Jamaica. From that time the colonists had constant connections with Mexico and Peru,
either by means of the Portuguese agents, or by the
captains of their own ships employed in this trade.
But this intercourse was somewhat slackened by the
war which broke out on account of the succession to
the throne of Spain.

At the peace, the Assiento treaty alarmed the people of Jamaica. They were afraid that the South Sea
Company, which was appointed to furnish the Spanish
colonies with Negroes, would entirely exclude them
from all access to the gold mines. All the efforts they
made to break this regulation, could not produce any
alteration in the measures of the English ministry.
They wisely foresaw that the activity of the Assientists

would prove a fresh motive of emulation for increasing the contraband trade formerly carried on ; and these views were found to be juft.

The illicit trade of Jamaica was carried on in a very fimple manner. An English veffel pretended to be in want of water, wood, or provifions ; that her maft was broken ; or that fhe had fprung a leak, which could not be difcovered or ftopped without unloading. The governor permitted the fhip to come into the harbour to refit : but, for form fake, and to exculpate himfelf to his court, he ordered a feal to be affixed to the door of the warehoufe where the goods were depofited ; while another door was left unfealed, through which the merchandife that was exchanged in this trade was carried in and out by ftealth. When the whole tranf-action was ended, the ftranger, who was always in want of money, requefted that he might be permitted to fell as much as would pay his charges ; and it would have been too cruel to refufe this permiffion. It was necef-fary that the governor, or his agents, might fafely dif-pofe in public of what they had previoufly bought in fecret ; as it would always be taken for granted, that what they fold could be no other than the goods that were allowed to be bought. In this manner were the greateft cargoes difpofed of.

The court of Madrid thought to put a ftop to thefe practices, by prohibiting the admiffion of all foreign fhips into the Spanifh harbours, on any pretence what-ever. But the people of Jamaica calling in force to the affiftance of artifice, fupported themfelves in this trade under the protection of the Englifh men of war, by allowing them five per cent. upon every article, to the fraudulent introduction of which they gave a fanc-tion.

To this open violation of public order, fucceeded a more private and lefs alarming one. The fhips dif-patched from Jamaica repaired to thofe ports of the Spanifh coaft which were leaft frequented, efpecially to that of Brew, five miles from Carthagena, and to that of Grout, four miles from Porto-Bello. A man

who fpoke the language of the country was immediately put afhore, to give notice in the adjacent country of the arrival of the fhips. The intelligence was
propagated with amazing fpeed to the moft diftant
parts ; the merchants haftened to the place, and the
trade began ; but with fuch precautions as experience
had taught them. The fhip's company was divided
into three parties. While the firft was entertaining
the purchafers, and treating them with great civilities,
at the fame time keeping a watchful eye to prevent
them from exercifing their inclination and dexterity
in ftealing, the fecond was employed in receiving the
vanilla, indigo, cochineal, gold and filver of the Spaniards, in exchange for flaves, quickfilver, filks, and
other commodities. The third divifion was, in the
meanwhile, under arms upon deck, to provide for the
fafety of the fhip, and to take care not to admit at
once a greater number of men than could be kept in
order.

When the tranfactions were finifhed, the Englifhman returned with his ftock, which he had commonly
doubled, and the Spaniard with his purchafe, of which
he hoped to make as great a profit, or greater. To
prevent a difcovery, he avoided the high-roads, and
went through by-ways, with the Negroes he had
bought, who were loaded with the merchandife, which
was divided into parcels of a convenient form and
weight for carriage.

This manner of trading had been carried on fuccefsfully for a long time, to the great emolument of
the colonies of both nations ; when, as Spain intended, it was greatly obftructed by fubftituting regifter-
fhips to the galleons. It has gradually diminifhed, and
of late years was reduced to a very low ebb. The Britifh miniftry, wifhing to revive it, judged, in 1766, that
the beft expedient to repair the loffes of Jamaica was
to make it a free port.

Immediately the Spanifh fhips in America flocked
thither from all parts, to exchange their gold and filver, and their commodities, for the manufactures of

England. This eagerneſs was attended with this con- venience, that the profit, of which it was the ſource, was acquired without riſk, and could not occaſion any diſputes: but it was to be expected that the court of Madrid would ſoon put a ſtop to an intercourſe ſo pre- judicial to their intereſts. This was the opinion of Great Britain; and in order to preſerve the riches of the neighbouring continent, they laid the foundation of a colony upon the Moſquito coaſts.

Whatever may one day be the fate of this new ſet- tlement, it is certain that the attention of Jamaica was for too long a time, and too much engaged in a ſmug- gling trade, while its cultures were too much neglect- ed. The firſt of theſe which the Engliſh devoted them- ſelves to was that of cocoa, which they found eſtabliſh- ed by the Spaniards. It proſpered as long as thoſe plantations laſted, which had been cultivated by a people who made this their principal food and their only traffic. The trees grew old, and it became ne- ceſſary to renew them; but, either for want of care or of ſkill, they did not ſucceed. Indigo was ſubſti- tuted to them.

This production was increaſing conſiderably, when the parliament laid a duty upon it which it was not able to bear, and which occaſioned the fall of this cul- ture in Jamaica, as well as in the other Engliſh iſlands. This imprudent tax hath been ſince ſuppreſſed, and even the encouragement of gratifications hath been ſubſtituted to it; but this tardy generoſity hath only occaſioned abuſes. In order to obtain the bounty, the Jamaica people contracted the habit of procuring this valuable dye from St. Domingo, and of introducing it into Great Britain as the growth of their own plan- tations.

The expence the government is at on this account cannot be looked upon entirely as a loſs, ſince it is of uſe to the nation. But it keeps up that miſtruſt, and we may ſay, that propenſity to fraud, which the ſpirit of finance has given riſe to in all our modern forms of legiſlation, between the ſtate and the citizens. Ever

B O O K since the magistrate has been inceffantly contriving
XIV.   means to appropriate to himfelf the money of the people, thefe have been ftudying artifices to elude the avidity of the magiftrates.   When there has been on one
fide no moderation in the expences, no limit to taxa-
tions, no equity in the repartition, no lenity in the recovery, there have been no longer any fcruples about
the violation of pecuniary laws on the other, nor any
honefty in the payment of the duties, nor probity in
the engagements of the fubject with the prince.   Oppreffion hath prevailed on one hand, and plunder on
the other; the finance hath extorted from commerce,
and commerce hath eluded or defrauded the finance.
The treafury hath pillaged the planters, and the planters have impofed upon the treafury by falfe entries.
Such are the manners of both hemifpheres.

In the New one there ftill exifted a few plantations
of indigo at Jamaica, when the culture of cotton began to be attended to.   This production had a rapid
fuccefs, which continued, becaufe it was advantage-
oufly, and without delay, difpofed of in England,
where it was manufactured with a degree of dexterity
which hath been rather imitated than equalled by the
rival nations.

Ginger hath been lefs ufeful to the colony.   The
favages who were found by the Europeans in the American iflands, moft generally made ufe of it; but their
confumption in this, as in every other article, was fo
fmall, that nature afforded them a fufficient quantity
without the affiftance of cultivation.   The ufurpers
grew paffionately fond of this fpice; they ate it in the
morning to fharpen their appetite; they ferved it up
at table, preferved in feveral different ways; they ufed
it after meals to facilitate digeftion, and at fea as an
antidote againft the fcurvy.   The Old World adopted
the tafte of the New; and this lafted till the price of
pepper, which had for a long while been extremely
high, was reduced.   Ginger then fell into a kind of
contempt; and its culture was dropped almoft every-
where, except at Jamaica.

This ifland produces and fells another fpice, improperly called Jamaica pepper. The tree which bears it
is a kind of myrtle, which commonly grows upon the
mountains, and rifes to the height of more than thirty
feet. It is very ftraight, moderately thick, and covered
with a grayifh, fmooth, and fhining bark. Its leaves,
which have a pleafant fmell, refemble, in form and
difpofition, thofe of the laurel; and the branches are
terminated by clufters of flowers entirely fimilar to
thofe of the common myrtle. The fruit by which
they are fucceeded is a fmall berry, fomewhat larger
than that of the juniper. Thefe berries are gathered
green, and fpread in the fun to dry. They turn brown,
and acquire a fpicy fmell, which in England hath given
the name of *all-fpice* to this pimento. It is very ufeful
to ftrengthen cold ftomachs; but what is this advantage compared with all thofe that are obtained from
fugar?

The art of managing this culture was unknown in
Jamaica till the year 1668. It was brought thither
by fome inhabitants of Barbadoes. One of them was
poffeffed of every requifite for that kind of produce
that depends on man. His name was Thomas Modi-
ford. His capital, together with his fkill and activity,
enabled him to clear an immenfe tract of land, and
raifed him in time to the government of the colony;
yet neither could the view of his fortune, nor his urgent folicitations, prevail upon men, who were moft
of them accuftomed to the idlenefs of a military life,
to apply to the labours of cultivation. Twelve hundred unfortunate men, who arrived in 1760 from Su-
rinam, which had juft been ceded to the Dutch, proved more tractable. Neceffity infpired them with refolution; and their example excited emulation, which
was kept up by the quantity of money conftantly
poured into the ifland by the Freebooters. Great part
of it was employed in erecting buildings, purchafing
flaves, implements of hufbandry, and furniture neceffary for the rifing plantations. In procefs of time, Jamaica exported great quantities of fugar, of an inferior

B O O K kind, indeed, to that which was made in moft of the
XIV.   other colonies, but the rum of which was exceedingly
fuperior.

The coffee-tree profpered in the Dutch and French
fettlements in the New World, before the Englifh
thought of appropriating it to themfelves; and, indeed, Jamaica was the only Britifh ifland which
thought proper to adopt it, but it never carried the
cultivation of it as far as the rival nations.

It was a generally received opinion in 1756, that
Jamaica had attained the greateft degree of profperity
of which it was fufceptible. An ifland, inhabited during a whole century by an active and enlightened
people, into which the riches of Mexico and Peru had
been conveyed without interruption, by piracy, and
by a fraudulent commerce, and in which no circumftance neceffary for cultivation had ever been wanting: an ifland, to which navigators muft have been
conftantly attracted, by the fafety of the coafts, and
by the excellence of the harbours; and the productions of which had always been in great requeft
throughout all Europe: fuch a fettlement muft have
appeared, even to the moft thinking perfons, to have
made all the progrefs of which nature had rendered
it fufceptible.

This illufion, fo reafonably adopted, was diffipated
by a war, which will for ever render this period memorable. A calamity, which fometimes overturns
ftates, and always exhaufts them, became a fource of
wealth to Jamaica. The Englifh merchants, enriched
with the fpoils of an enemy, conquered and fugitive
on all fides, found themfelves enabled to advance confiderable fums, and to grant a long credit to the planters. The colonifts themfelves, animated by the difcouragement of the French colonifts, whofe labours
had till that time been fo fortunate, eagerly availed
themfelves of the means which were put in their hands
by thefe unexpected events. Peace did not check the
impulfe they had received. This rapid increafe of activity hath continued, and the productions of the co-

lony are nearly one-third more confiderable than they

B O O K
XIV.

Prefent
ftate of Ja-
maica, con-
fidered in
every point
of view.

were thirty years ago.

The whole ifland may contain about three millions eight hundred thoufand acres of land, of which, according to the information of a judicious and ftudious man, who hath for a long time governed the colony, one million feven hundred twenty-eight thoufand four hundred and thirty-one acres are taken up by mountains, rocks, lakes, moraffes, rivers, and other places, which are unavoidably loft to the purpofes of every ufeful labour. Government hath fucceffively granted one million fix hundred and feventy-one thoufand five hundred and fixty-nine acres, which are cleared, or capable of being fo. There ftill remain four hundred thoufand to be difpofed of, which want nothing but men and means to cultivate them.

In 1658 Jamaica reckoned four thoufand five hundred white perfons, and fourteen hundred flaves; in 1670, feven thoufand five hundred white men, and eight thoufand flaves; in 1734, feven thoufand fix hundred and forty-four white men, and eighty-fix thoufand five hundred and forty-fix flaves; in 1746, ten thoufand white men, and one hundred and twelve thoufand four hundred and twenty-eight flaves; in 1768, feventeen thoufand nine hundred and forty-feven white men, and one hundred and fixty-fix thoufand nine hundred and fourteen flaves; in 1775, eighteen thoufand five hundred white perfons, three thoufand feven hundred blacks, or free Mulatoes, and one hundred and ninety thoufand nine hundred and fourteen flaves. One hundred and ten thoufand of thefe unfortunate people are placed on fix hundred and fourfcore fugar plantations; the remainder is employed in lefs valuable cultures, carried on in fourteen hundred and fixty habitations, in navigation, in domeftic fervices, and in other labours of primary neceffity.

The public expences of the colony amount annually to 817,750 livres [34,073l. 8s. 4d.] Thefe expences are fupplied by duties upon houfes, upon the feveral productions of the foil, upon foreign liquors, and by

B O O K a poll- tax upon the Negroes, which, in extraordinary
XIV.   cafes, is doubled. The perfons appointed, in the nineteen parifhes, to levy thefe taxes, which are decreed by
the general affembly, have obtained two and a half
per cent. as a reward for their trouble ; and the re-
ceiver-general retains five per cent. for himfelf.

The fpecie which is commonly circulated in the
ifland doth not exceed 954,041 livres [39,751l. 14s.
2d.]. This is more than fufficient, fince it is only ufed in the more minute details of trade. The flaves
brought from Africa, the merchandife fent from Europe, all things which are of great value, are paid by
bills of exchange payable in London, or in fome other
Britifh port, where the colonifts fend their commodities on their own account.

The profit arifing from thefe productions is not deftined entirely for the inceffant wants of Jamaica. A
great part of it is intended for the difcharge of the
debts, which an immoderate luxury, and accumulated
misfortunes, have obliged the inhabitants fucceffively
to contract. Thefe engagements, as far as we can
judge of them, amount to two-thirds of the apparent
riches of the colony. The greateft number of the
creditors are fettled in England ; the others are merchants temporarily fettled in the ifland, among whom
are reckoned a great many Jews. May thefe people,
who were flaves at firft, afterwards conquerors, and
then difgraced for the fpace of twenty centuries, one
day attain the legal poffeffion of Jamaica, or of fome
other rich ifland in the New World ! May they collect
all their children there, and bring them up in peace to
culture and commerce, fheltered from that fanaticifm
which rendered them odious to the world, and from
that perfecution which hath punifhed their errors with
too much rigour ! May the Jews live free, unmolefted,
and happy, in fome corner of the world ; fince, by the
ties of humanity, they are our brethren, and our fathers in the tenets of religion !

The colony, at prefent, fends annually to the mother country eight hundred thoufand quintals of fugar,

which, at the rate of 40 livres [1l. 13s. 4d.] the quin- B O O K
tal, produce 32,000,000 livres [1,333,333l. 6s. 8d.]; XIV.
four million gallons of rum, which, at the rate of
1 livre 10 fols [1s. 3d.] the gallon, produce 6,000,000l.
livres [250,000l.]; three hundred thousand gallons of
molasses, which, at the rate of 10 fols [5d.] the gallon, produce 150,000 livres [6250l.]; fix thousand
quintals of cotton, which, at the rate of 150 livres [6l.
5s.] the quintal, produce 900,000 livres [37,500l.];
fix thousand quintals of pimento, which, at the rate of
42 livres [1l. 6s. 8d.] the quintal, produce 252,000
livres [10,500l.]; eighteen thousand quintals of coffee, which, at the rate of 50 livres [2l. 1s. 8d.] the
quintal, produce 900,000 livres [37,500l.]; three
thousand quintals of ginger, which, at the rate of 70
livres [2l. 18s. 4d.] the quintal, produce 210,000
livres [8750l.]; and to the amount of 400,000 livres
[16,666l. 13s. 4d.] in wood for inlaying. All these
fums united, make the produce of Jamaica amount to
40,812,000 livres [1,700,500l.].

The veffels deftined for their exportation are very
numerous, but are only of the budren of one hundred
and fifty, or two hundred tons.

A fmall number of thefe veffels take up their cargoes at the harbour of Morant Point, which might be
confidered as a good harbour, were it more eafy of accefs. This road, fituated in the fouthern part of the
ifland, is only defended by an ill-conftructed battery,
improperly placed. Twelve men, commanded by a
ferjeant, are continually on guard there. Not far off
is a bay of the fame name, more convenient, and more
frequented by navigators.

The coaft affords no other anchorage, unlefs for
very fmall boats, till the fhips arrive at Port Royal,
where half of the productions of the colony deftined
for Europe are embarked.

At a greater diftance is the old harbour, which is
commonly well frequented. The neighbouring planters have often refolved to conftruct fome works there,
to protect the veffels which may take in their cargoes

B O O K at this place, againſt ſmall privateers. This expenſive
XIV. projeᶜt appears to be entirely laid aſide. It hath been
at length underſtood that the difficulty of entrance
would always be the beſt defence.

The bay of the Black River would require a good
battery, It might be ereᶜted without much expence,
and would enſure the ſafety of a great number of ſmall
ſhips that frequent it.

Savanna la Mar hath never much water, and its entrance is every where embarraſſed with ſhoals and
ſunken rocks. It is the worſt harbour of the colony ;
and yet it is become the ſtaple of a conſiderable trade,
ſince the neighbouring territory hath been cleared.
Formerly its inhabitants were deſirous of ſurrounding
themſelves with fortifications. Theſe works were forſaken, after more than one thouſand crowns [12,500l.]
had been expended upon them. Nothing remains of
theſe labours but a heap of ruins.

The iſland hath upon its weſtern coaſt, which is very
narrow, only one harbour, and that is Port Orange,
where ſeven or eight veſſels take in their cargoes annually.

The firſt harbour to the north is that of St. Lucia.
It is ſpacious and ſafe, and defended by a fort, capable
of making ſome reſiſtance, if it were repaired, and if
the artillery were put into a ſtate fit for ſervice. A
ſmall garriſon is always kept there.

Eight or nine leagues further, is the excellent bay
of Montego. The fifth part of the produᶜtions of the
colony is embarked in the ſmall town of Barnet-town,
defended by a battery of ten guns.

The entrance of Port St. Ann is rendered difficult
by ſhoals. It ſcarce receives annually fifteen or ſixteen veſſels.

Port Antonio is one of the ſafeſt harbours, but not
one of the moſt frequented, of the iſland. Its fort is
guarded by a detachment commanded by an officer.

The eaſtern coaſt hath no other harbour than the
Manchineel. Its anchorage is good, but in the neighbouring latitudes the ſea is always violently agitated

by the eaſterly winds. This is the ſpot moſt expoſed
to invaſions, and the battery of ten guns, which hath
been conſtructed there, would not ſhelter it from danger, if its riches were more conſiderable. The whole
defence of the colony is properly fixed at Port Royal.

The Engliſh had no ſooner made themſelves maſters
of Jamaica, than they attended to the rendering of
this conqueſt uſeful, and to the ſecuring of the poſſeſſion of it. The cultures undertaken by the Spaniards,
and the advantages of a ſafe, immenſe, and convenient
harbour, prudently inclined them to fix their views
upon Port Royal. The town they built there, though
placed in the midſt of ſands, upon a very narrow neck
of land, though deprived by nature of water fit for
drinking, and of all the other ſupports of life, became
a famous city in leſs than thirty years.

Means
which Ja-
maica hath
to preſerve
herſelf
from inva-
ſion.

This ſplendour was owing to a conſtant and quick
circulation of trade, formed by the commodities of
the iſland, the captures of the freebooters, and the
trade opened with the neighbouring continent. There
have been few ſtaples upon the face of the globe,
where the thirſt of wealth and pleaſure had united
more opulence and more corruption.

One moment deſtroyed, on the 27th of June 1692,
this beautiful appearance. The ſky, which was clear
and ſerene, grew obſcured and red throughout the
whole extent of Jamaica. A rumbling noiſe was heard
under ground, ſpreading from the mountains to the
plain ; the rocks were ſplit ; hills came cloſe together ; infectious lakes appeared on the ſpots where
whole mountains had been ſwallowed up ; immenſe
foreſts were removed ſeveral miles from the place
where they ſtood ; the edifices diſappeared, being either ſunk into the caverns of the earth, or overturned.
Thirteen thouſand lives were loſt by this dreadful
earthquake, and three thouſand by a contagious diſ-
temper that broke out ſoon after. It is ſaid, that ſince
this cataſtrophe, the climate is not ſo fine, the air not
ſo pure, nor the ſoil ſo fruitful, as it was before. This

B O O K terrible phenomenon fhould have taught the Euro-
   XIV. peans not to truft to the poffeffion of a world that
   ‿‿‿ trembles under their feet, and feems to flip out of their
rapacious hands.

In this general overthrow, Port Royal beheld buried
in the incenfed waves, or thrown at a diftance upon
defolate coafts, the numerous fhips, the proud flags
which rendered her fo vain. The city itfelf was deftroyed and overflown. In vain was it attempted to
rebuild the town upon its ruins; thefe labours were
all fruitlefs. The rifing walls were again blown down
by a hurricane. Port Royal, like Jerufalem, could
never be rebuilt. The earth feemed only digged to
fwallow it up anew. By a fingularity which baffles
all human efforts and reafonings to account for, the
only houfes that were left ftanding, after this frefh
fubverfion, were fituated at the extremity of a point
of land extremely narrow, which advances feveral
miles in the fea; as if the inconftant ocean had afforded a folid foundation to edifices which the firm ground
feemed to caft off.

The inhabitants of Port Royal, difcouraged by thefe
repeated calamities, retired to Kingfton, which is fituated in the fame bay. By their induftry and activity,
this town, which till then had been obfcure, foon became a pleafant and flourifhing city. Trade is even
gradually become more animated here, than it ever
was at any period in any of the marts to which it hath
fucceeded; becaufe the colony hath gained more by
the increafe of its cultures, than it hath loft by the decreafe of its fmuggling trade.

Yet Port Royal had never been, and Kingfton did
not become, the capital of the ifland. St. Yago de la
Vega, which the Englifh have named Spanifh-town,
continued ftill to enjoy this ufeful prerogative. This
town, built by the Spaniards, at the diftance of fome
leagues from the fea, upon the river Cobra, the moft
confiderable one of the country, though not navigable, was the feat of the legiflative body, the refi-
dence of the governor-general, the place where the

courts of juftice were holden, and, confequently, that B O O K
where the richeft planters dwelt.   XIV.

Admiral Knowles judged that this arrangement was
contrary to the public good ; and in 1756, he caufed
it to be decided by the general affembly, that all the
affairs, and all the powers of adminiftration, fhould
be united at Kingfton. Perfonal hatred againft the
projector of this plan ; the harfhnefs of the meafures
he employed to carry it into execution ; the attachment moft people are apt to take for places as well as
things; numberlefs private interefts that muft necefla-
rily be affected by this alteration : all thefe caufes raifed in the minds of feveral of the colonifts, unfurmount-
able objections to a plan, which was indeed liable to
fome inconveniencies, but which was founded on un-
anfwerable reafons, and offered great advantages. The
obftacles with which the opponents embarraffed the
new fyftem, did not put a ftop to the meafures of government. This was even the time they chofe for repairing Fort Charles, which ferves as a citadel to Port
Royal, and for increafing, on the other fide of the
bay, the very well executed fortifications of Mofquito
Point, which command the canal through which the
veffels deftined for Kingfton muft pafs. If, inftead of
entering the bay, the enemy fhould wifh to land to
the north of the new capital, they would be ftopped
in their march by Zock, a fort conftructed with fkill,
and maintained with care, in a very narrow defile, at
the diftance of a league from the city. Among thefe
different works, and in fome other lefs important
pofts, two regiments are ufually diftributed. They
receive pay from the mother-country : but the colony
adds to it a daily gratuity of 12 fols [6d.] for every
foldier, and a double gratuity for every officer. If
thefe troops were as well as they are ill difciplined,
they would not preferve the ifland from invafion, and
would foon be reduced to capitulate to a naval force
fuperior to that which might be deftined to fupport
them.

If Jamaica could even be preferved from the cala-

B O O K mities of a foreign invafion, it would no lefs be expof-
XIV   ed to domeftic dangers, ftill more alarming.

When the Spaniards were compelled to cede Jamaica to the Englifh, they left there a number of Negroes and Mulattoes, who, tired of their flavery, took
a refolution to retire into the mountains, there to preferve that liberty which they had recovered by the ex-
pulfion of their tyrants. Having entered into fome a-
greements neceffary to preferve their union, they planted maize and cocoa, in the moft inacceffible places of
their retreat ; but the impoffibility of fubfifting till
harveft, obliged them to come down into the plain to
pillage for fuftenance. The conquerors bore this plunder the more impatiently, as they had nothing to fpare;
and declared war againft them. Many were maffacred ;
the greater part fubmitted ; and only fifty or fixty fled
back to the rocks, there to live or die in freedom.

Policy, which fees every thing, but is never moved
by compaffion, thought it neceffary utterly to exterminate or reduce this handful of fugitives, who had
efcaped from flavery or carnage ; but the troops, who
were either perifhing or exhaufted with fatigue, were
averfe from this deftructive fcheme, which muft have
occafioned the effufion of more blood. It was therefore dropt, for fear of a revolt. This condefcenfion
was attended with fatal confequences. All the flaves,
grown defperate by the hardfhips they underwent, or
by the dread of punifhment, foon fought an afylum in
the woods, where they were fure of meeting with companions ready to affift them. The number of fugitives
increafed daily. In a fhort time they deferted by
troops, after having maffacred their mafters, and plundered and fet fire to the habitations. In vain were
active partizans fent out againft them; to whom a reward of 900 livres [37l. 10s.] was offered for the head
of every Negro they fhould bring. This feverity produced no alteration, and the defertion only became the
more general.

The rebels grew more daring as their numbers increafed. Till the year 1690, they had only fled ; but,

when they thought themfelves ftrong enough to attack, they fell upon the Englifh plantations, in feparate bands, and committed horrid ravages. In vain
were they driven back to their mountains with lofs;
in vain were forts erected and garrifoned at proper diftances, to prevent their inroads ; notwithftanding
thefe precautions, they renewed their depredations
from time to time. The refentment which the violation of the rights of nature by barbarous policy excited
in thefe Blacks, infpired them with fuch fury, that the
white people who had bought them, in order, as they
faid, to cut off the root of the evil, refolved, in 1735,
to employ all the forces of the colony, to deftroy a
juftly implacable enemy.

Immediately the military law took place of all civil
government. All the colonifts formed themfelves into regular bodies of troops. They marched towards
the rebels by different roads. One party undertook to
attack the town of Nauny, which the Blacks themfelves had built in the Blue Mountains. With cannon,
a town built without regularity and defended without
artillery, was foon deftroyed ; but the fuccefs of the
other enterprifes was frequently doubtful, fometimes
attended with much lofs. The flaves, more elated
by one triumph than difcouraged by ten defeats, were
proud of confidering their former tyrants merely as
enemies they were to contend with. If they were
beaten, they had at leaft fome revenge. Their blood
was at leaft mixed with that of their barbarous mafters.
They rufhed againft the fword of the European, to
plunge a dagger into his breaft. At laft, overpowered
by numbers, or by the dexterity of their antagonifts,
the fugitives intrenched themfelves in inacceffible
places, where they difperfed in fmall bands, fully determined never to ftir out ; and well affured that they
fhould never be conquered there. At length, after
various contefts and excurfions, that lafted nine months,
the Englifh gave up all thoughts of fubduing them.

Thus, fooner or later, will any people, made defperate by tyranny, or the oppreffion of conquerors, al-

BOOK
XIV.
ways get the better of numerous, experienced, and even well-difciplined armies; if they have but refolution enough to endure hunger rather than the yoke; to die rather than live in bondage; and, if they choofe, rather to fee their nation extinct than enflaved. Let them abandon the field to the multitude of troops; to the train of war; to the difplay of provifions, ammunition, and hofpitals: let them retire into the heart of the mountains, without baggage, without covering, without ftores; nature will provide for them and defend them. There let them remain for years, till the climate, idlenefs, and intemperance, have deftroyed thofe fwarms of foreign invaders, who have no booty to expect, nor any laurels to gather. Let them pour down upon them at intervals, like the torrents of their own mountains, furprife them in their tents, and ravage their boundaries. Laftly, let them defpife the opprobrious names of robbers and murderers, which will be lavifhed upon them by a great people, bafe enough to arm themfelves againft a handful of huntfmen, and weak enough to be unable to conquer them.

Such was the conduct of the Blacks with the Englifh. Thefe, weary of excurfions and fruitlefs armaments, fell into univerfal defpondency. The pooreft among them would not venture to accept the lands which the government offered them in the vicinity of the mountains. Even the fettlements at a greater diftance from thefe rebels, inured to war, were either neglected or forfaken. Many parts of the ifland, which from their appearance feemed likely to become the moft fruitful, were left in their uncultivated ftate.

In this fituation was the colony, when Trelawney was appointed governor. This prudent and humane commander was fenfible, that a fet of men, who for near a century paft lived upon wild fruits, went naked, and expofed to the inclemency of the weather; who, ever at war with an affailant ftronger than themfelves, and better armed, never ceafed fighting for the defence of their liberty; that fuch a fet of men would never be fubdued by open force. He, therefore, had recourfe

to conciliating measures. He offered them not only BOOK XIV.
lands as their own property, but likewise liberty and
independence.

These overtures were favourably received. The
treaty concluded with them in 1739, decided, that the
chief, whom they themselves should choose, should receive his commission from the English government;
that he should come every year to the capital of the
colony, if required; that two white men should constantly reside with him, in order to maintain a harmony
advantageous to both nations; and if the colony were
ever attacked, he and all his people should take up
arms.

While Trelawney was negotiating this accommodation in the name of the crown, the general assembly of
the colony proposed their separate plan. In this second agreement, the new people engaged to harbour
no more fugitive slaves; and they were promised a sti-
pulated sum for every deserter whom they should inform against, and a more considerable reward for those
whom they should bring back to their plantations.
Since this shameful contract, this small republic hath
been constantly declining. It now reckons no more
than thirteen hundred individuals, men, women, and
children, distributed in five or six villages.

Whether these events inspired them with boldness,
or whether they were exasperated at the ill usage they
met with from the English, the Negro slaves resolved
to be free likewise. While the flames of war, kindled
in Europe, were spreading in America, these miserable
men agreed, in 1760, to take up arms all in one day,
murder their tyrants, and seize upon the government.
But their impatience for liberty disconcerted the unanimity of the plot, by preventing the timely execution
of it. Some of the conspirators stabbed their masters,
and set fire to their houses before the appointed time;
but finding themselves unable to resist the whole force
of the island, which their premature exploit had collected in a moment, they fled to the mountains. From
this impenetrable recess they were incessantly making

B O O K destructive inroads. The English, in their distress, were
XIV. reduced to solicit the assistance of the wild Negroes,
whose independence they had been obliged to acknowledge by a solemn treaty. They even bribed
them, and promised a considerable sum for every slave
they should kill with their own hands. Those base
Africans, unworthy of the liberty they had recovered,
were not ashamed to sell the blood of their brethren :
they pursued them, and killed many of them by surprise. At last the conspirators, weakened and betrayed by their own nation, remained a long time silent
and inactive.

The conspiracy was thought to be effectually extinguished, when the rebels, reinforced by deserters
from the several plantations, appeared again with re-
doubled fury. The regular troops, the militia, and a
large body of sailors, all marched in pursuit of the
slaves; they fought and beat them in several skir-
mishes ; many were slain, or taken prisoners, and the
rest dispersed into the woods and rocks. All the prisoners were shot, hanged, or burnt. Those who were sup-
posed to be the chief promoters of the conspiracy, were
tied alive to gibbets, and there left to perish slowly,
exposed to the scorching sun of the torrid zone ; a far
more painful and more terrible death than that of being burnt alive. Yet their tyrants enjoyed the torments of these miserable wretches, whose only crime
was an attempt to recover by revenge, those rights of
which avarice and inhumanity had deprived them.

The measures that were taken to prevent future in-
surrections were dictated by the same spirit of barbarity. A slave is whipped in the public places, if he
plays at any game whatsoever ; if he presumes to go
a-hunting, or to sell any thing but milk or fish. He
cannot stir out of his master's plantation, unless attended by a white man, or with an express permission
in writing. If he should beat a drum, or make use of
any other noisy instrument, his master is condemned
to pay a fine of 225 livres [9l. 7s. 6d.] Thus do the
English, who are so jealous of their own liberty, sport

with that of other men. To this excefs of barbarity the Negro trade muft neceffarily have brought thefe ufurpers. Such is the progrefs of injuftice and violence. To conquer the New World, its inhabitants muft doubtlefs have been flaughtered. To replace them, Negroes muft be bought, as they alone are able to endure the climate and the labours of America. To remove thefe Africans from their native country, who were defigned to cultivate the land without having any poffeffions in it, it was neceffary to feize them by force, and to make them flaves. To keep them in fubjection, they muft be treated with feverity. To prevent their revolt, the natural confequence of feverity and fervitude, thefe men, whom we have made defperate, muft be reftrained by capital punifhments, by hard ufage, and atrocious laws.

But cruelty itfelf has a period in its own deftructive nature. In an inftant it may ceafe. An enemy who fhould be fo fortunate as to land at Jamaica, would foon convey arms to thefe men, who are full of rancour againft their oppreffors, and only wait a favourable opportunity to rife againft them. The French, not confidering that the revolt of the Blacks in one colony would probably occafion it in all the reft, will haften fuch a revolution in time of war. The Englifh, finding themfelves between two fires, will be difmayed; their ftrength and courage will fail them; and Jamaica will fall a prey to flaves and conquerors, who will contend for dominion with frefh enormities. Such is the train of evils that injuftice brings along with it! It attaches itfelf to man fo clofely, that the connection cannot be diffolved but by the fword. Crimes beget crimes; blood is productive of blood; and the earth becomes a perpetual fcene of defolation, tears, mifery, and affliction, where fucceffive generations rife to imbrue their hands in blood, to tear out each other's bowels, and to lay each other in the duft.

The lofs of Jamaica, however, would be a heavy one for England. Nature has placed this ifland at

B O O K the entrance of the gulf of Mexico, and made it a
XIV.   kind of key to that rich country.   All fhips going
war. Its   from Carthagena to the Havannah, are obliged to pafs
difadvan-   by its coafts ; it is more within reach of the feveral
tages for
navigation. trading ports on the continent, than any other ifland ;
the many excellent roads with which it is furrounded,
facilitate the launching of men of war on all fides of
the ifland.   Thefe feveral advantages are balanced by
fome inconveniencies.

If it be eafy to get at Jamaica by the trade-winds,
by taking a view of the Lefs Antilles, it is not fo eafy
to get away from thence, whether we go through
the Straits of Bahama, or determine for the Leeward
Paffage.

The firft of thefe two ways gives the full advantage
of the wind for two hundred leagues ; but as foon as
Cape St. Anthony is doubled, we meet the fame wind
againft us that before was favourable : fo that more
time is loft than was gained ; and there is alfo a rifk
of being taken by the guarda coftas of the Havannah.
This danger is fucceeded by another, which is the fhoals
on the coaft of Florida, towards which the winds and
currents drive with great violence.   The Elizabeth, an
Englifh man of war, would infallibly have been loft
there in 1746, had not Captain Edwards ventured
into the Havannah.   It was during the height of the
war, and the port belonged to the enemy.   " I come,"
faid the captain to the governor, " to deliver up my
" fhip, my failors, my foldiers, and myfelf, into your
" hands ; I only afk the lives of my men."   " I will
" not be guilty of any difhonourable action," replied
the Spanifh commander.   " Had we taken you in fight,
" in open fea, or upon our coafts, your fhip would
" have been ours, and you would have been our pri-
" foners.   But as you are overtaken by a ftorm, and
" are driven into this port from the fear of being fhip-
" wrecked, I do, and ought to forget that my nation
" is at war with yours.   You are men, and fo are we ;
" you are in diftrefs, and have a right to our pity.   You
" are at liberty to unload and refit your veffel ; and if

" you want it, you may trade in this port to pay your
" charges ; you may then go away, and you will have
" a pafs to carry you fafe beyond the Bermudas. If
" after this you fhould be taken, you will be a lawful
" prize ; but, at this moment, I fee in Englifhmen,
" only ftrangers for whom humanity claims our affift-
" ance."

Spaniards! incomprehenfible race of men, tell me,
fince fuch are your feelings, and fince you can fpeak thus
to an enemy, delivered into your power by the winds,
why have you not known how to refpect the innocent
favage, proftrate at your feet, who adored you? The
reafon of this I conceive to be, that Captain Edwards's
fhip was not loaded with that yellow duft, the fight
of which changes you into wild beafts. Perhaps I
have calumniated you : but I have feen you fo frequently below your own fpecies, that I have had good
reafon for doubting of your virtues ; efpecially when
you difplay them to me with a character of heroifm
which affects and aftonifhes me. I oppofe fufpicions,
perhaps unjuft ones to my admiration and to my tears
which are ready to flow.

The other way is attended with no lefs difficulty
and danger. It terminates at a fmall ifland, that the
Englifh call Crooked Ifland, which lies eighty leagues
off Jamaica. Ships that come this way muft commonly ftrive againft the eafterly wind through the whole
paffage, coaft along clofe under St. Domingo, in order
to keep clear of the flats of Cuba, and then pafs the
ftraits, between the points of thefe two great iflands,
where it is very difficult to efcape being intercepted
by their privateers or their men of war. The navigators coming from the Lucays do not meet with thefe
obftructions.

It is reckoned that there are about two hundred of
thefe iflands, all of them fituated to the north of Cuba,
and moft of which are nothing more than rocks juft
rifing above water. Columbus, who difcovered them
on his arrival in the New World, and who gave the
name of San Salvador to that on which he landed,

Revolu-
tions which
have hap-
pened in
the Lucaya
iflands.
State of
thefe
iflands.

B O O K   did not make any fettlement there.   Neither did the
XIV.   Caftilians afterwards fix upon it ; but, in 1507, they
         carried off all the inhabitants, who foon perifhed in
the mines, or in the pearl fifhery. This fmall Archipelago was entirely defert, when, in 1672, fome Englifhmen took poffeffion of Providence Ifland ; they
were driven from thence feven or eight years afterwards, by the orders of the court of Madrid, but returned in 1690, and were again expelled in 1703 by
the Spaniards and French united.   The ifland was
peopled again by a particular event.

In 1714, fome fhips richly laden were fwallowed up
by a ftorm upon the coafts of Florida.   The treafures
which they contained belonged to the Spaniards, who
caufed them to be dived for.   So rich a prey tempted
fome of the inhabitants of Jamaica.   The Spaniards
refufed to fhare with them, and Jennings, the boldeft
among them, had recourfe to arms, to fupport what
he called a natural and undeniable right.   The dread
of being feverely punifhed, for having difturbed the
peace which Europe had for fo long a time been anxious to obtain, obliged him to turn pirate.   His companions were foon numerous enough to make it neceffary to multiply his armaments.   The Lucays became
their place of retreat.   It was from thence that thefe
robbers fallied forth to attack all veffels without diftinction, Englifh as well as others.   The nations were
apprehenfive of feeing renewed, in the New World,
thofe fcenes of horror which had been difplayed there
by the ancient freebooters, when George I. roufed by
the clamours of his people and by the wifhes of his
parliament, fent out, in 1719, a fufficient force to fub-
due thefe pirates.   The moft determined of them refufed the amnefty which was offered them, and went
to infeft the coafts of Afia and Africa with their rob-
beries.   The reft increafed the colony which Woods
Rogers brought with him from Europe.

This colony may at this day confift of three or four
thoufand perfons, half of whom are fettled at Providence, where Fort Naffau hath been conftructed, and

which hath a harbour fufficient for fmall veffels; the
reft are diftributed in the other iflands. They fend
annually to England to the value of forty or fifty
thoufand crowns [from 5000l. to 6250l.] of cotton,
wood for dyeing, and live turtle ; and with their falt
they pay for the provifions which North America fupplies them with.

Although the foil of the Lucays cannot be compared to that of feveral of the other colonies, yet it would
be fufficient to afford plenty of fubfiftence, by labour,
to a population much more confiderable than that
which is at prefent found there, in free people or in
flaves. The great neglect of its cultures muft be attributed to the firft manners, and prefent propenfities,
of the inhabitants. Thefe iflands, which on one fide
are feparated from Florida by the channel of Bahama,
form on the other a long chain, which terminates at
the point of Cuba. It is there that begin the iflands
called Turk's Iflands, or Caicos, which continue the
chain as far as towards the middle of the northern
coaft of St. Domingo. So favourable a pofition for
piracy hath turned the views of the inhabitants towards a cruizing life. They are ever eager to engage
in hoftilities, which may put the Spanifh and French
productions into their hands. The Bermudas exhibit
a more tranquil fcene.

This fmall Archipelago, about three hundred leagues
diftant from that of the Antilles, was difcovered, in
1527, by the Spaniard John Bermudas, who gave his
name to it, but did not land there. Ferdinand Came-
lo, a Portuguefe, obtained in 1572, of Philip II. a grant
of it, which did not take effect. The French navigator Barbotiere was fhipwrecked there in 1593, but
thought no more of it after he had quitted it. The
fhip of George Sommers was broken to pieces there in
1609. With the wrecks of this fhip a fmall veffel was
conftructed, which had the good fortune to arrive fafe
in England.

Three years after, a company was formed in London to people the Bermudas, which were entirely un-

Poverty of
the Ber-
mudas.
Character
of the inha-
bitants.

BOOK
XIV.
inhabited. Sixty men were fent there, and they were foon followed by many more. They occupied at firft St. George, the one of thefe iflands which had the beft harbour; and in procefs of time they took poffeffion of all thofe which were fufceptible of culture. The land was exactly meafured, and diftributed among the inhabitants, in proportion as their families were more or lefs numerous.

The accounts that were propagated of the falubrity and mildnefs of the climate, attracted colonifts from all parts of the Britifh empire. Inhabitants reforted thither from the Antilles for the recovery of their health, and from the northern colonies to enjoy their fortune in peace. Many royalifts retired there, in expectation of the death of their oppreffor Cromwell. Waller, among the reft, that charming poet, who was an enemy to that tyrannical deliverer, croffed the feas, and celebrated thofe fortunate iflands, infpired by the influence of the air, and the beauty of the country, which are always favourable to the poet. He imparted his enthufiafm to the fair fex. The Englifh ladies never thought themfelves handfome or well dreffed, unlefs they had fmall Bermuda hats made with palm leaves.

But at laft the charm was broken, and thefe iflands fell into that contempt which their infignificance deferved. They are very numerous, and their whole compafs is but fix or feven leagues. The foil is very indifferent, and there is not a fingle fpring to water it. There is no water to drink but what is taken from wells and refervoirs. Maize, vegetables, and excellent fruits, afford plenty of wholefome food; but there are no fuperfluous commodities for exportation; yet chance has collected under this pure and temperate fky four or five thoufand inhabitants; poor, but happy in being unobferved. Their connections with England do not annually exceed 120,000 livres [5000l.], and thofe which they have formed with the American continent are fcarcely more extenfive.

In order to render the circumftances of this weak

colony more eafy, it hath been fucceffively propofed B O O K
to cultivate filk, vines, and cochineal there ; but none XIV.
of thefe projects have been carried into execution. Induftry hath been confined to the manufacturing of
fail-cloth, an occupation which is naturally connected
with the conftruction of thofe fmall veffels made of
cedar or acajou wood, which have never been equalled upon the globe, either for their failing or for their
duration.

The principal inhabitants of the Bermuda iflands
formed a fociety in 1765, the ftatutes of which are,
perhaps, the moft refpectable monument that ever
dignified humanity. Thefe virtuous citizens engaged
themfelves to form a library of all books of hufbandry, in whatever language they had been written ; to
procure to all capable perfons of both fexes an employment fuitable to their difpofition ; to beftow a reward on every man who had introduced into the colony any new art, or contributed to the improvement
of any one already known ; to give a penfion to every
daily workman, who, after having affiduoufly continued his labour, and maintained a good character for
forty years, fhould not have been able to lay by a
ftock fufficient to allow him to pafs his latter days in
quiet ; and laftly, to indemnify every individual who
fhould have been oppreffed either by the minifter or
the magiftrate.

May thefe advantages ever be preferved to thofe induftrious, though indigent people ; happy in their labour and in their poverty, which keeps their morals
untainted ! They enjoy, in a ftate of innocence, the
benefits of a pure and ferene fky, and preferve tranquillity of mind with health. The poifon of luxury
has never infected them. They are not themfelves addicted to envy, nor do they excite it in others. The
rage of ambition and war is extinguifhed upon their
coafts, as the ftorms of the ocean that furround them
are broken. The virtuous man would willingly crofs
the feas to enjoy the fight of their frugality. May the
winds never convey to them the account of the events

B O O K of the world in which we live! They then learn——
  XIV. ⌣ but, alas!——my imagination wanders, the pen drops
from my hand, and they fhall receive no information
from me.

Such were the poffeffions of the Englifh in the American Archipelago, when the fucceffes of the war which
ended in 1763 gave to the domains of that power a
confiderable increafe of extent, of which Granada was
the richeft part.

Granada
was firft oc-
cupied by
the French.
What the
firft colo-
nifts did
there.

This ifland hath twenty-one leagues in circumference, fix in its greateft breadth, which is from north
to fouth, and four from eaft to weft. Its territory,
though very uneven, is in general fertile, and fufceptible of fome kind of culture, according to its quality,
and to its expofure, which is not fufficiently attended
to. The foil, however, becomes lefs productive, in
proportion to its diftance from the coafts. The caufe
of this, perhaps, may be, that the rains, which are too
frequent at the foot of the mountains, even in thofe
feafons when the reft of the ifland is afflicted by
droughts, keep the neighbouring grounds, which are
almoft all clayey, in a ftate of frefhnefs and moifture,
which deftroys their richnefs, and confequently their
fertility.

The weftern part of the ifland is watered by ten rivers, the northern part by three, the eaftern part by
eight, and the fouthern part by five. Befide thefe
fprings, which are all confiderable enough to work fu-
gar-mills, there are feveral others lefs confiderable, but
very ufeful to the coffee plantations.

The neighbouring continent fhelters Granada from
thofe fatal hurricanes which carry defolation in fo many other iflands; and nature hath multiplied the creeks,
the bays, and the harbours, which are favourable for
the exportation of provifions. Its principal port is called Baffe-Terre, or St. George, which would furnifh a
fafe retreat to fixty men of war.

Though the French, acquainted with the fertility
of Granada, had formed, as early as the year 1638, the
project of fettling there, yet they never carried it into

execution till the year 1651. At their arrival they gave a few hatchets, fome knives, and a barrel of brandy, to the chief of the favages they found there; and imagining they had purchafed the ifland with thefe trifles, affumed the fovereignty, and foon acted as tyrants. The Caribs, unable to contend with them by open force, took the method which weaknefs always infpires to repel oppreffion; they murdered all whom they found alone and defencelefs. The troops that were fent to fupport the infant colony, found no fafer or more expeditious way than to deftroy all the natives. The remainder of thefe miferable favages took refuge upon a fteep rock, preferring rather to throw themfelves down alive from the top of it, than to fall into the hands of an implacable enemy. The French inconfiderately called this rock *le mont des fauteurs*, the hill of the leapers; and it ftill retains that name.

How was it poffible that thefe frivolous people could lofe, in diftant countries, that vein of pleafantry which they preferve in their own, even in the midft of the greateft calamities! They are not a cruel people; but the natural cheerfulnefs which accompanies the Frenchman in tents, in the midft of camps, upon the field of battle, upon a mattrafs in an hofpital, where he may have been laid, covered with wounds, and of which he is expiring, will fuggeft to him fome ridiculous expreffion, which will produce a fmile in the companions of his misfortunes; and this contraft of character with fituation will manifeft itfelf in the fame manner among all Frenchmen, and among fome perfons of a fingular turn in all the countries in the world.

They were juftly punifhed for all thefe cruelties, by a rapacious, violent, and inflexible governor. Moft of the colonifts, no longer able to endure his tyranny, retired to Martinico, and thofe who remained on the ifland condemned him to death. In the whole court of juftice that formally tried this mifcreant, there was only one man who could write, and his name was Archangeli. A farrier was the perfon that impeached, who, inftead of the fignature, fealed with a horfe-

BOOK
XIV.
ſhoe; and Archangeli, who performed the office of clerk, wrote gravely round it, *Marque de Monſieur de la Brie, conſeiller rapporteur:* MARK OF MR. DE LA BRIE, COUNSEL FOR THE COURT.

It was apprehended that the court of France would not ratify this extraordinary ſentence, paſſed with ſuch unuſual formalities, though dictated by common ſenſe. Moſt of the judges of the crime, and witneſſes of the execution, diſappeared from Granada. None remained, except thoſe whoſe obſcurity ſcreened them from the purſuit of the laws. The eſtimate taken in 1700 ſhows, that there were on the iſland no more than 251 white people, 53 free ſavages or mulattoes, and 525 ſlaves. The uſeful animals were reduced to 64 horſes, and 569 head of horned cattle. The whole culture conſiſted of three plantations of ſugar, and fifty-two of indigo.

The face of things was totally changed towards the year 1714; and this alteration was effected by Martinico. That iſland was then laying the foundation of a ſplendour that was to aſtoniſh all nations. It ſent immenſe productions to France, and received valuable commodities in return, which were moſt of them ſent to the Spaniſh coaſts. Its ſhips touched at Granada in their way, to take in refreſhments. The trading privateers, who undertook this navigation, taught the people of that iſland the value of their ſoil, which only required cultivation. The execution of every project is facilitated by commerce. Some traders furniſhed the inhabitants with ſlaves and utenſils to erect ſugar plantations. An open account was eſtabliſhed between the two colonies. Granada was clearing its debts gradually by its rich produce; and the balance was on the point of being cloſed, when the war in 1744 interrupted the communication between the two iſlands, and at the ſame time ſtopped the progreſs of the moſt important culture of the New World. At that time, cotton, cacao, and particularly coffee trees, were planted; and during the continuance of hoſtilities, they acquired a ſufficient growth to yield plenti-

fully. Thefe ufeful trees were not abandoned after
the peace of 1748; but the culture of the fugar-canes
was then pufhed with an eagernefs proportioned to
their importance. A feries of misfortunes, too much
merited, foon deprived the mother-country of the
great advantages it flattered itfelf with from this colony.

The paffionate defire of premature and unbounded
enjoyment, that malady which hath tainted the government of a nation which yet deferves the affection
of her mafters; that prodigality which reaps when it
fhould fow, which deftroys the paft with one hand,
and the future with the other, which exhaufts and
confumes the ftock by anticipating the income; that
confufion which refults from the diftreffes any ftate
muft neceffarily be reduced to, that has neither principles nor experience, that has power without views,
and means without conduct; that anarchy that prevails at the helm; that precipitation, that caballing
among inferiors; the impropriety, or total want of
projects; on one hand, the audacity of doing any
thing with impunity; on the other, the fear of fpeaking even for the public good: this concurrence of
long fucceeding evils has thrown Granada into the
hands of Great Britain, which is confirmed in the poffeffion of this conqueft by the treaty of 1763.

The Englifh did not make a fortunate beginning.
A great number of them refolved to have plantations
upon an ifland, of which the higheft opinion had previoufly been formed; and, in their enthufiafm, they
purchafed them for much more than their real value.
This paffion, which expelled the ancient colonifts, who
were inured to the climate, drew thirty-five or thirty-
fix millions of livres [from 1,458,333l. 6s. 8d. to
1,500,000l.] out of the mother-country. This imprudence was followed by another. The new proprietors,
mifled, no doubt, by national pride, have fubftituted
new methods to thofe of their predeceffors. They attempted to alter the mode of living among their flaves.
The Negroes, who from their ignorance are more at-

Events
which have
happened
at Granada
fince it is
fallen un-
der the Bri-
tifh govern-
ment.

B O O K tached to their old customs than other men, revolted.
    XIV.   It was found necessary to send out troops, and to shed
blood. The whole colony was filled with suspicions.
Masters, who had been under the necessity of using violent methods, were afraid of being burnt or massacred
in their own habitations. The labours declined, and
were even totally suspended. Tranquillity was at length
restored, but it was soon succeeded by a new storm.

Throughout the whole extent of the British empire,
the Roman Catholics are rigorously deprived of the
least influence in public affairs. When the ministry
established the English government at Granada, they
thought proper to deviate from these generally received principles; and they permitted all the ancient inhabitants, of whatever religion they might be, to give
their vote in the assemblies of the colony. This innovation met with the most obstinate resistance; but at
last parliament, which had got rid of some of its prejudices, declared in favour of the administration, and
Catholics, as well as others, were allowed to attend to
the common interests of the colony.

The predilection which George III. had shown for
the French, who were become his subjects, made him
imagine that his commands would meet with no opposition in a settlement of which they still formed the
greatest number. In this persuasion, he ordered that
the duty of four and a half per cent. upon productions
on their exportation, which, in an excess of zeal, all
the British islands, except Jamaica, had very anciently
granted, should be levied at Granada. The power of
doing this was disputed with him. The cause was formally tried, and the decision was not favourable to the
monarch.

This triumph elated the minds of the colonists. In
order to accelerate the cultures, they had borrowed
large sums from the monied people of the mother-
country. These debts, which amounted to 50,000,000
of livres [2,083,333l. 6s. 8d.], were not paid at the
appointed time. The creditors had recourse to the
rigour of the law, which authorised them to seize the

plantations that had been mortgaged to them, to put B O O K
them up to public fale, and to exact the full value of XIV.
them eight months after. This feverity fpread univerfal confternation. The legiflative body of the ifland,
in their defpair, paffed a bill on the 6th of June 1774,
which divided the value of the acquifition into five
payments, and which protracted the laft payment to
the term of thirty-two months. The fecret motive of
this fingular act was undoubtedly to put it in the power
of the debtors to bid for their own eftates, and by this
contrivance to procure them delays, which they would
in vain have expected from the commiferation of their
creditors.

A meafure fo bold excited a tumult throughout
England. It was generally thought an injurious thing,
that a very fmall part of the empire fhould arrogate
to itfelf a right of annihilating engagements contracted under the fanction of a law univerfally eftablifhed,
in the good faith of trade. This indignation was communicated even to the iflands of America, which underftood clearly, that no further credit could be expected, if confidence were not fettled upon a firm bafis. The Britons of the Old and of the New World
united in urging the fupreme power to repair without
delay this great breach made in the important and im-
prefcriptible right of property.

The parliament, whatever might be the diftrefs of Cultures of
this valuable acquifition, thought in the fame manner Granada,
as the people. and of the
Grana-
In 1771 and 1775, St. George was reduced to afhes dines.
by dreadful fires. The colony experienced other calamities ; and notwithftanding this, its productions
have increafed threefold fince it came out of the hands
of the French. It is become, under the other hemifphere, the fecond of the Englifh iflands. Its new
mother-country receives from it annually eighteen
millions weight of fugar, which, at 40 livres [1l. 13s.
4d.] the quintal, produce in Europe 7,200,000 livres
[300,000l.] ; one million one hundred thoufand gallons of rum, which, at one livre ten fols [1s. 3d.] the

B O O K gallon, produce 1,650,000 livres [68,750l.]; thirty
XIV. thousand quintals of coffee, which, at 50 livres [2l. 1s.
8d.] the quintal, produce 1,500,000 livres [62,500l.];
three thousand quintals of cacao, which, at 50 livres
[2l. 1s. 8d.] the quintal, produce 150,000 livres
[6250l.]; three hundred quintals of indigo, which, at
800 livres [33l. 6s. 8d.] the quintal, produce 240,000
livres [10,000l.]; thirteen thousand quintals of cotton,
which, at 150 livres [6l. 5s.] the quintal, produce
1,950,000 livres [81,250l.]: this makes in all
12,690,000 livres [528,750l.]: but in this revenue is
included that which the Granadines produce.

Thefe are a dozen of fmall iflands, from three to
eight leagues in circumference. They do not afford a
fingle river, and yet the climate is very wholefome.
The ground, covered only with thin bufhes, has not
been fcreened from the fun for many centuries, and it
may be cultivated without its exhaling at any time
thofe noxious vapours which generally attack the
planters perpetually elfewhere.

Cariacou, the only one of thefe iflands which the
French have occupied, was at firft frequented by
turtle fifhermen, who, in the intervals of leifure afforded them by their occupation, attempted fome
kinds of culture. Their fmall number was foon increafed by feveral of the inhabitants of Guadalupe,
who had been driven from their habitations by mifchievous infects. Thefe good people, affifted by eight
or nine hundred flaves, employed themfelves with fuccefs in the culture of cotton. This fhrub was conveyed
by the Englifh to the other Granadine iflands, and
they even formed a fugar plantation at Bequia, and
two at Cariacou.

The ifland   Tabago, which was acquired by Great Britain at
of Tabago, the fame period and by the fame treaty, is feparated
which was
the caufe of from the Spanifh ifland of Trinidad only by a channel
great dif- of nine leagues over. This poffeffion hath ten leagues
putes be-
tween the in length and four in its greateft breadth. It hath a
Dutch and harbour upon its eaftern coaft, in which there are
the French,
becomes a twenty-five or thirty feet of water, and another on its

northern coaft, which hath no more than twenty or B O O K
twenty-five. They are both fheltered from moft of XIV.
the winds, an advantage which that on the fouth fide British pof-
doth not enjoy. Among the fmall mountains which feffion.
occupy the centre of the ifland, there is one more
elevated, the black and reddifh colour of which
feems to indicate the ruins of an ancient volcano. It
is not expofed to thofe dreadful hurricanes that are fo
deftructive in other parts. Poffibly it owes this inef-
timable advantage to the vicinity of the continent.

Tabago has formerly been exceedingly populous, if
we may credit fome traditional accounts. The inhabitants long withftood the fierce and frequent attacks
of the favages from the continent, who were ftub-
born and irreconcileable enemies. At length, wea-
ried out with thefe inroads, which were inceffantly renewed, they difperfed into the adjacent iflands.

That which they had forfaken lay open to invafion
from Europe, when two hundred natives of Fleffin-
gen landed there in 1632, to lay the foundation of
a Dutch colony. The neighbouring Indians joined
with the Spaniards of the ifland of Trinidad, to oppofe an eftablifhment that gave umbrage to both.
Whoever attempted to ftop their fury, was murdered
or taken prifoner; and the few who efcaped into the
woods foon deferted the ifland.

For twenty years the Dutch forgot a fettlement
which was only noted for the difafters of its origin.
In 1654 a frefh colony was fent there, which was
driven away in 1666. The Englifh were foon deprived of this conqueft by the French; but Lewis
XIV. fatisfied with having conquered it, reftored it
to his ally the republic of Holland. This fettlement
fucceeded no better than the other colonies of that
commercial nation that were engaged in agriculture.
The motives that determine fo many perfons from
other countries to go to America, ought never to
have influenced the Dutch. Their own country affords every poffible advantage for trade, and they
have no need to go abroad to make their fortune. A

BOOK
XIV.

happy toleration, purchafed, like their liberty, with rivers of blood, hath at length left the confciences of all men free ; fo that no religious fcruples can induce timorous minds to banifh themfelves from their native country. The government makes fuch ample provifion for the relief and employment of the poor, that none are driven by defpair to go and clear a foreign land, which ufually deftroys the firft cultivators. Tabago, therefore, never had more than 1200 men, employed in the culture of a little tobacco, cotton, and indigo, and of fix fugar plantations.

The colony was confined to this fcanty exertion of induftry, when it was attacked by the very fame nation that had reftored it to its former rights of poffeffion and property. In the month of February 1677, a French fleet, deftined to feize upon Tabago, fell in with the Dutch fleet that was fent out to oppofe this expedition. They engaged in one of the roads of the ifland, which became famous for this memorable action in an age abounding with great events. The obftinacy and valour on both fides were fuch, that the fight ftill continued, when every fhip was difmafted and unrigged, and no failors left to work them. The engagement did not ceafe till twelve veffels were burnt, and a great number were funk. The affailers loft the feweft men, and the defendants kept poffeffion of the ifland.

But d'Eftrées, who was determined to take it, landed there the fame year in the month of December. There was then no fleet to obftruct or retard his progrefs. A bomb thrown from his camp, blew up their powder magazine. This proved, as it generally does, a decifive ftroke ; and the enemy, unable to refift, furrendered at difcretion. The conquerors availed themfelves to the utmoft of the right of war : not content with razing the fortifications, they burnt the plantations, feized upon all the fhips in the harbour, and tranfported the inhabitants from the ifland. The conqueft of this place was fecured to France by the peace that foon followed an action, in which defeat

was attended with no marks of difgrace, and victory
with no advantage.

The court of Verfailles neglected this important
ifland to fuch a degree, as not to fend a fingle man
thither. Perhaps, in the intoxication of falfe grandeur, they beheld with indifference whatever was
merely ufeful. They even entertained an unfavourable opinion of Tabago, and imagined it was only a
barren rock. This error gained ground from the behaviour of the French, who, finding themfelves too
numerous at Martinico, went over to the iflands of
St. Lucia, St. Vincent, and Dominica. Thefe were
precarious poffeffions, and the foil of which was of
an indifferent quality. Could they poffibly have been
preferred to an ifland where the land was better, and
the property inconteftable? Such was the reafoning
of a government, which was not then fufficiently enlightened concerning the trade and plantations of the
colonies, to difcern the true motives of this diflike the
fubjects had to Tabago.

An infant colony, efpecially when it is founded
with flender means, cannot fubfift without immediate
affiftance. It cannot make any progrefs but in proportion as it finds confumption for its firft productions.
Thefe are generally of a common fort, are not worth
the expences of exportation to any diftance, and
therefore will fcarce fell but in the neighbourhood,
and ought infenfibly, and by moderate profits, to lead
to the undertaking of thofe great cultures which are
the object of commerce between Europe and the Leeward Iflands. But Tabago was too remote from the
French fettlements, to attract inhabitants by fuch a
gradation of fuccefs. Lefs fruitful iflands, that were
nearer to their refources, were preferred.

The low condition into which it was fallen, did not
prevent it from attracting the attention of England.
That proud ifland, which thinks herfelf the queen of
all others, becaufe fhe is the moft flourifhing, pretended to have an undoubted right to that of Tabago, becaufe it had once been in her poffeffion for fix months.

B O O K   Her forces have confirmed her pretenſions; and the
   XIV.   peace of 1763 has juſtified the ſucceſs of her arms, by
⌣⌣⌣⌣⌣   ceding to her a poſſeſſion, which ſhe will turn to bet-
          ter account than the French ever did.

Plan for   Almoſt all the ſettlements in the Antilles have prov-
clearing the ed fatal to the firſt coloniſts, who, acting by chance
American   in times of little experience, without the concurrence
iſlands.   of the mother-country, committed perpetual blun-
          ders.   Their avidity would not ſuffer them to follow
          the method of the natives, who, to abate the influence
          of a conſtant ſcorching ſun, uſed to ſeparate the ſmall
          parcels of land which they were forced to clear, with
          large ſpaces covered with trees and ſhady thickets.
          Theſe ſavages, inſtructed by experience, fixed their
          dwellings in the middle of the woods, to preſerve
          themſelves from the quick and dangerous exhalations
          of a ground newly turned up.

          The deſtroyers of this prudent people, being too
          eager after their profits, neglected this method as too
          flow; and being impatient to cultivate all, precipi-
          tately cut down whole foreſts.   Thick vapours imme-
          diately aroſe from the ground, which was heated, for
          the firſt time, by the rays of the ſun.   Theſe increaſ-
          ed as the earth was ſtirred up for ſowing and planting.
          Their malignant particles inſinuated themſelves into
          every pore and every organ of the huſbandman; who,
          by hard labour, was conſtantly kept in a profuſe per-
          ſpiration.   The circulation of the fluids was ſtopped,
          all the viſcera were dilated, the body ſwelled, the ſto-
          mach could no longer perform its functions, and death
          enſued.   Thoſe who eſcaped theſe peſtilential influ-
          ences by day, loſt their lives by ſleeping in huts haſti-
          ly run up upon a freſh ſoil, where vegetation was too
          active, and ſo unwholeſome, that it conſumed the men
          before it could nouriſh the plants.

          From theſe obſervations it appears, that the follow-
          ing would be the beſt plan which could be purſued in
          the eſtabliſhing of a new colony.   At our firſt arri-
          val, it ſhould be obſerved what winds are moſt preva-
          lent in the Archipelago of America, and it will be

found that they blow regularly from the fouth-eaft and the north-eaft. If we were at liberty to choofe, and met with no obftacle from the nature of the ground, we fhould take care not to fix on the lee-ward fide, left the wind fhould be continually bring-ing to us the vapours of the new-tilled grounds, and infect, from the exhalations of the new plantations, a piece of land that might have been purified in time. Our colony fhould therefore be founded on the wind-ward fide of whatever country we mean to cultivate. Firft, all the habitations fhould be built in the woods, and not a tree be fuffered to be felled about them. The woods are wholefome ; the refrefhing fhade they afford, and the cool air we breathe in them, even in the heat of the day, are a prefervative againft that exceffive perfpiration, which is the deftruction of moft Europeans, by the drynefs and acrimony of an inflam-mable blood, deprived of its fluid parts. Fires fhould be kept in the huts all night, to difpel any noxious air that might have entered. This cuftom, which is con-ftantly practifed in fome parts of Africa, would be as fuccefsful in America, confidering the analogy between the two climates.

After having taken thefe precautions, we might be-gin to cut down the woods ; but it fhould be at leaft at fifty toifes diftance from the huts. When the ground is laid bare, the flaves fhould not be fent out to their work till ten o'clock in the morning, when the fun has had time to divide the vapours, and the wind to drive them away. The four hours loft after fun-rife, would be fully compenfated by fparing the ftrength of the labourers, and by the prefervation of the human race. This attention fhould be continued as long as any lands are clearing or fowing, till the ground was thoroughly purged and fettled ; when the colonifts might be allowed to fix upon it, and be em-ployed without the leaft apprehenfions at all hours in the day. Experience has already juftified the neceffi-ty of all thefe meafures.

Misfortunes
which the
Englifh
have fuffer-
ed at Taba-
go, for hav-
ing deviat-
ed from the
maxims
which we
have juft
laid down.

The Englifh and their flaves not having followed
the plan we have been tracing, perifhed in great numbers at Tabago, though moft of them came there together from the neighbouring colonies. Enlightened
by this difafter, they fettled to windward of the ifland,
and death ceafed its ravages. The cuftom which the
Britifh government have of felling the foil of the
iflands, and the formalities infeparable from fuch a
fyftem, retarded the formation of a fettlement, which
by purfuing other maxims, perhaps lefs prudent, might
have been begun immediately after the peace. It was
not till 1766, that fourteen thoufand acres of ground
were allotted and divided into fhares of five hundred
acres each. New allotments were afterwards made,
but no planter was ever allowed to purchafe more than
one fhare.

The ifland, the foil of which hath been found too
fandy, is yet inhabited only by four hundred white
people and eight thoufand Negroes. They were ftopped in the beginning of their career by ants, who have
devoured the greateft part of the fugar canes which
have been already planted. The forty thoufand quintals of fugar which were gathered from thirty plantations have been reduced to one half. This void hath
been filled up by cotton, the crop of which is eight
hundred thoufand pounds weight, and by indigo,
which yields twelve thoufand pounds. St. Vincent
hath not experienced a fimilar calamity.

Hiftory of
the favages
of St. Vin-
cent.

When the Englifh and French, who for fome years
had been ravaging the Windward Iflands, began to
give fome confiftence to their fettlements, in the year
1660 they agreed that Dominica and St. Vincent
fhould be left to the Caribs as their property. Some
of thefe favages, who till then had been difperfed, retired into the former, and the greater part into the latter. There thefe mild and moderate men, lovers of
peace and filence, lived in the woods, in fcattered families, under the guidance of an old man, whom his
age alone had advanced to the dignity of ruler. The

dominion paffed fucceffively into every family, where B o o K
the oldeft always became king, that is to fay, the guide XIV.
and father of the nation. Thefe ignorant favages were
ftill unacquainted with the fublime art of fubduing
and governing men by force of arms; of maffacring
the inhabitants of a country to get poffeffion of their
lands; of granting to the conquerors the property,
and to the conquered the labours of the conquered
country; and, in procefs of time, of depriving both of
the rights and the fruit of their toil by arbitrary taxes.

The population of thefe children of nature was fud
denly augmented by a race of Africans, whofe origin
was never pofitively afcertained. It is faid, that a fhip
carrying Negroes for fale, foundered on the coaft of
St. Vincent, and the flaves who efcaped the wreck
were received as brethren by the favages. Others
pretend that thefe Negroes were deferters, who ran
away from the plantations of the neighbouring colonies. A third tradition fays, that this foreign race
comes from the blacks whom the Caribs took from
the Spaniards in the firft wars between thofe Europeans and the Indians. If we may credit Du Tertre,
the moft ancient hiftorian who has written an account
of the Antilles, thofe terrible favages, who were fo inveterate againft their mafters, fpared the captive flaves,
brought them home, and reftored them to liberty, that
they might enjoy life, that is, the common bleffings of
nature, which no man has a right to withhold from
any of his fellow-creatures.

Their kindnefs did not ftop here : for, by whatever
chance thefe ftrangers were brought into the ifland,
the proprietors of it gave them their daughters in marriage; and the race that fprang from this mixture were
called Black Caribs. They have preferved more of the
primitive colour of their fathers than of the lighter hue
of their mothers. The red Caribs are of a low ftature;
the black Caribs tall and ftout; and this doubly favage
race fpeak with a vehemence that feems to refemble
anger.

B O O K
XIV.

The arrival
of the
French at
St. Vincent
raifes dif-
putes be-
tween the
red and the
black Ca-
ribs.

In procefs of time, however, fome differences arofe
between the two nations. The people of Martinico
perceiving this, refolved to take advantage of their divifions, and raife themfelves on the ruins of both parties. Their pretence was, that the black Caribs gave
fhelter to the flaves who deferted from the French
iflands. Impofture is always productive of injuftice.
Thofe who were falfely accufed were afterwards attacked without reafon. But the fmallnefs of the numbers fent out againft them; the jealoufy of thofe who
were appointed to command the expedition; the defection of the red Caribs, who refufed to fupply fuch
dangerous allies with any of the fuccours they had
promifed them to act againft their rivals; the difficulty of procuring fubfiftence; the impoffibility of coming up with enemies who kept themfelves concealed
in woods and mountains : all thefe circumftances confpired to difconcert this rafh and violent enterprife. It
was obliged to be given up, after the lofs of many valuable lives; but the triumph the favages obtained did
not prevent them from fuing for peace as fuppliants.
They even invited the French to come and live with
them, fwearing fincere friendfhip and inviolable concord. The propofal was agreed to; and the next
year, 1719, many of the inhabitants of Martinico removed to St. Vincent.

The firft who came thither fettled peaceably, not
only with the confent, but by the affiftance of the red
Caribs. This fuccefs induced others to follow their
example; but thefe, whether from jealoufy, or fome
other motive, taught the favages a fatal fecret. That
people, who knew of no property but the fruits of the
earth, becaufe they are the reward of labour, learnt
with aftonifhment that they could fell the earth itfelf,
which they had always looked upon as belonging to
mankind in general. This knowledge induced them
to meafure and fix boundaries; and from that inftant
peace and happinefs were banifhed from their ifland.
The partition of lands occafioned divifions amongft

men. The following were the caufes of the revolution produced by the fyftem of ufurpation.

When the French came to St. Vincent, they brought flaves along with them, to clear and till the ground. The black Caribs, fhocked at the thoughts of refembling men who were degraded by flavery, and fearing that fome time or other their colour, which betrayed their origin, might be made a pretence for enflaving them, took refuge in the thickeft parts of the foreft. In this fituation, in order to imprint an indelible mark. of diftinction upon their tribe, that might be a perpetual token of their independence, they flattened the foreheads of all their children as foon as they were born. The men and women, whofe heads could not bend to this ftrange fhape, dared no longer appear in public without this vifible fign of freedom. The next generation appeared as a new race. The flat-headed Caribs, who were nearly of the fame age, tall, proper men, hardy and fierce, came and erected huts by the fea-fide.

They no fooner knew the price which the Europeans fet upon the lands they inhabited, than they claimed a fhare with the other iflanders. This rifing fpirit of covetoufnefs was at firft appeafed by fome prefents of brandy, and a few fabres. But not content with thefe, they foon demanded fire-arms, as the red Caribs had ; and at laft they were defirous of having their fhare in all future fales of land, and likewife in the produce of paft fales. Provoked at being denied a part in this brotherly repartition, they formed into a feparate tribe, fwore never more to affociate with the red Caribs, chofe a chief of their own, and declared war.

The numbers of the combatants might be equal, but their ftrength was not fo. The black Caribs had every advantage over the red, that induftry, valour, and boldnefs, muft foon acquire over a weak habit and a timorous difpofition. But that fpirit of equity, which is feldom deficient in favages, made the conqueror confent to fhare with the vanquifhed all the

BOOK territory lying to the leeward. It was the only one
XIV. which both parties were defirous of poffeffing, becaufe
there they were fure of receiving prefents from the
French.

The black Caribs gained nothing by the agreement
which they themfelves had drawn up. The new planters who came to the ifland always landed and fettled
near the red Caribs, where the coaft was moft acceffible. This preference roufed that enmity which was
but ill extinguifhed. The war broke out again. The
red Caribs, who were always beaten, retired to windward of the ifland. Many took to their canoes, and
went over to the continent, or to Tabago; and the
few that remained lived feparate from the blacks.

The black Caribs, conquerors and mafters of all the
leeward coaft, required of the Europeans that they
fhould again buy the lands they had already purchafed. A Frenchman attempted to fhow the deed of his
purchafe of fome land which he had bought of a red
Carid; *I know not*, fays a black Carib, *what thy paper
fays; but read what is written on my arrow. There
you may fee, in characters which do not lie, that if you
do not give me what I demand, I will go and burn your
houfe to night.* In this manner did a people, who had
not learnt to read, argue with thofe who derived fuch
confequence from knowing how to write. They made
ufe of the right of force, with as much affurance, and
as little remorfe, as if they had been acquainted with
divine, political, and civil right.

Time, which brings on a change of meafures with a
change of interefts, put an end to thefe difturbances.
The French became, in their turn, the ftrongeft. They
no longer fpent their time in breeding poultry, and
cultivating vegetables, caffava, maize, and tobacco, in
order to fell them at Martinico. In lefs than twenty
years, more important cultures employed eight hundred white men and three thoufand Blacks. Such was
the fituation of St. Vincent when it fell into the hands
of the Englifh; and was fecured to them by the treaty
of 1763.

This ifland, which may have forty leagues in circum- ference, is mountainous, but interfected by excellent valleys, and watered by a few rivers. It was in the weftern part of it that the French had begun the cul- ture of cacao and of cotton, and had made confider- able advances in that of coffee. The conquerors formed there fome fugar plantations. The impoffibili- ty of multiplying them upon an uneven foil, which is full of ravines, made them defirous of occupying the plains towards the Eaft. The favages, who had taken refuge there, refufed to quit them ; and recourfe was had to arms to compel them to it. The refiftance which they oppofed to the thunders of European ty- ranny, was not, and could not poffibly be maintained without great difficulty.

An officer was meafuring out the ground which had juft been taken poffeffion of, when the detachment that accompanied him was unexpectedly attacked, and almoft totally deftroyed, on the 25th of March 1775. It was generally believed that the unfortunate perfons who had juft been deprived of their poffeffions, were the authors of this violence ; and the troops put them- felves in motion to deftroy them.

Fortunately, it was determined in time, that the Caribs were innocent ; that they had taken or maf- facred feveral fugitive flaves who had been guilty of fuch cruelties ; and that they had fworn not to ftop till they had purged the ifland of thofe vagabonds, whofe enormities were often imputed to them. In or- der to confirm the favages in this refolution, by the al- lurement of rewards, the legiflative body paffed a bill to enfure a gratuity of five moïdes, or 120 livres [5l.], to any one who fhould bring the head of a Negro, who fhould have deferted within three months.

Great Britain hath not hitherto gained any great ad- vantage from thefe barbarities. St. Vincent ftill reckons no more than five hundred white men, and feven or eight thoufand Negroes. Their labours yield no more than twelve hundred quintals of cotton, fix millions weight of very fine fugar, and three hundred and fixty

B O O K thoufand gallons of rum. Thefe productions grow
XIV. upon a very light kind of foil, and which for that reafon, it is thought, will be foon exhaufted. This is an
opinion generally received in America ; and it will be
proper to examine whether it be well founded.

Undoubtedly, the rains which fall in torrents upon
a broken country, muft more readily carry away a
fandy foil than a clayey one, the particles of which
fhall adhere more ftrongly to each other. But is it
underftood in what manner a foil can be exhaufted?
Can it be by the lofs of thofe earthy particles, into
which the plants it produces are at length reduced,
and of which it feems to be deprived, when the plants
do not rot upon the fpot where they have been cultivated? In anfwer to this, it is proved from the experiments of Van Helmont, that plants do not take away
any fenfible weight from the foil ; and that it is the
moifture with which the earth is watered, that is the
only caufe of vegetation. If this exhaufting of the
foil be fuppofed to arife from the lofs of the falts which
it furnifhes for the fucceffive growth of the plants, it
is equally proved, by the numerous experiments of M.
Tillet, and of feveral other natural philofophers, that
the ground is nothing more than a matrix, in which
the germina of plants receive their growth, which they
feem only to derive from heat and moifture. All thefe
experiments collected, feem alfo to prove, that the water alone, whether conveyed by natural or artificial
means, contains all the falts and all the principles that
are to concur in producing this growth.

Let us therefore content ourfelves with faying, that
fuch or fuch a fpecies of earth may be more or lefs eafily put into a ftate fit to receive and to preferve the
quantity of water neceffary for completing vegetation.
The moft trifling labour ftirs up a light foil : it is then
eafily penetrated by the flighteft rain : but a hard rain
preffes it together, and the fun eafily raifing the moifture, which in this ftate of compreffion it could only
imbibe to a very little depth, deprives it of the only
fpecies of nourifhment which it furnifhed to the plant,

and without which the plant could not fubfift. Never- B O O K
thelefs, the feafon is not called in queftion ; and much XIV.
lefs the ignorance of him who knows not how to moderate its effects. Prejudice determines the foil to be
exhaufted and ruined. In future, it is worked only
with regret, and confequently very ill. It is abandoned, while nothing more was wanting than a proper
fpecies of culture to enrich the proprietor who neglects
it.

A fomewhat lefs degree of friability conftitutes what
is called a ftrong foil, which requires more tillage, and
of a more laborious nature ; but when once it is prepared, manured, and watered, the ftiff foil preferves for
a much longer time its moifture, which is a neceffary
vehicle of the falts, whether they be continually conveyed, and fucceffively renewed by the rains, or by artificial watering.

Of what ufe then, it will be faid, is dung? It ferves
to raife up more eafily, and more generally, the foil,
by the fermentation which it excites in it, and to keep
it for a longer time raifed and fupplied, either by its
active particles, which can only unfold themfelves
gradually in the compact foils, fuch as thofe of the fecond fpecies, which are divided by heating them, or by
its oily particles, which fattening the foil of the firft
fpecies, retain in it, for a longer time, the moifture which
its too great laxity, and the incoherence of its particles,
would foon allow to efcape.

Dung, therefore, properly applied, and according to
its quality, partly fupplies the place of tillage ; but can
tillage fupply the place of dung? We are inclined to
think it would not for light foils, which, fortunately,
require but little dunging ; but we believe it would in
ftrong foils, and thefe require a great deal of dung.
But nothing can fupply the place of rain ; which, in
America, when it is plentiful, renders all the foils nearly equal. Some fruits brought forward by the feafon,
rot in the moft excellent foils : but almoft all of them
arrive at perfection in the moft ordinary foils. In A-
merica there is no rainy feafon which is not fruitful ;

B O O K while, in a dry feafon, the income diminifhes fometimes
XIV.   by one half.

The only object that deferves the attention of the
inhabitants of St. Vincent's, as well as of all perfons
who are in poffeffion of a light foil, in whatever zone
it may be fituated, muft therefore be, to fix their plantations upon their loweft mountains, to prefer the culture of fuch plants as will cover the foil fooneft, and
will leave it lefs expofed to the immediate fhock of
heavy rains, which comprefs it more and more when
it is not tilled, and which drag it away when it is prepared ; to choofe efpecially that plan of cultivation,
which, while it fhall not counteract the efforts of the
plant too much, fhall fupply it with a degree of growth
neceffary to defend the foil, at the time when it ftands
moft in need of it, in that feafon when it would be in
danger of being ftripped, in procefs of time, down to
the fand.   While the foil fhall remain covered with
any kind of earth, we need not fear its being barren.
The foil which hath once been fufficient for the nutri-
tion of any plant, when brought into its primitive ftate
by the care of the cultivator, will for ever be fufficient
for the fame purpofes.

Great Bri-   Dominica was inhabited by its own children. In
tain takes   1732 nine hundred and thirty-eight Caribs were found
poffeffion of
Dominica.   there, diftributed in thirty two carbets ; and three
hundred and forty-nine Frenchmen occupied a part of
the coaft, which the favages had left to them.   Thefe
Europeans had no other affiftance, or rather companions of their labours, except twenty-three free Mulattoes, and three hundred and thirty-eight flaves.   They
were all employed in breeding poultry, in raifing provifions for the confumption of Martinico, and in cultivating feventy-two thoufand two hundred cotton
fhrubs.   Thefe trifling productions were afterwards increafed by the addition of coffee. At length the ifland,
at the peace of 1763, when it became an Englifh poffeffion, reckoned fix hundred white people, and two
thoufand Negroes.

Since the end of the laft century, Great Britain,

which was advancing towards the dominion of the seas,
while she accused France of aspiring to the monarchy
of the continent, had showed as much eagerness for
Dominica, as she had in the late negotiations, when
victory gave her a right to choose. Nine parishes have
successively been established upon this island, where,
on the first of January 1778, the population consisted
of fifteen hundred and seventy-four white people, men,
women, and children ; five hundred and seventy-four
Mulattoes, or free Negroes, and fourteen thousand
three hundred and eight slaves.

The cattle of the island did not exceed two hundred
and eighty-eight horses, seven hundred and seven mules,
thirty-four asses, eighteen hundred and thirty head of
horned cattle, nine hundred and ninety-nine hogs, and
two thousand two hundred and twenty-nine sheep, or
goats.

Its cultures consisted of sixty-five sugar plantations,
which occupied five thousand two hundred and fifty-
seven acres of ground ; three thousand three hundred
and sixty-nine acres planted with coffee, at the proportion of one thousand feet per acre ; two hundred
and seventy-seven acres planted with cacao, at the proportion of five hundred feet per acre ; fourscore and
nine acres planted with cotton, at the proportion of
one thousand feet per acre; sixty-nine acres of indigo,
and sixty trees of black cassia.

Its provisions consisted of twelve hundred and two
acres of banana trees, sixteen hundred and forty-seven
acres of yams or potatoes, and two thousand seven
hundred and twenty nine trenches of manioc.

Nineteen thousand four hundred and seventy-eight
acres were taken up by the woods ; four thousand two
hundred and ninety-six by pasturages and savannas ;
three thousand six hundred and fifty-five acres were
reserved for the crown, and three thousand four hundred and thirty-four were entirely barren.

This was all that fifteen years of labour had been
able to effect upon a soil which was exceedingly hilly,
and not very fertile.

BOOK
XIV.

Disturb-
ances be-
tween the
Englifh of
Dominica,
and the
French of
the neigh-
bouring
iflands.

This fettlement was expofed in its infancy to a moſt flagrant act of diſhoneſty. Several of the planters had obtained confiderable advances from trade. To avoid paying their debts, they took refuge, with their ſlaves, in the French iſlands, where an open protection was granted them. In vain they were claimed ; in vain was it required that they ſhould be compelled to fatis-fy their creditors : every folicitation was uſeleſs. The legiſlative body then made a law, which fecured to all French emigrants the advantage of enjoying, without moleſtation, all the riches they ſhould bring into Do-minica.

Let us examine without partiality the conduct of the two nations, and we ſhall find it faulty on both ſides.

And firſt, with reſpect to the French, let me aſk them, if theſe refugees were not at the ſame time thieves? Why therefore did they grant them an aſy-lum? Why did they refuſe to give them up, when they were claimed? Let us even ſuppoſe that the re-quiſition had been made in an imperious manner ; the buſineſs was to examine the juſtice of the claim, not the manner in which it was made. This was not an occaſion in which it was proper to give a petulant an-ſwer to a haughty demand. An action which we are urged to by juſtice, can never be humiliating. Let the French, for a moment, put themſelves in the place of the creditors, and tell me, whether they would not have ſent to the court of London the ſame repreſentations, and the ſame complaints? and whether they would not have been equally exaſperated by its filence, or by its refuſal? There cannot be two ſyſtems of juſtice.

On the other hand, when by way of repriſal the Engliſh offered an aſylum to the French emigrants, did they not double the ſame fault? Did they not ex-cite to robbery and to defertion thoſe fraudulent debt-ors who were inclined to eſcape from the legal pur-ſuit of their creditors? If the nations, who divided the New World among themſelves, had adopted, in imi-tation of them, the ſame meaſures, who would have advanced to their colonifts the fums they might have wanted? What would have become of America, if this pernicious fyftem had manifefted itfelf at the origin of the conquefts? What would ftill become of it if it were univerfally adopted? Let us reflect a moment, and we fhall be convinced, that a general fufpenfion of juftice would become one of the moft dreadful calamities that could poffibly afflict mankind. We fhall perceive, that fo fatal an agreement among nations would bring the world back to that ftate of plundering and barbarifm of which we have not even an idea. What advantage will the Englifh find, in infefting themfelves with our villains, and in fending theirs to us? What concern can we have, or what confidence can we repofe, in men who are deftitute of faith towards their fellow-citizens? Do the Englifh expect more honefty from ours? If they receive them, why fhould a third nation expel them? Is it intended that perfidy fhould wander, with impunity, from one country to another, and fpread itfelf over the whole furface of the globe? I may perhaps exaggerate the confequences of this proceeding: but in order to judge properly of an action, we muft confider the utmoft extent of its effects. This is a certain way of impreffing the mind more forcibly with them.

But I may be afked, in what manner fhould the Englifh have acted? In the firft inftance, they were right in making the demand. Afterwards, they fhould have gone down fword in hand into the afylums of their deferters, and fhould have laid them wafte. Thus it is that they would have fhown themfelves brave and upright men. The blood that would have been fpilt would not have been imputed to them; and they would have been applauded by all the people of Europe, interefted in the fame caufe.

We need not however be furprifed that both the Englifh and French fhould reciprocally grant a retreat to their malefactors, when we daily fee them arrogating to themfelves the right of fending them to each other, by banifhing them from their own country; a law, which is as contrary to the common right, as that which fhould authorife a citizen, whofe dog fhould run mad, to let him loofe in the houfe of his neighbour, would be contrary to the right of individuals.

But a man who has two hands, is always a fpecies of valuable property.—He ought therefore not to be concealed.—It may alfo be urged, that we have fome reafon to expect, fince there are a few inftances of it, that a wicked man may amend.—It is true, there may be one inftance in a hundred of fuch an amendment.—But the queftion is, whether, for the chance of having one bad man who may forfake his evil ways, it be prudent to keep a hundred incorrigible villains?

In what confifts the importance of Dominica? There was however another diftant object, exclusive of the care of fettling plantations, which entered into the extenfive views of the Englifh. They wifhed to attract the productions of the French colonies to Dominica, in order that they might fecure the trade of them to themfelves. It was to carry this great project into execution, that, in 1766, all the ports of the ifland were made free. A number of active and enterprifing men immediately came from Europe and from North America. Immenfe ftores of corn, falt fifh, and flaves, were formed at Rofeau. This town fupplied the wants of Martinico, of Guadalupe, and of St. Lucia; and received in payment, commodities of greater or lefs value. Thefe exchanges would have been even more confiderable, if by an ill judged avidity of of the treafury, Great Britain had not herfelf put a reftraint upon thefe fraudulent connections.

The events which have detached the American continent from England, and the efforts which the French are making to extend their connections in Africa, muft foon reduce the ftaple of Dominica to nothing, or to a trifle; but it can never be deprived of the advantage of its pofition. Situated between Guadalupe and Martinico, at only feven leagues diftance from each, it threatens them equally. At both its extremities, to the North and to the South, are two excellent harbours, from whence the privateers and the fleets may intercept the navigation between the mother-country and its colonies, and even the communication between the two fettlements. What would be the confequence if the northern port, known by the name of Prince Rupert, were changed, as it might eafily be, into a harbour, and furrounded with fortifications? This plan, it is faid, hath been determined upon in the council of George III. Every circumftance induces us to believe that it will never be carried into execution; the nation hath too much confidence in its naval forces, ever to incur fuch an expence.

Dominica, in thefe latter times, hath drawn the attention of all America, by an event, the caufes of which may almoft be traced as far back as the difcovery of the New World.

Scarce had the Europeans marked the foil of the other hemifphere with their fanguinary fteps, than it became neceffary to procure flaves from Africa, in order to clear it. Women were found among this degraded race, whom the fcarcity of females rendered agreeable to the firft colonifts. From this alliance, which feemed to be reprobated by nature, there arofe a mixed generation, whofe chains were often broken by paternal tendernefs. A fentiment of goodnefs, innate in man, gave liberty, on fome occafions, to other flaves; and a ftill greater number of captives purchafed their freedom. In vain did a fufpicious and provident fyftem of policy exclaim, with vehemence, againft this cuftom, applauded by humanity: the beftowing of freedom upon flaves was ftill continued; and even became more frequent.

The freedmen, however, were not put upon an entire equality with their former mafters. The laws generally imprinted a mark of inferiority on this clafs of men. They were ftill more degraded by prejudice, in the frequent occurrences of civil life. Their fituation was never any thing more than an intermediate ftate between flavery and original liberty.

Diftinctions fo humiliating filled the minds of thefe freedmen with rage. The flave is commonly in fo ab-

B O O K XIV.

Laws peculiar to Dominica.

B O O K ject a ftate, that he doth not dare to defy his tyrant;
XIV. he can do nothing more than hate him.   But the
heart of a man whofe chains have been fhaken off,
hath a greater degree of energy ; he both hates, and
bids defiance to the white men.

The dangerous effects of thefe finifter difpofitions
fhould have been prevented. In the focieties of Europe, where all the members are equals, where the intereft of each individual is the intereft of the whole
community ; we are not allowed to fuppofe that a citizen would intentionally do any thing injurious to
the general good, unlefs there are ftrong proofs of it.
But in Ameiica, where an enormous and fingular body of men, divided in opinions, is compofed of three
different claffes, it is thought right to facrifice the two
laft to the fecurity of the former. The flaves are
kept in a perpetual ftate of oppreffion, and the freedmen are thrown into prifon upon the flighteft fufpicion.   Their averfion for the white people is confidered as a delinquency of a very ferious nature, and juf-
tifies, in the eyes of authority, all the precautions that
are taken againft them.   It is to this ftrange feverity that moft of the nations have wifhed to attribute
the kind of tranquillity which they have enjoyed in
their fettlements in the New World.

In the Englifh colonies alone the free Negro is upon the fame footing as the white man.   The ftrongeft
prefumptions are not fufficient to authorife an attack
upon the liberty of the one, any more than of the
other.   Hence it happens that the law, which is very
cautious, for fear of a miftake, in fixing upon the criminal, fometimes remains inactive for a longer time
than is confiftent with the public advantage.   The
freedmen have fometimes abufed thefe indulgences in
the Britifh iflands ; and their feditious commotions
have obliged Dominica to alter its fyftem.

It was determined, by a bill paffed in the month of
September 1774, that no colonift fhould, for the future, be allowed to grant liberty to any flave, before
he had paid 100 piftoles [41l. 13s. 4d.] into the pub-

lic treafury. But if the freedman could afterwards B O O K prove that he could not gain a fubfiftence by his la- XIV. bour, he was to receive 80 livres [3l. 6s. 8d.] every fix months, till he fhould be enabled, by more favourable circumftances, to do without this affiftance.

Every freedman, convicted by the depofition of two witneffes, either free or flaves, before two juftices of the peace, of being guilty of any offence that is not capital, is to be whipped, or to pay a fine, or to be imprifoned, according as the magiftrates fhall determine. The fame punifhments are to be inflicted upon him for having difturbed the public peace, or for having infulted, threatened, or beaten a white man.

A freedman who fhall have affifted a flave to defert, who fhall have granted an afylum to him, or accepted of his fervices, fhall be condemned to a fine of 2000 livres [83l. 6s. 8d.], to be applied to public ufe. If the culprit fhould be unable to pay the fum, he fhall undergo three months imprifonment, or be whipped, according to the decifion of the juftices of the peace.

No free Negro, Mulatto, or Meftee, fhall be allowed to vote at the election of a reprefentative of his parifh, in the general affembly of the colony. Neither protection nor fortune can ever efface this mark of reprobation.

After having given a feparate account of each of the three neutral iflands which England acquired by the treaty of 1763, it is incumbent upon us to ftate the means which that power hath thought proper to employ, in order to derive folid advantages from their profperity.

Plan conceived by the Britifh miniftry to render flourifhing the three iflands which were formerly neutral.

At firft, government thought proper to fell the different portions of the extenfive foil which the fuccefs of the war had given to them. Had they been gratuitoufly beftowed, they would have been obtained by favour and intrigue, and they would not have been ufeful for a long time. But the nation was well convinced, that every citizen who fhould have employed part of his capital in the acquifition of an eftate, would

B O O K not fail to lay out upon it what was neceffary for him
XIV. to make the moft of his property.

It might, however, be improper to exact the immediate payment of the ceded lands, becaufe the new
plantations require fuch great expences in buildings,
in cattle, and in flaves. On this account, it was fettled, that the purchafer fhould not be obliged to pay
more than twenty per cent. in the firft inftance, ten
per cent. the two following years, and afterwards
twenty per cent. every year after, till the payment
was completed. He was to be divefted of all his privileges, if he did not fulfil his engagements at the ftated periods.

In order to foften what might appear too fevere in
this law, the planter was allowed to change this debt
into a perpetual annuity ; and even the firft payment
was not to begin till a twelvemonth after the clearing
of the land.

As the vaft extent of the eftates had vifibly dimi-
niſhed the mafs of the productions in the iflands, which
England had poffeffed for a long time, it was thought
proper to take meafures to avoid this inconvenience in
the new acquifitions. It was decreed, that no perfon
fhould be allowed to purchafe more than one plantation ; and that the largeft of them fhould not exceed
five hundred acres. It was even limited to three hundred for Dominica, the pofition and deftination of
which required a greater number of Europeans. Government alfo decreed, that five of every hundred
acres fhould be annually cleared, till half the plantation fhould be cultivated ; and that thofe who fhould
not have fulfilled this obligation fhould pay a fine of
112 livres 10 fols [4l. 13s. 9d.] annually, for every
acre of ground which fhould not have been cultivated
in the limited time. Every colonift was obliged alfo
to put one white man, or two white women, upon
every hundred acres of his territory, under the penalty of paying every year to the treafury 900 livres [37l.
10s.] for every man, and half of that fum for every

woman, that fhould be wanting to make up the number he ought to have.

This laſt precaution might give ſome conſiſtence to
the new ſettlements ; but it was thought they would
one day ſtand in need of further aſſiſtance. In order
to procure it for them in time, gratuitous conceſſions
of land, from ten to thirty acres, have been granted
in favour of the poor who chooſe to ſettle in thoſe
iſlands. This was a ſufficient portion of land to enable them to live by their labour, in thoſe eaſy circumſtances which they would never have experienced in
the Old Hemiſphere. From an apprehenſion that
they might lend their name to ſome rapacious man,
or might afterwards ſell their property to him, it was
ordained, that they fhould themſelves take poſſeſſion
of the land three months after it had been granted to
them ; that they fhould dwell upon it for twelve
months conſecutively ; and that they fhould keep it
for ſeven whole years. After this time, they were to
pay a fine of 12 ſols [6d.] for every acre which fhould
be cultivated, and one of 12 livres 5 ſols [11s. 8d.] for
thoſe which fhould remain uncultivated.

The Engliſh iſlands had for a long while complained of the want of rain, becauſe all their foreſts had
been levelled. In order to prevent this inconvenience
in the new poſſeſſions, the commiſſaries were ordered
to preſerve for the crown a ſufficient quantity of the
woods to attract the clouds, and to keep up that degree of moiſture which is more or leſs neceſſary for all
the plants peculiar to America.

Laſtly, None of the ſums acquired by the ſale of
the lands were to belong to government. They were
all to be conſecrated to the harbours, to the fortifications, and to other objects of uſe in thoſe iſlands.

The fate of the French, reſiding in great numbers
at Dominica and at St. Vincent, remained ſtill to be
ſettled. Theſe planters were under no kind of apprehenſion for their property. They had obtained or
purchaſed it from the Indians, and had been confirmed in their poſſeſſion by the government of Martinico,

B O O K who required of them a flight duty in return. The
XIV. firft of thefe titles could be of no weight in the eyes
of a conqnering power ; and the fecond was manifeft-
ly contrary to the conventions between the courts of
London and of Verfailles, who had engaged themfelves not to allow their refpective fubjects to fettle in
the neutral iflands.

The expectations, therefore, of thofe active men,
who would have accelerated the progrefs of the two
colonies which they themfelves had founded, were entirely fruftrated. Whether the Britifh miniftry were
apprehenfive of difgufting the Englifh, in obliging
them to pay for a territory, which their ancient rivals
continued to poffefs gratuitoufly, or whether a wifh
prevailed of getting rid of thofe foreigners, who, by
their religion and their habits, might be too ftrongly
attached to their former country, it was regulated,
that the French fhould, for the future, enjoy their
plantations only upon perpetual leafes.

This hard reftraint, fo contrary to the maxims of
found policy, difperfed them. The emigration was
not, however, univerfal. After the firft effects of dif-
fatisfaction, the wifeft of them became fenfible that
they fhould ftill gain more by repurchafing the lands
which they already enjoyed, than if they were to fettle upon a frefh fpot that would coft them nothing.

Obftacles   Great Britain entertained great expectations from
which have the meafures which fhe had taken for the profperity
prevented
the profpe- of her conquefts. The fuccefs hath not been anfwer-
rity of the able ; and the caufes of this fingular difappointment
neutral
iflands. are well known.

The three neutral iflands were no fooner fecured to
England by the treaties, than it became a general paffion to form fettlements upon them. This epidemical
madnefs made the lands which were fold by government rife to an extravagant price. As a bold fpirit of
enterprife was the only fortune moft of the purchafers
had, credit became their only refource. They found
it in London, and in fome other trading places, the
merchants of which, mifled by the fame illufion, bor-

rowed confiderable fums at a low intereft, in order to lend them to thefe enterprifing fpeculators at an advanced intereft.

The new proprietors, moft of whom had purchafed a foil, without taking the trouble of examining it, proceeded with the fame levity in the formation of their plantations. The coafts, and the interior parts of the iflands, were foon covered with mafters and flaves, equally inexperienced in the laborious and difficult art of clearing the lands. This occafioned numberlefs faults and misfortunes. The evil became extreme, and foon broke out.

The colonifts had borrowed at eight per cent. in 1766, or about that period, and the loan was to be paid five years after. The impoffibility they found of fulfilling thefe engagements alarmed their European creditors. Difappointed of the remittances they expected, thefe rapacious lenders were at length undeceived; and the greater their credulity had been, the more active did their anxiety become. Having recourfe to the authority of the law, they expelled from their plantations the unhappy men who had been unfortunately feduced by rafh expectations. Thus ended the delufive profpect of the new Englifh colonies.

But this great commotion muft be attended with favourable confequences. The manures undertaken by men without powers, and who are reduced to their original poverty, will procure to the nation the fame advantages that ufually refult from an irregular and diforderly ferment in the ftate. A foil which languifhed in the hands of the firft poffeffors will be cultivated with better means, with more intelligence and economy. While we are expecting the effects of this new effort of induftry and activity, let us refume the account of the Englifh poffeffions in the American Archipelago. To afcertain the value of the colonies of a maritime and commercial power, is to make an eftimate of its ftrength.

The Britifh iflands in the Weft Indies are in general more extenfive than they are fertile. Mountains, Prefent ftate of the Englifh iflands.

B O O K which cannot be cultivated, occupy a great space in
XIV. some of them; and others are entirely, or partly, formed of a chalky soil, which produces but very little.
The best have been cleared for a long time, and require the assistance of manures, which are imperfect
and scarce in this part of the New World. Most of
them have been stripped of the forests, by which they
were originally sheltered, and are exposed to droughts,
which often ruin the labours undertaken with the
strictest attention, and carried on at a great expence.

Accordingly, the increase of provisions hath not
been proportioned to the number of hands employed
in obtaining them. There are at this time in those
colonies four hundred thousand slaves, who by their
labours scarce produce two thirds of the income that
is collected from a richer soil with the same means.

The number of white people hath generally diminished in proportion to the increase of the Negroes.
Not but that there were as many idle or indigent men
in England to replace those who perished, or who difappeared with the fortunes they had acquired, as at
the time of the first emigration; but the spirit of ad-
venture, which the novelty of the object, and the concurrence of circumstances had excited, was either
checked or annihilated. On one hand, the space
which was occupied by the smaller cultures hath been
successively filled with sugar plantations, which require an immense extent of territory; and on the
other, the proprietors of these great plantations have
reduced, as much as possible, the number of their
agents, whose salaries were become a heavy burden.

Since this revolution, the British islands have still
greater reason than ever to be apprehensive of plunder
and of invasion. Their colonists, who are all enlisted,
were formerly strong enough at least to repel a weak
and ill-armed enemy. Most of them might at present
be taken by surprise, should the navy of the mother-
country ceafe one moment to protect them. It is a
great point, if in the present state the militia are able
to contain the Negroes, who are more unfortunate un-

der the Englifh dominion than under any other: for B O O K
it fhould feem, that the hardfhips of flavery were fo XIV.
much the greater among free nations, in proportion
as it is more unjuft, and more foreign to the conftitution. Such is the progrefs of man towards independence, that, after having fhaken off the yoke, he wifhes
to impofe it upon others; and that thofe who are the
moft impatient of fervitude become the fondeft of dominion!

The Weft Indies were never fubjected to any impoft
by Great Britain. But in 1663, Barbadoes, and the
other iflands, except Jamaica, voluntarily engaged to
pay a perpetual tax of four per cent. upon all their
productions which fhould be exported. So great an
act of generofity hath fince appeared burdenfome, and
the weight of it was alleviated as much as poffible. As
this obligation is paid in commodities, there are fcarce
any delivered to government, except fuch as are in
fome refpect faulty; and the colonifts are not more
fcrupulous with regard to their weight than to their
quality. Thus it is that the treafury receives only
two-thirds of the gift which was formerly granted to
them.

This is ftill too much for fettlements that are obliged
to defray their internal expences themfelves. Thefe
were very confiderable when thofe colonies regulated
all their own affairs, or erected the fortifications judged neceffary for their fecurity. The taxes were multiplied at this period; and every difagreeable event
brought on frefh ones, becaufe it was thought more
prudent to require contributions of the citizens, than
to have recourfe to public engagements. Time hath
diminifhed the wants, and it has been found neceffary
to provide for thofe which remained with more economy, becaufe the planters have not the fame refources. The taxes are at prefent inconfiderable, and
they might ftill be reduced, if thofe who fill the pofts
of adminiftration, in manifeft contradiction to the republican fpirit, which is that of difinterestednefs, did
not require large falaries.

B O O K   But this is an unavoidable inconvenience attending
   XIV.   a commercial nation.   Whether free or not, they ul-
timately love or value nothing but wealth.   The thirst
of gold being more the work of imagination than of
necessity, we are not satiated with riches, as we are
with the objects that gratify our other passions.   The
latter are distinct and transient; they either counteract or succeed each other; whereas the thirst of gold
feeds and satisfies all the other passions, at least it sup-
plies their place, in proportion as it exhausts them, by
the means it contributes towards the gratification of
them.   There is no habit which is more confirmed by
custom than that of amassing riches.   It seems equally
to be excited by the enjoyments of vanity, and by the
self-denial of avarice.   The rich man always wants to
fill or to increase his treasure.   This is a constant ob-
servation, which extends from individuals to nations.

   Since large fortunes have been raised in England
by trade, the desire of wealth is become the universal
and ruling passion.   Such citizens as have not been
able, or did not choose to follow this lucrative profes-
sion, have still turned their views to that gain which
the manners and opinion of the times have made necessary.   Even in aspiring to honours, they hunt after
riches.   In following the career of those laws and virtues, which ought ever mutually to assist each other,
even in obtaining the honour of a seat in parliament,
they have found out the way of aggrandizing their
fortune.   In order to be chosen members of this powerful body, they have bribed the votes of the people;
and have not been more ashamed of selling these very
people to the court, than they were of having bought
them.   Every vote in the senate of the empire is become venal.   A celebrated minister had a book of
rates of the probity of each member, and openly boasted of it, to the disgrace of the English.   It was the duty of his office, he said, to buy off the representatives
of the nation, in order that they should vote, not
against, but according to their conscience.   But what
can conscience avail against the allurements of gain?

If the mercantile fpirit hath been able to diffufe in the B o o K mother-country the contagion of perfonal intereft, how XIV. is it poffible that it fhould not have infected the colonies, of which it is the principal and the fupport? Is it then true, that, in proud Albion, a man who fhould be generous enough to ferve his country for the mere love of glory would be confidered as a man of another world, and of the laft age? Vain-glorious ifland, may thine enemies renounce this fordid fpirit of intereft, and thou wilt one day reftore to them all they have loft!

Neverthelefs, opulence feems to prevail in the Englifh fettlements in the Weft Indies. This is becaufe the proceedings of arbitrary authority, which afflict fo many other countries, are unknown here: becaufe there are none of thofe vile inftruments of the treafury, who deftroy the bafis of property, in order to eftablifh the forms of it: becaufe the culture of fugar hath been fubftituted there, to that of productions of little value: becaufe the plantations belong in general to rich men, or to powerful affociations, which never fuffer them to want the neceffary means for their improvement: becaufe if fome unfortunate cafualty fhould reduce the colonift to the neceffity of borrowing, he obtains the loan eafily, and at a cheap rate; for his poffeffions are mortgaged to his creditor, and the payment is fecured at the ftated times: becaufe thefe iflands are lefs expofed to devaftation and invafion than the poffeffions of other powers, that are rich in productions, and poor in fhips: becaufe the events of the moft obftinate and moft deftructive wars never prevent, and feldom retard, the exportation of their commodities: in a word, it is becaufe the Britifh ports always open to their principal crops a more advantageous mart than their rivals can expect anywhere elfe. Accordingly, the lands conftantly bear a very high price in the Englifh iflands, both the Europeans and the Americans being equally eager to purchafe them.

Thefe lands would ftill have been in greater requeft,

BOOK if the accefs to the Weft Indies had been lefs rigidly
XIV. prohibited to foreign navigators ; if they had been at
liberty to choofe their own purchafers throughout the
globe. But a fet of laws, the regulations of which
it hath never been poffible to elude, have concentrated their connections within the limits of their own
empire, with the national provinces of both hemifpheres.

Thefe colonies do not find upon their own territory,
either provifion for their own fubfiftence, or beafts of
burden for their labours, or woods for their buildings.
They were fupplied with thefe objects of primary neceffity by North America, which received in payment
rum and other productions, to the amount of three or
four millions of livres [from 125,000l. to 166,666l.
13s. 4d.] every year. The troubles which have divided Old and New England have interrupted this
communication, to the great detriment of the iflands.
Till neceffities of an urgent nature fhall caufe it to be
opened again, or till other connections fhall be formed,
to be fubftituted to it, the Weft Indies will have no
other vent for their productions than that which Great
Britain will furnifh them.

At the prefent period, England receives annually
from the iflands fhe occupies in the Weft Indies, to
the amount of about ninety-three millions of livres
[3,875,000l.] in commodities, including fixteen or feventeen millions [from 666,666l. 13s. 4d. to 708,333l.
6s. 8d.] which they pay to government, and the rum
which Ireland receives directly in payment for the falt
provifions which it furnifhes to the colonies.

Almoft all the fugar, which forms three-fourths of
the produce of the iflands, is confumed in the kingdom itfelf, or is carried to Ireland. It is feldom that
any of it is fent to Hamburgh or to other markets.

The exports which Great Britain makes of the production of the iflands do not annually exceed feven
or eight millions of livres [from 291,666l. 13s. 4d. to
333,333l. 6s. 8d.]. If we add to this fum what fhe
muft gain upon her cottons, which fhe manufactures

with fo much fuccefs, and which are diffufed throughout a great part of the globe, we fhall have a tolerably
exact idea of the advantages which this empire derives
from the Weft Indies.

The iflands receive in payment their furniture and
clothing, the utenfils neceffary for their manufactures,
a great deal of hardware, and flaves for the working
of their lands. But the things that are fent to them
are infinitely inferior in value to thofe which are received from them. We muft deduct the expences of
navigation and of infurance, the commiffion, or the
profit of the merchant. We muft deduct the intereft of fixteen millions Sterling, which thefe colonies
owe to the mother-country. We muft deduct what
the rich proprietors of the plantations fpend in England, where they habitually refide. If we except
the poffeffions acquired or fecured by the treaties
of 1763, the infant plantations of which are ftill in
want of advances, the other poffeffions of the Weft
Indies fcarce receive in their harbours the fourth part
of the value which they fend out from them.

It was the capital of the empire, which formerly fent
out almoft all the exports, and received almoft all the
returns. Men of enlightened underftanding were very
properly incenfed at this evil. But London is at leaft
the fineft port in England. It is there that fhips are
built, and manufactures are carried on. London furnifhes feamen for navigation, and hands for commerce,
It ftands in a temperate, fruitful, and central country.
Every thing has a free paffage in and out of it. It
may be truly faid to be the heart of the body politic,
from its local pofition. That city is not filled with
proud and idle men, who only encumber and opprefs
the laborious people. It is the feat of the national
affembly. There the king's palace is neither vaft nor
empty. He reigns in it by his prefence, which ani-
mates every thing. There the fenate dictates the laws,
agreeable to the fenfe of the people it reprefents. It
neither fears the eye of the monarch, nor the frowns
of the miniftry. London has not arrived to its pre-

B O O K fent greatnefs by the influence of government, which
XIV. ftrains and over-rules all natural caufes; but by the
ordinary impulfe of men and things, and by a kind
of attraction of commerce. It is the fea, it is England,
it is the whole world, that makes London rich and
populous.

Neverthelefs, this immenfe ftaple hath loft, in procefs of time, fomething of that fpecies of monopoly
which it exercifed over the colonies and over the provinces. Briftol, Liverpool, Lancafter, and Glafgow,
have taken a confiderable fhare in this great circulation. A more general competition would even have
been eftablifhed, if a new fyftem of manners, a diflike for a retired life, the defire of approaching the
throne, and an effeminacy and corruption which have
exceeded all bounds, had not collected at London,
or within its diftrict, a third part of the population
of the whole kingdom, and efpecially the great con-
fumers.

Summary The hiftory of the great American Archipelago
of the cannot be better concluded, than by a recapitulation
riches that
Europe of the advantages it procures to thofe powers which
draws from
the Ameri- have fucceffively invaded it. It is only by the im-
can iflands. pulfe which the immenfe productions of this Archipelago have given to trade, that it muft ever hold a
diftinguifhed place in the annals of nations; fince, in
fact, riches are the fpring of all the great revolutions
that difturb the globe. The colonies of Afia Minor
occafioned both the fplendour of that quarter of the
earth, and the downfal of Greece. Rome, which was
at firft defirous of fubduing nations only to govern
them, was ftopped in the progrefs of her greatnefs,
when fhe acquired the poffeffion of the treafures of the
Eaft. War feemed to flumber for a while in Europe,
in order to invade a New World : and has fince been
fo often renewed there, merely to divide the fpoils.
Poverty, which will always be the lot of the greater
part of mankind, and the choice of a few wife men,
makes no difturbance in the world. Hiftory, therefore, can only treat of maffacres or riches.

The iſlands of the other hemiſphere yield annually B O O K fifteen millions of livres [625,000l.] to Spain; eight XIV. millions [333,333l. 6s. 8d.] to Denmark; thirty mil-lions [1,250,000l.] to Holland; eighty-two millions [3,416,666l. 13s. 4d.] to England; and one hundred and twenty-ſix millions [5,250,000l.] to France. The pro-ductions therefore gathered in fields that were totally uncultivated within theſe three centuries, are ſold in our continent for about two hundred and ſixty-one millions of livres [10,875,000l.]

This is not a gift that the New World makes to the Old. The people who receive this important fruit of the labour of their ſubjects ſettled in America, give in exchange, though with evident advantage to them-ſelves, the produce of their ſoil and of their manu-factures. Some conſume the whole of what they draw from theſe diſtant poſſeſſions; others make the over-plus the baſis of a proſperous trade with their neigh-bours. Thus every nation that is poſſeſſed of property in the New World, if it be truly induſtrious, gains ſtill leſs by the number of men it maintains abroad, with-out any expence, than by the population which thoſe procure it at home. To ſubſiſt a colony in America, it is neceſſary to cultivate a province in Europe; and this additional labour increaſes the inward ſtrength and real wealth of the nation. The whole globe is ſenſible of this impulſe.

The labours of the people ſettled in thoſe iſlands are the ſole baſis of the African trade: they extend the fiſheries and the cultures of North America, af-ford a good market for the manufactures of Aſia, and double, perhaps treble, the activity of all Europe. They may be conſidered as the principal cauſe of the rapid motion which now agitates the univerſe. This ferment muſt increaſe, in proportion as cultures, that are ſo capable of being extended, ſhall approach nearer to their higheſt degree of perfection.

Nothing would be more likely to haſten this happy The beſt period, than to give up the excluſive trade, which every mode to be nation has reſerved to itſelf in its own colonies. An adopted for increaſing

B O O K unlimited freedom to trade with all the iflands would
XIV.   be productive of the greateft efforts, by exciting a ge-
the produc- neral competition.   Men who are infpired with the
tions of the love of humanity, and are enlightened by that facred
American
Archipela- fire, have ever wifhed to fee every obftacle removed
go.   that intercepts a direct communication of all the ports
of America with all thofe of Europe.   The feveral governments, which, being almoft all corrupt in their
origin, cannot be influenced by this principle of univerfal benevolence, have imagined that affociations,
moftly founded on the feparate intereft of each nation,
or of one fingle individual, ought to be formed, in order to confine all the connections of every colony to
its refpective mother-country.   The opinion is, that
thefe reftraining laws fecure to each commercial nation in Europe the fale of its own territorial productions, the means of procuring fuch foreign commodities as it may ftand in need of, and an advantageous
balance with all the other trading nations.

This fyftem, which was long thought to be the beft,
has been vigoroufly oppofed, when the theory of commerce had once fhaken off the fetters of prejudice.   It
has been alleged, that no nation can fupply all the real
or imaginary wants of its colonies out of its own property.   There is not one that is not obliged to get
fome articles from abroad, in order to complete the
cargoes deftined for America.   From this neceffity
arifes at leaft an indirect communication of all nations
with thofe diftant poffeffions.   Would it not be more
eligible to convey each article to its deftination in a
direct line, than by this indirect way of exchange?
This plan would be attended with lefs expence ; would
promote both culture and confumption, and bring an
increafe of revenue to the public treafury : an infinite
number of advantages would accrue to the mother-
countries, which would make them full amends for the
exclufive right they all claim, to their reciprocal injury.

Thefe maxims are true, folid, and ufeful, but they
will not be adopted.   The reafon is this : A great re-

volution is preparing in the trade of Europe, and is al- B O O K
ready too far advanced not to be completed.   Every   XIV.
government is endeavouring to do without the affiftance of foreign induftry. Moft of them have fucceeded, and the reft will not be long before they free themfelves from this dependence. Already the Englifh and
the French, who are the great manufacturers of Europe, fee their mafter-pieces of workmanfhip refufed on
all fides.   Will thefe two nations, which are at the
fame time the greateft planters in the iflands, open
their ports to thofe who force them, as it were, to fhut
up their manufactures at home? The more they lofe
in the foreign markets, the lefs they will confent to a
competition in the only market they have left.   They
will rather ftrive to extend it, that they may have a
greater demand for their commodities, and a greater
fupply of American productions. It is by thefe returns
that they will preferve their advantage in the balance
of trade, without being apprehenfive that the plenty of
thefe productions will lower their value. The progrefs
of induftry in our continent muft increafe population
and wealth, and of courfe the confumption and value
of the productions of the Antilles.

But what will become of this part of the New World? What will
Will the fettlements that render it fo flourifhing, al- be the fate
ways remain in the hands of their original poffeffors ; rican iflands
or will the mafters of them be changed? If a revolu- hereafter?
tion fhould take place in them, by what means will it
be brought about, and what people will reap the advantage of it? Thefe are queftions that afford much
room for conjecture, which may be affifted by the following reflections.

The iflands depend totally upon Europe for a fupply
of all their wants.   Thofe which only refpect wearing
apparel and implements of hufbandry will admit of delay ; but the leaft difappointment, with regard to provifions, fpreads a general alarm, and caufes univerfal
defolation, which rather tempts the people to wifh for,
than to fear the approach of an enemy. And, indeed,
it is a common faying in the colonies, that they will

B O O K never fail to capitulate with a fquadron ftored with
XIV. barrels of flour inftead of gunpowder. If we pretend
to obviate this inconvenience, by obliging the inhabitants to cultivate for their own fubfiftence, we defeat
the very end of thefe fettlements, without any real advantage. The mother-country would deprive herfelf
of a great part of the rich produce of her colonies, and
would not preferve them from invafion.

In vain fhould we hope to repulfe an invafion by
the help of Negroes, born in a climate where effeminacy
ftifles the feeds of courage, and who are ftill more
enervated by flavery, and, confequently, but little concerned in the choice of their tyrants. In fuch hands,
the beft weapons muft be ufelefs. It might even be
apprehended that they would turn them againft their
mercilefs oppreffors.

The white people appear to be better defenders of
the colonies. Befide the courage which liberty naturally infpires, they muft alfo be animated with that
which exclufively belongs to great proprietors. They
are not men debafed by coarfe labours, by obfcure occupations, or by indigence. The abfolute fway which
they exercife in their plantations, muft have infpired
them with pride and greatnefs of foul. But, difperfed
as they are among vaft poffeffions, what can their fmall
number avail? And would they even prevent an invafion, were they able to do it?

All the colonifts hold it as a maxim, that their iflands
are to be confidered as thofe great cities in Europe,
which, lying open to the firft-comer, change their dominion without an attack, without a fiege, and almoft
without being fenfible of the war. The ftrongeft is
their mafter. The inhabitants exclaim, *God fave the
conqueror!* in imitation of the Italians, who have paffed
and repaffed from one yoke to another in the courfe of
a campaign. Whether the city fhould return, at the
time of peace, under its former government, or fhould
remain in the hands of the victor, it has loft nothing of
its fplendour ; while towns, that are defended by ramparts, and difficult to be taken, are always depopulated

and reduced to a heap of ruins. Accordingly, there is scarce, perhaps, one inhabitant in the American iflands, who does not confider it to be a fatal prejudice to expose his fortune for the fake of his country. Of what importance is it to this rapacious calculator whofe laws he obeys, if his crops are left ftanding? Is it to enrich himfelf that he has croffed the feas? If he preferves his treafure, his purpofe is anfwered. Can the mother-country that forfakes him, and frequently after having tyrannized over him; that is ready to give him up, or, perhaps, to fell him, at the conclufion of a peace, have any claim to the facrifice of his life? It is no doubt a glorious thing to die for one's country. But a ftate, where the profperity of the nation is facrificed to forms of government; where the art of impofing upon men is the art of training up fubjects; where flaves are wanted inftead of citizens; where war is declared, and peace concluded, without confulting the opinion or the wifhes of the people; where evil defigns are always countenanced by the intrigues of debauchery, or the practices of monopoly; and where ufeful plans are only adopted with fuch reftrictions as prevent their being carried into execution: is this the country for which our blood fhould be facrificed?

The fortifications erected for the defence of the colonies, will fecure them no better than the efforts of the inhabitants. Even if they were ftronger, and better guarded and ftored than they have ever been, they muft always furrender unlefs they are fuccoured. Should the refiftance hold out above fix months, that circumftance would not difcourage the befiegers, who, being within reach of a conftant fupply of refrefhments, both by land and by fea, could better endure the feverity of the climate, than a garrifon could refift the duration of a fiege.

There is no other way to preferve the colonies but by a formidable navy. It is on the docks and in the harbours of Europe, that the baftions and ramparts of the American colonies muft be raifed. While the mother-country fhelters them, as it were, under the wings

BOOK
XIV.
of her ships; so long as she shall fill up with her fleets the vast interval that separates her from these islands, the offspring of her industry and power, her parental attention to their prosperity will secure their attachment to her. In future, therefore, the maritime forces will be the great object that will attract the attention of all proprietors of land in America. European policy generally secures the frontiers of states by fortified towns; but for maritime powers, there ought, perhaps, to be citadels in the centre, and ships on the circumference. A commercial island, indeed, wants no fortified towns. Her rampart is the sea, which constitutes her safety, her subsistence, her wealth; the winds are at her command, and all the elements conspire to promote her glory.

In this respect, Great Britain might lately have undertaken any thing, with the greatest hopes of success. Her islands were secure, while those of her rivals were open to invasion. The opinion which the English had conceived of their own valour; the terror which their arms had inspired; the fruits of a fortunate experience acquired by their admirals; the number and the excellence of their fleets; all these several modes of aggrandizement must have been annihilated during the calm of a long peace. The pride of past success; the very restlessness inseparable from prosperity; even the burden of conquests, which seems to be the punishment of victory; all these circumstances were so many incitements to war. The projects formed by their active ambition, have been annihilated by the revolution which hath detached North America from their empire: but is the possession of the islands, which are become very wealthy, and have been placed by nature in the vicinity of that great continent, which is still in a state of poverty, better secured to the nations that have cultivated them? It is in the position, in the interests, in the spirit of the new republics, that we must endeavour to explore the secret of our future destiny.

BOOK XV.

*Settlements of the French in North America. Upon what
Bafis was founded the Hope of their Profperity. Confequence of thefe Settlements.*

HITHERTO we have vifited thofe regions where
the rays of the fun are peipendicular. We fhall now
pafs on to thofe where they are oblique. It is no
longer gold which our rapacious and cruel Europeans
are going in fearch of at fo great a diftance from their
country. If they again crofs the feas, it will be for a
lefs extravagant motive; it will be to withdraw themfelves from the calamities of their own regions; it will
be to find reft and liberty; to clear uncultivated lands;
to caft their nets on fhores abounding with fifh; to go
in fearch of animals upon the tops of mountains, and
in the midft of forefts, in order to ftrip them of their
valuable furs.

The favage poffeffors of the regions we are going to
pervade are not a race of degenerate men, without
ftrength of body, or elevation of foul: but we fhall
find them huntfmen, warriors, inured to labour, brave,
eloquent, jealous of their independency; men, in a
word, who alternately difplay inftances of the moft
unheard-of ferocioufnefs, of the moft heroic magnanimity, and of the moft abfurd fuperftition.

Superftition, that fatal plant, is then indigenous in
all climates: it grows equally in the plains, and upon
the rocks; under the ardour of the line, under the
fnows of the pole, and in the temperate interval which
divides them. Doth the generality of this phenomenon point out in all parts a tendency of the ignorant
and timid man towards the Author of his exiftence,
and the Difpofer of good and evil? Doth it indicate
the anxiety of a child feeking his father in the dark?

Spain was miftrefs of the rich empires of Mexico Reafons
which pre-
vented the
and Peru, of the gold of the New World, and of almoft all South America. The Portuguefe, after a long French, for

B O O K
XV.

a long time,
from pur-
fuing the
plan of
forming
fettlements
in the New
World.
feries of victories, defeats, enterprifes, miftakes, conquefts, and loffes, had kept the moft valuable fettlements in Africa, in India, and in the Brazils. The
French government had not even conceived it poffible
to eftablifh colonies, or imagined that any advantage
could be derived from having poffeffions in thofe diftant regions.

Their ambitious views were turned entirely towards
Italy. Some ancient claims on the Milanefe and the
two Sicilies had involved them in expenfive wars, in
which they had been engaged for a long time. Their
internal commotions diverted them ftill more from the
great object of eftablifhing a diftant and extenfive commerce, and from the idea of increafing their dominions
by acquifitions in the Eaft and Weft Indies.

The authority of kings, though not openly contefted, was oppofed and eluded. Some remains of the
feudal government were ftill fubfifting, and many of
its abufes had not yet been abolifhed. The prince was
continually employed in reftraining the reftlefs fpirit of
a powerful nobility. Moft of the provinces that compofed the monarchy were governed by diftinct laws
and forms of their own. Every fociety, every order
in the ftate, enjoyed peculiar privileges, which were
either perpetually contefted, or carried to excefs. The
government was a complicated machine, which could
only be regulated by the management of a variety of
delicate fprings. The court was frequently under a
neceffity of having recourfe to the fhameful refources
of intrigue and corruption, or to the odious means of
oppreffion and tyranny; and the nation was continually negotiating with the prince. Regal authority was
unlimited, without having received the fanction of the
laws; and the people, though frequently too independent, had yet no fecurity for their liberty. Hence
arofe continual jealoufies, apprehenfions, and ftruggles.
The whole attention of the government was not directed to the welfare of the nation, but to the means
of enflaving it. The people were fenfible of their
wants, but ignorant of their powers and refources.

They found their rights alternately invaded or tramp- B O O K
led upon by their nobles or their fovereigns. XV.

France, therefore, fuffered the Spaniards and Por- Errors and
tuguefe to difcover new worlds, and to give laws to misfortunes
unknown nations.   Their attention was at length ex- which rendered me-
cited by Admiral Coligny, a man of the moft exten- morable
five, fteady, and active genius, that ever flourifhed in the firft expeditions of
that powerful empire.   This great politician, attentive the French
in the New
to the interefts of his country, even amidft the horrors Hemi-
of a civil war, fent John Ribaud to Florida, in 1562. fphere.
This vaft tract of North America then extended from
Mexico to the country which the Englifh have fince
cultivated under the name of Carolina.   The Spaniards
had paffed over it in 1512, but without fettling there.
The motives that engaged them to make this difcovery, and thofe which induced them to relinquifh it, are
equally unaccountable.

All the Indians of the Caribbee iflands believed, upon the credit of an ancient tradition, that nature had
concealed a fpring, or fountain, fomewhere on the continent, the waters of which had the property of reftoring youth to all old men who were fo fortunate as to
tafte of them.   The notion of immortality was always
the paffion of mankind, and the comfort of old age.
This idea delighted the romantic imagination of the
Spaniards.   The lofs of many, who were the victims
of their credulity, did not difcourage the reft.   Far
from fufpecting that the firft had perifhed in an attempt, of which death would prove the moft certain
confequence, they concluded that they did not return,
becaufe they had found the art of enjoying perpetual
youth, and had difcovered a fpot fo delightful, that
they did not choofe to leave it.

Ponce de Leon was the moft famous of the navigators who were infatuated with this chimerical idea.
Fully perfuaded of the exiftence of a third world, the
conqueft of which was referved to advance his fame,
but thinking that the remainder of his life was too
fhort for the immenfe career that was opening before
him, he refolved to endeavour to renew it, and recover

BOOK that youthful vigour fo neceffary to his defigns. He
XV. immediately bent his courfe towards thofe climates
where fable had placed the Fountain of Youth, and
difcovered Florida; from whence he returned to Porto-Rico, vifibly more advanced in years than when he
fet out. Thus chance immortalized the name of an
adventurer, who made a real difcovery, merely by being in purfuit of an imaginary one. His fate was the
fame as that of the alchemift, who, while he is fearching for gold which he does not find, difcovers fome
valuable thing which he was not feeking after.

There is fcarce any ufeful and important difcovery
made by the human mind, that has not been rather
the effect of a reftlefs imagination, than of induftry
excited by reflection. Chance, which is the imperceptible courfe of nature, is never at reft, and affifts
all men without diftinction. Genius grows weary, and
is foon difcouraged; it falls to the lot only of a few,
and exerts itfelf merely at intervals. Its utmoft efforts
frequently ferve only to throw it in the way of chance,
and invite its affiftance. The only difference between
a man of genius and one of common capacity is, that
the former anticipates and explores what the latter ac-
cidentally hits upon. But even the man of genius
himfelf more frequently employs the advantages which
chance prefents to him. It is the lapidary who gives
the value to the diamond, which the peafant has digged up without knowing its worth.

The Spaniards had neglected Florida, becaufe they
did not difcover there, either the fountain that was to
make them all grow young, or gold, which haftens the
period of old age. The French found there a more
real and valuable treafure; a clear fky, a fruitful foil,
a temperate climate, and favages who were lovers of
peace and hofpitality; but they themfelves were not
fenfible of the worth of thefe advantages. Had they
followed the directions of Coligny; had they tilled the
ground, which only wanted the affiftance of man to
call forth its treafures; had a due fubordination been
maintained among the Europeans; had not the rights

of the natives of the country been violated; a colony might have been founded, which in time would have become flouriſhing and permanent. But ſuch prudent meaſures were not to be expected from the levity of the French. The proviſions were laviſhed; the fields were not ſown; the authority of the chiefs was diſregarded by untractable ſubalterns; the paſſion for hunting and war engroſſed all their attention; in a word, every duty was neglected.

To complete their misfortune, the civil diſturbances in France diverted the ſubjects from an undertaking which had never engaged the attention of government. Theological diſputes alienated the minds, and divided the hearts, of all ranks of people. Government had violated that ſacred law of nature, which enjoins all men to tolerate the opinions of their fellowcreatures; and the rules of policy, which are inconſiſtent with an unſeaſonable exertion of tyranny. The reformed religion had made great progreſs in France, when it was perſecuted; a conſiderable part of the nation was involved in the proſcription, and took up arms.

Spain, though not leſs intolerant, had prevented religious diſturbances, by ſuffering the clergy to aſſume that authority which has been continually increaſing, but which, for the future, will be conſtantly on the decline. The inquiſition, always ready to oppoſe the leaſt appearance of innovation, found means to prevent the Proteſtant religion from making its way into the kingdom, and by this means ſpared itſelf the trouble of extirpating it. Philip II. wholly taken up with America, and accuſtomed to conſider himſelf as the ſole proprietor of it, being informed of the attempts made by ſome Frenchmen to ſettle there, and of their being neglected by their own government, fitted out a fleet from Cadiz to deſtroy them. Menendez, who was the commander of it, landed in Florida, where he found the enemies he went in ſearch of ſettled at Carolina fort. He attacked all their intrenchments, carried them ſword in hand, and made a dreadful maſ-

BOOK XV.

facre. Thofe who efcaped the rage of the fword were hanged on a tree, with this infcription: *Not as Frenchmen, but as heretics.*

Far from feeking to revenge this infult, the miniftry of Charles IX. fecretly rejoiced at the mifcarriage of a projeƈt, which, though they had approved it, was not countenanced by them; becaufe it had been contrived by the head of the Huguenots, and might refleƈt honour on their party. The indignation of the public only confirmed them in their refolution of fhowing no refentment. It was referved for a private man to execute what the ftate ought to have done.

Dominic de Gourgues, born at Mount Marfan in Gafcony, a fkilful and intrepid feaman, an enemy to the Spaniards, from whom he had received perfonal injuries; paffionately fond of his country, of hazardous expeditions, and of glory; fold his eftate, built fome fhips, and with a feleƈt band of his own ftamp, embarked to attack the murderers in Florida. He drove them from all their pofts with incredible valour and aƈtivity, defeated them in every rencounter, and, by way of retaliation for the contemptuous infult they had fhown, hung them up on trees; with this infcription: *Not as Spaniards, but as affaffins.*

Had the Spaniards been content with maffacring the French, the latter would never have had recourfe to fuch cruel reprifals; but they were offended at the infcription, and were guilty of an atrocious aƈt, in revenge for the derifion to which they had been expofed. This is not the only inftance in hiftory which may lead one to imagine, that it is not the thing that has made the word, but the word that has made the thing.

The expedition of the brave de Gourgues was attended with no further confequences. He blew up the forts he had taken, and returned home, either for want of provifions fufficient to enable him to remain in Florida, or becaufe he forefaw that no fuccours were to be expeƈted from France, or thought that friendfhip with the natives would laft no longer than the means of purchafing it, or that he would be attacked

by the Spaniards. He was received by all true patriots with the applaufe due to his merit; but neglected by the court, which was too defpotic and fuperftitious, not to ftand in awe of virtue.

From the year 1567, when this intrepid Gafcon
evacuated Florida, the French neglected America.
Bewildered in a chaos of unintelligible doctrines, they
loft their reafon and their humanity. The mildeft and
moft fociable people upon earth became the moft barbarous and fanguinary. Scaffolds and ftakes were infufficient; as they all appeared criminal in each other's
eyes, they were all mutually victims and executioners.
After having condemned one another to eternal deftruction, they affaffinated each other at the inftigation
of their priefts, who breathed nothing but the fpirit of
revenge and bloodfhed. At length, the generous
Henry foftened the minds of his fubjects; his compaffion and tendernefs made them feel their own calamities; he revived their fondnefs for the fweets of focial
life; he prevailed upon them to lay down their arms;
and they confented to live happy under his parental
laws.

In this ftate of tranquillity and freedom, under a
king who poffeffed the confidence of his people, they
began to turn their thoughts to fome ufeful projects,
and undertook the eftablifhment of colonies abroad.
Florida was the firft country that naturally occurred
to them. Except Fort St. Auguftine, formerly built
by the Spaniards, at the diftance of ten or twelve
leagues from the French colony, the Europeans had
not a fingle fettlement in all that vaft and beautiful
country. The inhabitants were not a formidable fet
of men; and the foil had every promifing appearance
of fertility. It was likewife reported to be rich in gold
and filver mines, both thofe metals having been found
there; whereas, in fact, they came from fome fhips
that had been caft away upon the coafts. The remembrance of the great actions performed by fome
Frenchmen could not yet be erafed. Probably the
French themfelves were rather afraid of irritating

BOOK
XV.

Spain, which was not yet difpofed to fuffer the leaft fettlement to be made on the Gulf of Mexico, or even near it. The danger of provoking a nation, fo formidable in thofe parts, determined them to keep at a diftance as much as poffible, and therefore they gave the preference to the more northern parts of America: that road was already chalked out.

The French turn their views towards Canada.

Francis I. had fent out Verazani, a Florentine, in 1523, who only took a view of the ifland of Newfoundland, and fome coafts of the continent, but made no ftay there.

Eleven years after, James Cartier, a fkilful navigator of St. Malo, refumed the projects of Verazani. The two nations, which had firft landed in America, exclaimed againft the injuftice of treading in their footfteps. *What!* faid Francis I. pleafantly, *fhall the kings of Spain and Portugal quietly divide all America between them, without fuffering me to take a fhare as their brother? I would fain fee the article of Adam's will that bequeaths that vaft inheritance to them.*

Cartier proceeded further than his predeceffor. He went up the river St. Lawrence; but, after having bartered fome European commodities with the favages for fome of their furs, he re-embarked for France, where an undertaking, which feemed to have been entered upon merely from imitation, was neglected from levity.

It happened fortunately that the Normans, the Britons, and the Bifcayans, continued to carry on the cod-fifhery on the great fand-bank along the coafts of Newfoundland, and in all the adjacent latitudes. Thefe intrepid and experienced men ferved as pilots to the adventurers, who, fince the year 1598, have attempted to fettle colonies in thofe defert regions. None of thofe firft fettlements profpered, becaufe they were all under the direction of exclufive companies, which had neither abilities to choofe the beft fituations, nor a fufficient capital to wait for their returns. One monopoly followed another in a rapid fucceffion without any advantage: they were purfued with gree-

dineſs, without a plan, or any means to carry them into execution. All theſe different companies ſucceſſively ruined themſelves; and the ſtate was no gainer
by their loſs. Theſe numerous expeditions had coſt
France more men, more money, and more ſhips, than
other ſtates would have expended in the foundation of
great empires. At laſt Samuel de Champlain went a
conſiderable way up the river St. Lawrence; and, in
1608, upon the borders of that river laid the foundation of Quebec, which became the origin, centre, and
capital of New France, or Canada.

The unbounded track, that opened itſelf to the view
of this colony, diſcovered only dark, thick, and deep
foreſts, the height of which alone was a proof of their
antiquity. Numberleſs large rivers came down from
a conſiderable diſtance to water theſe immenſe regions.
The intervals between them were full of lakes. Four
of theſe meaſured from two to five hundred leagues in
circumference. Theſe ſort of inland ſeas communicated with each other; and their waters, after forming
the great river St. Lawrence, conſiderably increaſed
the bed of the ocean. Every thing in this rude part
of the New World appeared grand and ſublime. Nature here diſplayed ſuch luxuriancy and majeſty as
commanded veneration, and a multitude of wild graces,
far ſuperior to the artificial beauties of our climates.
Here the imagination of a painter or a poet would
have been raiſed, animated, and filled with thoſe ideas
which leave a laſting impreſſion on the mind. All
theſe countries exhaled an air fit to prolong life. This
temperature, which, from the poſition of the climate,
muſt have been extremely pleaſant, loſt nothing of its
wholeſomeneſs by the ſeverity of a long and intenſe
winter. Thoſe who impute this merely to the woods,
ſprings, and mountains, with which this country a-
bounds, have not taken every thing into conſideration.
Others add to theſe cauſes of the cold, the elevation
of the land, a pure aerial atmoſphere, ſeldom loaded
with vapours, and the direction of the winds, which
blow from north to ſouth over ſeas always frozen.

B O O K
XV.

Government, cus-
toms, vir-
tues, vices,
and wars,
of the fa-
vages that
inhabited
Canada.
Notwithſtanding this, the inhabitants of this ſharp and bleak climate were but thinly clad. Before their intercourſe with us, a cloak of buffalo or beaver ſkin, bound with a leathern girdle, and ſtockings made of a roe-buck's ſkin, was the whole of their dreſs. The additions they have ſince made give great offence to their old men, who are ever lamenting the degeneracy of their manners.

Few of theſe ſavages knew any thing of huſbandry ; they only cultivated maize, and that they left entirely to the management of the women, as being beneath the dignity of independent men. Their bittereſt imprecation againſt an enemy, was the ſame as the curſe pronounced by God againſt the firſt man, that he might be reduced to till the ground. Sometimes they would condeſcend to go a-fiſhing ; but their chief delight, and the employment of all their life, was hunting. For this purpoſe, the whole nation went out as they did to war, every family marched in ſearch of ſuſtenance. They prepared for the expedition by ſevere faſting, and never ſtirred out till they had implored the aſſiſtance of their gods ; they did not pray for ſtrength to kill the beaſts, but that they might be ſo fortunate as to meet with them. None ſtaid behind except infirm and old men ; all the reſt ſallied forth ; the men to kill the game, and the women to dry and bring it home. The winter was with them the fineſt ſeaſon of the year : the bear, the roe-buck, the ſtag, and the elk, could not then run with any degree of ſwiftneſs through ſnow that was four or five feet deep. The ſavages, who were ſtopped neither by the buſhes, the torrents, the ponds, nor the rivers, and who could outrun moſt of the ſwifter animals, were ſeldom unſucceſsful in the chaſe. When they were without game, they lived upon acorns ; and, for want of theſe, fed upon the ſap or inner ſkin that grows between the wood and the bark of the aſpen tree and the birch.

In the interval between their hunting parties, they made or mended their bows and arrows, the rackets for running upon the ſnow, and the canoes for croſſing the lakes and rivers. Thefe travelling implements, B O O K and a few earthen pots, were the only fpecimens of art XV. among thefe wandering nations. Thofe who were col-lected in towns, added to thefe the labours requifite for their fedentary way of life, for the fencing of their huts, and fecuring them from being attacked. The favages, at that period, gave themfelves up to total in-action, in the moft profound fecurity. The people, content with their lot, and fatisfied with what nature afforded them, were unacquainted with that reftleff-nefs which arifes from a fenfe of our own weaknefs, that lothing of ourfelves and every thing about us, that neceffity of flying from folitude, and eafing our-felves of the burden of life by throwing it upon others.

Their ftature in general was beautifully proportion-ed; but they had more agility than ftrength, and were more fit to bear the fatigues of the chafe than hard la-bour. Their features were regular; and there was a kind of fiercenefs in their afpect, which they contract-ed in war and hunting. Their complexion was of a copper colour; and they derived it from nature, by which all men who are conftantly expofed to the open air are tanned. This complexion was rendered ftill more difagreeable by the abfurd cuftom that prevails among favages, of painting their bodies and faces, ei-ther to diftinguifh each other at a diftance, to render themfelves more agreeable to their miftreffes, or more formidable in war. Befide this varnifh, they rubbed themfelves with the fat of quadrupeds, or the oil of fifh, a cuftom common and neceffary among them, in order to prevent the intolerable ftings of gnats and in-fects, that fwarm in uncultivated countries. Thefe ointments were prepared and mixed up with certain red juices, fuppofed to be a deadly poifon to the mof-chetos. To thefe feveral methods of anointing them-felves, which penetrate and difcolour the fkin, may be added, the fumigations they made in their huts againft thofe infects, and the fmoke of the fires they kept all the winter to warm themfelves, and to dry their meat. This was fufficient to make them appear frightful to

BOOK our people, though beautiful, without doubt, or at leaft
XV. not difagreeable to themfelves. Their fight, fmell, and
hearing, and all their fenfes, were remarkably quick,
and gave them early notice of their dangers and wants.
Thefe were few, but their difeafes were ftill fewer.
They hardly knew of any but what were occafioned
by too violent exercife, or eating too much after long
abftinence.

They were not a very numerous people; and, poffibly, this might be an advantage to them. Polifhed
nations muft wifh for an increafe of population, becaufe, as they are governed by ambitious rulers, who
are the more inclined to war from not being perfonal-
ly engaged in it, they are under a neceffity of fighting, either to invade or repulfe their neighbours; and
becaufe they never have a fufficient extent of territory to fatisfy their enterprifing and expenfive way of
life. But unconnected nations, who are always wandering, and guarded by the deferts which divide them;
who can fly when they are attacked, and whofe poverty preferves them from committing or fuffering any
injuftice; fuch favage nations do not feel the want of
numbers. Perhaps nothing more is required, than to
be able to refift the wild beafts, occafionally to drive
away an infignificant enemy, and mutually to affift
each other. Had they been more populous, they
would the fooner have exhaufted the country they inhabited, and have been forced to remove in fearch of
another; the only, or, at leaft, the greateft misfortune
attending their precarious way of life.

Independent of thefe reflections, which poffibly did
not occur fo ftrongly to the favages of Canada, the
nature of things was alone fufficient to check their increafe. Though they lived in a country abounding in
game and fifh, yet in fome feafons, and fometimes for
whole years, this refource failed them: and famine
then occafioned a great deftruction among people who
were at too great a diftance to affift each other. Their
wars, or tranfient hoftilities, the refult of former ani-
mofities, were very deftructive. Men conftantly ac-

cuftomed to hunt for their fubfiftence, to tear in pieces
the animal they had overtaken, to hear the cries of
death, and fee the fhedding of blood, muft have been
ftill more cruel in war, if poffible, than our own people, who live partly on vegetables. In a word, notwithftanding all that has been faid in favour of inuring children to hardfhips, which mifled Peter the
Great to fuch a degree that he ordered that none of
his failors children fhould drink any thing but fea-
water (an experiment which proved fatal to all who
tried it); it is certain, that a great many young favages perifhed through hunger, thirft, cold, and fatigue.
Even thofe whofe conftitution was ftrong enough to
bear the ufual exercifes of thofe climates, to fwim
over the broadeft rivers, to go two hundred leagues
on a hunting party, to live many days without fleep,
to fubfift a confiderable time without any food; fuch
men muft have been exhaufted, and totally unfit for
the purpofes of generation. Few were fo long-lived
as our people, whofe manner of living is more uniform and tranquil.

The aufterity of a Spartan education, the cuftom
of inuring children to hard labour and coarfe food,
has been productive of dangerous miftakes. Philofophers, defirous of alleviating the miferies incident to
mankind, have endeavoured to comfort the wretched
who have been doomed to a life of hardfhips, by
perfuading them that it was the moft wholefome and
the beft. The rich have eagerly adopted a fyftem,
which ferved to render them infenfible to the fufferings of the poor, and to difpenfe them from the duties of humanity and compaffion. But it is an error
to imagine, that men, who are employed in the more
laborious arts of fociety, live as long as thofe who enjoy the fruit of their toil. Moderate labour ftrength-
ens the human frame; exceffive labour impairs it. A
peafant is an old man at fixty; while the inhabitants
of towns, who live in affluence, and with fome degree of moderation, frequently attain to fourfcore and
upward. Even men of letters, whofe employments

B O O K are by no means favourable to health, afford many in-
XV. ftances of longevity. Let not then our modern writings propagate this falfe and cruel error, to feduce
the rich to difregard the groans of the poor, and to
transfer all their tendernefs from their vaffals to their
dogs and horfes.

Three original languages were fpoken in Canada,
the Algonquin, the Sioux, and the Huron. They
were confidered as primitive languages, becaufe each
of them contained many of thofe imitative words
which convey an idea of things by found. The dia-
lects derived from them were nearly as numerous as
their towns. No abftract terms were found in thefe
languages, becaufe the infant mind of the favages feldom extends its view beyond the prefent object and
the prefent time ; and, as they have but few ideas,
they feldom want to reprefent feveral, under one and
the fame fign. Befides, the language of thefe people, almoft always animated by a quick, fimple, and
ftrong fenfation, excited by the great fcenes of nature,
contracted a lively and poetical caft from their ftrong
and active imagination. The aftonifhment and admiration which proceeded from their ignorance, gave
them a ftrong propenfity to exaggeration. They expreffed what they faw ; their language painted, as it
were, natural objects in ftrong colouring ; and their
difcourfes were quite picturefque. For want of terms
agreed upon to denote certain compound or complex
ideas, they made ufe of figurative expreffions. What
was ftill wanting in fpeech, they fupplied by their gef-
tures, their attitudes, their bodily motions, and the mo-
dulations of the voice. The boldeft metaphors were
more familiar to them in common converfation, than
they are even in epic poetry in the European languages.
Their fpeeches in public affemblies, particularly, were
full of images, energy, and pathos. No Greek or Roman orator ever fpoke, perhaps, with more ftrength
and fublimity than one of their chiefs. It was thought
neceffary to perfuade them to remove at a diftance
from their native foil. *We were born*, faid he, *on this*

fpot, our fathers lie buried in it. Shall we fay to the
bones of our fathers, Arife, and come with us into a fo-
reign land ?

It may eafily be imagined, that fuch nations could
not be fo gentle nor fo weak as thofe of South America. They fhowed that they had that degree of activity and ftrength which the people of the northern nations always poffefs, unlefs they are, like the Lapland-
ers, of a very different fpecies from ours. They had
but juft attained to that degree of knowledge and civilization, to which inftinct alone may lead men in the
fpace of a few years ; and it is among fuch people
that a philofopher may ftudy man in a ftate of nature.

They were divided into feveral fmall nations, whofe
form of government was nearly fimilar. Some had
hereditary chiefs ; others elected them ; the greater
part were only directed by their old men. They were
mere affociations, formed by chance, and always free ;
and though united, they were bound by no tie. The
will of individuals was not even overruled by the general one. All decifions were confidered only as matter of advice, which was not binding, or enforced by
any penalty. If, in one of thefe fingular republics, a
man was condemned to death, it was rather a kind of
war againft a common enemy, than an act of juftice
exercifed againft a fubject or a fellow-citizen. Inftead
of coercive power, good manners, example, education,
a refpect for old men, a parental affection, maintained
peace in thefe focieties, where there was neither law
nor property. Reafon, which had not been mifled by
prejudice, or corrupted by paffion, as it is with us,
ferved them inftead of moral precepts and regulations
of police. Harmony and fecurity were maintained
without the interpofition of government. Authority
never encroached upon that powerful inftinct of nature, the love of independence ; which, enlightened by
reafon, produces in us the love of equality.

Hence arifes that regard which the favages have for
each other. They lavifh their expreffions of efteem,
and expect the fame in return. They are obliging, but

referved; they weigh their words, and liften with great
attention. Their gravity, which appears like a kind
of melancholy, is particularly obfervable in their national affemblies. Every one fpeaks in his turn, according to his age, experience, and fervices. No one
is ever interrupted, either by indecent reflections or ill-
timed applaufe. Their public affairs are managed with
fuch difintereftednefs as is unknown in our governments, where the welfare of the ftate is hardly ever
promoted but from felfifh views or party fpirit. It is
no uncommon thing to hear one of thefe favage orators, when his fpeech has met with univerfal applaufe,
telling thofe who agreed to his opinion, that another
man is more deferving of their confidence.

This mutual refpect among the inhabitants of the
fame place, prevails between the feveral nations, when
they are not in actual war. The deputies are received
and treated with that friendfhip that is due to men who
come to treat of peace and alliance. Wandering nations, who have not the leaft notion of increafing their
territory, never negotiate for conqueft, or for any interefts relative to dominion. Even thofe who have fixed
fettlements, never contend with others for coming to
live in their diftrict, provided they do not moleft them.
The earth, fay they, is made for all men ; no one muft
poffefs the fhare of two. All the politics, therefore, of
the favages, confift in forming leagues againft an enemy who is too numerous or too ftrong, and in fufpend-
ing hoftilities that become too deftructive. When they
have agreed upon a truce or league of amity, it is rati-
fied by mutually exchanging a belt, or ftring of beads,
which are a kind of fnail-fhells. The white ones are
very common ; but the purple ones, which are rare,
and the black, which are ftill more fo, are much
efteemed. They work them into a cylindrical form,
bore them, and then make them up into necklaces.
The branches are about a foot long, and the beads are
ftrung upon them one after another in a ftraight line.
The necklaces are broad belts, on which the beads are
placed in rows, and neatly tacked down with little

flips of leather. The fize, weight, and colour of thefe B O O K shells, are adapted to the importance of the bufinefs. XV. They ferve as jewels, as records, and as annals. They are the bond of union between nations and individuals. They are the facred and inviolable pledge which is a confirmation of words, promifes, and treaties. The chiefs of towns are the keepers of thefe records. They know their meaning; they interpret them; and by means of thefe figns, they tranfmit the hiftory of the country to the fucceeding generation.

As the favages poffefs no riches, they are of a benevolent turn. A ftriking inftance of this appears in the care they take of their orphans, widows, and infirm people. They liberally fhare their fcanty provifion with thofe whofe crops have failed, or who have been unfuccefsful in hunting or fifhing. Their tables and their huts are open night and day to ftrangers and travellers. This generous hofpitality, which makes the advantages of a private man a public bleffing, is chiefly confpicuous in their entertainments. A favage claims refpect, not fo much from what he poffeffes, as from what he gives away. The whole ftock of provifions collected during a chafe that has lafted fix months, is frequently expended in one day; and he who gives the entertainment enjoys more pleafure than his guefts.

None of the writers who have defcribed the manners of the favages have reckoned benevolence among their virtues. But this may be owing to prejudice, which has made them confound the antipathy arifing from refentment, with natural temper. Thefe people neither love nor efteem the Europeans, nor are they very kind to them, The inequality of conditions, which we think fo neceffary for the well-being of fociety, is, in their opinion, the greateft folly. They are fhocked to fee, that among us, one man has more property than feveral others collectively, and that this firft injuftice is productive of a fecond, which is, that the man who has moft riches is on that account the moft refpected. But what appears to them a meannefs be-

BOOK low the brute creation, is, that men who are equal by
XV. nature fhould degrade themfelves fo far as to depend
upon the will or the caprice of another. The refpect
we fhow to titles, dignities, and efpecially to hereditary
nobility, they call an infult, an outrage to human nature. Whoever knows how to guide a canoe, to beat
an enemy, to build a hut, to live upon little, to go a
hundred leagues in the woods, with no other guide
than the wind and fun, or any provifion but a bow and
arrows ; he acts the part of a man, and what more can
be expected of him? That reftlefs difpofition, which
prompts us to crofs fo many feas in queft of fugitive
advantages, appears to them rather the effect of poverty than of induftry. They laugh at our arts, our manners, and all thofe cuftoms which infpire us with a
greater degree of vanity, in proportion as they remove
us further from the ftate of nature. Their franknefs
and honefty are roufed to indignation by the tricks
and cunning which have been practifed in our dealings
with them. A multitude of other motives, fome
founded on prejudice, but frequently on reafon, have
rendered the Europeans odious to the Indians. They
have made reprifals, and are become harfh and cruel in
their intercourfe with us. The averfion and contempt
they have conceived for our manners, have always
made them avoid our fociety. We have never been
able to reconcile any of them to our indulgent manner
of living; whereas we have feen fome Europeans
forego all the conveniencies of civil life, retire into
the forefts, and take up the bow and the club of the
favage.

An innate fpirit of benevolence, however, fometimes
brings the favages back to us. At the beginning of the
winter a French veffel was wrecked upon the rocks of
Anticofti. The failors who had efcaped the rigour of
the feafon and the dangers of famine in this defert and
favage ifland, built a bark out of the remains of their
fhip, which, in the following fpring, conveyed them to
the continent. They were obferved in a languid and
expiring ftate, by a hut filled with favages. *Brethren,*

said the chief of this lonely family, addreffing himfelf
affectionately to them, *the wretched are entitled to our
pity and our affiftance. We are men, and the misfortunes
incident to any of the human race affect us in the fame
manner as if they were our own.* Thefe humane expreffions were accompanied with every token of friendfhip thefe generous favages had it in their power to
fhow.

Europeans, who are fo proud of your government,
of your laws, of your inftitutions, of your monuments,
of every thing that you call your wifdom, fuffer me to
engage your attention for a moment. I have juft defcribed, in a plain and artlefs way, the life and manners
of the favages. I have not concealed from you their
vices, nor have I exaggerated their virtues. I entreat
you to preferve the fenfations which my narrative hath
raifed in you, till the man of the firft genius and of the
greateft eloquence among you, fhall have prepared
himfelf to defcribe to you, with all the ftrength and
with all the magic of his colouring, the good and the
evil of your civilized countries. His picture will undoubtedly tranfport you with admiration ; but do you
imagine that it will leave in your minds that delicious
emotion which you experience at prefent? Will the
writer infpire you with thofe fentiments of efteem,
love, and veneration, which you have juft granted the
favages? You would only be miferable favages if you
were to live in the forefts, and the loweft of the favages
would be a refpectable man in your cities.

One thing only was wanting to complete the felicity
of the Americans, and that was the happinefs of being
fond of their wives. Nature hath in vain beftowed on
their women, a good fhape, beautiful eyes, pleafing
features, and long black hair. All thefe accomplifh-
ments are no longer regarded than while they remain
in a ftate of independence. They no fooner fubmit to
the matrimonial yoke, but even their hufband, who is
the only man they love, grows infenfible to thofe
charms they were fo liberal of before marriage. The
ftate of life, indeed, to which this condition fubjects

BOOK them, is by no means favourable to beauty. Their
XV. features alter, and they lofe at once the defire and the
power of pleafing. They are laborious, indefatigable,
and active. They dig the ground, fow, and reap;
while their hufbands, who difdain to ftoop to the
drudgeries of hufbandry, amufe themfelves with hunting, fifhing, fhooting with the bow, and afferting the
dominion of man over the earth.

Many of thefe nations allow a plurality of wives;
and even thofe that do not practife polygamy, have
ftill referved to themfelves the liberty of a divorce. The
very idea of an indiffoluble tie never once entered the
thoughts of a people who are free till death. When
thofe who are married difagree, they part by confent,
and divide their children between them. Nothing appears to them more repugnant to nature and reafon,
than the contrary fyftem which prevails among Chri-
ftians. The Great Spirit, fay they, hath created us all
to be happy; and we fhould offend him, were we to
live in a perpetual ftate of conftraint and uneafinefs.
This fyftem agrees with what one of the Miamis faid
to one of the miffionaries, *My wife and I were continually at variance. My neighbour difagreed equally
with his. We have exchanged wives, and are both fatisfied.*

A celebrated writer, whom we cannot but admire,
even when we differ from him in opinion, has obferved, that love among the Americans is never productive
of induftry, genius, and character, as it is among the
Europeans; becaufe the former, fays he, have a fixth
fenfe, weaker than it is among the latter. The favages,
it is faid, are neither acquainted with the torments nor
the delights of this moft violent of all paffions. The
air and the climate, the moifture of which contributes
fo powerfully to vegetation, does not beftow upon
them any great warmth of conftitution. The fame fap
which covers the countries with forefts, and the trees
with leaves, occafions among men, as among women,
the growth of long, fmooth, thick, ftrong, and fturdy
hair. Men who have little more beard than eunuchs

have, cannot abound in generating principles. The B O O K
blood of thefe people is watery and cold; the males XV.
have fometimes milk in their breafts. Hence arifes
their tardy inclination to the fex; their averfion for
them at certain periods, and in times of pregnancy;
and that feeble and tranfient ardour, which is excited
only at certain feafons of the year. Hence arifes that
quicknefs of imagination, which renders them fuperftitious, fearful as children in the dark, and as much
prone to revenge as women; which makes them poets,
and figurative in their difcourfe; men of feeling, in a
word, but not of ftrong paffions. Hence, in fhort,
hath proceeded that want of population which hath
always been obferved in them. They have few children, becaufe they are not fufficiently fond of women.
And this is a national defect, with which the old men
were inceffantly reproaching the young people.

But may it not be faid, that the paffion of the favages for women is lefs languid from the nature of
their conftitution, than from their moral character?
The pleafures of love are too eafily indulged among
them, to excite any ftrong defires. Accordingly, a-
mong ourfelves, it is not in thofe ages, where luxury
encourages incontinence, that we fee the men moft
attached to the women, and the women bear the moft
children. In what country hath love ever been a
fource of heroifm and virtue, when the women have
not encouraged their lovers to thefe purfuits by chafte
refufals, and by the fhame they had affixed to the
weaknefs of their fex? It is at Sparta, at Rome, and
even in France, in the ages of chivalry, that love hath
given rife to great undertakings, and hath occafioned
the enduring of great hardfhips. There it is, that,
uniting itfelf to public fpirit, it affifted patriotifm, or
fupplied the place of it. As it was a more difficult
thing always to pleafe one woman, than to feduce feveral, the fway of moral love prolonged the power of
natural love, by fuppreffing it, by directing it to proper objects, by deceiving it even with hopes which
kept up defires, and maintained the paffion in all its

B O O K ſtrength. But this love, though ſtinted in enjoy-
XV. ments, was productive of great effects. To love was
not then an art, but a paſſion, which being engen-
dered in innocence itſelf, was kept alive by ſacrifices,
inſtead of being extinguiſhed in voluptuouſneſs.

With reſpect to the ſavages, if they ſhould not be
ſo fond of women as civilized people are, it is not,
perhaps, for want of powers or inclination to population. But the firſt wants of nature may, perhaps, re-
ſtrain in them the claims of the ſecond. Their ſtrength
is almoſt all exhauſted in procuring their ſubſiſtence.
Hunting and other expeditions leave them neither the
opportunity nor the leiſure of attending to the increaſe
of their ſpecies. No wandering nation can ever be
numerous. What muſt become of women obliged to
follow their huſbands a hundred leagues, with children at their breaſt or in their arms? What would
become of the children themſelves, if deprived of the
milk that muſt neceſſarily fail during the fatigues of
the journey? Hunting prevents, and war deſtroys,
the increaſe of mankind. A ſavage warrior reſiſts the
ſeducing arts of young women, who ſtrive to allure
him. When nature compels this tender ſex to make
the firſt advances, and to purſue the men that avoid
them, thoſe who are leſs inflamed with military ardour than with the charms of beauty, yield to the
temptation. But the true warriors, who have been
early taught that an intercourſe with women enervates
ſtrength and courage, do not ſurrender. It is not,
therefore, owing to natural defects that Canada is un-
peopled, but to the tract of life purſued by its inhabitants. Though they are as fit for procreation as our
northern people, all their ſtrength is employed for
their own preſervation. Hunger does not permit them
to attend to the paſſion of love. If the people of the
ſouth ſacrifice every thing to this latter deſire, it is
becauſe the former is eaſily ſatisfied. In a country
where nature is very prolific, and man conſumes but
little, all the ſtrength he has to ſpare is entirely turned to population; which is likewiſe aſſiſted by the

warmth of the climate. In a climate where men con- B O O K
fume more than nature affords them without pains, XV.
the time and the faculties of the human fpecies are
exhaufted in fatigues that are detrimental to population.

But a further proof, that the favages are not lefs
inclined to women than we are, is, that they are
much fonder of their children. Their mothers fuckle
them till they are four or five years old, and fometimes till fix or feven. From their earlieft infancy,
their parents pay a regard to their natural independence, and never beat or chide them, left they fhould
check that free and martial fpirit, which is one day
to conftitute their principal character. They even
forbear to make ufe of ftrong arguments to perfuade
them, becaufe this would be in fome meafure a reftraint upon their will. As they are only taught what
they want to know, they are the happieft children
upon earth. If they die, the parents lament them
with deep regret; and will fometimes go fix months
after, to weep over the grave of their child : and the
mother will fprinkle it with her own milk.

The ties of friendfhip among the favages are more
lafting than thofe of nature. Friendfhip is not abfolutely a duty, fince it cannot be commanded : but it
is a more agreeable, a more tender, and even a ftronger union, than thofe which are formed by nature, or
by focial inftitutions. All perfons who are connected
by that delightful fentiment, agree in giving mutual
advice to each other in difficult conjunctures ; in admi-
niftering comfort in misfortunes; in granting affiftance
in undertakings, and fuccours in adverfity. Imagination, far from feeking to diminifh the obligations incumbent upon this virtue, delights in exaggerating
them. It is thought that it cannot fubfift without an
entire neglect of one's felf, a total renunciation of all
perfonal interefts in favour of the friend truly beloved.

It is not given to all men to enjoy the fweets of
friendfhip. Several can neither feel it themfelves,
nor infpire it to others, on account of the coldnefs and

B O O K XV.

ſtiffneſs of their character. How is it poſſible that it ſhould enter into the heart of the rich? They have no other concern but their preſent opulence, the deſire of increaſing it, and the dread of loſing it. The powerful man requires none but flatterers, who ſcarce can venture to raiſe their timid looks up to him; and mean ſouls, who ſervilely implore his protection. What pleaſure could he find in an intimate friendly connection, which the loweſt claſs of citizens might enjoy as well, or better, than he? The diſſipated man is equally incapable of ſtrong or laſting affection; he is wholly abſorbed in ſhow, and in a variety of pleaſures. His enjoyments are external, and his heart totally unconnected with his attachments.

Friendſhip among ſavages is never broken by that variety of claſhing intereſts, which in our ſocieties weaken even the tendereſt and the moſt ſacred connections. When a man hath once made his choice, he depoſits in the breaſt of his aſſociate his inmoſt thoughts, his ſentiments, his projects, his ſorrows, and his joys. The two friends ſhare every thing in common; their union is for life; they fight ſide by ſide; and if one ſhould fall, the other certainly expires upon the body of his friend. Even then they cheriſh the flattering perſuaſion, that their ſeparation will be only momentary, and that they ſhall rejoin each other in another world, where they ſhall never part, and where they ſhall perpetually render each other the moſt important ſervices. An Iroquois, who was a Chriſtian, but who did not live according to the maxims of the goſpel, was threatened with eternal puniſhments. He aſked whether his friend, who had been buried a few days, was in hell? I have ſtrong reaſons to believe, replied the miſſionary, that he hath not been ſent to that place of torment. If that be the caſe, replied the ſavage, I will not go there either. He immediately promiſed to alter his manners, and after this, always led a very exemplary life.

The ſavages ſhow a degree of penetration and ſagacity, which aſtoniſhes every man who has not obſerved

how much our arts and methods of life contribute to
render our minds dull and inactive : becaufe we are
feldom under a neceffity of thinking, and have only
the trouble to learn. If however they have never improved any thing, any more than thofe animals, in
which we obferve the greateft fhare of fagacity, it is
probably becaufe, as they have no ideas but fuch as
relate to their prefent wants, the equality that fubfifts
between them lays every individual under a neceffity
of thinking for himfelf, and of fpending his whole life
in acquiring this common ftock of knowledge; hence
it may be reafonably inferred, that the fum total of
ideas in a fociety of favages is no more than the fum
of ideas in each individual.

Inftead of abftrufe meditations, the favages delight
in fongs. They are faid to have no variety in their
finging; but it is uncertain whether thofe who have
heard them had an ear properly adapted to their
mufic. When we firft hear a foreign language fpoken,
the whole feems one continued found, and appears to
be pronounced with the fame tone of voice, without
any modulation or profody. It is only by continued
habit that we learn to diftinguifh the words and fylla-
bles, and to perceive that the found of fome is dull,
and that of others fharp, and that it is more or lefs
lengthened out. Would it not require at leaft as much
time to enable us to determine any thing certain with
regard to the mufic of any nation, which muft always
be fubordinate to their language?

Their dances are generally an emblem of war, and
they ufually dance with their weapons in their hands.
There is fomething fo regular, rapid, and terrible, in
thefe dances, that an European, when firft he fees
them, cannot help fhuddering. He imagines that the
ground will in a moment be covered with blood and
fcattered limbs, and that none of the dancers or the
fpectators will furvive. It is fomewhat remarkable,
that in the firft ages of the world, and among favage
nations, dancing fhould be an imitative art, and that
it fhould have loft that characteriftic in civilized coun-

B O O K
XV.

tries, where it feems to be reduced to a fet of uniform fteps without meaning, But it is with dances as with languages, they grow abftracted like the ideas they are intended to reprefent. The figns of them are more allegorical, as the minds of the people become more refined. In the fame manner as a fingle word, in a learned language, expreffes feveral ideas; fo, in an allegorical dance, a fingle ftep, a fingle attitude, is fufficient to excite a variety of fenfations. It is owing to want of imagination, either in the dancers, or the fpectators, if a figured dance be not, or do not appear to be, expreffive. Befides, the favages can exhibit none but ftrong paffions and ferocious manners, and thefe muft be reprefented by more fignificant images in their dances, which are the language of gefture, the firft and fimpleft of all languages. Nations living in a ftate of civil fociety, and in peace, have only the gentler paffions to reprefent, which are beft expreffed by delicate images, fit to convey refined ideas. It might not, however, be improper fometimes to bring back dancing to its firft origin, to exhibit the old fimplicity of manners, to revive the firft fenfations of nature by motions which reprefent them, to depart from the antiquated and fcientific mode of the Greeks and Romans, and to adopt the lively and fignificant images of the rude Canadians.

Thefe favages, always totally devoted to the purfuit of the prefent paffion, are extravagantly fond of gaming, as is ufual with all idle people, and efpecially of games of chance. The fame men, who are commonly fo fedate, moderate, and difinterefted, and have fuch a command of themfelves, are outrageous, greedy, and turbulent at play; they lofe their peace, their fenfes, and all they are poffeffed of. Deftitute of almoft every thing, coveting all they fee, and when they like it, eager to have and enjoy it, their attention is entirely turned to the moft fpeedy and readieft way of acquiring it. This is a confequence of their manners, as well as of their character. The profpect of prefent happinefs always prevents them from difcerning the evils

that may enfue. Their forecaft does not even reach B o-o k
from day to night., They are alternately filly children xv.
and violent men. Every thing depends with them on
the prefent moment.

Gaming alone would lead them to fuperftition, even
if they were not naturally fubject to that fcourge of
the human race. But as they have few phyficians or
empirics of this kind to have recourfe to, they fuffer
lefs from this diftemper of the mind than more polifhed nations, and are better difpofed to attend to the
fuggeftions of reafon, which abate the violence of it.
The Iroquois have a confufed notion of a firft Being
who governs the world at pleafure. They never repine at the evil which this Being permits. When
fome mifchance befals them, they fay, *the man above
will have it fo ;* and there is, perhaps, more philofophy
in this fubmiffion, than in all the reafonings and de-
clamations of our philofophers. Moft other favage nations worfhip thofe two firft principles of good and evil,
which occur to the human mind as foon as it has acquired any conception of invifible fubftances. Sometimes they worfhip a river, a foreft, the fun or the
moon; in fhort, any beings in which they have obferved a certain power and motion ; becaufe, wherever
they fee motion, which they cannot account for, they
fuppofe there is a foul.

They feem to have fome notion of a future ftate ;
but, having no principles of morality, they do not
think the next life is a ftate of reward for virtue and
punifhment for vice. They believed that the indefatigable huntfman, the fearlefs and mercilefs warrior,
who has flain or. burnt many enemies, and made his
own town victorious, will after death pafs into a country, where he will be fupplied with plenty of all kinds
of animals to fatisfy his hunger ; whereas thofe who
are grown old in indolence, and without glory, will be
for ever banifhed into a barren land, where they will
be eternally expofed to famine and ficknefs. Their
tenets are fuited to their manners and their wants.
They believe in fuch pleafures and fuch fufferings as

they are acquainted with. They have more hopes than fears, and are happy even in their delusions. They are, however, often tormented with dreams.

Ignorance is naturally prone to connect something mysterious with dreams, and to ascribe them to the agency of some powerful being, who takes the opportunity, when our faculties are suspended and lulled asleep, of watching over us in the absence of our senses. It is, as it were, a soul, distinct from our own, that glides into us, to inform us of what is to come, when we cannot yet see it; though futurity be always present to that Being who created all things.

In the bleak and rough climates of Canada, where the people live by hunting, their nerves are apt to be painfully affected by the inclemency of the weather, and by fatigue and long abstinence. Then these savages have melancholy and troublesome dreams: they imagine they are surrounded with enemies; they see their town surprised, and deluged in blood; they receive injuries and wounds; their wives, their children, their friends, are carried off. When they awake, they take these visions for a warning from the gods; and that fear which first inspired them with this idea adds to their natural ferocity, by the melancholy cast it gives to their thoughts, and their gloomy complexions. The old women, who are useless in the world, dream for the safety of the commonwealth. Some weak old men also, like them too, dream on public affairs, in which they have no share or influence. Young men who are unfit for war or laborious exercises, will dream too, that they may bear some part in the administration of the clan. In vain hath it been attempted, during two centuries, to remove illusions so deeply rooted. The savages have constantly replied, *You Christians laugh at the faith we have in dreams, and yet require us to believe things infinitely more improbable.* Thus we see in these untutored nations the seeds of priestcraft, with all its train of evils.

Were it not for these melancholy fits and dreams, there would scarce ever be any contentions among

them. Europeans, who have lived long in thofe countries, affure us they never faw an Indian in a paffion.
Without fuperftition, there would be as few national
as private quarrels.

Private differences are moft commonly adjufted by
the majority of the people. The refpect fhown by the
nation to the aggrieved party fooths his felf-love, and
difpofes him to peace. It is more difficult to prevent
quarrels, or to put an end to hoftilities between two
nations.

War often takes its rife from hunting. When two
companies, which were feparated by a foreft a hundred
leagues in extent, happen to meet, and to interfere
with each other's fport, they foon quarrel, and turn
thofe weapons againft one another which were intended for the deftruction of bears. This flight fkirmifh
is a fource of eternal difcord. The vanquifhed party
vows implacable vengeance againft the conquerors; a
national hatred which will be maintained by their pofterity, and be rekindled from their afhes. The mutual wounds which both parties fuffer in fkirmifhes of
this kind fometimes put a ftop to thefe contentions;
when on each fide they happen to be occafioned by
fome impetuous young men, who in the heat of youth
may have been tempted to remove to a confiderable
diftance, in order to make a trial of their military fkill.
But the contentions between whole nations are not
eafily excited.

The declaration of war, when it appears neceffary,
is not left to the judgment and decifion of one man.
The nation meets, and the chief fpeaks. He ftates the
nature of the injury, and caufes of complaint. The
matter is confidered; the dangers and the confequences
of a rupture are weighed. The orators fpeak directly
to the point, without hefitation, without digreffion, or
without miftaking the cafe. The arguments are difcuffed with a ftrength of reafoning and eloquence that
arifes from the evidence and fimplicity of the matter
in difpute; and even with an impartiality which is lefs
affected by their ftrong paffions, than it is among us by

a combination of ideas. If war be unanimoufly determined by their giving a general fhout, the allies are invited to join in it, which they feldom refufe, as they
always have fome injury to revenge, or fome flain to
replace by prifoners.

The favages next proceed to the election of a chief.
When a certain number of men affemble to execute
an enterprife, in which common intereft is concerned,
one perfon among them muft be appointed to guide
the motions of the multitude, of whom he muft be the
common foul ; a foul which muft command them all
as imperioufly as its orders are iffued to the members
of the body which it inhabits, and which muft be o-
beyed with as much difpatch and punctuality. Whenever this identity ceafes, diforder is introduced. It is
no longer an army which hath the fame object in
view; it is a fet of diftinct officers and foldiers who
have each of them their particular defigns. That fubordination which connects one hundred thoufand men
with all their powers to one commander, is the chief
circumftance of diftinctions between modern and ancient warriors. Among the latter, every man ufed to
fingle out his enemy, and bid him defiance in the
midft of the throng. An engagement was nothing
more than a great number of duels fought at the fame
time upon a field of battle. It is not fo at prefent:
our armies confift of deep, large, and clofe bodies of
men, placed upon a line, preffed together, and moving
in all directions as one fingle body. Formerly an engagement was a duel between man and man ; at prefent, it is a duel of one body of men againft another.
The leaft want of fubordination would bring on confufion, and confufion would occafion a horrid maffacre
and a humiliating defeat.

The diflike which the favages of Canada have for
whatever may reftrain their independence, hath not
prevented them from perceiving the neceffity of having a military chief. They have always been led to
action by commanders, and phyfiognomy hath been
always attended to in the choice they have made of

them. This might be a very fallacious, and even ri- BOOK
diculous, way of forming a judgment of men, where XV.
they have been trained up from their infancy to difguife their real fentiments, and where, by a conftant
practice of diffimulation and artificial paffions, the
countenance is no longer expreffive of the mind. But
a favage, who is folely guided by nature, and is acquainted with its workings, feldom miftakes in the
judgment he forms at firft fight. The chief requifite,
next to a warlike afpect, is a ftrong voice; becaufe, in
armies that march without drums or clarions, in order
more effectually to furprife the enemy, nothing is fo
proper to found an alarm, or to give the fignal for the
onfet, as the terrible voice of a chief, who fhouts and
ftrikes at the fame time. But the beft recommenda-
tions for a general are his exploits. Every one is at
liberty to boaft of his victories, in order that he may
be the firft to expofe himfelf to march foremoft to
meet danger; to tell what he has done, in order to
fhow what he will do: and the favages think felf-
commendation not unbecoming a hero who can fhow
his fcars.

He who is chofen to be chief, and to lead on the
reft in the path of glory, never fails to harangue them.
" Comrades," fays he, " the bones of our brethren are
" ftill uncovered. They cry out againft us; we muft
" fatisfy them. Young men, to arms; fill your qui-
" vers; paint yourfelves with gloomy colours that
" may ftrike terror. Let the woods ring with our
" war-fongs. Let us footh the dead with the fhouts
" of vengeance. Let us go and bathe in the blood of
" our enemies, take prifoners, and fight as long as wa-
" ter fhall flow in the rivers, and as long as the fun
" and moon fhall remain fixed in the firmament."

At thefe words, thofe brave men who are eager for
war, go to the chief, and fay, *We will fhare the danger
with thee. So you fhall*, replies the chief; *we will fhare
it together.* But as no perfuafions are made ufe of to
induce any one to join the army, left a falfe point of
honour fhould compel men of no courage to take the

B O O K field, a man muſt undergo many trials before he can
  XV   be admitted as a ſoldier. If a young man, who has
never yet faced the enemy, ſhould betray the leaſt impatience, when, after long abſtinence, he is expoſed to
the ſcorching heat of the ſun, the intenſe froſts of the
night, or the ſtings of inſects, he would be declared incapable and unworthy to bear arms. Are the ſoldiers
of our militias and armies formed in this manner? On
the contrary, what a mournful and ominous ceremony
is ours! Men who have not been able to eſcape being
preſſed into the ſervice, or could not procure an exemption by purchaſe, or by virtue of ſome privilege,
march heavily along, with downcaſt looks, and pale
dejected faces, before a magiſtrate, whoſe office is odious to the people, and whoſe honeſty is doubtful. The
afflicted and trembling parents ſeem to be following
their ſon to the grave. A black ſcroll, iſſuing from a
fatal urn, points out the victims which the prince de-
votes to war. A diſtracted mother in vain preſſes her
ſon to her boſom, and ſtrives to detain him; he is torn
from her arms, and ſhe bids him an eternal farewell,
curſing the day of her marriage, and that of her deli-
very. It is not certainly by ſuch ſacrifices that good
ſoldiers are to be acquired. It is not with ſuch ſcenes
of diſtreſs and conſternation that the ſavages go to
meet victory. They march out in the midſt of feſti-
vity, ſinging, and dancing. The young married women follow their huſbands for a day or two, without
ſhowing any ſigns of grief or ſorrow. Theſe women,
who do not even utter a groan in the pangs of child-
birth, would ſcorn to ſoften the minds of the defenders and avengers of their country, by the tears even of
tenderneſs and compaſſion.

    The weapons of theſe ſavage nations are a kind of
ſpear, armed with ſharp bones, and a ſmall club of
very hard wood, of a round figure, and with one cutting edge. Inſtead of theſe laſt, ſince their acquaint-
ance with the Europeans, they make uſe of a hatchet,
which they manage with amazing dexterity. Moſt of
them have no inſtrument of defence: but if they at-

tack the pallifades that furround a town, they cover their body with a thin plank. Some of them ufed to wear a kind of cuirafs, made with plaited reeds; but they left it off, on finding it was not proof againft fire-arms.

The army is followed by dreamers, who affume the name of jugglers, and are too often fuffered to deter-mine the military operations. They march without any colours. All the warriors, who are almoft naked, that they may be the more alert in battle, rub their bodies with coal, to appear more terrible, or with mould, that they may not be fo eafily feen at a di-ftance, and by that means may be better able to fur-prife the enemy. Notwithftanding their natural in-trepidity and averfion for all difguife, their wars are carried on with artifice. Thefe ftratagems, common to all nations, whether favage or civilized, are become neceffary to the petty nations of Canada. They would have totally deftroyed one another, had they not made the glory of their chiefs to confift in bringing home all their companions, rather than in fhedding the blood of their foes. Honour, therefore, is to be gained by falling upon the enemy before he is prepared. Thefe people, whofe fenfes have never been impaired, are ex-tremely quick in their fmell, and can difcover the places where men have trode. By the keennefs of that and of their fight, it is faid they can trace footfteps that are made upon the fhorteft grafs, upon the dry ground, and even upon ftone; and from the nature of the footfteps can difcover to what nation the ad-venturers belong. Perhaps they may do this by the leaves from the forefts, which always cover the ground.

When they are fo fortunate as to furprife the ene-my, they difcharge a whole volley of arrows, and fall upon them with their clubs or hatchets. If they are upon their guard, or well intrenched, they retreat if they can; if not, they fight till they conquer or die. The victorious party difpatch the wounded whom they cannot carry off, fcalp the dead, and take fome prifoners.

BOOK
XV.

The conqueror leaves his hatchet upon the field of battle, having previoufly engraven upon it the mark of his nation, that of his family, and efpecially his own picture ; that is to fay, an oval with the figures marked on his own face. Others paint all thefe enfigns of honour, or rather trophies of victory, on the ftump of a tree, or on a piece of the bark, with coal mixed up with feveral colours. To this they add the hiftory, not only of the battle, but of the whole campaign, in hieroglyphic characters. Next to the picture of the general, the number of his foldiers is marked by fo many lines, that of the prifoners by fo many little images, and that of the dead by fo many human figures without heads. Such are the expreffive and technical figns which, in all original focieties, have preceded the art of writing and printing, and the voluminous libraries which fill the palaces of the rich and idle, and embarrafs the minds of the learned.

The hiftory of an Indian war is but a fhort one; they make hafte to defcribe it, for fear the enemy fhould rally and fall upon them. The conqueror glories in a precipitate retreat, and never ftops till he reaches his own territory and his own town. There he is received with the warmeft tranfports of joy, and finds his reward in the applaufes of his countrymen. A debate then enfues, how the prifoners, who are the only advantage of their victory, fhall be difpofed of.

The moft fortunate of the captives are thofe who are chofen to replace the warriors who fell in the late action, or in former battles. This adoption has been wifely contrived, to perpetuate nations, which would foon be deftroyed by frequent wars. The prifoners being once incorporated into a family, become coufins, uncles, fathers, brothers, hufbands ; in fhort, they fucceed to any degree of confanguinity in which the deceafed ftood, whofe place they fupply ; and thefe affectionate titles convey all their rights to them, at the fame time that they bind them to all their engagements. Far from being averfe for attaching themfelves with all proper affection to the family that has

adopted them, they will not refuse even to take up B O O K
arms againft their own countrymen. Yet this is fure- XV.
ly a ftrange inverfion of the ties of nature. They muft
be very weak men, thus to fhift the object of their regard with the viciffitudes of fortune. The truth is,
that war feems to cancel all the bonds of nature, and
to confine a man's feelings to himfelf alone Hence
arifes that union between friends among the favages,
which is obferved to be ftronger than that which fubfifts between relations. Thofe who are to fight and
die together, are more firmly attached than thofe who
are born together, or under the fame roof. When
war or death has diffolved that confanguinity which
is cemented by nature, or has been formed by choice,
the fame fate which loads the favage with chains, gives
him new relations and friends. Cuftom and common
confent have authorifed this fingular law, which undoubtedly fprang from neceffity.

But it fometimes happens that a prifoner refufes this
adoption; fometimes that he is excluded from it. A
tall handfome prifoner had loft feveral of his fingers
in battle. This circumftance was not noticed at firft.
Friend, faid the widow to whom he was allotted, *we
had chofen you to live with us; but in the condition you
appear, unable to fight and to defend us, of what ufe is
life to you? Death is certainly preferable. I am of the
fame opinion*, anfwered the favage. *Well then*, replied
the woman, *this evening you fhall be tied to the ftake.
For your own glory, and for the honour of your family,
who have adopted you, remember to behave like a man of
courage.* He promifed he would, and kept his word.

For three days he endured the moft cruel torments,
with a conftancy and cheerfulnefs that fet them all
at defiance. His new family never forfook him, but
encouraged him by their applaufe, and fupplied him
with drink and tobacco in the midft of his fufferings.
What a mixture of virtue and ferocioufnefs! Every
thing is great in thefe people who are not enflaved.
This is the fublime of nature, in all its horrors and its
beauties.

BOOK   The captives whom none choofe to adopt, are foon
XV.   condemned to death. The victims are prepared for
it by every thing that may tend to infpire them with
a fondnefs for life. The beft fare, the kindeft ufage,
the moft endearing names, are lavifhed upon them.
They are even fometimes indulged with women to the
very moment of their fentence. Is this compaffion,
or is it a refinement of barbarity? At laft a herald
comes, and acquaints the wretch that the pile is ready.
Brother, fays he, *be patient, you are going to be burnt.
Very well brother*, fays the prifoner, *I thank you.*

These words are received with general applaufe;
but the women are the moft violent in their expreffions of the common joy. She to whom the prifoner
is delivered up, inftantly invokes the fhade of a father, a hufband, a fon, the deareft friend, whofe death
is ftill unrevenged. *Draw near*, fhe cries, *I am preparing a feaft for thee. Come and drink large draughts
of the broth I intend to give thee. This warrior is going
to be put into the cauldron. They will apply hot hatchets
all over his body: they will fcalp him: they will drink out
of his fkull: thou fhalt be avenged and fatisfied.*

This furious woman then rufhes upon her victim,
who is tied to a poft near the fiery pile, and by ftriking or maiming him, fhe gives the fignal for the intended cruelties. There is not a woman or child in
the clan whom this fight has brought together, who
does not take a part in torturing and flaying the miferable captive. Some pierce his flefh with firebrands;
others cut it in flices; fome tear off his nails; while
others cut off his fingers, roaft them, and devour them,
before his face. Nothing ftops his executioners but
the fear of haftening his end: they ftudy to prolong
his fufferings for whole days, and fometimes they make
him linger for a week.

In the midft of thefe torments, the hero fings, in a
barbarous but heroic manner, the glory of his former
victories: he fings the pleafure he formerly took in
flaying his enemies. His expiring voice is raifed, to
exprefs the hope he entertains of being revenged;

and to tell his perfecutors that they know not how to avenge their anceſtors, whom he hath maſſacred. He chooſes to bid defiance to his executioners, the moment when their rage appears rather ſlackened ; and he endeavours to excite it anew, in order that the exceſs of his ſufferings may diſplay the exceſs of his courage. It is a conflict between the victim and his tormentors ; a dreadful challenge between conſtancy in ſuffering and obſtinacy in torturing. But the ſenſe of glory predominates. Whether this intoxication of enthuſiaſm ſuſpends, or wholly benumbs, all ſenſe of pain ; or whether cuſtom and education alone produce theſe prodigies of heroiſm ; certain it is, that the ſufferer dies without ever ſhedding a tear or heaving a ſigh. Let fanatics of all falſe religions no longer boaſt the conſtancy of their martyrs : the ſavage of nature goes beyond all their miraculous accounts.

How ſhall we account for this inſenſibility ? Is it owing to the climate, or to the manner of life ? Colder blood, thicker humours, a conſtitution rendered more phlegmatic by the dampneſs of the air and the ground, may doubtleſs blunt the irritability of the nervous ſyſtem in Canada. Men who are conſtantly expoſed to all the inclemencies of the weather, the fatigues of hunting, and the perils of war, contract ſuch a rigidity of fibres, ſuch a habit of ſuffering, as makes them inſenſible to pain. It is ſaid, the ſavages are ſcarce ever convulſed in the agonies of death, whether they die of ſickneſs or of a wound. As they have no apprehenſions, either of the approaches or the conſequences of death, their imagination does not ſuggeſt that artificial ſenſibility againſt which nature has guarded them. Their whole life, whether conſidered in a natural or moral view, is calculated to inſpire them with a contempt for death, which we ſo much dread ; and to enable them to overcome the ſenſe of pain, which is increaſed by our indulgences.

But a circumſtance ſtill more aſtoniſhing in the character of the Indians than their reſolution in ſupporting tortures, is the rancour that appears in their re-

B O O K venge.   It is dreadful to think that man may become
XV.   the moft cruel of all animals.   In general, revenge is
not profecuted with cruelty either among nations, or
between individuals who are governed by good laws;
which, at the fame time that they protect the fubject,
reftrain him from committing injuries.   Vengeance is
not a very lively principle in wars that are carried on
between great nations, becaufe they have but little to
fear from their enemies.   But in thofe petty nations,
where a confiderable fhare of the power of the ftate
belongs to each individual, where the lofs of one man
endangers the whole community, war is nothing elfe
than a fpirit of revenge that actuates the whole body.
Among independent men, who entertain a degree of
efteem for themfelves, which can never be felt by men
who are under fubjection; among favages whofe affections are very lively, and confined to a few objects,
injuries muft neceffarily be refented to the greateft degree, becaufe they affect the perfon in the moft fenfible
manner: the affaffination of a friend, of a fon, of a
brother, or of a fellow-citizen, muft be avenged by the
death of the affaffin.   Thefe beloved fhades are continually calling out for vengeance from their graves.
They wander about in the forefts, amidft the mournful accents of the birds of night; they appear in the
phofphorus and in the lightning; and fuperftition
pleads for them in the afflicted or incenfed hearts of
their friends.

When we confider the hatred which the hordes of
thefe favages bear to each other; the hardfhips they
undergo; the fcarcity they are often expofed to; the
frequency of their wars; the fmall number of inhabitants; the numberlefs fnares we lay for them; we
cannot but forefee that, in lefs than three centuries,
the whole race will be extinct.   What judgment will
pofterity form of this fpecies of men, who will exift
only in the defcriptions of travellers? Will not the accounts given of the favages appear to them in the
fame light as the fables of antiquity do to us? It will
fpeak of them, as the Centaurs and Lapithæ are fpoken

of by us. How many contradictions will not posterity difcover in their cuftoms and manners! Will not
fuch of our writings as may then have efcaped the deftructive hand of time, pafs for romantic inventions,
like thofe which Plato has left us concerning the ancient Atlantic?

The character of the North Americans, as we have
defcribed it, had fingularly difplayed itfelf in the war
between the Iroquois and the Algonquins. Thefe
two nations, the moft numerous in Canada, had formed a kind of confederacy. The former, who tilled the
ground, imparted their productions to their allies, who
in return fhared with them the fruits of their chafe.
Connected by their reciprocal wants, they mutually
defended each other. During the feafon when all the
labours of agriculture were interrupted by the fnow
on the ground, they lived together. The Algonquins
went a-hunting; and the Iroquois ftaid at home, to
fkin the beafts, cure the flefh, and drefs the hides.

The French
imprudent-
ly take a
part in the
wars of the
favages.

It happened one year that a party of Algonquins,
who were not very dexterous, or much ufed to the
chafe, proved unfuccefsful. The Iroquois, who attended them, defired leave to try whether they fhould
fucceed better. This requeft, which had fometimes
been complied with, was not granted. Irritated at
this unfeafonable refufal, they went out privately in
the night, and brought home a great number of animals. The Algonquins greatly mortified, to blot out
the very remembrance of their difgrace, waited till
the Iroquois huntfmen were afleep, and put them all
to death. This maffacre occafioned a great alarm.
The offended nation demanded juftice, which was
haughtily refufed; and they were given to underftand
that they muft not expect the fmalleft fatisfaction.

The Iroquois, enraged at this contemptuous treatment, vowed that they would either be revenged, or
that they would perifh in the attempt. But not being
powerful enough to venture to attack their haughty
adverfaries, they removed to a greater diftance in order to try their ftrength, and improve their military

BOOK
XV.

kill, by making war againſt ſome leſs formidable nations. As ſoon as they had learnt to approach like foxes, to attack like lions, and to fly like birds, as they expreſs themſelves, they were no longer afraid to encounter the Algonquins; and, therefore, carried on a war againſt them with a degree of ferocioufneſs proportionable to their reſentment.

It was juſt at the time when theſe animoſities were kindled throughout Canada, that the French made their firſt appearance in that country. The Montagnez, who inhabited the lower parts of the river St. Lawrence; the Algonquins, who were ſettled upon its banks, from Quebec to Montreal; the Hurons, who were diſperſed about the lake that bears that name; and ſome leſs conſiderable nations, who wandered about in the intermediate ſpaces; were all inclined to favour the ſettlement of the ſtrangers: theſe ſeveral nations combined againſt the Iroquois, and, unable to withſtand them, imagined that they might find in their new gueſt an unexpected reſource, which would enſure them ſucceſs. From the opinion they entertained of the French, which ſeemed as if it were formed upon a thorough knowledge of their character, they flattered themſelves they might engage them in their quarrel, and were not diſappointed. Champlain, who ought to have availed himſelf of the ſuperior knowledge of the Europeans to effect a reconciliation between the Americans, did not even attempt it. He warmly eſpouſed the intereſts of his neighbours, and accompanied them in purſuit of their enemy.

The country of the Iroquois was near eighty leagues in length, and more than forty in breadth. It was bounded by the lake Erie, the lake Ontario, the river St. Lawrence, and the celebrated countries ſince known by the names of New York and Pennſylvania. The ſpace between theſe vaſt limits was watered by ſeveral fine rivers, and was inhabited by five nations, which could bring about twenty thouſand warriors into the field, though they are now reduced to leſs than fifteen hundred. They formed a kind of league or aſſociation, not unlike that of the Swifs or the Dutch. Their de- puties met once a-year, to hold their feaft of union, and to deliberate on the interefts of the common-wealth.

Though the Iroquois did not expect to be again attacked by enemies who had fo often been conquered, they were not unprepared. The engagement was begun with equal confidence on both fides ; one relying on their ufual fuperiority ; the other on the affiftance of their new ally, whofe fire-arms could not fail of enfuring the victory. And, indeed, no fooner had Champlain, and the two Frenchmen who attended him, fired a fhot, which killed two chiefs of the Iroquois, and mortally wounded a third, than the whole army fled in the utmoft amazement and confternation.

This alteration in the mode of attack induced them to think of changing their mode of defence. In the next campaign, they judged it neceffary to intrench themfelves, to elude the force of weapons they were unacquainted with. But their precaution was ineffectual. Notwithftanding an obftinate refiftance, their intrenchments were forced by the Indians, fupported by a brifker fire from a greater number of Frenchmen, than appeared in the firft expedition. The Iroquois were almoft all killed or taken. Thofe who had efcaped from the engagement were precipitated into a river, and drowned.

This nation would probably have been deftroyed, or compelled to live in peace, had not the Dutch, who in 1610 founded the colony of New Belgia in their neighbourhood, furnifhed them with arms and ammunition. Poffibly too they might fecretly foment their divifions, the furs taken from the enemy during the continuance of hoftilities being a greater object than thofe they could procure from their own chafe. However this may be, this connection reftored the balance between both parties. Various hoftilities and injuries were committed by each nation, which weakened the ftrength of both. This perpetual ebb and flow of fuccefs, which, in governments actuated by motives of intereft rather than of revenge, would infallibly have restored tranquillity, served but to increase animosities, and to exasperate a number of little clans, bent upon each other's destruction. The consequence was, that the weakest of these petty nations were soon destroyed, and the rest were gradually reduced to nothing.

The French settlement makes no progress. The cause of this.   These destructive events did not however contribute to advance the power of the French. In 1627, they had only three wretched settlements, surrounded with pales. The largest of these contained but fifty inhabitants, including men, women, and children. The climate had not proved destructive to the people sent there: though severe, it was wholesome, and the Europeans strengthened their constitutions without endangering their lives. The little progress they made was entirely owing to an exclusive Company, whose chief designs were not so much intended to create a national power in Canada, as to enrich themselves by the fur trade. This evil might have been immediately removed, by abolishing this monopoly, and allowing a free trade ; but it was not then time to adopt so simple a theory. The government, however, chose only to employ a more numerous association, composed of men of greater property and credit.

They gave them the disposal of the settlements that were or should be formed in Canada, together with a power of fortifying and governing them as they thought proper, and of making war or peace, as should best promote their interest. The whole trade by sea and land was allowed them for a term of fifteen years, except the cod and whale fisheries, which were left open to all. The beaver and all the fur trade was granted to the Company for ever.

To all these were added further encouragements. The king made a present of two large ships to the Company, which consisted of seven hundred proprietors. Twelve of the principal were raised to the rank of nobility. Gentlemen, and even the clergy, already too rich, were invited to share in this trade. The Company were allowed the liberty of sending and export-

ing all kinds of commodities and merchandife, free of BOOK
any duty whatfoever. A perfon who exercifed any XV.
trade in the colony for the fpace of fix years, was entitled to the freedom of the fame trade in France. The
laft favour granted them was the free entry of all goods
manufactured in thofe diftant regions. This fingular
privilege, the motives of which it is not eafy to difcover, gave the manufacturers of New France an infinite
advantage over thofe of the mother-country, who were
encumbered with a variety of duties, letters of mafter-
fhip, charges for ftamps, and with all the impediments
which ignorance and avarice had multiplied without
end.

In return for fo many marks of partiality, the Company, which had a capital of a hundred thoufand
crowns [12,500l.], engaged to bring into the colony,
in the year 1628, which was the firft year they enjoyed their charter, two or three hundred artificers of
fuch trades as were fitteft for their purpofe ; and fixteen thoufand men before the year 1643. They were
to provide them with lodging and board, to maintain
them for three years, and afterwards to give them as
much cleared land as would be neceffary for their fubfiftence, with a fufficient quantity of grain to fow it the
firft year.

Fortune did not fecond the endeavours of government in favour of the new Company. The firft fhips
they fitted out were taken by the Englifh, who were
lately at variance with France, on account of the fiege
of Rochelle. Richelieu and Buckingham, who were
enemies from jealoufy, from perfonal character, from
ftate intereft, and from every motive that can excite
an irreconcileable enmity between two ambitious minifters, took this opportunity to fpirit up the two kings
they governed, and the two nations they were endeavouring to opprefs. The Englifh, who fought for their
interefts, gained the advantage over the French ; and
the latter loft Canada in 1629. The council of Lewis
XIII. were fo little acquainted with the value of this
fettlement, that they were inclined not to demand the

B O K reſtitution of it; but the pride of the leading man,
XV.　who, being at the head of the Company, conſidered
the encroachments of the Engliſh as a perſonal inſult,
prevailed with them to alter their opinion. They met
with leſs difficulty than they expected; and Canada
was reſtored to the French, with peace, in 1631, by
the treaty of St. Germain en Laye.

The French were not taught by adverſity. The
ſame ignorance, the ſame negligence, prevailed after
the recovery of Canada as before. The monopolizing
Company fulfilled none of their engagements. This
breach of faith, far from being puniſhed, was in a manner rewarded by a prolongation of their charter. The
clamours of all Canada were diſregarded at ſuch a diſtance; and the deputies ſent to repreſent its wretched ſituation were denied acceſs to the throne, where
timid truth is never ſuffered to approach, but is awed
into ſilence by threats and puniſhments. This behaviour, equally repugnant to humanity, private intereſt,
and good policy, was attended with ſuch conſequences
as might naturally be expected from it.

The French had formed their ſettlement improperly. In order to have the appearance of reigning over
an immenſe track of country, and to draw nearer to
the furs, they had placed their habitations at ſuch a
diſtance from each other, that they had ſcarce any
communication, and were unable to afford each other
any aſſiſtance. The misfortunes which were the re-
ſult of this imprudence had not produced any alteration in their conduct. The intereſt of the moment
made them always forget the paſt, and prevented them
from foreſeeing the future. They were not properly
in a ſocial ſtate, ſince the magiſtrates could not ſuper-
intend their morals, nor government provide for the
ſafety of their perſons and property.

The audacious and ardent Iroquois ſoon perceived
the defect of this conſtitution, and purſued meaſures
to avail themſelves of it. The weak bands of ſavages
which had been ſheltered from their fury, deprived of
that ſupport which conſtituted their ſecurity, ſoon fled

before them. This firſt ſucceſs inſpired the Iroquois with the hopes of compelling their protectors to croſs the ſea again, and even of being able to deprive theſe foreigners of their children, that with them they might fill the place of thoſe warriors they had loſt in the preceding wars. To avoid theſe calamities and humiliations, the French were obliged to erect, in each of the diſtricts which they occupied, a kind of fort, where they took refuge, and where they ſheltered their proviſions and their cattle, at the approach of theſe irreconcileable foes. Theſe paliſadoes, commonly ſupported by ſome indifferent guns, were never forced, and perhaps even never blocked up; but whatever was found on the outſide of the intrenchments was either deſtroyed or carried off by theſe barbarians. Such was the miſery and deplorable ſtate of the colony, that it was reduced to ſubſiſt upon the charitable contributions which the miſſionaries received from Europe.

The French miniſtry, at length awakened from their lethargy by that general commotion which at that time agitated every nation, ſent a body of four hundred well-diſciplined troops to Canada in 1662. This corps was reinforced two years after. The French gradually recovered an abſolute ſuperiority over the Iroquois. Three of their nations, alarmed at their loſſes, made propoſals for an accommodation; and the other two were ſo much weakened, that they were induced to accede to it in 1668. At this time the colony firſt enjoyed a profound peace, which paved the way for its proſperity; and a freedom of trade contributed to ſecure it. The beaver trade alone continued to be monopolized.

This revolution in affairs excited induſtry. The former coloniſts, whoſe weakneſs had till then confined them within their ſettlements, now ventured to extend their plantations, and cultivated them with greater confidence and ſucceſs. All the ſoldiers who conſented to ſettle in the New World obtained their diſcharge, together with a grant of ſome property. The officers had lands given them in proportion to their

The French are rouſed from their inactivity. Means by which this change was effected.

rank. The former fettlements were improved; and new ones eftablifhed, wherever the intereft or fafety of the colony required it. This fpirit and activity occafioned an increafe of traffic with the Indians, and revived the intercoufe between both continents. This profperity feemed likely to receive additional advantages from the care taken by the fuperintendants of the colony, not only to preferve friendfhip with the neighbouring nations, but likewife to eftablifh peace and harmony among themfelves. Not a fingle act of hoftility was committed throughout an extent of four or five hundred leagues; a circumftance, perhaps, unheard of before in North America. It fhould feem that the French had kindled the war at their arrival, only to extinguifh it the more effectually.

But this concord could not continue among people who were always armed for the chafe, unlefs the power that had effected it fhould preferve it by the fuperiority of its forces. The Iroquois, finding this precaution was neglected, refumed that reftlefs difpofition arifing from their love of revenge and dominion. They were, however, careful to continue on good terms with all who were either allies or neighbours to the French. Notwithftanding this moderation, they were told that they muft immediately lay down their arms, and reftore all the prifoners they had taken, or expect to fee their country deftroyed, and their habitations burnt down. This haughty fummons incenfed their pride. They anfwered, that they fhould never fuffer the leaft incroachment on their independence; and that they fhould make the French fenfible, that they were friends not to be neglected, and enemies not to be defpifed. But, as they were ftaggered with the air of authority that had been affumed, they complied in part with the terms required of them; and the affair was thus compromifed.

But this kind of humiliation rather increafed the refentment of a people more accuftomed to commit than to fuffer injuries. The Englifh, who in 1664 had difpoffeffed the Dutch of New Belgia, and remained mafters of the territory they had acquired, which they had called New York, availed themfelves of the difpofitions of the Iroquois. They not only excited the fpirit of difcord, but added prefents to induce them to break with the French. The fame artifices were ufed to feduce the reft of their allies. Thofe who adhered to their allegiance were attacked. All were invited, and fome compelled to bring their beaver and other furs to New York, where they fold at a higher price than in the French colony.

Denonville, who had lately been fent to Canada to enforce obedience to the authority of the proudeft of monarchs, was impatient of all thefe infults. Though he was in a condition not only to defend his own frontiers, but even to encroach upon thofe of the Iroquois; yet, fenfible that this nation muft not be attacked without being deftroyed, it was agreed that the French fhould remain in a ftate of feeming inaction, till they had received from Europe the neceffary reinforcements for executing fo defperate a refolution. Thefe fuccours arrived in 1687; and the colony had then 11,249 perfons, of whom about one-third were able to bear arms.

Notwithftanding this fuperiority of forces, Denonville had recourfe to ftratagem, and difhonoured the French name among the favages by an infamous perfidy. Under pretence of terminating their differences by negotiation, he bafely abufed the confidence which the Iroquois repofed in the Jefuit Lamberville, to allure their chiefs to a conference. As foon as they arrived, they were put in irons, embarked at Quebec, and fent to the galleys.

On the firft report of this treachery, the old men fent for their miffionary, and addreffed him in the following manner: " We are authorifed by every motive " to treat you as an enemy, but we cannot refolve to " do it. Your heart has had no fhare in the infult " that has been put upon us; and it would be unjuft " to punifh you for a crime you deteft ftill more than " ourfelves. But you muft leave us. Our rafh young

" men might confider you in the light of a traitor,
" who has delivered up the chiefs of our nation to
" fhameful flavery." After this fpeech, thefe favages,
whom the Europeans have always called barbarians,
gave the miffionary fome guides, who conducted him
to a place of fafety; and then both parties took up
arms.

The French prefently fpread terror among the Iroquois bordering upon the great lakes; but Denonville
had neither the activity nor the expedition neceffary
to improve thefe firft fucceffes. While he was taken
up in deliberating, inftead of acting, the campaign was
clofed without the acquifition of any permanent advantage. This increafed the boldnefs of the Iroquois
who lived near the French fettlements, where they repeatedly committed the moft dreadful ravages. The
planters, finding their labours deftroyed by thefe depredations, which deprived them of the means of repairing the damages they had fuftained, ardently wifhed for peace. Denonville's temper coincided with their
wifhes; but it was no eafy matter to pacify an enemy
rendered implacable by ill ufage. Lamberville, who
ftill maintained his former afcendant over them, made
overtures of peace, which were liftened to.

While thefe negotiations were carrying on, a Ma-
chiavel, born in the forefts, known by the name of
Le Rat, the braveft, the moft refolute, the moft intelligent favage ever found in the wilds of North America, arrived at Fort Frontenac with a chofen band of
Hurons, fully determined upon exploits worthy of the
reputation he had acquired. He was told that a treaty
was actually on foot; that the deputies of the Iroquois
were upon the road to conclude it at Montreal; and
that it would be an infult upon the French governor,
if hoftilities fhould be carried on againft a nation with
which they were negotiating a peace.

Le Rat, piqued that the French fhould thus enter
into negotiations without confulting their allies, refolved to punifh them for their prefumption. He lay
in wait for the deputies, fome of whom were killed,

and the reft taken prifoners. When the latter told him the purport of their voyage, he feigned the great- er furprife, as Denonville, he faid, had fent him to inter- cept them. In order to carry on the deceit more fuc- cefsfully, he immediately releafed them all, except óne, whom he pretended to keep, to replace one of his Hu- rons who had been killed in the fray. He then haftened to Michillimakinac, where he prefented his prifoner to the French commandant, who, not knowing that De- nonville was treating with the Iroquois, caufed the un- happy favage to be put to death. Immediately after this, Le Rat fent for an old Iroquois, who had long been a prifoner among the Hurons, and gave him his liberty to go and acquaint his nation, that, while the French were amufing their enemies with negotiations, they continued to take prifoners and murder them. This artifice, worthy of the moft infamous European policy, fuceeded as the favage Le Rat defired. The war was renewed with greater fury than ever, and lafted the longer, as the Englifh, who about that period were engaged in a conteft with France, on account of the depofition of James II. thought it their intereft to make an alliance with the Iroquois.

An Englifh fleet, which failed from Europe in 1690, appeared before Quebec in October, to lay fiege to the place. They had reafon to expect but a faint refift- ance, as the favages were to make a powerful diver- fion, to draw off the principal land-forces of the co- lony. But they were compelled fhamefully to relin- quifh the enterprife, after having fuftained great loffes. The caufes of this difappointment merit fome difcuffion.

When the Britifh miniftry projected the reduction of Canada, they determined that the land and fea forces fhould arrive there at the fame time. This wife plan was executed with the utmoft exactnefs. As the fhips were failing up the river St. Lawrence, the troops marched by land, in order to reach the fcene of ac- tion at the fame inftant as the fleet. They were near- ly arrived, when the Iroquois, who conducted and fup- ported them, recollected the hazard they ran in lead-

B O O K ing their allies to the conqueſt of Quebec. Situated
   XV as we are between two European nations, ſaid they in
a council which they held, each powerful enough to
deſtroy us, both intereſted in our deſtruction, when
they no longer ſtand in need of our aſſiſtance; what
better meaſure can we take, than to prevent the one
from being victorious over the other? Then will each
of them be compelled to court our alliance, or to bribe
us to a neutrality. This ſyſtem, which ſeemed to be
dictated by the ſame kind of deep policy as that which
directs the balance of Europe, determined the Iroquois
to return to their reſpective homes under various pre-
tences. Their defection obliged the Engliſh to retreat;
and the French, now in ſecurity on their lands, united
all their forces with as much unanimity as ſucceſs for
the defence of their capital.

The Iroquois, from motives of policy, ſtifled their
reſentment againſt the French, and were attached rather to the name than to the intereſts of England.
Theſe two European powers, therefore, irreconcileable
rivals to each other, but ſeparated by the territory
of a ſavage nation, equally apprehenſive of the ſuperiority of either, were prevented from doing each other
ſo much injury as they could have wiſhed. The war
was carried on merely by a few depredations, fatal to
the coloniſts, but of little conſequence to the ſeveral
nations concerned in them. During the ſcene of
cruelties exerciſed by the ſeveral parties of Engliſh
and Iroquois, French and Hurons, whoſe ravages extended one hundred leagues from home, ſome actions
were performed, which ſeemed to render human nature ſuperior to ſuch enormities.

Some French and Indians having joined in an expedition that required a long march, their proviſions
began to fail. The Hurons caught plenty of game,
and always offered ſome to the French, who were not
ſuch ſkilful huntſmen. The latter would have declined accepting this generous offer; *You ſhare with
us the fatigues of war*, ſaid the ſavages; *it is but reaſon-
able that we ſhould ſhare with you the neceſſaries of life;*

we should not be men if we acted otherwise with men. If
similar instances of magnanimity may have sometimes
occurred among Europeans, the following is peculiar
to savages.

A party of Iroquois being informed that a party of
the French and their allies were advancing with superior forces, they fled with precipitation. They were
headed by Onontague, who was a hundred years old.
He scorned to fly with the rest, and chose rather to
fall into the hands of the enemy; though he had nothing to expect but exquisite torments. What a spec-
tacle to see four hundred barbarians eager in torment-
ing an old man; who far from complaining, treated
the French with the utmost contempt, and upbraided
the Hurons with having stooped to be the slaves of
those vile Europeans! One of his tormentors, provoked at his invectives, stabbed him in three places to
put an end to his repeated insults. *Thou dost wrong,*
said Onontague calmly to him, *to shorten my life; thou
wouldst have had more time to learn to die like a man.*
And are these the men whom the French and English
have been conspiring to extirpate for a century past?
But, perhaps, they would be ashamed to live among
such models of heroism and magnanimity.

The peace of Ryswick put a sudden end to the calamities of Europe and the hostilities in America. The
Hurons and the Iroquois, as well as the French and
English, were sensible that they required a long continuance of peace, to repair the losses they had sus-
tained in war. The Indians began to recover themselves; the Europeans resumed their labours; and the
fur trade, the first that could be entered into with a
nation of huntsmen, was more firmly established.

Before the discovery of Canada, the forests with which
it was over-run were little more than the extensive haunt
of wild beasts, which had multiplied prodigiously; because the few men who lived in those deserts having no
flocks or tame animals, left more room and more food
for such as were wandering and free like themselves. If
the nature of the climate did not afford an infinite vari-

The furs are
the founda-
tion of the
connections
between
the French
and the In-
dians.

B O O K ety, each species produced, at least, a multitude of indi-
    XV.   viduals.   But they at last paid tribute to the sovereign-
ty of man, that cruel power which hath always been
exercised in a manner so fatal to every living creature.
Having neither arts nor husbandry to employ them,
the savages fed and clothed themselves entirely with
the wild beasts they destroyed.   As soon as luxury
had led us to make use of their skins, the natives
waged a perpetual war against them ; which was the
more active, as it procured them plenty, and a variety of gratifications which they were unaccustomed
to ; and the more destructive, as they had adopted the
use of our fire arms.   This fatal industry exercised in
the woods of Canada, occasioned a great quantity and
prodigious variety of furs to be brought into the ports
of France ; some of which were consumed in the
kingdom, and the rest disposed of in the neighbouring countries.   Most of these furs were already known
in Europe ; they came from the northern parts of our
hemisphere, but in too small quantities to supply a
general demand.   Caprice and novelty have made
them more or less in fashion, since it has been found
to be for the interest of the American colonies that
they should be valued in the mother countries.   It
may not be improper to give some account of those
that are still in request.

   The otter is a voracious animal, which runs or swims
along the banks of the lakes or rivers, commonly lives
upon fish, and, when that fails, will feed upon grass, or
the rind of aquatic plants.   From his manner and place
of living he has been ranked amongst amphibious animals, who can equally live in the air and under water ;
but improperly, since the otter, like all other land animals, cannot live without respiration.   He is found in
all those countries which abound in water, and are
temperate, but is more common and much larger in
the northern parts of America.   His hair is nowhere
so black or so fine ; a circumstance the more fatal to
him, as it exposes him more to the pursuits of man.

   The pole-cat is in equal estimation among the Ca-

nadian huntfmen. There are three fpecies of this ani- B O O K
mal : the firft is the common pole-cat; the fecond is XV.
called the mink ; and the third, the ftinking pole-cat,
becaufe his urine, which he voids in his fright when
he is purfued, is fo offenfive, that it infects the air at a
great diftance. Their hair is darker, more gloffy, and
more filky than in Europe.

Even the rat in North America is valuable for his
fkin. There are two forts efpecially whofe fkin is an
article of trade. The one, which is called the Opof-
fum, is twice as large as an European rat. His hair is
commonly of a filver grey, fometimes of a clear white.
The female has a bag under her belly, which fhe can
open and fhut at pleafure. When fhe is purfued, fhe
puts her young ones into this bag, and runs away with
them. The other, which is called the Mufk-rat, becaufe his tefticles contain mufk, has all the characteriftic qualities of the beaver, of which he feems to be
a diminutive ; and his fkin is employed for the fame
purpofes.

The ermine, which is about the fize of a fquirrel,
but not quite fo long, has the fame lively eyes, keen
look, and his motions are fo quick that the eye cannot
follow them. The tip of his long and bufhy tail is as
black as jet. His hair, which is yellow as gold in fummer, turns as white as fnow in winter. This lively
and light animal is one of the beauties of Canada ;
bùt, though fmaller than the fable, is not fo common.

The martin is only to be met with in cold countries, in the centre of the forefts, far from all habitations, is a beaft of prey, and lives upon birds. Though
it is but a foot and a half long, it leaves prints on the
fnow that appear to be the footfteps of a very large
animal ; becaufe it always jumps along, and leaves the
marks of both feet together, Its fur is much efteemed, though far inferior to that fpecies which is diftinguifhed by the name of the Sable. This is of a fhining black. The fineft among them are thofe whofe
fkin is the moft brown, and reaches along the back
quite to the tip of the tail. The martins feldom quit

the inmoft receffes of their impenetrable woods more than once in two or three years. The natives think it portends a good winter ; that is, a great quantity of fnow, and confequently good fport.

The animal which the ancients called Lynx, known in Siberia by the name of the Ounce, is only called the Wild-cat in Canada, where it is fmaller than in our hemifphere. This animal, to whom vulgar error would not have attributed very piercing eyes, if he were not endowed with the faculty of feeing, hearing, and fmelling at a diftance, lives upon what game he can catch, which he purfues to the very tops of the talleft trees. His flefh is known to be very white and well flavoured ; but he is hunted chiefly for the fake of his fkin ; the hair of which is very long, and of a fine light grey, but lefs efteemed than that of the fox.

This carnivorous and mifchievous animal is a native of the frozen climates, where nature, affording few ve- getables, feems to compel all animals to eat one ano- ther. In warmer climates he has loft much of his ori- ginal beauty, and his fur is not fo fine. In the north, it has remained long, foft, and full, fometimes white, fometimes brown, and often red or fandy. The fineft of any is that which is black ; but this is more fcarce in Canada than in Mufcovy, which lies further north, and is not fo damp.

Befide thefe fmaller furs, North America fupplies us with fkins of the ftag, the deer, and the roe-buck ; of the mooze-deer, called there Caribou ; and of the elk, which is called Orignal. Thefe two laft kinds, which in our hemifphere are only found towards the polar circle, the elk on this fide, and the mooze-deer beyond, are to be met with in America in more fouth- ern latitudes. This may be owing to the cold being more intenfe in America, from fingular caufes, which make an exception to the general law of nature ; or it may poffibly arife from thefe frefh lands being lefs frequented by deftructive man. Their ftrong, foft, and warm fkins, make excellent garments, which are very light. All thefe animals are hunted by the Europeans; but the favages have referved the chafe of the bear to themfelves, it being their favourite fport, and beft adapted to their warlike manners, their ftrength, and their bravery, and efpecially to their wants.

In a cold and fevere climate, the bear is moft commonly black. As he is rather fhy than fierce, inftead of a cavern, he choofes for his lurking-place the hollow rotten trunk of an old tree. There he fixes himfelf in winter, as high as he can climb. As he is very fat at the end of autumn, very much covered with hair, takes no exercife, and is almoft always afleep, he muft lofe but little by perfpiration, and confequently muft feldom want to go abroad in queft of food. But he is forced out of his retreat by its being fet fire to; and as foon as he attempts to come down, he falls under a fhower of arrows before he can reach the ground. The Indians feed upon his flefh, rub themfelves with his greafe, and clothe themfelves with his fkin. Such was the defign of their purfuit after the bear, when a new intereft directed them towards the beaver.

This animal poffeffes all the friendly difpofitions fit for fociety, without being fubject, as we are, to the vices or misfortunes attendant upon it. Formed by nature for focial life, he is endowed with an inftinct adapted to the prefervation and propagation of his fpecies. This animal, whofe tender plaintive accents, and whofe ftriking example, draw tears of admiration and pity from the humane philofopher, who contemplates his life and manners; this harmlefs animal, who never hurts any living creature, neither carnivorous nor fanguinary, is become the object of man's moft earneft purfuit, and the one which the favages hunt after with the greateft eagernefs and cruelty: a circumftance owing to the unmerciful rapacioufnefs of the moft polifhed nations of Europe.

The beaver is about three or four feet long, but his weight amounts to forty or fixty pounds, which is the confequence of the largenefs of his mufcles. His head, which he carries downwards, is like that of a

BOOK XV.

Figure of the beavers. Their difpofition, and form of government.

rat, and his back raifed in an arch above it like that of a moufe. Lucretius has obferved, not that man has hands given him to make ufe of them, but that he had hands given him, and has made ufe of them. Thus the beaver has webs at his hinder feet, and he fwims with them. The toes of his fore-feet are feparate, and anfwer the purpofe of hands; the tail, which is flat, oval, and covered with fcales, he ufes to carry loads and to work with; he has four fharp incifors or cutting teeth, which ferve him inftead of carpenter's tools. All thefe inftruments, which are in a manner ufelefs while he lives alone, and do not then diftinguifh him from other animals, are of infinite fervice when he lives in fociety, and enable him to difplay a degree of ingenuity fuperior to all inftinct.

Without paffions, without a defire of doing injury to any, and without craft, when he does not live in fociety, he fcarcely ventures to defend himfelf. He never bites unlefs he be caught. But in the focial ftate, in lieu of weapons, he has a variety of contrivances to fecure himfelf without fighting, and to live without committing or fuffering any injury. This peaceable and even tame animal is neverthelefs independent: he is a flave to none, becaufe all his wants are fupplied by himfelf: he enters into fociety, but will not ferve, nor does he pretend to command: and all his labours are directed by a filent inftinct.

It is the common want of fubfiftence and propagation that calls the beavers home, and collects them together in fummer to build their towns againft winter. As early as June or July, they come in from all quarters, and affemble, to the number of two or three hundred; but always by the water fide, becaufe thefe republicans are to live on the water, to fecure themfelves from invafion. Sometimes they give the preference to ftill lakes in unfrequented diftricts, becaufe there the waters are always at an equal height. When they find no pools of ftanding water, they make one in the midft of rivers or ftreams, by means of a caufeway or dam. The very plan of this contrivance im-

plies such a complication of ideas, as our short-sighted B O O K
reason would be apt to think above any capacity but XV.
that of an intelligent being. The first thing to be
erected is a pile a hundred feet long, and twelve feet
thick at the basis, which shelves away to two or three
feet in a slope answerable to the depth of the waters.
To save work, or to facilitate their labour, they choose
the shallowest part of the river. If they find a large
tree by the water-side, they fell it, so that it falls across
the stream. If it should be larger in circumference
than a man's body, they saw it through, or rather
gnaw the foot with their four sharp teeth. The
branches are soon lopped off by these industrious
workmen, who want to fashion it into a beam. A
number of smaller trees are felled and prepared for
the intended pile. Some drag these trees to the river-
side, others swim over with them to the place where
the causeway is to be raised. But the question is, how
these animals are to sink them in the water with the
assistance only of their teeth, tail, and feet : their contrivance is this. With their nails they dig a hole in
the ground, or at the bottom of the water. With
their teeth they rest the large end of the stake against
the bank of the river, or against the great beam that
lies across. With their feet they raise the stake, and
sink it with the sharp end downwards into the hole,
where it stands upright. With their tails they make
mortar, with which they fill up all the vacancies between the stakes, which are bound together with twist-
ed boughs ; and thus the pile is constructed. The
slope of the dam is opposite to the current, to break
more effectually the force of the water by a gradual
resistance, and the stakes are driven in obliquely, in
proportion to the inclination of the plane. The stakes
are planted perpendicularly on the side where the water is to fall ; and, in order to open a drain which may
lessen the effect of the slope and weight of the causeway, they make two or three openings at the top of
it, by which part of the waters of the river may run
off.

B O O K   When this work is finifhed by the whole body of
   XV.   the republic, every member confiders of a lodging for
himfelf. Each company builds a hut in the water upon the pile. Thefe huts are from four to ten feet in
diameter, upon an oval or round fpot. Some are two
or three ftories high, according to the number of families or houfeholds. Each hut contains at leaft two
or three, and fome ten or fifteen. The walls, whether
high or low, are about two feet thick, and are all arch-
ed at the top, and perfectly neat and folid both within
and without. They are varnifhed with a kind of ftuc-
co, impenetrable by the water and by the external air.
Every apartment has two openings ; one on the land
fide, to enable the beavers to go out and fetch provifions ; the other on the fide next the ftream, to facilitate their efcape at the approach of the enemy, that
is, of man, the deftroyer of cities and commonwealths.
The window of the houfe opens to the water. There
they take the frefh air in the day-time, plunged into
the river up to their middle. In winter it ferves to
fence them againft the ice, which collects to the thicknefs of two or three feet. The fhelf, intended to prevent the ice from ftopping up this window, refts upon
two ftakes that flope fo as to carry off the water from
the houfe, and leave an outlet to efcape, or to go and
fwim under the ice. The infide of the houfe has no
other furniture than a flooring of grafs, covered with
the boughs of the fir-tree. No filth of any kind is
ever feen in thefe apartments.

The materials for thefe buildings are always to be
found in their neighbourhood. Thefe are alders, pop-
lars, and other trees, delighting in watery places, as
thefe republicans do who build their aparments of
them. Thefe citizens have the fatisfaction, at the
fame time that they fafhion the wood, to nourifh
themfelves with it. Like certain favages of the frozen
ocean, they eat the bark. The favages, indeed, do
not like it till it is dried, pounded, and properly dreffed ; whereas the beavers chew it, and fuck it when
it is quite green.

Provisions of bark and tender twigs are laid up in
separate storehouses, for every hut, proportionable to the number of its inhabitants. Every beaver knows his own storehouse, and not one of them steals from that of his neighbour. Each party live in their own habitation, and are contented with it, though jealous of the property they have acquired in it by their labour. The provisions of the community are collected and expended without any contest. They are satisfied with that simple food which their labour prepares for them. The only passion they have, is that of conjugal affection, the basis and end of which is the increase of their species.

Two of these animals, matched together and united by inclination and reciprocal choice, after being acquainted with each other by being mutually employed in the public labours during the summer-months, agree to pass the winter together. They prepare for this by the stock of provisions they lay up in September. The happy couple retire into their hut in the autumnal season, which is not less favourable to love than the spring. If the season of flowers invite the birds of the sky to propagate in the woods, the season of fruits, perhaps, excites the inhabitants of the earth as powerfully to the reproduction of their species. The winter at least gives leisure for amorous pursuits, and in this circumstance compensates the advantages of other seasons. The couple then never quit each other. Their whole time is consecrated to love; from which neither labour nor any other object can divert them. The females conceive, and bear the endearing pledges of this universal passion of nature. If some sunshiny day should chance to enliven this melancholy season, the happy couple go out of their hut, to walk on the borders of the lake or the river, there to eat some fresh bark, and to breathe the salutary exhalations of the earth. Towards the end of winter, however, the mothers bring forth their young ones, which have been conceived in autumn; and while the father ranges all the woods, allured by the fweets of the fpring, leaving to his little family the room he took up in his narrow cell, the mother fuckles and nurfes them, to the number of two or three; then fhe takes them out along with her in her excurfions, in fearch of cray and other fifh, and green bark, to recruit her own ftrength, and to feed them, till the feafon of labour returns.

Thus doth this republic live in focieties, which might diftantly be compared to a large Carthufian convent. But they have only the appearance of it; and if happinefs may be faid to dwell in thefe two forts of communities, it muft be acknowledged that it is by very oppofite means; fince, in the former, happinefs confifts in following nature; while in the latter, it confifts in thwarting and deftroying her. But man, in his folly, thinks he has found out the path of wifdom. A number of perfons live together in a kind of fociety, which precludes for ever all intercourfe between the two fexes. The men and the women are placed in diftinct cells, where, to make them happy, nothing more would be required than that they fhould live together. There they confume their beft days, in ftifling, or in execrating the propenfity that attracts them to each other, even through the prifons and grates of iron, which have been raifed to prevent them from indulging every tender and innocent emotion of the heart. Can any thing be more injurious, as well as inhuman, than thefe gloomy and ferocious inftitutions, which deprive man of his nature, and render him ftupid and filly, under pretence of making him fimilar to angels? God of Nature! It is at thy tribunal that we muft appeal againft all thofe laws which injure the moft beautiful among thy works, by condemning them to a ftate of fterility, contrary to thine own inftitutions! For art thou not a truly plaftic and fruitful Being; thou who hath created man from nothing, and taken him out of chaos; thou, who doth continually caufe life to be renewed even from death itfelf? Who is it that beft fings forth thy praifes, the folitary being who difturbs the filence of the night to cele-

brate thee among the tombs, or the happy people who
glorify thee, in perpetuating the wonders of thy works?

Such is the fyftem of the republican, induftrious,
intelligent beaver, fkilled in architecture, provident
and fyftematical in its plans of police and fociety,
whofe gentle and inftructive manners we have been
defcribing. Happy, if his coat did not tempt mercilefs and favage man to deftroy his buildings and his
race. It has frequently happened, when the Americans have demolifhed the fettlements of the beavers,
that thofe indefatigable animals have had the refolution to rebuild them in the very fame fituation for feveral fummers fucceffively. The winter is the time
for attacking them. Experience then warns them of
their danger. At the approach of the huntfmen, one
of them ftrikes a hard ftroke with his tail upon the
water: this fignal fpreads a general alarm throughout
all the huts of the commonwealth, and every one tries
to fave himfelf under the ice. But it is very difficult
to efcape all the fnares that are laid for this harmlefs
tribe.

Sometimes the huntfmen lie in wait for them: but
as thefe animals fee and hear at a great diftance, it feldom happens that they are fhot by the water-fide; and
they never venture fo far upon land as to be caught
by furprife. If the beaver be wounded before he takes
to the water, he has always time enough to plunge in;
and, if he dies afterwards, he is loft, becaufe he finks,
and never rifes again.

A more certain way of catching beavers is, by laying traps in the woods, where they eat the tender bark
of young trees. Thefe traps are baited with frefh flips
of wood; and as foon as the beavers touch them, a
great weight falls, and crufhes their loins. The man,
who is concealed near the place, haftens to it, feizes
the animal, and having killed it, carries it off.

There are other methods more commonly and fuccefsfully practifed. The huts are fometimes attacked,
in order to drive out the inhabitants, who are watched
at the edges of the holes that have been bored in the

ice, where they cannot avoid coming to take in freſh air. The inſtant they appear, they are killed. At other times, the animal, driven out of his retreat, is entangled in the nets, ſpread for ſome toiſes round his hut, the ice being broken for that purpoſe. If the whole colony is to be taken at once, inſtead of breaking down the ſluices to drown the inhabitants, a ſcheme that might, perhaps, be tried with effect in Holland, the cauſeway is opened, in order to drain off the water from the pool where the beavers live. When they are thus left dry, defenceleſs, and unable to eſcape, they may be caught at pleaſure, and deſtroyed at any time; but care is always taken to leave a ſufficient number of males and females to preſerve the breed; an act of generoſity which in reality proceeds only from avarice. The cruel foreſight of man only ſpares a few, in order to have the more to deſtroy. The beaver, whoſe plaintive cry ſeems to implore his clemency and pity, finds in the ſavage, rendered cruel by the Europeans, only an implacable enemy, whoſe enterpriſes are undertaken, not ſo much to ſupply his own wants, as to furniſh ſuperfluities to another world.

If we compare the manners, the police, and the induſtry of the beavers, with the wandering life of the ſavages of Canada, we ſhall be inclined to admit, making allowance for the ſuperiority of man's faculties above thoſe of animals, that the beaver was much further advanced in the arts of ſocial life than his purſuer, when the Europeans firſt brought their talents and improvements to North America.

The beaver, an older inhabitant of that world than man, and the quiet poſſeſſor of regions ſo well adapted to his ſpecies, had employed that tranquillity he had enjoyed for many ages, in the improvement of his faculties. In our hemiſphere, man has ſeized upon the moſt wholeſome and fertile regions, and has driven out or ſubdued all other animals. If the bee and the ant have preſerved their laws and government from the jealous and deſtructive dominion of tyrant man, it has been owing to the ſmallneſs of their ſize. It is thus

we fee fome republics in Europe, without fplendour or
ftrength, maintain themfelves by their very weaknefs,
in the midft of vaft monarchies, which muft fooner or
later fwallow them up. But the focial quadrupeds,
banifhed into uninhabited climates, unfit for their increafe, have been unconnected in all places, incapable
of uniting into a community, or of improving their natural fagacity; while man, who has reduced them to
that precarious ftate, exults in their degradation, and
fets a high value on that fuperior nature, and thofe ra-
tional powers, which conftitute a perpetual diftinction
between his fpecies and all others.

Brutes, we are told, bring nothing to perfection:
their operations, therefore, can only be mechanical,
and do not imply any principle fimilar to that which
actuates man. Without examining in what perfection
confifts; whether the moft civilized being be in reality the moft perfect; whether he does not lofe in the
property of his perfon what he acquires in the property of things; or, whether what is added to his enjoyments is not fo much fubtracted from his duration: it
muft be acknowledged, that the beaver, which in Europe is a wandering, folitary, timorous, and ftupid animal, was in Canada acquainted with civil and domeftic
government, knew how to diftinguifh the proper feafons for labour and reft, was acquainted with fome
rules of architecture, and with the curious and learned
art of conftructing dikes; yet he had attained to this
degree of improvement with feeble and imperfect tools.
He can hardly fee the work he performs with his tail.
His teeth, which anfwer the purpofes of a variety of
tools, are circular, and confined by the lips. Man, on
the contrary, with hands fit for every purpofe, hath
in this fingle organ of the touch all the combined
powers of ftrength and dexterity. Is it not to this advantage of organization, that he owes the fuperiority
of his fpecies above all others? It is not becaufe his
eyes are turned toward heaven, as thofe of all birds
are, that he is the lord of the creation; it is becaufe
he is provided with hands, capable of every exertion,

B O O K and of adapting themfelves to every fpecies of indu-
   XV.   ftry; hands, ever ready to ftrike terror into his enemies, to defend or to affift him. His hand is his fceptre,
that arm which he lifts up to heaven, to find out, as it
were, his origin; he, at the fame time, marks his dominion with it over the earth, by deftroying and ravaging the face of the globe. The fureft fign of the
population of mankind is the depopulation of other
fpecies. That of the beavers gradually decreafes and
difappears in Canada, fince the Europeans have been
in queft of their fkins.

Their fkins vary with the climate, both in colour
and quality. In the fame diftrict, however, where the
colonies of civilized beavers are found, there are fome
that are wild and folitary. Thefe animals, who are
faid to be expelled the fociety for their ill behaviour,
live in a fubterraneous retreat, and have neither lodging nor ftorehoufe. They are called earth beavers.
Their coat is dirty, and the hair on their backs is worn
off by rubbing againft the cave which they dig for
their habitation. The hole they make, and which
commonly opens into fome pond or ditch full of water, fometimes extends above a hundred feet in length,
and rifes gradually in a flope, to facilitate their efcape
from inundations when the waters fwell. Some of
thefe beavers are fo wild as to difclaim all communication with their natural element, and live entirely on
land. In this they refemble our otters in Europe.
Thefe wild beavers have not fuch fleek hair as thofe
that live in focieties; their furs are anfwerable to their
manners.

Beavers are found in America from the thirtieth to
the fixtieth degree of north latitude. There are but
few towards the fouth; but they increafe in number,
and grow darker, as we advance towards the north.
In the country of the Illinois, they are yellow and
ftraw-coloured; higher up in the country, they are of
a light chefnut; to the north of Canada, of a dark
chefnut; and fome are found that are quite black,
and thefe are reckoned the fineft. Yet, in this cli-

mate, the coldeſt that is inhabited by this ſpecies, ſome
among the black tribes are quite white; others white,
ſpeckled with grey, and ſometimes with ſandy ſpots
on the rump; ſo much does nature delight in ſhowing
the gradations of warmth and cold, and their various
influences, not only on the figure, but on the very covering of animals. The value that is ſet upon them
depends upon the colour of their ſkins. Some of them
are ſo little in eſteem, that it is not thought worth
while to kill them; but theſe are not commonly
found.

In what
places, and
in what
manner, the
fur trade
was carried
on.

The fur trade was the firſt which the Europeans
carried on in Canada. It was begun by the French
colony at Tadouſac, a port ſituated thirty leagues below Quebec. About the year 1640, the town of Les
Trois Rivieres, at the diſtance of twenty-five leagues
above the capital, became a ſecond mart. In proceſs
of time, all the fur trade centered in Montreal. The
ſkins were brought thither on canoes made of the bark
of trees in the month of June. The number of Indians
who reſorted to that place increaſed, as the fame of
the French ſpread further. The account of the reception they had met with, the ſight of the things
they had received in exchange for their goods, all
contributed to increaſe this traffic. Whenever they
returned with a freſh ſupply of furs, they always
brought a new nation along with them. Thus a kind
of fair was opened, to which the ſeveral tribes of that
vaſt continent reſorted.

The Engliſh grew jealous of this branch of wealth;
and the colony they had founded at New York ſoon
found means to divert the ſtream of this great circulation. As ſoon as they had ſecured a ſubſiſtence, by
beſtowing their firſt attention upon agriculture, they
began to think of the fur trade, which was at firſt confined to the country of the Iroquois. The five nations
of that name would not ſuffer their lands to be tra-
verſed, in order to give an opportunity of treating with
other ſavage nations, who were at conſtant enmity with
them; nor would they allow thoſe nations to come up-

B O O K on their territories,.to fhare in competition with them
　XV.　 the profits of the trade they had opened with the Europeans.　But time having extinguifhed, or rather fuf-
pended, the national hoftilities between the Indians,
the Englifh fpread themfelves over the country, and
the favages flocked to them from all quarters.　This
nation had infinite advantages to give them the preference to their rivals the French.　Their voyages were
carried on with greater facility, and confequently they
could afford to underfell them.　They were the only
manufacturers of the coarfe cloths that were moft fuitable to the favages.　The beaver trade was free among
them; whereas, among the French, it was, and ever
has been, fubject to the tyranny of monopoly.　It was
by this freedom, and thefe privileges, that they engroffed moft of the trade that rendered Montreal fo
famous.

At this time the French in Canada indulged them-
feves more freely in a cuftom, which at firft had been
confined within narrow bounds.　Their inclination for
frequenting the woods, which was that of the firft colonifts, had been wifely reftrained within the limits of
the territory belonging to the colony.　Permiffion was,
however, granted every year to twenty-five perfons to
go beyond thefe limits, in order to trade with the Indians.　The fuperiority which New York was acquiring, was the caufe of increafing the number of thefe
permiffions.　They were a kind of patents, which the
patentees might make ufe of either in perfon or by
proxy, and continued a year or more.　The produce
of the fale of thefe patents was affigned, by the governor of the colony, to the officers, or their widows
and children, to hofpitals and miffionaries, to fuch as
had diftinguifhed themfelves by fome great action, or
fome ufeful undertaking; and fometimes even to the
creatures of the governor, who fold the patents himfelf.　The money he did not give away, or did not
choofe to keep, was put into the public coffers; but
he was not accountable to any one for the management of it.

This cuftom was attended with fatal confequences. B O O K Many of thefe traders fettled among the Indians, to XV. defraud their partners, whofe goods they had difpofed of. A greater number fettled among the Englifh, where the profits were greater. The immenfe lakes, frequently agitated with violent ftorms; the cafcades, which render navigation fo dangerous up the broadeft rivers in the whole world ; the weight of the canoes, the provifions, and the bales of goods, which they were forced to carry upon their fhoulders at the *carrying places*, where the rapidity or fhallownefs of the water obliged them to quit the rivers, and purfue their journey by land, proved the deftruction of feveral perfons. Some perifhed in the fnow and on the ice, by hunger, or by the fword of the enemy. Thofe who returned to the colony with a profit of fix or feven hundred per cent. were not always on that account more ufeful members, as they gave themfelves up to the greateft exceffes, and by their example produced in others a diflike to attention and induftry. Their fortunes were diffipated as fuddenly as they were amaffed, like thofe moving mountains which a whirlwind raifes and deftroys at once, on the fandy plains of Africa. Moft of thefe travelling traders, exhaufted with the exceffive fatigues which their avarice prompted them to undergo, and the licentioufnefs of a wandering and diffolute life, dragged on a premature old age in indigence and infamy. The government took cognizance of thefe irregularities, and changed the manner of carrying on the fur trade.

The French had for a long time been inceffantly employed in erecting a number of forts, which were thought neceffary for the prefervation and aggrandizement of their fettlements in North America. Thofe built on the weft and fouth of the river St. Lawrence were large and ftrong, and were intended to reftrain the ambition of the Englifh. Thofe which were conftructed on the feveral lakes in the moft important pofitions, formed a chain which extended northward to the diftance of a thoufand leagues from Quebec ; but

they were only miferable pallifades, intended to keep
the Indians in awe, to fecure their alliance, and the
produce of their chafe. There was a garrifon in each,
more or lefs numerous, according to the importance of
the poft, and of the enemies who threatened it. It was
thought proper to intruft the commandant of each of
thefe forts with the exclufive right of buying and felling in the whole diftrict under his dominion. This privilege was purchafed; but as it was always advantageous, and fometimes was the means of acquiring a confiderable fortune, it was only granted to officers that
were moft in favour. If any of thefe had not a ftock
fufficient for the undertaking, he could eafily prevail
with fome monied men to join with him. It was pretended that this fyftem, far from being detrimental to
the fervice, was a means of promoting it, as it obliged
the military men to keep up more conftant connections with the natives, to watch their motions, and to
neglect nothing that could fecure their friendfhip. It
was not forefeen, or at leaft pretended not to be fo by
any, that fuch an arrangement muft neceffarily prevail
over every principle, except that of intereft, and would
be a fource of perpetual oppreffion.

This tyranny, which foon became univerfal, was feverely felt at Frontenac, at Niagara, and at Toronto.
The farmers of thofe three forts, making an ill ufe of
their exclufive privilege, fet fo low a value upon the
merchandife that was brought them, and rated their
own fo high, that, by degrees, the Indians, inftead of
ftopping there, reforted in great numbers to Choua-
guen, on the lake Ontario, where the Englifh traded
with them upon more advantageous terms. The
French court, alarmed at the account of thefe new
connections, found means to weaken them, by taking
the trade of thefe three pofts into their own hands, and
treating the Indians ftill better than they were treated
by their rivals the Englifh.

In confequence of this ftep, the refufe of all thofe
furs that were not faleable became the fole property
of the king; and all the fkins of thofe beafts that were

killed in summer and autumn were readily given him ; B O O K XV. in a word, all the moſt ordinary furs, the thinneſt, and moſt eaſily ſpoiled, were reſerved for the king. All theſe damaged furs, bought without examination, were carelefsly depoſited in warehouſes, and eaten up by the moths. At the proper ſeaſon for ſending them to Quebec, they were put into boats, and left to the diſcretion of ſoldiers, paſſengers, and watermen, who, having had no concern in thoſe commodities, did not take the leaſt care to keep them dry. When they came into the hands of the managers of the colony, they were ſold for one half of the ſmall value they had. Thus the returns were rather leſs than the ſums advanced by the government in ſupport of this loſing trade.

But though this trade was of no conſequence to the king, it is ſtill a matter of doubt, if it were advantageous to the Indians, though gold and ſilver were not the dangerous medium of their traffic. They received, indeed, in exchange for their furs, ſaws, knives, hatchets, kettles, fiſh-hooks, needles, thread, ordinary linen, and coarſe woollen ſtuffs; all which may be conſidered as the means or pledges of intercourſe with them. But articles were likewiſe ſold them that would have proved prejudicial to them, even as a gift or a preſent; ſuch as guns, powder and ſhot, tobacco, and eſpecially brandy.

This liquor, the moſt fatal preſent the Old World ever made to the New, was no ſooner known to the ſavages, than they grew paſſionately fond of it. It was equally impoſſible for them to abſtain from it, or to uſe it with moderation. It was ſoon obſerved that it diſturbed their domeſtic peace, deprived them of their judgment, and made them furious; and that it occaſioned huſbands, wives, children, brothers, and ſiſters, to abuſe and quarrel with one another. In vain did ſome worthy Frenchmen expoſtulate with them, and endeavour to make them aſhamed of theſe exceſſes. It is you, anſwered they, who have taught us to drink this liquor; and now we cannot do without it. If you refuſe to give it us, we will apply to the En-

BOOK glifh. You have done the mifchief, and it admits not
XV. of a remedy.

The court of France, upon receiving contradictory information with refpect to the diforders occafioned by this pernicious trade, hath alternately prohibited, tolerated, and authorifed it, according to the light in which it was reprefented to the miniftry. Notwithftanding all thefe various alterations, the intereft of the merchants was nearly the fame. The fale of brandy was feldom decreafed. It was, however, confidered by judicious people as the principal caufe of the diminution of the human race, and confequently that of the fkins of beafts; a diminution which became every day more evident.

This decline of the fur trade was not yet fo remarkable as it has been fince, when the promotion of the duke of Anjou to the throne of Charles V. fpread an alarm over all Europe, and plunged it once more into the horrors of a general war. The conflagration extended beyond the feas, and was advancing even to Canada, had not the Iroquois put a ftop to it. The Englifh and French had long been contending to fecure an alliance with that nation. Thefe marks of efteem or fear had fo far increafed their natural pride, that they confidered themfelves as the umpires of the two rival nations, and pretended that the conduct of both was to be regulated by their intereft. As they were inclined to peace at that time, they haughtily declared that they would take up arms againft either of the two nations, which fhould commence hoftilities againft the other. This refolution was favourable to the fituation of the French colony, which was ill prepared for a war, and expected no affiftance from the mother-country. The people of New York, on the contrary, whofe forces were already confiderable, and received daily reinforcements, wifhed to prevail upon the Iroquois to join with them. Their infinuations, prefents, and negotiations, were, however, ineffectual till 1709; at which period they fucceeded in feducing four of the five nations; and their troops, which till

then had remained inactive, marched out, supported
by a great number of Indian warriors.

The army was confidently advancing towards the centre of Canada with the greatest probability of fuccefs, when one of the chiefs of the Iroquois, who had never approved of their proceedings, plainly faid to his people, " What will become of us, if we fhould " fucceed in driving away the French ? " Thefe few words, uttered with a myfterious and anxious look, immediately recalled to the minds of all the people their former fyftem, which was to keep the balance even between the two foreign nations, in order to fecure their own independence. They inftantly refolved to relinquifh a defign they had been too precipitately engaged in, contrary to the public intereft; but as they thought it would be fhameful openly to defert their affociates, they imagined that fecret treachery might ferve the purpofe of open defection. The lawlefs favages, the virtuous Spartans, the religious Hebrews, the wife and warlike Greeks and Romans; all people, whether civilized or not, have always made what is called the right of nations confift either in craft or violence.

The army had halted on the banks of a little river to wait for the artillery and ammunition. The Iroquois, who fpent their leifure hours in hunting, flayed all the beafts they caught, and threw their fkins into the river, a little above the camp. The waters were foon infected. The Englifh, who had not any fufpicion of fuch an inftance of treafury, continued unfortunately to drink of the waters that were thus rendered poifonous; in confequence of which, fuch confiderable numbers of them immediately died, that it became neceffary to fufpend the military operations.

A ftill more imminent danger threatened the French colony. A numerous fleet, deftined againft Quebec, and which had five or fix thoufand troops on board, entered the river St. Lawrence the following year, and would probably have fucceeded, had it reached the place of its deftination. But the rafhnefs of the admiral, joined to the violence of the elements, was the

B O O K cause of its being lost in the paſſage. Thus was Ca-
XV.   nada at once delivered from its fears both by ſea and
land, and had the glory of maintaining itſelf, without
ſuccours and without loſs, againſt the ſtrength and policy of the Engliſh.

France is   France, in the mean time, which for forty years had
compelled
to cede part ſingly withſtood the combined efforts of all Europe,
of the pro- vanquiſhed or repulſed all the nations united againſt
vinces that
were united her, gained that point under Lewis XIV. which Charles
to Canada. V. had not been able to do with the innumerable troops
of his ſeveral kingdoms ; France, which had at that
period produced as many great men as would have
rendered immortal a ſeries of twenty reigns, and under one in particular had ſignalized herſelf by as many
great actions as might have raiſed the glory of twenty
different nations, was then upon the point of crown-
ing all her glorious ſucceſſes by placing a branch of
the houſe of Bourbon on the throne of Spain. She
had then fewer enemies, and a greater number of allies, than ſhe ever had in the moſt brilliant periods of
her proſperity. Every thing concurred to promiſe her
an eaſy ſucceſs, a ſpeedy and deciſive ſuperiority.

It was not fortune, but nature itſelf, that changed
her deſtiny. Proud and flouriſhing under a king endowed with the graces and vigour of youth, after having riſen with him through the ſeveral degrees of glory and grandeur, ſhe ſank with him through all the
periods of decay incident to human nature. The ſpirit of bigotry, which had been introduced into the
court by an ambitious woman, determined the choice
of miniſters, generals, and governors ; and this choice
was always blind and unfortunate. Kings, who, like
other men, have recourſe to heaven when they are
ready to quit the earth, ſeem in their old age to ſeek
for a new ſet of flatterers, who ſooth them with hopes,
at the time when all realities are diſappearing. It is
at this time that hypocriſy, always ready to avail itſelf
of the firſt and ſecond childhood of life, awakens in
the mind of princes the ideas that had been early im-
planted in it ; and, under pretence of guiding him to

the only happinefs that remains for him, affumes an B O O K
abfolute empire over his will.   But as this laft age, as XV.
well as the firft, is a ftate of weaknefs, a continual
fluctuation muft, therefore, prevail in the government.
Cabals grow more violent and more powerful than
ever ; the expectations of intriguing men are raifed,
and merit is lefs rewarded ; men of fuperior talents
are afraid to make themfelves known ; folicitations of
every kind are multiplied ; places are cafually beftowed upon men all equally unfit to fill them, and
yet prefumptuous enough to think they deferve them ;
men who rate the eftimation of themfelves by the contempt they entertain for others.   The nation then lofes
its ftrength with its confidence, and every thing is carried on with the fame fpirit it was undertaken ; that is,
without defign, vigour, or prudence.

To raife a country from a ftate of barbarifm, to
maintain it in the height of its glory, and to check
the rapidity of its decline, are three objects very difficult to accomplifh ; but the laft is certainly the moft
arduous tafk of them all.   A nation rifes out of barbarifm by fudden efforts exerted at intervals ; it fup-
ports itfelf at the fummit of its profperity by the powers it has acquired ; it declines in confequence of an
univerfal languor, which has been brought on by almoft imperceptible gradations.   Barbarous nations require a long-continued reign ; but fhort reigns are
beft calculated to maintain a ftate in its profperity.
But the long dotage of a declining monarch lays the
foundation of evils for his fucceffor, which it is almoft
impoffible to remedy.

Such was the latter part of the reign of Lewis XIV.
After a feries of defeats and mortifications, he was ftill
happy that he could purchafe peace by facrifices which
made his humiliation evident.   But he feemed to wifh
to conceal thefe facrifices from his people, by making
them chiefly beyond fea.   It is eafy to judge how
much his pride muft have fuffered, in giving up to the
Englifh Hudfon's Bay, Newfoundland, and Acadia,
three poffeffions, which, together with Canada, form-

B O O K ed that immenfe tract of country known by the glo-
XV.   rious name of New France. We fhall fee in the next
book by what means this power, accuftomed to conqueft, endeavoured to repair its loffes.

BOOK XVI.

*A new Order of Things is eftablifhed in the French Co-
lonies in North America. Refult of thefe Arrangements.*

B O O K THE war carried on for the Spanifh fucceffion had
XVI.   raifed a ferment in the four quarters of the world,
which for the two laft centuries have felt the effects of
that reftlefs fpirit with which Europe hath been agitated. All kingdoms were fhaken by the contefts excited on account of one, which, under the dominion
of Charles V. had ftricken terror into them all. The
influence of a houfe whofe fovereignty extended over
five or fix ftates, had raifed the Spanifh nation to a
pitch of greatnefs which could not but be extremely
flattering to her. At the fame time another houfe,
whofe power was ftill fuperior, becaufe with a lefs extent of territory it had a greater degree of population,
was ambitious of giving the law to that haughty nation. The names of Auftria and Bourbon, which had
been rivals for two hundred years, were now exerting
their laft efforts to acquire a fuperiority, which fhould
no longer be confidered as precarious or doubtful between them. The point of conteft was, which fhould
have the greateft number of crowns, to boaft the poffeffion of. Europe, divided between the claims of the
two houfes, which were not altogether groundlefs, was
inclined to allow them to extend their branches, but
would not permit that feveral crowns fhould centre in
one houfe, as they formerly did. Every power took
up arms to difperfe or divide a vaft inheritance; and
refolved to difmember it, rather than fuffer it to be
attached to one, which, with this additional weight of

ſtrength, muſt infallibly deſtroy the balance of all the reſt. As the war was ſupported by each party with numerous forces and great ſkill, with warlike people and experienced generals, it continued a long time: it deſolated the countries it ſhould have ſuccoured, and even ruined nations that had no concern in it. Victory, which ſhould have determined the conteſt, was ſo variable, that it ſerved only to increaſe the general flame. The ſame troops that were ſucceſsful in one country were defeated in another. The people who conquered by ſea were routed on land. The news of the loſs of a fleet and the gaining of a battle arrived at the ſame time. Succeſs alternately favoured each party, and by this inconſtancy ſerved only to complete the mutual deſtruction of both. At length, when the blood and treaſure of the ſeveral ſtates were exhauſted, and after a ſeries of calamities and expences that had laſted twelve years, the people who had profited by their misfortunes, and were weakened by their conteſts, were anxious of recovering the loſſes they had ſuſtained. They endeavoured to find in the New World the means of peopling and re-eſtabliſhing the Old. France firſt turned her views towards North America, to which ſhe was invited by the ſimilarity of ſoil and climate, and the iſland of Cape-Breton became immediately the object of her attention.

The Engliſh conſidered this poſſeſſion as an equivalent for all the French had loſt by the treaty of Utrecht; and not being entirely reconciled to them, ſtrongly oppoſed their being allowed to people and fortify it. They ſaw no other method of excluding them from the cod-fiſhery, and making the entrance into Canada difficult for their ſhips. The moderation of Queen Anne, or, perhaps, the corruption of her miniſters, prevented France from being expoſed to this freſh mortification: and ſhe was authoriſed to make what alterations ſhe thought proper at Cape-Breton.

This iſland is ſituated at the entrance of the Gulf of St. Lawrence, between the 45th and 47th degrees of north latitude. Newfoundland lies to the eaſt, on

The French, to recover their former loſſes, people and fortify Cape-Breton; and eſtabliſh conſiderable fiſheries there.

the fame gulf, and is only 15 or 16 leagues diftant from it ; and to the weft, Acadia is only feparated from the ifland by a ftrait not more than three or four leagues over. Cape-Breton, thus fituated between the territories ceded to its enemies, threatened their poffef-fions, while it protected thofe of France. The ifland meafures about 36 leagues in length, and 22 in its greateft breadth. It is furrounded with little fharp-pointed rocks, feparated from each other by the waves, above which fome of their tops are vifible. All its harbours open to the eaft, turning towards the fouth. On the other parts of the coaft there are but a few anchoring-places for fmall veffels, in creeks, or be-tween iflets. Except in the hilly parts, the furface of the country has but little folidity, being every where covered with a light mofs and with water. The damp-nefs of the foil is exhaled in fogs, without rendering the air unwholefome. In other refpects, the climate is very cold, which is owing either to the prodigious quantity of lakes, which cover above half the ifland, and remain frozen a long time, or to the number of forefts, that totally intercept the rays of the fun, the effect of which is befides decreafed by perpetual clouds.

Though fome fifhermen had long reforted to Cape-Breton every fummer, not more than twenty or thirty had ever fixed there. The French, who took poffef-fion of it in Auguft 1713, were properly the firft in-habitants. They changed its name into that of Ifle Royale, and fixed upon Fort Dauphin for their prin-cipal fettlement. This harbour was two leagues in circumference. The fhips, which came to the very fhore, were completely fheltered from winds. Forefts affording oak fufficient to build and fortify a large city, were near at hand ; the ground appeared lefs barren than in other parts ; and the fifhery was more plenti-ful. This harbour might have been made impreg-nable at a trifling expence ; but the difficulty of ap-proaching it (a circumftance that had at firft made a ftronger impreffion than the advantages refulting from it), occafioned it to be abandoned after great labour had been beftowed upon it. The French then turned their views to Louifbourg, the accefs to which was eafier, and convenience was thus preferred to fecurity.

The harbour of Louifbourg, fituated on the eaftern coaft of the ifland, is at leaft a league in depth, and above a quarter of a league broad in the narroweft part. Its bottom is good, the foundings are ufually from fix to ten fathom, and it is eafy to tack about in it either to fail in or out even in bad weather. It includes a fmall gulf, very commodious for refitting fhips of all fizes, which may even winter there, with proper precautions. The only inconvenience attending this excellent harbour is, that it is frozen up from November till May, and frequently continues fo till June. The entrance, which is naturally narrow, is alfo guarded by Goat Ifland; the cannon of which playing upon a level with the furface of the water, would fink fhips of any fize, that fhould attempt to force the paffage. Two batteries, one of thirty-fix, the other of twelve twenty-four pounders, erected on the two oppofite fhores, would fupport and crofs this formidable fire.

The town is built on a neck of land that runs into the fea, and is about half a league in circuit. The ftreets are broad and regular. Almoft all the houfes are made of wood. Thofe that are of ftone were conftructed at the expence of the government, and are deftined for the reception of the troops. A number of wharfs have been erected, that project a confiderable way into the harbour, and are extremely convenient for loading and unloading the fhips.

The fortification of Louifbourg was only begun in 1720. This undertaking was executed upon very good plans, and is fupplied with all the works that can render a place formidable. A fpace of about a hundred toifes only was left without ramparts on the fide next the fea, which was thought fufficiently defended by its fituation. It was clofed only with a fimple dyke. The fea was fo fhallow in this place, that it made a kind of narrow canal, inacceffible, from

B O O K the number of its reefs, to any shipping whatever. The
XVI.   fire from the side bastions completely secured this spot
from any attack.

The necessity of bringing stone from Europe, and
other materials proper for these great works, sometimes
retarded their progress, but never made them be dis-
continued.   Thirty millions [1,250,000l.] were expended upon them.   This was not thought too great
a sum for the support of the fisheries, for securing the
communication between France and Canada, and for
obtaining a security or retreat to ships in time of war
coming from the southern islands.   Nature and sound
policy required that the riches of the south should be
protected by the strength of the north.

In the year 1714, the French fishermen, who till
then had lived in Newfoundland, arrived in this island.
It was expected that their number would soon have
been increased by the Acadians, who were at liberty,
by the treaties, to remove with all their effects, and
even to dispose of their estates.   But these hopes were
disappointed ; the Acadians chose rather to retain their
possessions under the dominion of England, than to
give them up for any precarious advantage they
might derive from their attachment to France.   Their
place was supplied by some distressed adventurers
from Europe, who came over from time to time
to Cape-Breton, and the inhabitants of the colony
gradually increased to the number of four thousand.
They were settled at Louisbourg, Fort Dauphin, Port
Toulouse, Nericka, and on all the coasts, where they
found a proper beach for drying the cod.

The inhabitants never applied themselves to agriculture, the soil being unfit for it.   They have often
attempted to sow corn, but it seldom came to matu-
rity ; and when it did thrive so much as to be worth
reaping, it had degenerated so considerably, that it
was not fit for seed for the next harvest.   They have
only continued to plant a few pot-herbs that are tolerably well tasted, but the seed of which must be renewed every year.   The poorness and scarcity of pas-

tures has likewife prevented the increafe of cattle. In B O O K
a word, the foil of Cape-Breton feemed calculated to XVI.
invite none but fifhermen and foldiers.

Though the ifland was entirely covered with forefts
before it was inhabited, its wood has fcarce ever been
an object of trade. A great quantity, however, of
foft wood was found there fit for firing, and fome that
might be ufed for timber; but the oak has always
been very fcarce, and the fir never yielded much
refin.

The peltry trade was a very inconfiderable object.
It confifted only in the fkins of a few lynxes, elks,
mufk rats, wild cats, bears, otters, and foxes, both of
a red and filver grey colour. Some of thefe were procured from a colony of Mickmac Indians, who had
fettled on the ifland with the French, and never could
raife more than fixty men able to bear arms. The
reft came from St. John's, or the neighbouring continent.

Greater advantages might poffibly have been derived
from the coal mines which abound in the ifland. They
lie in a horizontal direction, and being no more than
fix or eight feet below the furface, may be worked
without digging deep, or draining off the waters. Notwithftanding the prodigious demand for this coal from
New-England, from the year 1745, to the year 1749,
thefe mines would, probably, have been forfaken, had
not the fhips which were fent out to the French iflands
wanted ballaft.

The whole induftry of the colony has conftantly
been exerted in the cod fifhery. The lefs wealthy inhabitants employed yearly two hundred boats in this
fifhery, and the richeft, fifty or fixty veffels from thirty
to fifty tons burden. The fmall craft always kept
within four or five leagues of the coaft, and returned
at night with their fifh, which, being immediately
cured, was always in the utmoft degree of perfection
it was capable of. The larger fmacks went to fifh
further from fhore, kept their cargo for feveral days,
and as the cod was apt to be too falt, it was lefs valu-

able. But this inconvenience was compenfated by the advantage it gave them of purfuing the fifh, when the want of food compelled it to leave the ifland; and by the facility of carrying, during the autumn, the produce of their labours to the fouthern iflands, or even to France.

Befide the fifhermen fettled on the ifland, others came every year from France to dry their fifh, either in the habitations, in confequence of an agreement made with the owners, or upon the beach, which was always referved for their ufe.

The mother-country regularly fent them fhips laden with provifions, liquors, wearing apparel, houfehold goods, and all things neceffary for the inhabitants of the colony. The largeft of thefe fhips, having no other concern but this trade, returned to Europe as foon as they had bartered their lading for cod. Thofe from fifty to a hundred tons burden, after having land-ed their little cargo, went a-fifhing themfelves, and did not return till the feafon was over.

The people of Cape-Breton did not fend all their fifh to Europe. They fent part of it to the French fouthern iflands, on board twenty or twenty-five fhips, from feventy to a hundred and forty tons burden. Be-fide the cod, which made at leaft half their cargo, they exported to the other colonies, timber, planks, thin oak boards, falted falmon and mackarel, train oil, and fea-coal. All thefe were paid for in fugar and coffee, but chiefly in rum and molaffes.

The ifland could not confume all thefe commodi-ties. Canada took off but a fmall part of the over-plus: it was chiefly bought by the people of New-England, who gave in exchange fruits, vegetables, wood, brick, and cattle. This trade of exchange was allowed; but a fmuggling trade was added to it, con-fifting of flour, and a confiderable quantity of falt fifh.

Notwithftanding this circulation, which was all car-ried on at Louifbourg, moft of the colonies were ex-tremely poor. This was owing to the dependence their indigence had fubjected them to on their firft arrival. Unable to procure the necessary implements B O O K for the fishery, they had borrowed some at an excessive interest. Even those who were not at first reduced to this necessity, were soon obliged to submit to the hard terms of borrowing. The dearness of salt and provisions, together with the ill success of their fishery, soon compelled them to it; and they were inevitably ruined by being obliged to pay twenty or five and twenty per cent. a year for every thing they borrowed.

Such is, at every instant, the relative situation of the indigent man, who solicits assistance, and of the opulent citizen, who grants it only on terms so hard, that they become, in a short time, fatal to the borrower and to the creditor; to the borrower, because the profit he reaps from the sum borrowed cannot yield as much as it hath cost him; and to the creditor, because in the end he can no longer be paid by a debtor, whom his usury soon renders insolvent. It is a difficult matter to find out a remedy to this inconvenience; for the lender must finally have his securities, and it is necessary that the interest of the sum lent should increase in proportion to the risk of the security.

There is on both sides an error of calculation, which a little justice and benevolence on the part of the lender might remedy. The lender should say to himself: The unhappy man who applies to me is skilful, laborious, and economical; I will assist him, in order to raise him from misery. Let us see what his industry, turning out to the best advantage, will yield, and let us not lend to him; or if we should resolve to lend to him, let the interest we require upon the sum borrowed be less than the produce of his labour. If the interest and the produce were equal, the debtor would always remain in a state of misery; and the least unexpected accident would bring on his bankruptcy, and the loss of my capital. If, on the contrary, the produce should exceed the interest, the fortune of the debtor will be annually increasing, and consequently the security of the capital I have intrusted to him will become greater.

But, unfortunately, a rapacious spirit doth not argue in the same manner as a spirit of prudence and humanity. There are scarce any contracts and leases between the rich and the poor, to which those principles are not applicable. If a man should wish to be paid by his farmer, in good as well as bad seasons, he must not rigorously exact from him all that his land can yield; otherwise, if his barns should be set on fire, it is at the landlord's expence that they are consumed. A desire to prosper alone often makes prosperity escape from us. It is seldom that the profit of one man can be totally separated from that of another. A man will always be the dupe of him who knowingly promises more than he can perform; while the latter will be the dupe of the former, should he be ignorant of the event. He who unites prudence with honesty, will neither deceive others, nor be deceived himself.

Settlement
of the
French in
the island
of St. John.
Tendency
of this un-
dertaking. All the French colonies of New France were not from their first establishment destined to such distress. The island of St. John, more favourably situated, has been more favourable to its inhabitants. It lies further up the gulf of St. Lawrence, is twenty-two leagues long, and not much above a league at its greatest breadth. It bends in the form of a crescent, both ends terminating in a sharp point. Though the right of this island had never been disputed with France, yet she seemed to pay no regard to it till the peace of Utrecht. The loss of Acadia and Newfoundland drew their attention to this small remaining spot, and the government began to inquire what use could be made of it.

It appeared that the winters were long there, the cold extreme, with abundance of snow, and prodigious quantities of insects; but that these defects were compensated by a healthy coast, a good sea-port, and commodious harbours. The country was flat, enriched with fine pastures, watered by an infinite number of rivulets and springs; the soil exceedingly diversified, and fit for the culture of every kind of grain. There was plenty of game, and multitudes of wild

beafts; amazing fhoals of fifh of all forts; and a greater number of favage inhabitants than were found on
any other of the iflands. This circumftance alone was
a proof how much it was fuperior to the reft.

The report that was fpread of this in France gave
rife to a Company in 1619, which formed the defign
both of clearing this fertile ifland, and of eftablifhing
a great cod fifhery there. Unfortunately, intereft,
which had brought the adventurers together, fet them
at variance again, before they began to execute the
plan they had projected. St. John was again forgotten, when the Acadians began to remove to that ifland
in 1749. In procefs of time they increafed to the
number of three thoufand one hundred and fifty-four.
As they were for the moft part hufbandmen, and particularly accuftomed to the breeding of cattle, the government thought proper to confine them to this employment; and the cod fifhery was only allowed to be
carried on by thofe who fettled at Tracadia and St.
Peter.

Prohibitions and monopolies, while they are a reftraint upon induftry, are equally detrimental to the
labours that are permitted, and to thofe that are forbidden. Though the ifland of St. John does not afford
a fufficient extent of fea-fhore fit for drying the vaft
quantities of cod that come in fhoals to the coafts, and
though the fifh is too large to be eafily dried, yet it
was incumbent upon a power whofe fifheries are not
fufficient for the confumption of its own fubjects, to
encourage this kind of employment. If there were
too few drying places for the quantity that could be
caught, that which is called green cod might eafily
have been prepared, which alone would have made a
valuable branch of commerce.

By confining the inhabitants of St. John to agriculture, they were deprived of all refource in thofe unfortunate feafons that happen frequently on the ifland,
when the crops are devoured by the field mice and
grafshoppers. The exchanges which the mother country could and ought to have made with her colony

B O O K were reduced to nothing. Laftly, in attempting to
XVI. favour agriculture, its progrefs was obftructed, by laying the inhabitants under an impoffibility of procuring
the neceffary articles for extending it.

Only one or two fmall veffels came annually to the
ifland from Europe, and landed at Port la Joie, where
they were fupplied with all they wanted from Louifbourg, and paid for it in wheat, barley, oats, pulfe,
oxen, and fheep. A party of fifty men ferved rather
to regulate their police, than to defend them. Their
commanding officer was dependent on Cape-Breton,
which was itfelf under the controul of the governor
of Canada. The command of this laft officer extended to a great diftance, over a vaft continent, the richeft
part of which was Louifiana.

Difcovery   This extenfive and beautiful country, which the
of the Mif- Spaniards formerly comprehended under the name of
fiffippi by   Florida, was for a long time unknown to the inhabi-
the French. tants of Canada. It was not till 1660 that fuch a
country was fuppofed to exift. At this period they
were told by the favages, that to the weft of the colony there was a great river, which flowed neither to
the north nor to the eaft; and they concluded that it
muft therefore empty itfelf into the gulf of Mexico, if
its courfe were fouthward, or into the South Sea, if it
were weftward. The care of afcertaining thefe two
important facts was committed, in 1673, to Joliet, an
inhabitant of Quebec, a very intelligent man, and to
the Jefuit Marquette, whofe mild and benevolent manners had fecured to him the general affection of all the
inhabitants.

Thefe two men, equally difinterefted, equally active,
and equally zealous for their country, immediately fet
out together from the lake Michigan, entered the river
of the Foxes, which empties itfelf into that lake, and
went up almoft to the head of the river, notwithftanding the currents, which render that navigation difficult.
After fome days march, they again embarked on the
river Ouifconfing, and, keeping always weftward, came
to the Miffiffippi, and failed down that river as far as

the Akanſas, about the 33d degree of latitude. Their zeal would have carried them further, but they were in want of proviſions; they were in an unknown country, and they had only three or four men along with them: beſides, the object of their voyage was fulfilled, ſince they had diſcovered the river they had been in ſearch of, and were certain of its courſe. Theſe conſiderations determined them to return to Canada, acroſs the country of the Illinois, a numerous people, who were well inclined to a friendly intercourſe with the French nation. Without concealing or exaggerating any particular, they communicated to the chief of the colony all the information they had procured.

Among the inhabitants of New France at that time, was a Norman, named La Salle, who was equally deſirous of making a great fortune, and of eſtabliſhing a brilliant reputation. This man had ſpent his younger years among the Jeſuits, where he had contracted that activity, enthuſiaſm, and firmneſs, which thoſe fathers ſo well know how to inſtil into their diſciples, when they meet with young men of quick parts, with whom they are fond of recruiting their order. La Salle, who was a bold and enterpriſing man, fond of availing himſelf of every opportunity to diſtinguiſh himſelf, and anxious even to ſeek out ſuch opportunities, beheld in the diſcovery that had been made a vaſt career open to his ambition and to his genius. In concert with Frontenac, governor of Canada, he embarked for Europe, went to the court of Verſailles, was liſtened to, almoſt even with admiration, at a time when both the prince and the people were inſpired with a paſſion for great actions. He returned loaded with favours, and with orders to complete what had been ſo fortunately begun.

This was a great project: but in order to render the execution of it uſeful and permanent, it was neceſſary, by forts placed at different diſtances, to ſecure the poſſeſſion of the countries that ſeparated the Miſſiſſippi from the French ſettlements; and to gain the affection of the colonifts, either wandering or fedentary, that were contained in this vaft fpace. Thefe operations, flow in their nature, were ftill retarded by unexpected incidents, by the malevolence of the Iroquois, and by the repeated mutinies of the foldiers, who were continually irritated by the defpotifm and reftleffnefs of their chief. Accordingly, La Salle, who had begun his preparatives in the month of September 1678, could not fail till the fecond of February 1682, on the great river, which was the end of his wifhes and expectations. On the 9th of April he difcovered the mouth of it; which, as it had been conjectured, was in the gulf of Mexico: and he returned to Quebec in the fpring of the following year.

He immediately fet out for France, to propofe the difcovery of the Miffiffippi by fea, and the eftablifhment of a great colony upon the fertile fhores watered by that river. He perfuaded the court by his eloquence or by his arguments; and four fmall veffels were given to him, with which he fet fail towards the Gulf of Mexico. This fmall fleet miffed the place of their deftination, by fteering too far weftward, and arrived, in the month of February 1685, in the bay of St. Bernard, diftant a hundred leagues from the mouth of the river where it was intended to enter. The irreconcileable hatred which was conceived between La Salle and Beaujeu, commander of the fhips, rendered this error infinitely more fatal than it ought to have been. Thefe two haughty men, impatient of feparating from each other, refolved to land the whole of their embarkation upon the very coaft where they had been conducted by chance. After this defperate meafure the fhips went away, and there only remained upon thefe unknown coafts one hundred and feventy men, moft of them very corrupt, and all of them difpleafed, not without reafon, with their fituation. They had but few tools, a fmall quantity of provifions, and little ammunition. The remainder of what was to ferve for the foundation of the new ftate, was fwal-

lowed up by the waves, from the perfidy or wicked- B O O K
nefs of the fea-officers intrufted with the landing of <u>XVI.</u>
them.

The proud and unfhaken foul of La Salle was not,
however, depreffed by thefe misfortunes. Sufpecting
that the rivers, which difcharged themfelves in the bay
where he had entered, might be fome of the branches
of the Miffiffippi, he fpent feveral months in clearing
up his doubts. Undeceived in thefe expectations, he
neglected the object of his expedition. Inftead of
looking for guides among the favages, who would
have directed him to the place of his deftination, he
chofe to penetrate into the inland countries, and to
inform himfelf of the famous mines of St. Barbe. He
was wholly taken up with this abfurd project, when
he was maffacred by fome of his companions, who
were incenfed at his haughtinefs, and the violence of
his difpofition.

The death of La Salle foon occafioned the reft of
his company to difperfe. The villains who had murdered him fell by each others hand. Several incorporated with the natives. Many perifhed by hunger
and fatigue. The neighbouring Spaniards loaded fome
of thefe adventurers with chains, and they ended their
days in the mines. The favages furprifed the fort
which had been erected, and facrificed every thing to
their fury. Seven men only efcaped thefe numerous
difafters; and thefe, wandering as far as the Miffiffippi, came to Canada by the Illinois country. Thefe
diftreffes foon made the French lofe fight of a region
which was ftill but little known.

The attention of the miniftry was again roufed in
1697, by Yberville, a gentleman of Canada, who had
diftinguifhed himfelf by fome very bold and fortunate
attempts at Hudfon's Bay, in Acadia, and Newfoundland. He was fent out from Rochfort with two fhips,
and difcovered the Miffiffippi in 1699. He failed up
the river as far as the country of the Natchez; and
after having afcertained, by his own obfervation, every advantageous circumftance that had been reported

The French
settle in the
country
that is wa-
tered by the
Miſſiſſippi,
and call it
Louiſiana.

of it, he conſtructed, at the mouth of it, a ſmall fort,
which did not continue more than four or five years,
and proceeded to another ſpot to ſettle his colony.

Between the river and Penſacola, a ſettlement newly erected by the Spaniards in Florida, is a coaſt of
about forty leagues in extent, where no veſſel can
land. The ſoil is ſandy, and the climate burning.
Nothing grows there but a few ſcattered cedars and
fir-trees. In this large track there is a diſtrict called
Biloxi. This ſituation, the moſt barren and moſt in-
convenient upon the whole coaſt, was made choice of
for the reſidence of the few men whom Yberville had
brought thither, and who had been allured by the
moſt ſanguine expectations.

Two years after a new colony arrived. The firſt
was removed from the parched ſands on which it had
been ſettled, and they were both united upon the
banks of the Mobile. This river is navigable only for
Indian boats, and the lands that are watered by it are
not fertile. Theſe were ſufficient motives for giving
up the idea of ſuch a ſettlement ; which, however,
was not done. It was determined that theſe diſad-
vantages would be compenſated by the facility of
communication with the neighbouring ſavages, with
the Spaniards, with the French iſlands, and with Europe. The harbour which was to form theſe communications was not attached to the continent. It was
placed, by chance, either fortunately or otherwiſe, at
ſome leagues diſtance from the coaſt, in a deſert, barren, and ſavage iſland, which was decorated with the
great name of Dauphin Iſland.

A colony ſettled on ſuch bad foundations could not
poſſibly proſper. The death of Yberville at ſea, who
periſhed gloriouſly before the Havannah in 1706, in
the ſervice of his country, put an end to the ſmall remaining hopes of the moſt ſanguine coloniſts. France
was ſo deeply engaged in an unhappy war, that no aſſiſtance could be expected from her. The coloniſts
thought themſelves totally forſaken ; and thoſe who
entertained ſome hopes of finding a ſettlement in ano-

ther place, haftened to go in fearch of it. The colo- B O O K
ny was reduced to twenty-eight families, each more XVI.
wretched than the other, when, to the aftonifhment
of every one, Crofat petitioned for and obtained the
exclufive trade of Louifiana in 1712.

This was a famous merchant, who by his vaft and
prudent undertakings had raifed an immenfe fortune.
He had not given up the thoughts of increafing his
wealth, but he was defirous that his new projects
fhould contribute to the profperity of the monarchy.
This noble ambition made him turn his views towards
the Miffiffippi. The clearing of its fertile foil was not
his aim. His intention was to open communications,
both by land and fea, with Old and New Mexico, to
pour all kinds of merchandife into thofe parts, and to
draw from thence as much ore as he could The place
he afked for appeared to him to be the natural and
neceffary mart for his vaft operations; and all the fteps
taken by his agents were regulated upon this noble
plan. But being undeceived by feveral unfuccefsful
attempts, he relinquifhed his fcheme, and in 1717 re-
figned his charter to a company whofe fuccefs aftonifhed all nations.

This Company was formed by Law, that celebrated Louifiana
Scotchman, of whom no fettled judgment could be becomes
very fa-
formed at the time he appeared, but whofe name now mous in the
ftands between the crowd of mere adventurers and the time of
fhort lift of great men. This daring genius had made tem. Rea-
it his bufinefs, from his infancy, to obferve attentively fon of this.
the feveral powers of Europe, to examine their vari-
ous fprings, and to calculate the ftrength of each.
The ftate into which the inordinate ambition of Louis
XIV. had plunged the kingdom of France, particularly attracted his attention, which was now fixed upon a
heap of ruins. An empire, which, during the fpace of
forty years, had excited fo much jealoufy and fo much
anxiety among all its neighbours, no longer difplayed
any degree of vigour or animation. The nation was
exhaufted by the demands of the treafury, and the
treafury by the enormity of their engagements. In

vain had the puclic debts been reduced, in hopes of
enhancing the value of thofe that ftill remained. This
bankruptcy of government had but imperfectly produced that kind of good that was expected from it.
The bills of government were ftill infinitely below
their original value.

It became neceffary to open a mart for thefe bills,
to prevent them from falling into total difcredit. The
mode of reimburfement was impracticable; for the intereft for the fums due abforbed, almoft entirely, the
revenues of government. Law contrived another expedient. In the month of Auguft 1717, he eftablifhed, under the title of the Weftern Company, an affociation whofe funds were to confift in government
bills. This paper was received for its whole value,
although it loft fifty per cent. in the courfe of trade.
Accordingly, the capital, which was only of 100,000,000
of livres [4,166,666l. 13s. 4d.], was completed in a
few days. It is true, that, with thefe fingular proceedings, it was not poffible to found a powerful colony
in Louifiana, as the exclufive charter feemed to require : but the author of thefe novelties was fupported by an expectation of another kind.

No fooner had Ponce de Leon landed at Florida,
in 1512, than a rumour was fpread, throughout the
Old and the New World, that this region was full of
metals. Thefe had not been difcovered, either by
Francis de Cordova, or by Velafquez de Ayllon, or
by Philip de Narvaez, or by Ferdinand de Soto, although thefe enterprifing men had fearched for them
with incredible fatigue during thirty years. Spain had
at length renounced thefe hopes ; fhe had not even
left any trace of her enterprifes ; and notwithftanding
this, a vague report had remained among the minds of
the people, that thefe countries concealed immenfe
treafures. No one pointed out the precife fpot where
thefe riches might lie; but this circumftance itfelf
tended to encourage the exaggeration of them. If at
intervals the enthufiafm grew cooler, it was only to
feize upon the minds of men more powerfully fome

time after. This general difpofition towards an eager credulity might become a wonderful inftrument in the hands of fkilful perfons.

In times of misfortune, the people are agitated by their hopes, in the fame manner as they are by their fears, or by their rage. When they are actuated with rage, all the public places are in an inftant filled with a multitude in commotion, which threatens and roars aloud. The citizen fhuts himfelf up in his houfe; the magiftrate trembles on his tribunal; the fovereign is oppreffed with anxiety in his palace. When night comes on, the tumult ceafes, and tranquillity is re-ftored. When the people are under the impreffion of terror, univerfal confternation diffufes itfelf in an in-ftant from one city to another, and plunges the whole nation into a ftate of defpondency. When the people are elated with hopes, the phantom of happinefs pre-fents itfelf not lefs rapidly on all fides. It raifes the fpirits of all men, and the noify tranfports of joy fuc-ceed to the gloomy filence of misfortune. On one day every thing is loft, on the other all is faved.

Of all the paffions that are kindled in the heart of man, there is none which is fo violent in its intoxica-tion as the paffion for gold. We are all acquainted with the country where the moft beautiful women are to be found, and yet we are not tempted to vifit it. Sedentary ambition exerts itfelf in a narrow compafs. The rage of conqueft is the malady of a fingle man, who draws the multitude after him. But let us fup-pofe all the people of the earth to be equally civilized, and the thirft of gold will difplace the inhabitants of one and of the other hemifphere. Setting out from the two extremities of the diameter of the equator, they will crofs each other in their way from one pole to the other.

Law, to whom this great fpring of action was well known, eafily perfuaded the French, who were moft of them ruined, that the mines of Louifiana, which had fo long been fpoken of, were at length difcover-ed; and that they were even far richer than they were

generally fuppofed to be. To give the greater weight
to this falfe report, which had already gained too much
credit, a number of miners were fent over to work
thefe mines, which were imagined to be fo valuable,
with a body of troops fufficient to defend them.

It is inconceivable what a fudden impreffion this
ftratagem made upon a nation naturally fond of novelty. Every man exerted himfelf to acquire the right
of partaking of this fource of wealth, which was confidered as inexhauftible. The Miffiffippi became the
centre of all mens wifhes, hopes, and fpeculations.
It was not long before fome wealthy and powerful
men, moft of whom were thought to be perfons of
underftanding, not fatisfied with fharing the general
profit of the monopoly, became defirous of obtaining
a private property in a region which paffed for one
of the beft countries in the world. Cultivators were
wanted for the clearing of thofe domains, and were
abundantly fupplied by France, Switzerland, and Germany. Thefe men, after having worked three years
without falary, for the perfons who had been at the
expence of conveying them to the fpot, were to become citizens, and be put in poffeffion of lands, in order to clear them on their own account.

During the courfe of this frenzy, or in the years
1718 and 1719, all thefe unfortunate people were promifcuoufly crowded together in fhips. They were not
landed at Dauphin Ifland, the harbour of which had
lately been choked up by fands; nor were they fet on
fhore at Mobile, which had loft every thing fince it
had loft its port: but it was at Biloxi, that dreadful
fpot, where all the natives, as well as foreigners who
had been feduced, were placed. There they all perifhed by thoufands, with want and vexation. In order to preferve them, it was only neceffary to have
conveyed them up the Miffiffippi, and landed them
immediately upon the country they were to clear;
but fuch was the unfkilfulnefs or neglect of the managers of the enterprife, that they never thought of
conftructing the boats neceffary for fo fimple a ma-

nœuvre. Even after they found that the ſhips com- ing from Europe could moſt of them ſail up the river, Biloxi ſtill continued to be the grave of thoſe unhappy and numerous victims who had fallen a ſacrifice to a political impoſture. The head-quarters were not removed to New-Orleans till five years after, that is, till hardly any were left of thoſe unfortunate people who had been weak enough to quit their native country upon ſuch uncertain proſpects.

But at this period, when it was too late, the charm was diſſolved, and the mines vaniſhed. Nothing remained but the ſhame of having been miſled by chimerical notions. Louiſiana ſhared the fate of thoſe extraordinary men who have been too highly extolled, and are afterwards puniſhed for this unmerited fame, by being degraded below their real worth. Men ſtrive, by the exceſs of cenſure, to perſuade others that they have not given into the common error ; for how can it be ſuppoſed that they would violently perſiſt in ſpeaking ill of themſelves? This inchanted country was now holden in execration. Its very name became a reproach. The Miſſiſſippi was the terror of free men. No recruits were to be found to ſend thither, but ſuch as were taken from priſons and houſes of ill fame. It became the receptacle of the loweſt and moſt profligate perſons in the kingdom.

What could be expected from a ſettlement compoſed of ſuch perſons? Vicious men will neither people a country, nor labour, nor continue long in any place. Many of thoſe miſerable perſons who had been tranſported into theſe ſavage climates, went into the Engliſh or Spaniſh ſettlements, to exhibit the diſagreeable view of their diſtreſs and miſery. Others ſoon periſhed, from the infection they had brought along with them. The greater number wandered in the woods, till hunger and wearineſs put an end to their exiſtence. Nothing was yet begun in the colony, though twenty-five millions of livres [1,041,666l. 13s. 4d.] had been ſunk there. The managers of the Company that advanced theſe vaſt ſums fooliſhly pretended, that in

B O O K the capital of France they could lay the plan of such
XVI. undertakings as were fit for America. Paris, unacquainted with its own provinces, which it despises and
exhausts, would have submitted every thing to the
operations of these hasty and frivolous calculators.
From the office of the Company, they pretended to
regulate and direct all the inhabitants of Louisiana,
and to impose or withhold such restraints as were
judged favourable or unfavourable to the monopoly.
Had they granted some trifling encouragements to citizens of character, who might have been invited to settle
in the colony, by securing to them that liberty which
every man covets, that property which every man has
a right to expect from his own labour, and that protection which is due from every society to its members; such encouragements as these, given to proprietors well informed of their real interest and property, directed by the circumstances of the place,
would have been productive of far greater and more
lasting effects; and would have established more extensive, solid, and profitable settlements, than all those
an exclusive charter could ever have formed with all its
treasures, dispensed and managed by agents who could
neither have the knowledge requisite to conduct so
many various operations, nor even be influenced by
any immediate interest in their success.

The ministry, however, thought it conducive to the
welfare of the state, to leave the concerns of Louisiana in the hands of the Company; which were under a necessity of exerting all their interest to obtain
permission to alienate that part of their privilege.
They were even obliged to purchase this favour in
1731, by paying down the sum of 1,450,000 livres
[60,416l. 13s. 4d.]. For there are some states, where
the right of being involved in ruin, and that of being
preserved from it, or that of acquiring wealth, are
equally sold; because good or evil, whether public or
private, may prove an object of finance.

During all the time that an exclusive charter had
kept Louisiana in shackles, it had required, accord-

ing to the diftances, fifty, fixty, fourfcore, and a hun- B O O K
dred per cent. profit, upon all the merchandife which   XVI.
it ufed to fend there ; and had alfo regulated, by a
rate ftill more oppreffive, the price of the commodities which the colony delivered to it. How was it
poffible that an infant fettlement could make any progrefs under the yoke of a tyranny fo atrocious? Accordingly, the difcouragement became univerfal. To
reftore to the minds of men their energy, government was defirous that a poffeffion, which was become
a truly national one, fhould experience a happier fate.
With this view they decreed, that every article which
the trade of France fhould convey into this country,
and every thing it fhould bring back from thence,
fhould be exempted for ten years from all duties of
export and import. Let us fee to what degree of
profperity an arrangement fo prudent raifed this celebrated region.

Louifiana is a vaft country, bounded on the north   Extent, foil,
by the fea ; on the eaft by Florida and Carolina ; on   of Louifi-
the weft by New Mexico ; and on the north by Ca-   ana.
nada, and by unknown lands, which are fuppofed to
extend as far as Hudfon's Bay. It is impoffible to afcertain precifely the exact length of it; but its mean
breadth is two hundred leagues.

Throughout fuch an extent, the climate varies confiderably. Fogs are too frequent in Lower Louifiana,
in fpring and autumn ; the winters are rainy, and at
diftant intervals attended with a flight froft : moft of
the fummer days are fpoilt by violent ftorms. The
heats are not fo exceffive in any part of this extenfive territory as might be expected from its latitude.
This phenomenon, which feems extraordinary to a
common obferver, may be accounted for by natural
philofophers, from the thick forefts, which prevent the
rays of the fun from heating the ground ; the numberlefs rivers, which keep it conftantly damp; and
the winds, which blow from the north over a long extent of land.

Though difeafes are not very common in Upper

Louifiana, they are ftill more unfrequent in the Lower. This is, however, nothing more than a flip of
land of two or three leagues in extent, overrun with
infects, with ftagnated waters, and with vegetable fubftances, which putrify in a damp and warm atmofphere, the conftant principle of the diffolution of bodies. In this climate, where all dead bodies generally undergo a rapid putrefaction, men enjoy a more
fettled ftate of health, than in thofe regions which to
all appearance are more healthy. Except the tetanos,
which carries off half the Negro children before they
are twelve days old, and a great number of white children, there is fcarce any difeafe known in that country, except fome hyfterical affections, and obftructions,
which may even be confidered as a natural confequence
of the kind of life which is led there. From whence
can the falubrity of the air proceed? Perhaps it is
owing to the frequent thunders which are heard upon
this narrow foil. Perhaps to the winds which almoft
conftantly prevail there. Perhaps to the fires which
it is neceffary to kindle in order to deftroy the numerous reeds which impede the cultures.

This foil muft have appeared extremely fertile, before any trials had been made of it, fince it abounded
with wild fruits. It furnifhed a liberal provifion for
a great number of birds and fallow-deer. The meadows, formed by nature alone, were covered with roe-
bucks and bifons. The trees were remarkable for
their bulk and height, and woods for dyeing were only wanting, for thofe grow merely between the tropics.
Thefe favourable omens have been fince confirmed by
fortunate experiments.

The fource of the river which divides this immenfe
country from north to fouth, hath not yet been difcovered. The boldeft travellers have fcarce gone higher than two hundred leagues above the fall of St.
Anthony, which ftops the courfe of it by a cafcade
of fome height, about the 46th degree of latitude.
From thence to the fea, that is, throughout the fpace
of 700 leagues, the navigation is not interrupted. The

Miffiffippi, after being enlarged by the river of the B O O K
Illinois, the Miffouri, the Ohio, and a great number XVI.
of fmall rivers, maintains an uninterrupted courfe,
till it falls into the ocean. All circumftances concur to prove, that the bed of this river is confiderably extended, and that its bottom is almoft recent
ground, fince not a fingle ftone is to be found in it.
The fea throws up here a prodigious quantity of mud,
leaves of reeds, boughs and ftumps of trees, that the
Miffiffippi is continually wafhing down; which different materials being driven backward and forward,
and being collected together, form themfelves into a
folid mafs, continually tending to the prolongation of
this vaft continent.

The river hath not any regular periods of increafe
or decreafe; but, in general its waters are higher from
the month of January to that of June, than they are
through the reft of the year. The bed of the river
being very deep at the upper part, it feldom over-
flows on the eaft fide, till it comes within fixty leagues
of the fea, nor on the weft, till within a hundred leagues;
that is to fay, in the low lands, which we imagine to
be recent. Thefe muddy grounds, like all others that
have not yet acquired a due confiftence, produce a
prodigious quantity of large reeds, in which all ex-
traneous bodies wafhed down the river are entangled.
Thefe bodies all joined together, and added to the
flime that fills up the interftices, in procefs of time
form a mafs, that raifes the banks higher than the
adjacent ground, which forms on each fide an inclined
plane. Hence it happens, that the waters having once
got out of their natural courfe, never get into it again,
and are therefore obliged to run on to the ocean, or
to form themfelves into fmall lakes.

When the breadth and depth of the Miffiffippi are
alone confidered, we are induced to think that the
navigation is eafy. It is, on the contrary, very tedious, even in coming down; becaufe it would be dangerous by night in dark weather, and becaufe inftead
of the light canoes made of bark, which are fo con-

B O O K venient in the reft of America, it is neceffary to em-
XVI.   ploy larger boats, which are confequently heavier, and
         not fo eafily managed. Without thefe precautions,
the boats would be in continual danger of ftriking
againft the boughs or roots of trees, which are dragged along in great quantities by the ftream, and are
frequently fixed under water. The difficulties are
greater ftill in going up the river.

At fome diftance from land, before we enter the
Miffiffippi, care muft be taken to keep clear of the
floating wood that is come down from Louifiana. The
coaft is fo flat, that it can hardly be feen at the diftance of two leagues, and it is not eafy to get up to
it. The river empties itfelf into the fea by a great
number of openings. Thefe openings are conftantly
varying, and moft of them have but little depth of
water. When the fhips have happily furmounted all
thefe obftacles, they may fail without any difficulty
ten or twelve leagues, over a country funk under water, where the eye perceives nothing but reeds, and
a few fhrubs. Then, upon each fhore, they meet with
thick forefts, which they pafs by in two or three days,
unlefs calms, which are rather frequent in fummer,
fhould retard their progrefs. The reft of the navigation, upon a ftream fo rapid, and fo full of currents,
is performed in boats that go with oars and fails, and
are forced to pafs on from one point of land to another; and though they fet out by break of day, are
thought to have made a confiderable progrefs, if they
have advanced five or fix leagues by the clofe of the
evening. The Europeans engaged in this navigation,
are attended by fome Indian huntfmen, who follow
by land, and fupply them with fubfiftence during the
three months and a half that are employed in going
from one extremity of the colony to the other.

Thefe difficulties of fituation are the greateft which
the French have had to furmount in forming fettlements at Louifiana.

The Englifh, fettled in the Eaft, have been always
fo affiduoufly employed in their plantations, that they

have never thought of any thing but of extending and improving them. The fpirit of conqueft or of plunder hath not diverted them from their labours. Had they been inclined to jealoufy, the French did not behave fo as to excite it.

The Spaniards, unfortunately for themfelves, were more turbulent in the Weft. The defire of removing an active neighbour from New Mexico induced them, in 1720, to adopt the fcheme of forming a confiderable colony far beyond the boundaries within which they had hitherto confined themfelves. The numerous caravans that were to compofe this colony fet out from Santa Fé. They directed their march towards the Ozages, whom they wifhed to induce to take up arms againft their eternal enemies, the Miffourys, whofe territory they had refolved to occupy. The Spaniards miffed their way, and came directly to that nation, the ruin of which they were meditating; and miftaking thefe Indians for the Ozages, communicated their defign without any referve.

The chief of the Miffourys, who became acquainted, by this fingular miftake, with the danger that threatened him and his people, diffembled his refentment. He told the Spaniards, he would gladly concur in promoting the fuccefs of their undertaking, and only defired eight-and-forty hours to affemble his warriors. When they were armed, to the number of two thoufand, they fell upon the Spaniards, whom they had amufed with fports, and flew them in their fleep. All were maffacred, without diftinction of age or fex. The chaplain, who alone efcaped the flaughter, owed his prefervation to the fingularity of his drefs. This cataftrophe having fecured the tranquillity of Louifiana, on the fide where it was moft threatened, the colony could only be molefted by the natives; but thefe, although more numerous at that time than they are in our days, were ftill not very formidable.

Thefe favages were divided into feveral nations, all of them very feeble, and all at enmity with each other, though feparated by immenfe deferts. Some of them

General character of the favages of

B O O K
XVI

Louisiana,
and of the
Natchez in
particular.
had a fixed abode. Their dwellings were only made of leaves interwoven with each other, and fastened to a number of stakes. Those who did not go quite naked, were only covered with the skins of fallow-deer. They lived upon the produce of hunting and fishing, upon maize, and some fruits. Their customs were nearly the same as those of the savages of Canada, but they had not the same degree of strength and courage, of quickness and sagacity; and their character was less marked.

Among these nations, the Natchez were the most remarkable. They paid obedience to one man, who styled himself GREAT SUN; because he bore upon his breast the image of that luminary, from which he claimed his descent. The whole business of government, war, and religion, depended upon him. All the world could not, perhaps, have produced a sovereign more absolute. His wife enjoyed the same authority and the same honours. When any of these enslaved savages had the misfortune to displease either of these masters, they used to say to their guards, *Rid me of that dog*, and were instantly obeyed. Every thing of the best that was afforded by hunting, fishing, or culture, the savages were compelled to bring to them. On the demise of either the husband or the wife, it was necessary that many of their subjects should also die, that they might attend and serve them in the next world. The religion of the Natchez was limited to the adoration of the Sun: but this belief was accompanied with many ceremonies, and consequently attended with mischievous effects. There was, however, but one temple for the whole nation: it was once set on flames by the fire which is perpetually, or at least habitually, kept in it; and this event occasioned a general consternation. Many fruitless efforts were made to stop the progress of the flames. Some mothers threw their children into them, and at length the fire was extinguished. The next day these barbarous heroines were extolled in a discourse delivered by the despotic pontiff. It is thus that his authority was

maintained. It is aftonifhing how fo poor and fo favage a people could be fo cruelly enflaved. But fuperftition accounts for all the unreafonable actions of
men. That alone could deprive a nation of its liberty, which had little elfe to lofe.

B O O K
XVI.

Moft of the accounts affirm, upon the uncertain
faith of fome tradition, that the Natchez occupied for
a long time the eaftern coaft of the Miffiffippi, from
the river Yberville to the Ohio; that is to fay, a fpace
of four hundred leagues. In that cafe they muft have
formed the moft flourifhing nation of North America.
It may be fufpected, that the yoke under which they
were kept by an oppreffive and arbitrary government
difgufted them of their native country. They muft
have difperfed themfelves: and this opinion feems to
be in fome meafure confirmed by the circumftance of
our finding various traces of their worfhip at great diftances in thefe regions. It is certain, that, when the
French appeared in Louifiana,this people confifted of
no more than two thoufand warriors, and formed only
a few towns, fituated at a confiderable diftance from
each other, but all of them near the Miffiffippi.

This want of population did not prevent the country of the Natchez from being excellent. The climate is wholefome and temperate; the foil fufceptible
of rich and varied cultures; the territory fufficiently
elevated to preclude all fears from the inundations of
the river. This country is generally open, extenfive,
well-watered, and covered with pleafant hillocks, agreeable meadows, and delicious woods, as far as the Apalachian mountains. Accordingly, the firft Frenchmen
who came there judged, that, notwithftanding its diftance from the fea, this would become in time the
centre of the colony. This opinion drew numbers of
them to this fpot. They were favourably received by
the favages, and affifted in the fettlement of the plantations which they wanted to eftablifh. Exchanges
that were reciprocally ufeful laid the foundation of a
friendfhip, apparently fincere, between the two nations. It might have become permanent, had not the

B O O K ties of it been daily weakened by the avidity of the
XVI. Europeans. Thefe foreigners had at firft demanded
the productions of the country only as honeft merchants, but afterwards imperioufly dictated the conditions of the trade, and at length feized upon what they
were tired of paying for, even at a low price. Their
audacity increafed to fuch a degree, as to expel the
natives from the fields they had tilled themfelves.

This tyranny was atrocious. In vain did the Natchez endeavour to put a ftop to it by the moft humiliating fupplications. Driven to defpair, they endeavoured to engage in their refentment all the eaftern
nations, whofe difpofitions they were acquainted with;
and towards the latter end of the year 1729, they fucceeded in forming an almoft univerfal league, the purport of which was, to exterminate in one day the whole
race of their oppreffors. This negotiation was carried
on with fuch fuccefs, as not to be difcovered either by
the favages who were friends to the French, or by the
French themfelves. Nothing but fome cafually fortunate event could prevent the fuccefs of the plot; and
this event took place.

According to the accounts of the times, the Natchez fent to the confpiring nations, who were not better acquainted with the art of writing than themfelves,
fome parcels, confifting of an equal number of bits of
wood. That there might be no miftake made refpecting the time when the common hatred was to break
out, it was agreed, that one of thefe bits of wood fhould
be burnt every day in each town, and the laft was to
be the fignal for the bloody fcene that was to be exhibited. It happened that the wife or the mother of
the great chief was informed of the plot by a fon fhe
had by a Frenchman. She feveral times warned the
officer of that nation, who commanded in the neighbourhood, of the circumftance. The indifference, or
the contempt that was fhown for her advice, did not
ftifle in her heart the affection fhe had for thefe foreigners. Her rank entitled her to enter the temple of
the Sun at any hour fhe chofe. This prerogative put

it in her power to carry off fucceffively the bits of BOOK
wood which had been depofited in it; and fhe deter- XVI.
mined to do it, in order to difturb the calculations of
the confpirators, at the hazard of haftening, fince it
was neceffary, the deftruction of the Frenchmen fhe
was fond of, in order to infure the fafety of the reft
who were unknown to her. Every thing happened as
fhe expected. At the fignal agreed upon, the Natchez
fell unawares upon the enemy, not doubting but all
their allies were at the fame time engaged in the fame
bufinefs; but as there had been no treafon anywhere
elfe, every thing remained quiet, as it muft neceffarily
have done.

This account appears very fabulous; but it is very
certain, that the period agreed upon between the members of the confederacy to deliver Louifiana from a foreign yoke was foreftalled by the Natchez. They were,
perhaps, not able to contain their hatred any longer.
They were, perhaps, feduced by meeting with unexpected facility in the execution of their defign. Perhaps they were properly or improperly apprehenfive
that their intentions began to be fufpected. It is a certain fact, however, that of two hundred and twenty-
two French, who were then in this fettlement, two
hundred were maffacred; that the women who were
pregnant, or who had young children, did not fhare a
more fortunate deftiny; and that the reft, who remained prifoners, were expofed to the brutality of the murderers of their fons and of their hufbands.

The whole colony thought themfelves loft upon the
firft news of this event. They had nothing to oppofe
to a number of enemies threatening them on all fides,
except a few half-rotten pallifades, and a few vagabonds badly armed and ill difciplined. Perrier, in
whom the authority was vefted, had not a better opinion of the fituation of affairs. However, he fhowed
a firm countenance; and this boldnefs ferved him inftead of forces. The favages thought him not only
able to defend himfelf, but alfo to attack them. In
order to difpel the fufpicions that might have been

BOOK
XVI

conceived againft them, or in hopes of obtaining a pardon, feveral of thefe nations joined their warriors to
his, in order to affift in his revenge.

Other troops were wanting, befide ill-affected allies
or foldiers, forced into the fervice, to have infured fuccefs. This militia marched towards the country of
the Natchez, with a degree of flownefs which afforded
no good omen ; and they attacked the forts with that
indifference from which no good effect could be expected. Fortunately, the befieged offered to releafe
all the prifoners they had in their poffeffion, if the
troops would withdraw ; and this propofal was acced-
ed to with extreme joy.

But Perrier, having received fome reinforcements
from Europe, recommenced hoftilities, in the beginning of the year 1731. The profpect of this new danger fpread diffenfions among the Natchez, and this
mifunderftanding brought on the ruin of the whole
nation. A few feeble corps of thefe favages were put
to the fword, and a great number were fent flaves to
St. Domingo. Thofe who efcaped flavery or death
took refuge among the Chickafaws.

Thefe were the moft intrepid people of thofe regions : their intimate connections with the Englifh
were well known, and their favourite virtue was hofpitality. All thefe reafons prevented the French at
firft from requiring them to deliver up the Natchez, to
whom they had afforded refuge. But Bienville, who
fucceeded Perrier, thought himfelf authorifed to demand the ceffion of them. The Chickafaws, with courage and indignation, refufed to comply. Both fides
took up arms in 1736. The French were defeated in
the open field, and driven back with lofs under the
pallifades of their enemy. They tried their fortune
again four years after, encouraged by fome fuccours
they had received from Canada. They were upon the
point of being defeated a fecond time, when fome fortunate incident brought on a reconciliation with thefe
favages. Since that period, the tranquillity of Louifiana hath never been difturbed. Let us now fee to

what degree of prosperity this long peace hath raised
the colony.

The coasts of Louisiana, which are all situated upon
the gulf of Mexico, are in general flat, and covered
with a barren sand. They are neither inhabited, nor
capable of being so. No forts have ever been erected
upon them.

Though the French must have been desirous of
drawing near to Mexico, they have formed no settlement upon the coast which lies to the west of the Mississippi. They were undoubtedly apprehensive of of-
fending the Spaniards, who would not patiently have
suffered them in this neighbourhood.

To the east of the river is situated Fort Mobile, on
the banks of a river which derives its source from the
Apalachian mountains. It served to maintain the
Chactaws, the Alimabous, and other less numerous colonies in alliance with the French, and to secure their
fur trade. The Spaniards of Pensacola drew some provisions and merchandise from this settlement.

There are a great number of outlets at the mouth
of the Mississippi, which are always varying. Many
of them are entirely dry at times. Some can only admit canoes or sloops. That towards the east, the only
one frequented at present by ships, is very tortuous,
affords only a very narrow passage, and hath no more
than eleven or twelve feet of water in the highest tides.
The small fort called La Balise, which formerly defended the mouth of the river, is no longer of any use,
since its canal hath been filled up, and since the ships
sail out of the reach of its cannon.

New Orleans, situated at the distance of thirty
leagues from the sea, is the first settlement that pre-
sents itself. This city, which was intended for a staple
to carry on all the intercourse between the mother-
country and the colony, was built upon the eastern
border of the river, round a crescent, which is accessi-
ble to all ships, and where they ride in perfect safety.
The foundations of it were laid in 1717; but it was
not till 1722 that it had made any progress, and be-

BOOK came the capital of Louiſiana. Its population never
XVI. conſiſted of more than ſixteen hundred inhabitants,
partly free men and partly ſlaves. The huts which
originally covered it have been ſucceſſively transform-
ed into convenient houſes, but built with wood upon
bricks, becauſe the ſoil was not ſufficiently firm to
ſupport heavier buildings.

The city is placed on an iſland, which is ſixty leagues
in length, and hath a moderate breadth. This iſland,
the greateſt part of which is not ſuſceptible of culture,
is formed by the ocean, by the river Miſſiſſippi, by
the lake Pontchartrain, and by the Manchac, or the
river of Yberville, a canal which the Miſſiſſippi hath
digged for itſelf, in order to pour into it the ſuperflu-
ous part of its waters, in the ſeaſon when they moſt
abound. There may be upon this territory about a
hundred plantations, upon which are found four or five
hundred white men, and four thouſand Negroes, principally employed in the culture of indigo. A few enterpriſing proprietors have endeavoured to grow ſugar
there; but ſome trifling froſts, which are fatal to this
rich production, have rendered this attempt ineffectual.
The plantations are ſeldom contiguous to each other,
but are moſtly ſeparated by ſtagnating waters and mo-
raſſes, eſpecially in the interior part of the iſland.

Oppoſite to New Orleans, and on the weſtern ſhore
of the Miſſiſſippi, were ſettled, in 1722, three hundred
Germans, the unfortunate remains of ſeveral thouſand
who had been removed from their country. Their
number hath trebled ſince that period, which is not a
very diſtant one, becauſe they have always been the
moſt laborious men of the colony. Aſſiſted by about
two thouſand ſlaves, they cultivate maize for their
food, and rice and indigo for exportation. They formerly attended to the culture of cotton; but they
have abandoned it ſince it has been found too ſhort
for the European manufactures.

A little higher up, on the ſame coaſt, eight hundred
Acadians were ſituated, who had arrived in Louiſiana
immediately after the laſt peace. Their labours have

been hitherto confined to the breeding of cattle, and
to the cultivation of articles of primary neceffity. If
their means fhould increafe, they will attend to the
production of vendible commodities.

All thofe productions which enrich the lower part of
the colony, terminate at the fettlement of the Pointe
Coupée, formed at the diftance of forty-five leagues
from New Orleans. It furnifhes, moreover, the greateft part of the tobacco that is confumed in the country, and a great deal of wood for foreign trade. Thefe
labours employ five or fix hundred white men, and
twelve hundred Negroes.

Throughout the whole extent of the lands which
are cultivated in thefe feveral fettlements belonging to
Lower Louifiana, there runs a caufeway deftined to
fecure it from the inundations of the river. Large and
deep ditches, which furround every field, afford an iffue to the waters which would either have penetrated
or rifen above the dike. This foil is entirely muddy;
and when it is to be cultivated, the large reeds which
cover it are cut at the bottom. As foon as they are
dry, they are fet on fire. Then, however lightly the
earth be turned up, it becomes fertile in all productions requiring a damp foil. Corn does not thrive upon it; for the blades grow, but contain no feed. Moft
of the fruit trees fucceed no better: they grow up very faft, and are in bloffom twice in a year; but the
fruit, which is attacked by the worms, dries, and generally falls off before it is ripe. The peach, the orange,
and the fig-tree, are the only ones, the fertility of which
cannot be too much extolled.

The nature of the country is very different in Upper Louifiana. To the eaft of the Miffiffippi, this diftrict begins a little above the river of Yberville. Its
territory, which hath been anciently formed, is fufficiently raifed to be free from inundations, and hath
only a proper degree of moifture; it therefore requires
lefs care, and promifes a greater variety of productions.
This was the opinion of the firft Frenchmen who appeared in thefe countries. They fettled in the diftrict

B. O O K of the Natchez, and after having attempted feveral
   X V I. cultures, which were all fuccefsful, confined themfelves
to that of tobacco, which foon acquired in the mother-
country the reputation it deferved. Government expected foon to receive from this fettlement a fufficient
quantity for the fupply of the whole monarchy, when
the tyranny of its agents occafioned its ruin. Since
this fatal period, this inexhauftible foil hath remained
uncultivated, till Great Britain, having acquired the
property of it by treaties, fhall have conveyed there a
population fufficient to fertilize it.

A little higher up, but on the weftern fhore, the
Red River empties itfelf into the Miffiffippi. It is at
thirty leagues diftance from the mouth of it, and upon
the territory of the Natchitoches, that the French on
their arrival in Louifiana erected a few pallifades. The
object of this poft was to draw from New Mexico the
fheep and horned cattle, which a rifing colony is always in want of; and it was alfo to open a fmuggling
trade with the Spanifh fort of the Adages, which is
only feven leagues diftant. It is long. fince the multiplication of the cattle in thofe fields, to which it was
neceffary to accuftom them, hath put an end to the
firft of thefe connections; and it was ftill earlier underftood, that the latter, with one of the pooreft fettlements in the world, could never have any real utility. Accordingly, the territory of the Natchitoches
was foon forfaken by thofe whom the hopes of making a great fortune had drawn there. Upon this diftrict there are only now to be feen the defcendants of
a few foldiers, who have fettled there at the end of the
time they were engaged for in the fervice. Their
number does not exceed two hundred. They live
upon maize, or upon the vegetables which they cultivate, and fell the fuperfluous part of their productions
to their indolent neighbours. The money they receive from this feeble garrifon enables them to pay for
the liquors and the clothing which they are obliged to
get from elfewhere.

The fettlement formed among the Akanfas is ftill

more wretched. It would infallibly have become very B O O K
flourifhing, if the troops, the arms, the bondfmen, the XVI.
provifions, and the merchandife, which Law had fent
there on his own private account, had not been firft
confifcated after the difgrace of that enterprifing man.
Since that time fome few Canadians only have fettled
upon this excellent foil, who have taken to themfelves
wives among the women of the country. From thefe
connections hath foon arifen an almoft favage race,
confifting only of a few families, living feparate from
each other, and fcarce attending to any other employment except that of the chafe.

To go from the Akanfas to the Illinois country, it
is neceffary to travel three hundred leagues; for the
nations in America are not contiguous to each other,
as they are in Europe, and are therefore the more independent. They have no chiefs connected among
themfelves, alternately to feize upon, or to facrifice
them, and to render them fo unhappy, that they fhall
have nothing to gain or to lofe by a change of country and of mafter. The Illinois, fituated in the moft
northern part of Louifiana, were continually beaten,
and always upon the point of being deftroyed by the
Iroquois, or by other warlike nations. They ftood in
need of a defender; and the French took that part
upon themfelves, by occupying a portion of their territory, at the mouth of their river, and upon the more
pleafant and more fruitful banks of the Miffiffippi.
Under this protection, the Illinois have avoided the
deftiny of moft of the nations in the New World, of
whom there fcarce remains any remembrance. Neverthelefs, their number hath diminifhed, in proportion as that of their protectors hath increafed. Thefe
foreigners have gradually formed a population of two
thoufand three hundred and fourfcore free perfons,
and of eight hundred flaves, diftributed in fix villages,
five of which are fituated upon the eaftern border of
the river.

Unfortunately, moft of thefe people have entertained a paffion for running about the woods to buy up

the peltries, or have indulged themfelves with remaining in their warehoufes, waiting till the favages brought
them the produce of their chafe. They would have
worked more ufefully for themfelves, for the colony,
and for France, had they digged the excellent foil upon which chance had placed them ; and had they required of it the feveral kinds of corn produced in the
Old World, which Louifiana hath been obliged to
draw from Europe, or from North America. But
how much hath the fettlement formed by the French
in the country of the Illinois, and how much have
their other fettlements, fallen fhort of this profperity ?

Never did the colony, in its greateft fplendour, rec-
kon more than feven thoufand Negroes, exclufive of
the troops, the number of which varied from three
hundred to two thoufand men. This feeble population was fcattered along the borders of the Miffiffippi,
throughout a fpace of five hundred leagues ; and was
defended by a few fmall forts, fituated at an immenfe
diftance from each other. Neverthelefs, thefe men
were not defcended from that fcum of Europe which
France had, as it were, vomited forth into the New
World at the time of Law's fyftem. All thofe miferable men had perifhed without leaving any iffue.
The colonifts were robuft men, arrived from Canada,
or difbanded foldiers, who had fenfibly preferred the
labours of agriculture to a life of idlenefs, in which
prejudice and pride had confirmed them. Every inhabitant received from government a fuitable piece of
ground, with feed to fow it, a gun, an ax, a mattock,
a cow and a calf, a cock and fix hens, with a plentiful fupply of wholefome provifions for three years.
Some officers, and fome rich men, had formed confiderable plantations, which occupied eight thoufand
flaves.

This colony fent to France fourfcore thoufand weight
of indigo, fome hides, and much peltry. It fent to the
iflands tallow, fmoked meats, pulfe, rice, maize, pitch,
tar, and timber for fhips and for houfe-building. Thefe
feveral articles collected, might be worth 2,000,000 of

livres [83,333l. 6s. 8d.]. This fum was paid for in European merchandife, and in the productions of the Eaft Indies. The colony even received more than it gave, and derived this fingular advantage from the expences of fovereignty.

The public expences were always too confiderable at Louifiana. They often exceeded, even in times of full peace, the whole produce of the fettlement. Perhaps the agents of government would have been more circumfpect had the bufinefs been tranfacted with money. The unfortunate facility of paying every thing with bills, which were not to be difcharged till their arrival in the mother-country, rendered them generally lavifh, and fome of them were even difhoneft. For their own private emoluments, they ordered the conftruction of forts, which were of no kind of ufe, and which coft twenty times more than they ought to have done. They multiplied, without reafon, as without meafure, the annual prefents which the court of Verfailles were accuftomed to fend to the favage tribes.

The exports and imports of Louifiana were not carried on upon fhips belonging to itfelf; for it had never thought of having one fingle veffel. Sometimes it received fome feeble embarkations from the ports of France, and fometimes large boats from the fugar iflands. But moft frequently, fhips difpatched from the mother-country to St. Domingo, left part of their cargo in this rich fettlement; and after having fold the reft of it in the Miffiffippi, ufed to load themfelves, on their return to it, with every thing that might be wanted at St. Domingo, or which might be fuitable to the mother-country.

Louifiana, which nature feemed to invite to a great degree of profperity, would undoubtedly have attained to it, if government had had the prudence to attend to the wifhes of the French Proteftants, who had taken refuge in the colonies fettled by the Englifh to the north of the New World.

Under the moft brilliant reign, and at the moft fortunate period of that reign, three hundred thoufand

France might have derived great advantages from Louifiana. Faults that have impeded this fuccefs.

B O O K Calvinist families were enjoying peaceably in France
XVI. the rights of men and of citizens; rights which had
been confirmed to them by the famous edict, which
had quieted so many troubles, and put an end to so
many calamities, the edict of Nantes. Louis XIV.
the terror of his neighbours, and the idol of his subjects, had neither enemies to fear without, nor rebels
within his provinces. The Protestants, quiet from
motives of duty as well as interest, thought of nothing
but serving the state, and of contributing towards its
power and its glory. They were placed at the head
of several new manufactures; and being dispersed in
the maritime countries, a navy, which was formidable
in its infancy, derived its principal strength from them.
Where an easy and decent competency prevails, the
fruit of labour and of industry, there we generally
meet with good morals. The Protestants, in particular, were distinguished by them, because they were the
least numerous and most laborious of the subjects, and
because they had to justify their faith by their virtues.

Every thing, I say again, was quiet in the interior
part of the kingdom; but sacerdotal pride and phari-
saical ambition were not so. The clergy of France,
Rome, and the Jesuits, were continually importuning
the throne with their scandalous remonstrances. It
was represented, that Frenchmen who did not humble
themselves before a confessor; who saw nothing but
bread in the consecrated host; who never said mass;
who never brought any offering to the altar; who
married their cousins without purchasing dispensa-
tions; it was represented, that such Frenchmen could
not love their country nor their sovereign. It was
said, that they were in fact nothing more than traitors
and hypocrites; who, in order to shake off the yoke
of obedience, waited only for a favourable circumstance, which sooner or later they would find some
opportunity to excite.

When imposture shall awaken the apprehensions of
the sovereign, with respect to the fidelity of his subjects, it is difficult to prevent its being listened to with

attention. Neverthelefs, we fhall venture to afk, whe- ther Louis XIV. was excufable, when he feemed not to know how much his Proteftant fubjects were ufeful to him? We fhall venture to afk, if he could ferioufly believe that they would become more fo when they were turned Catholics ; and if the toleration of a ma- fter, fo powerful and fo abfolute, could ever bring on any of thofe difagreeable confequences with which he was inceffantly threatened? The Proteftants had been feditious, it is true; but they had been perfecuted, and had been made, alternately with Catholics, the fport of the turbulent ambition of the great. The idea of fo much blood fpilt in the preceding reigns, fhould it not have made him apprehenfive of fhedding more? Paft events fhould have taught him, that a king hath no power over religious opinions; that the confciences of men are not to be compelled; that for- tune, life, and dignities, are nothing in comparifon of eternal punifhments; and that if it be right in a coun- try, where only one form of worfhip is obferved, to forbid accefs to any foreign fuperftition, yet power will never exclude that which is already eftablifhed there; Louis XIV. experienced this. You monarchs, who are intrufted with the care of governing men, make it your bufinefs to be acquainted with them. Study their paffions, in order that you may govern them by their paffions. Know that a prince who fays to his fubjects, your religion difpleafes me, it is my pleafure that you fhould renounce it, has nothing to do but to raife the gallows, and to prepare the wheel, and let his executioners hold themfelves in readinefs.

Louis XIV. intrufted with the execution of his pro- ject, which was impious in religion and abfurd in po- licy, two minifters impetuous as himfelf; two men who hated the Proteftants, becaufe Colbert had em- ployed them. One of thefe was Le Tellier, a harfh and fanatic man; the other Louvois, a cruel and fan- guinary minifter; he who gave it as his opinion, that all Holland fhould be funk under water, and who af- terwards caufed the Palatinate to be reduced to afhes.

B O O K Immediately, on the flighteft pretence, the churches
XVI. of the Calvinifts are fhut up ; they themfelves are excluded from every office in the public revenue ; they
cannot be admitted into any corporation ; their clergy are fubjected to taxation ; their mayors are deprived of nobility ; the legacies left to their confifto-
ries are applied to hofpitals ; the officers of the king's
houfehold, the fecretaries of the king, the notaries, the
counfellors, and the attorneys, have orders to quit their
functions, or to renounce their faith. Thefe acts of
violence are fucceeded by abfurdity. A declaration
of council, in the year 1681, authorifes children of feven years of age to renounce their faith. Children of
feven years of age who have a faith, who have a civil
will, and who enter into public engagements ! Thus
it is that the fovereign and the prieft can equally make
children of men, and men of children !

But it became neceffary to withdraw children from
the authority of their parents ; for which purpofe force
was employed. Soldiers were appointed to carry them
off from their paternal dwelling, and took poffeffion of
it in their ftead. The cry of defolation refounded
from one end of the kingdom to the other. The people began to think of removing at a diftance from the
oppreffor. Whole families deferted ; their houfes were
converted into guard-rooms. The powers that were
the rivals of France offered them an afylum. Amfterdam was enlarged with a multitude of houfes prepared for their reception. The provinces were depopulated. The government beheld thefe emigrations,
and were difturbed. The punifhment of the gallies
was decreed againft the fugitive artifan and the failor.
All the paffages were clofed. Nothing was forgotten
that could poffibly enhance the merit of the facrifice ;
and more than five hundred thoufand ufeful citizens
made their efcape, at the rifk of receiving in their way
the crown of martyrdom.

It was in 1685, in the midft of thefe horrors, that
the fatal revocation of the edict of Nantes appeared.
The clergy who were fteady in their opinions were

ordered to quit the kingdom within a fortnight, on B O O K pain of death. Children were torn from the arms of ̲ ̲ ̲XVI.̲ their fathers and mothers. And thefe horrible acts were authorifed by a fet of deliberate men ; by an af-fembly of grave perfons ; by a fupreme court ! They were fathers, and yet they did not fhudder while they gave orders for the infringement of the moft facred laws of nature !

In the meanwhile, the minds of men were inflam-ed. The Poteftants affembled ; they were attacked ; they defended themfelves, and dragoons were fent a-gainft them. And now the hamlets, the villages, the fields, the highways, and the gates of the cities, were planted with fcaffolds, and drenched with blood. The intendants of the provinces vied with each other in cruelty. Some minifters, venturing to preach and to write, were feized upon, and put to death. The pri-fons were foon incapable of holding the number of the perfecuted ; and it was the will of a fingle man that could make fo many perfons unfortunate ! At his word, all the civil and moral ties were broken ! At his word, a thoufand citizens, revered for their virtues, their dignities, and their talents, were devoted to death and to infamy ! O ye people ! ye herd of weak and mean men !

And thou, blind tyrant ! becaufe thy priefts have not the art of perfuafion to make their arguments vic-torious ; becaufe they cannot efface from the minds of thofe innocent men the profound traces which edu-cation had engraved in them ; becaufe thefe men will neither be bafe, nor hypocritical, nor infamous ; be-caufe they choofe rather to obey their God than to obey thee, muft thou deprive them of their property, put chains upon them, burn them, hang them up, and drag their carcafes upon a hurdle ? When thou with-draweft thy protection from them, becaufe they do not think as thou doft, why fhould they not withdraw their obedience from thee, becaufe thou thinkeft dif-ferently from them ? It is thou who doft break the compact.

BOOK   The churches of the Proteftants were deftroyed.
XVI.   Their minifters were either put to death, or they fled.
But this did not put a ftop to the defertion of the perfecuted perfons.   What fteps were therefore to be taken to prevent it? It was imagined that flight would
be lefs frequent when the gates were laid open.   This
proved to be a miftake; and after the paffages had
been opened, they were fhut again a fecond time with
as little fuccefs as at firft.

The dreadful wound which fanaticifm then inflicted
on the nation hath continued bleeding down to our
days, and will ftill remain open.   Armies deftroyed
are recruited ; provinces that are invaded are recovered : but the emigration of ufeful men, who convey to
foreign nations their induftry and their talents, and
raife them at once to a level with the nation which
they have quitted, is an evil which cannot be remedied.   The citizen of the world, whofe comprehenfive
mind embraces the intereft of all the human race, will
perhaps be comforted on this occafion ; but the true
patriot will never ceafe to deplore the event.

This patriot is the man who at this inftant addreffes
himfelf to kings in the following terms : " Rulers of
" the world, when a man, under the name of prieft,
" fhall contrive to connect his interefts with the pre-
" tended interefts of a God ; when his fufpicious hat-
" red can induce him to make ufe of the name of that
" God, whom he will not fail to reprefent as jealous
" and cruel, in order to excite perfecution againft the
" man who fhall not think as he does; or, to fpeak
" with greater precifion, who fhall not think as the
" prieft would have him think ; woe to you and to
" your fubjects, if you fhould liften to fuch infinua-
" tions !"

In the meanwhile, the French Proteftants, fcattered over the feveral parts of the globe, were every
where turning their forrowful looks towards their former country.   Thofe who had found an afylum in the
northern part of America, defpairing ever to be able
to revifit their former habitations, wifhed at leaft to

be connected with the amiable nation from which ty-BOOK
ranny had feparated them. They offered to convey XVI.
their induftry and their capitals to Louifiana, provided they might be allowed to follow their mode of
worfhip there. Unfortunately for the ftate, the fuperftition of Louis XIV. and the weaknefs of the regent,
occafioned thefe propofals to be rejected.

Neverthelefs, what analogy is there between the
tenets of religion and the fpeculations of the miniftry? Not more, it fhould feem, than there is between the prefcriptions of the phyfician and the doctrine he profeffes. Hath the patient ever thought of
afking his phyfician whether he went to church or to
meeting? whether he believed in God or not? Rulers
of the earth, he who caufes the fun indifcriminately
to fhine on orthodox or on heretic regions; he who
fuffers his fertile dew to fall equally on their fields;
doth he not declare to you, with fufficient evidence
and energy, how much it ought to be indifferent to
you by what men they are peopled, and by what
hands they are cultivated? It is yours to protect them;
it is yours to animate their labours; it is yours to encourage their induftry and their virtues. It is the
part of God to fearch into their hearts, and to judge
them. Doth he render the mothers of the Calvinifts
barren? Or doth he ftifle the child in the womb of the
Lutheran women when they are pregnant? How therefore, do ye dare to condemn to exile, to death, or to
mifery worfe than thefe, that being, whom the Sovereign of all Sovereigns, your Father and theirs, permits to live and to profper? Becaufe mafs hath not
been performed, or vefpers fung at Louifiana, have the
productions of the foil been lefs plentiful, lefs valuable, and lefs ufeful? Had the country been peopled
with orthodox perfons, and that fome reafon of ftate
had induced you to attempt the conqueft of it, you
would have put them all to the fword without hefitation; and yet you fcruple to intruft the culture of
them to heretics. With what ftrange madnefs are
you affected? A conformity of worfhip puts no ftop

BOOK to your ferociousnefs, and a difference of worship ex-
XVI. cites it.   Is it then confiftent with the dignity of the
chief of the ftate, to regulate his conduct by the fanatic fpirit and narrow views of the director of a religious feminary ? Is it confiftent with his wifdom, to
admit among the number of his fubjects none but the
flaves of his priefts ? I fhould not be in the leaft furprifed, after having determined an old pufillanimous
monarch humbled by a long feries of calamities, to
complete them all by the revocation of a falutary
edict, that the fuperftitious and hypocritical men who
furrounded him fhould have led him on, from one
circumftance to another, to reject the advantageous
propofals of the religious people in the New World;
but that confiderations, which may be called mona-
ftic, fhould have had the fame influence over the enlightened prince who held the reins of the empire after
the old monarch, and who certainly was never accufed
of bigotry, is a circumftance which I cannot explain.

Independently of this fatal fyftem, Louifiana would
not probably have languifhed for fo long a time, had
it not been for an original error adopted, of granting
lands indifcriminately to every perfon who applied for
them, and in the manner in which he defired them.
Immenfe deferts would not then have feparated the
colonifts from each other.   Being brought near to a
common centre, they would have affifted each other,
and would have enjoyed all the advantages of a well
regulated fociety.   As population increafed, the lands
would have been cleared to a greater extent.   Inftead
of a few hordes of favages, we fhould have feen a
rifing colony, which might in time have become a
powerful nation, and procured infinite advantages to
France.

The French, who annually purchafe from eighteen
to twenty millions weight of tobacco, might have encouraged the cultivation of it in Louifiana, and might
have drawn from that fettlement a fufficient quantity
of it for their own confumption.   Such were the hopes
that government entertained, when they ordered all

the tobacco plants in France to be rooted up. Convinced that the lands in their provinces were adapted
to more important and richer cultures, they thought
it would be advantageous both to the mother-country
and the colony, to fecure to this infant fettlement a
market for that production which required the leaft
capital, the leaft time and experience. When Law,
the projector of this undertaking, fell into difcredit,
this fcheme, the advantages of which were fo evident,
was forgotten, and fhared the fame fate as thofe which
were merely the offspring of a difordered imagination.
The blindnefs of the miniftry was kept up by the private interefts of the agents of the treafury ; and this
is not one of the leaft mifchiefs the finance has done
to the monarchy.

The wealth which tobacco would have procured to
the colony, would have made it fenfible of the advantages that might be derived from the fpacious and
beautiful meadows with which that country abounds.
They would foon have been covered with numerous
herds, whofe hides would have prevented the mother-
country from purchafing any from other nations, and
whofe flefh, when prepared and falted, would have
been difpofed of in the iflands, inftead of foreign beef.
Horfes and mules, multiplying in the fame proportion, would have freed the French colonies from the
dependence they have always had upon the Englifh
and Spaniards for this neceffary article.

As foon as the colonifts had begun to exert themfelves, they would have proceeded from one branch
of induftry to another. They could not poffibly avoid
building fhips ; for the country was covered with
wood fit for the hull, and the fir-trees, that grew in
great plenty along the coaft, would have afforded mafts
and tar. There was no want of oak for the planks,
and if there had been, it might have been fupplied
by cyprefs, which is lefs apt to fplit, bend, or break,
and the additional thicknefs of which might have
compenfated for its want of ftrength and hardnefs.
They might eafily have grown hemp for the fails and

BOOK rigging. Nothing, perhaps, need have been import-
XVI. ed but iron ; and it is even more than probable that
there are iron mines in Louifiana.

The forefts being thus cleared without any expence,
and even with advantage, would have left the foil fit
for the culture of corn and indigo. The production of
filk might even have been undertaken with fuccefs, when
once the colony had been fufficiently populous to attend to an employment, which the mildnefs of the
climate, the number of mulberry trees, and fome fuccefsful trials, had conftantly invited them to. In a
word, what might not have expected from a country,
where the air is temperate, and the foil even, frefh,
and fertile ; and which, properly fpeaking, had never
been inhabited, but traverfed carelefsly by vagabonds
equally deftitute of fkill and conduct ?

Had Louifiana attained to that degree of perfection
it was capable of, its harbour would foon have been
made more eafy of accefs. This might perhaps have
been effected, by ftopping up all the fmall paffes with
the floating trees waihed down by the waters ; and
by collecting the whole force of the ftream in one
fingle channel. If the foftnefs of the foil, the rapidity of the river, or the ebbing of the fea, had oppofed
infurmountable obftacles to this project, genius might
have found fome refources againft them. Every art,
and every ufeful improvement, would have fucceffively appeared to form a flourifhing and vigorous colony in that fpacious plain of America.

This profpect, which had never been feen but at a
diftance, feemed to be drawing near at the laft peace.
The inhabitants, to whom the treafury owed feven
millions of livres [291,666l. 13s. 4d.], moftly acquired by criminal manœuvres, defpairing of ever obtaining the payment of this difhoneft debt, or being only
able to flatter themfelves that they fhould obtain it
at a diftant period, and in part only, turned their attention to fome important cultures with fuccefs. Their
trade was increafed with part of the peltry trade, which
had formerly belonged to Canada. The French iflands,

the wants of which were continually increasing, while their resources were diminishing, required of them more wood, and more articles of subsistence. The fraudulent connections with Mexico, which the war had interrupted, were renewed. The traders of the mother country, excluded from some of the markets they had frequented, failed towards the Missisippi, the borders of which, too long neglected, were at length going to be inhabited. Already had two hundred Acadian families fixed there; and the unfortunate remains of that nation, dispersed among the English settlements, were preparing to follow them. The same dispositions were observed in several colonists of St. Vincent's and Granada, dissatisfied with their new masters. Twelve or fifteen hundred Canadians had already begun their march to Louisiana, and were to be followed by many more. There are even strong reasons to think, that several Catholics were preparing to quit the British possessions, in order to go into this spacious and beautiful country.

Such was the state of things, when the court of Versailles announced to the inhabitants of Louisiana, on the 21st of April 1764, that by a secret treaty made the 3d of November 1762, the property of this island had been given up to the court of Madrid. The languid state of the colony, the obstacles which prevented its improvement, the impossibility of puting it in a situation to resist the whole force of the enemy united upon the frontier, these considerations must easily have determined the French ministry to this cession, apparently so considerable. But what motive could induce Spain to accept it? Would it not have been better for them to sacrifice Florida without any indemnification, for the restoration of public tranquillity, than to receive in exchange a possession which it was impossible for them to defend? If it were a barrier against the enterprises which an ambitious, active, and powerful nation might form against Mexico, was it not for the interest of Spain that a faithful ally should sustain the first shock, which would warn them

The French ministry cede Louisiana to Spain. Had they a right to do it?

B O O K of the ftorm, and might perhaps give them time to dif-
XVI.   fipate it?

But in whatever manner this event may be confidered in a political view, will it not be looked upon as an
offence againft morality, thus to have fold or given
away the members of the community to a foreign
power? For what right has a prince to difpofe of his
fubjects without their confent?

What becomes of the rights of the people, if all is
due from the nation to the prince, and nothing from
the prince to the nation? Are there then no rights
but thofe of princes? Thefe pretend to derive their
power from God alone. This maxim, which is in-
vented by the clergy, only with a defign of raifing
kings above the people, that they themfelves may
command even kings in the name of the Deity, is no
more than an iron chain, to bind a whole nation under the power of one man. It is no longer a mutual
tie of love and virtue, of intereft and fidelity, that
gives to one family the rule in the midft of a fociety.

But why fhould the fovereign authority wifh to conceal its being derived from men? Kings are fufficiently informed by nature, experience, hiftory, and their
own confcioufnefs, that it is of the people they hold
all they poffefs, whether conquered by arms or acquired by treaty. As they receive from the people all
the marks of obedience, why fhould they refufe to accept from them all the rights of authority? Nothing
is to be apprehended from voluntary fubmiffion, nor
is any thing to be obtained by the abufe of ufurped
power. It can only be fupported by violence; and is
it poffible that a prince can be happy who commands
only by force, and is obeyed only through fear? He
cannot fit eafy upon his throne, when he cannot
reign without afferting that he holds his crown from
God alone. Every man may more truly affirm, that
he holds from God, his life, his liberty, the unalienable right of being governed only by reafon and
juftice. The welfare, then, and fecurity of the people, is the fupreme law on which all others depend.

This is, undoubtedly, the real fundamental law of all fociety. It is by this we muft interpret every particular law which muft be derived from this principle, and ferve to explain and fupport it.

If we apply this rule to the treaties of divifion and ceffion which kings make between themfelves, will it appear that they have the right of buying, felling, or exchanging their fubjects, without their confent? Shall princes then arrogate to themfelves the barbarous right of alienating or mortgaging their provinces and their fubjects as they would their effects or eftates; while the fupplies granted for the fupport of their houfe, the forefts of their domain, the jewels of their crown, are all facred unalienable effects, which we muft never have recourfe to, even in the moft preffing exigencies of the ftate?——Methinks I hear the voice of a numerous colony exclaiming from America, and addreffing the mother-country in the following terms:

" What have I done to thee, that thou fhouldft de-
" liver me up into the hands of a ftranger? Did I not
" fpring from thy loins? Have I not fown, planted,
" cultivated, and reaped for thee alone? When thy
" fhips conveyed me to thefe fhores, fo different from
" thy own happy climate, didft thou not engage for
" ever to protect me with thy fleets and armies? Have
" I not fought in fupport of thy rights, and defended
" the country thou gaveft me? After having fertilized
" it by my labour, have I not maintained it for thee
" at the expence of my blood? Thy children were
" my parents or my brethren; thy laws my boaft,
" and thy name my pride; that name which I have
" ftriven to render illuftrious among nations to whom
" it was unknown. I have procured thee friends and
" allies among the favages. I flattered myfelf with
" the thought that I might one day come in competi-
" tion with thy rivals, and be the terror of thine ene-
" mies. But thou haft forfaken me. Thou haft bound
" me without my confent, by a treaty, the very con-
" cealment of which was a treachery. Unfeeling, un-
" grateful parent, how couldft thou break, in oppofi-

B O O K " tion to the dictates of nature, the ties by which I
XVI.   " was attached to thee, even from my birth?   While
       " with inceffant and painful toil I was reftoring to
       " thee the tribute of nourifhment and fubfiftence I
       " had received from thee, I wifhed for no other com-
       " fort than that of living and dying under thy law.
       " That comfort thou haft refufed me. Thou haft torn
       " me from my family, to deliver me up to a mafter
       " whom I did not approve. Reftore my parent to
       " me ; reftore me to him whofe name I have been
       " ufed to call upon from my earlieft infancy. It is
       " in thy power to make me fubmit, againft my will,
       " to a yoke which I abhor ; but this fubmiffion will
       " only be temporary. I fhall languifh and perifh with
       " grief and weaknefs ; or if I fhould recover life and
       " vigour, it will only be to withdraw myfelf from con-
       " nections I deteft ; though I fhould even be compel-
       " led to deliver myfelf up to thy enemies."

Conduct of   This averfion which the inhabitants of Louifiana
the Spani- had to the Spanifh government, did not alter the ar-
ards at
Louifiana. rangements made between the courts of Madrid and
Verfailles. On the 28th February 1766, M. Ulloa arrived in the colony with fourfcore Spaniards. According to the ufual form, he ought to have taken poffeffion immediately on his landing. But this was not the
cafe : the orders ftill continued to be given out in the
name of the king of France ; the French magiftrates
ftill acted in that capacity, and the troops ftill continued to do the duties of the fervice under French ban-
ners ; the perfon who reprefented Lewis XV. ftill retained the command. Thefe circumftances perfuaded
the inhabitants, that Charles III. was caufing the country to be examined ; and that he would determine to
accept or reject it, according as he fhould find it to the
advantage or difadvantage of his power. This examination was made by an officer who appeared to have
no favourable opinion of the region which he had come
to reconnoitre ; and it was natural to hope that he
would put his mafter out of conceit with it.

This illufion was in general prevailing, when a law

came from Spain, to forbid Louifiana from carrying
on any trading connections with the markets where it
had hitherto fold its productions. This fatal decree
was accompanied, according to every teftimony, with
intolerable haughtinefs, with odious monopolies, and
with repeated acts of arbitrary authority; evils, which
were the more oppreffive, as they appeared to be the
work of the French commander, over whom Ulloa
had acquired fuch an afcendant, as to make him the
vile inftrument of all his caprices. Thefe accufations
were, perhaps, exaggerated. But the Spaniards fhould
not have difdained to take every ftep which might
have undeceived the prejudiced people, and foftened
their irritated minds.

This contemptuous behaviour, which was confidered as the greateft outrage, and as the utmoft ftretch of
tyranny, drove the people to defpair. An infallible
way of acquiring happinefs and tranquillity prefented
itfelf to them. They had only to go acrofs the river
to obtain it. The Englifh government folicited them
to accept an excellent territory, together with every
kind of encouragement for the culture of it, and all
the prerogatives of liberty; but they were attached to
their country by a facred and beloved tie. They chofe
rather to petition the council, that Ulloa fhould be
obliged to retire; and fince he had deferred till then
to take poffeffion, that he fhould not be allowed to do
it, till the court of Verfailles had heard the reprefentations of the colony. On the 28th October 1766,
the tribunal pronounced the decree which was required, and the Spaniards quietly reimbarked upon the
frigate which had brought them there. There was not
the leaft tumult, nor indecent act committed in New
Orleans, during the three days that this crifis lafted.
When it was at an end, the inhabitants of the city,
and thofe of Lower Louifiana, who had united their
refentments, in order to bring about the revolution,
reaffumed their labours with the comfortable hopes
that their conduct would be approved by the court of
France.

B O O K   The fuccefs did not anfwer their expectation. The
XVI.   deputies of the colony did not arrive in Europe till fix
weeks after Ulloa; and they found that the miniftry
of Verfailles were either exceedingly difpleafed with
what had paffed, or at leaft affected to be fo. Thefe
difpofitions were openly cenfured by the French nation, who confidered the colonifts of Louifiana in no
other light than as a generous fet of men, whofe only
crime was an unlimited attachment to their mother-
country. A clamour fo unanimous and fo powerful
was excited in their favour, that the government could
not decently refufe to fhow fome concern for thefe unfortunate people. This tardy compaffion was of no
effect. The court of Madrid, who had forefeen it,
had caufed M. Orelly to fet out with fpeed for the
ifland of Cuba. From thence this commander took
three thoufand men of regular troops or of militia,
which he embarked upon twenty-five tranfports; and
on the 25th of July 1769, he hoifted his flag at the
mouth of the Miffiffippi.

Upon this intelligence, the minds of all men were
incenfed with inexpreffible rage againft a mother-
country which made a free facrifice of an affectionate
colony, and againft a power which pretended to reign
over a people who rejected their inhuman yoke. Steps
were taken to prevent the landing of the troops, and
to burn the fhips which conveyed them. Nothing was
more eafy, if we may credit thofe who were well acquainted with the fituation of the place. The confequences of this bold refolution were not fo dangerous
as they might appear at firft fight. The inhabitants of
Louifiana migh hope to form an independent republic.
Should Spain and France attack them with too great
a force, they might put themfelves under the protection of England; and fhould Great Britain find itfelf
in a fituation that would not allow her to grant them
her fupport, their laft refource would have been to pafs
over to the eaftern fhore of the river, with their flaves,
their flocks, and their moveables.

Terrible events were expected, when the promifes

of the Spanish general, the supplications of Aubry, that weak French commander, whose imbecility had occasioned the loss of every thing, and the vehement speeches of an eloquent magistrate, quieted the ferment. No man impeded the progress of the small fleet which arrived before New Orleans on the 17th of August. The next day all the citizens were freed from the allegiance which they owed to their first country. Possession was taken of the colony in the name of its new master; and the following days, those of the inhabitants who consented to submit to the Castilian yoke took the oaths of allegiance.

Every thing was now completed, except revenge. Victims were required. Twelve were chosen out from among the most distinguished persons in the army, the magistracy, and trade. Six of these generous men atoned with their blood for the consideration which they enjoyed. The others, perhaps more unfortunate, were sent to languish out their lives in the dungeons of the Havannah; and this horrible tragedy was ordered by the Spanish ministry, while the French ministry showed no indignation at it!

Inhuman and cruel masters, who will be inclined to belong to you? Who will be tempted to be called your subjects? By whom will you be served, since you dispose of your colonists, and cede them without their consent, in opposition to the laws of nature, and to the rights of mankind, as you would dispose of a herd of cattle? And if they had come out against you, armed with torches in one hand, and daggers in the other; if they had burnt the ships of the Spaniards; if they had assassinated the person who was charged with the orders of the court of Madrid; what mortal would be so vile as to blame them for it? Would the French government have had a right to be offended at an insurrection, the violence of which would only have been proportionate to the attachment professed for themselves? Would not the Spanish government have received the chastisement they deserved? But the colonists remained quiet; they

BOOK
XVI.
submitted with refignation to the new yoke that was impofed upon them; they ftifled their inward murmurs, and took the oath of allegiance that was required of them. Barbarous, fanguinary, and perfidious Spaniards! they fwore to be faithful to you, and at that very inftant you were marking out from among them the firft victims of your authority. Stupid and bafe colonifts, where do you conceal yourfelves? What outrages are you fubmitting to? Your friends, your relations, your chiefs, your defenders, the objects of your affection and of your veneration, are dragging to the fcaffold, and are going to be plunged into obfcure dungeons; and you remain motionlefs! At what period then, and for what reafon, will you expofe yourfelves to death? Learn, at leaft, to know the power under whofe authority you are to live. Vile rabble, come and learn the fate that awaits you, by that of citizens who are better than yourfelves.

Thofe of the inhabitants who had been drawn to the colony by the interefts of their commercial affairs, terrified with thefe atrocious acts, carried their activity elfewhere. Defpair made feveral proprietors of rich plantations forfake them. The remainder lived in mifery and oppreffion. Thefe unfortunate people would have had no market for their productions, nor any means of procuring the common neceffaries of life, had it not been for fome clandeftine connections which they carried on with the Englifh, who trade on the Miffiffippi, one of the two fhores of which they poffefs and enrich. Their deftiny muft in time become rather lefs difagreeable, becaufe the communication between Spain and her colonies is freed from many fhackles, and becaufe the French iflands have had the liberty granted them of obtaining from that great province, upon their own fhips, wood and fubfiftence. The court of Madrid, however, hath fo many more important concerns in the New Hemifphere, that it may be foretold they will never attend ferioufly to the profperity of Louifiana.

But can the wretched fituation of thefe colonifts,

who have fuffered their fellow-citizens to be maffacred, excite any great degree of compaffion? Is not their mifery a juft punifhment, which they have deferved? Doth not their confcience, that fevere judge of all our obligations, inceffantly reproach them in the following terms: " You had honeft and virtuous magiftrates, " whofe care was employed all day in contributing to " your happinefs, and in watching over your fafety in " the night, and over your interefts during the whole " year: you had among you fellow-citizens, who lov- " ed and who fuccoured you; and moft of them were " attached to you by the moft facred ties. They were " either your fathers, your brothers, or your children; " and you have quietly fuffered them to be led to the " fcaffold, or loaded with chains. You walk with " unfeeling indifference over the ftones which they " have ftained with their blood! You bow yourfelves " down before their executioners, and obey their or- " ders! Your cowardice muft be punifhed with the " coward's fate; and the punifhment muft ftill conti- " nue, till the exertions of a noble refentment fhall " juftify you to yourfelves and to us."

Let us now fee what has been the fate of Canada, which hath likewife changed its mother country.

At the peace of Utrecht, this vaft country was in a ftate of weaknefs and mifery not to be conceived. This was owing to the French who firft came there, and who rather threw themfelves into this country than fettled in it. Moft of them had done nothing more than run about the woods; the more fenfible among them had attempted fome cultures, but without choice or plan. A piece of ground, haftily tilled and built upon, was as haftily forfaken. The expences, however, the government had laid out, together with the profits of the fur trade, afforded at intervals to the inhabitants a tolerable fubfiftence; but a feries of unfortunate wars foon deprived them of thefe advantages. In 1714, the exports from Canada did not exceed a hundred thoufand crowns [12,500l.]. This fum, added to 350,000 livres [14,583l. 6s. 8d.], which the go-

State of Canada at the peace of Utrecht.

B O O K vernment fent over every year, was all the colony had
XVI.   to depend upon, for the payment of the goods they
received from Europe. And, indeed, thefe were fo
few, that the generality were reduced to wear fkins
like the Indians. Such was the diftrefsful fituation of
the far greater part of twenty thoufand French, fuppofed to inhabit thefe immenfe regions.

Population   The happy fpirit which at that time animated the
of Canada,   feveral parts of the world roufed Canada from that
and diftri-
bution of   ftate of lethargy in which it had fo long been plunged.
its inhabi- It appears from the eftimates taken in 1753 and 1758,
tants.   which were nearly equal, that the inhabitants amounted to 91,000 fouls, exclufive of the regular troops,
whofe numbers varied according to the different exigencies of the colony.

This calculation did not include the many allies
difperfed throughout an extent of 1200 leagues in
length, and of confiderable breadth, nor the 16,000
Indians who dwelt in the centre of the French fettlements, or in their neighbourhood. None of thefe were
ever confidered as fubjects, though they lived in the
midft of a great European colony : the fmalleft clans
ftill preferved their independence. All men talk of liberty, but the favage only enjoys it. Not only the
whole nation, but every individual, is truly free. The
confcioufnefs of his independence influences all his
thoughts and actions. He would enter the palace of
an Afiatic monarch in the fame manner as he would
the cottage of a peafant, and neither be dazzled with
his fplendour, nor awed by his power. It is his own
fpecies, it is mankind, it is his equal, that he loves and
refpects; but he would hate a mafter, and deftroy him.

Part of the French colony was centered in three cities. Quebec, the capital of Canada, is 1500 leagues
diftant from France, and 120 leagues from the fea. It
is built in the form of an amphitheatre, on a peninfula,
made by the river St. Lawrence and the river St.
Charles, and commands a profpect over extenfive
fields, which ferve to enrich it, and over a very fafe
road that will admit upwards of two hundred fhips.

It is three miles in circumference. Two thirds of this circuit are defended by the water and the rocks, which are a better fecurity than the fortifications erected on the ramparts that divide the peninfula. The houfes are tolerably well built. The inhabitants were computed at about 10,000 at the beginning of the year 1759. This place was the centre of commerce, and the feat of government.

The city of the Trois Rivieres, built ten years later than Quebec, and fituated thirty leagues higher, was raifed with a view of encouraging the trade with the northern Indians. But this fettlement, though promifing at firft, never contained more than 1500 inhabitants, becaufe the fur trade was foon diverted from this market, and carried entirely to Montreal.

Montreal is an ifland, ten leagues long, and almoft four broad, formed by the river St. Lawrence, fixty leagues above Quebec. It is the moft temperate, pleafant, and fruitful fpot in all the country. A few huts thrown up there as it were by chance in 1640, were improved to a regular built town, which contained four thoufand inhabitants. At firft it lay expofed to the infults of the favages; but was afterwards enclofed with flight pallifades, and then with a wall, conftructed about fifteen feet high, with battlements. It fell to decay, when the inroads of the Iroquois obliged the French to erect forts higher up the country, to fecure the fur trade.

The other colonifts, who were not contained within the walls of thefe three cities, did not live in towns, but were fcattered along the banks of the river St. Lawrence. None were to be feen near the mouth of that river, where the foil is uneven and barren, and where no corn will ripen. The firft habitations to the fouth were built at fifty leagues, and to the north, at twenty leagues below Quebec; they were at a great diftance from each other, and their produce was but indifferent. No very fertile fields were to be found but in the neighbourhood of its capital, and they improved as one approached Montreal. There cannot be a more beautiful profpect than the rich borders of that long and broad canal. Detached woods adding beauty to the tops of the verdant mountains, meadows covered with flocks, fields crowned with ripening corn, fmall ftreams of water flowing down to the river, churches and caftles feen at intervals through the trees, exhibited a fucceffion of the moft inchanting views. This interefting fcene did not extend far beyond the river, and for the following reafon : when the French miniftry undertook to form a fettlement in Canada, they gave fome extent to thofe active or unfortunate men who were defirous of fettling there. But as the cuftom obferved at Paris, which ordains that all the defcendants of the head of a family fhall have an equal fhare in the inheritance, was introduced in the colony at the fame time, this domain was reduced to little or nothing by a number of fhares which were divided among a long feries of generations.

If the whole of the eftate had been fecured to the eldeft fon, as the public good required, the province would have taken another turn. The father, urged to economy and labour by the defire of providing for his other children, would have required more lands, covered them with buildings, flocks, and cultures; and upon thefe plantations he would have placed his numerous pofterity. The new proprietors would in their turn have followed this proper example of paternal affection ; and the whole colony would in time have been entirely peopled and cultivated.

The advantages of this policy, which had efcaped the attention of the court of Verfailles, were at length perceived by them in 1745. They forbade the further divifion of any plantation which fhould not have an acre and a half in front, and thirty or forty in depth. This regulation did not remedy the mifchiefs occafioned by two ages of ignorance ; but it put a ftop to an inconvenience, which in the end muft have deftroyed the colony.

This plan of inequality in the divifion of eftates will be confidered by the vulgar as a fyftem of inhumanity

contrary to the laws of nature; but can there be any
foundation for fuch a reproach? Can a man who hath
ended his career preferve any rights? Doth he not lofe
them all when he ceafes to breathe? When the Al-
mighty deprives him of life, doth he not deprive him
of every thing that had any relation to it? Ought his
laft will to have any influence over the generations
which fucceed him? Certainly not. As long as he
lived, he hath enjoyed with reafon the lands which
he cultivated. At his death they belong to the firft
perfon who fhall take poffeffion of them and cultivate
them. This is the law of nature. If another order
of things hath been eftablifhed throughout almoft the
whole of the globe, this is a neceffary confequence of
focial inftitutions. Their laws have derogated from
thofe of nature, to fecure tranquillity, to encourage
induftry, and to confirm liberty. The government
will have a right to act as they have done, when they
fhall think it proper for the interefts and for the common happinefs of the members of the community, and
confequently in a more or lefs favourable manner to
one individual or another. Among the feveral poffible
inftitutions refpecting the inheritance of the citizens
after their deceafe, there is one which would perhaps
meet with fome approbation. This is, that the eftates
of the deceafed fhould return to the mafs of the public funds, to be employed firft towards the relief of the
indigent, and after that, to reftore perpetually a kind
of equality between the fortunes of individuals; when
thefe two important objects had been fulfilled, the reft
fhould be appropriated to the rewarding of virtue and
the encouraging of talents.

But to return to Canada: there Nature herfelf directed the labours of the hufbandman, and taught him
that watery and fandy grounds, and thofe where the
pine, the fir-tree, and the cedar grew folitary, were
unfavourable to agriculture; but wherever he found
a foil covered with maple, oak, beech, hornbeam, and
fmall cherry trees, he might reafonably expect an a-

B O O K bundant crop of wheat, rye, maize, barley, flax, hemp,
XVI. tobacco, pulfe, and pot-herbs in great plenty, and of
all kinds.

Moft of the inhabitants had a fcore of fheep, whofe
wool was very valuable to them ; ten or a dozen milk
cows, and five or fix oxen for the plough. The cattle
were fmall, but their flefh was excellent ; and thefe
people lived much better than our country people do
in Europe.

With this kind of affluence, they could afford to
keep a number of horfes ; which were not fine, but
fit for drudgery, and able to perform journeys of a-
mazing length upon the fnow. And indeed the colonifts took fuch delight in increafing the breed of
them, that in winter time they would feed them with
the corn which they themfelves wanted fometimes at
another feafon.

Such was the fituation of the 83,000 French, difperfed or collected on the banks of the river St. Lawrence. Above the head of the river, and in what is
called the Upper-country, there were 8000 more, who
were rather addicted to hunting and trade than to hufbandry.

Their firft fettlement was Catarakui, or Fort Frontenac, built in 1671, at the entrance of the lake Ontario, to ftop the inroads of the Englifh and Iroquois.
The bay of this place ferved as a harbour for the men
of war and trading veffels belonging to this great lake,
which might with more propriety be called a fea, and
where ftorms are almoft as frequent and as dreadful as
on the ocean.

Between the lakes Ontario and Erie, each of which
meafures three hundred leagues in circumference, lies
a tract of land fourteen leagues in extent. This tract
is interfected towards the middle by the famous fall of
Niagara, which from its height, breadth, and fhape,
and from the quantity and impetuofity of its waters,
is juftly accounted the moft wonderful cataract in the
world. It was above this grand and awful waterfall

that France had erected fortifications, with a defign to prevent the Indians from carrying their furs to the rival nation.

Beyond the lake Erie is an extent of land, diftinguifhed by the name of the Streight, which exceeds all Canada for the mildnefs of the climate, the beauty and variety of the landfcapes, the richnefs of the foil, and the profufion of game and fifh. Nature has lavifhed all her bleffings to enrich this beautiful fpot. But this was not the motive that determined the French to fettle there in the beginning of the prefent century. It was the vicinity of feveral Indian nations, who could fupply them with confiderable quantities of furs; and, indeed, this trade increafed very faft.

The fuccefs of this new fettlement proved fatal to the poft of Michillimakinach, a hundred leagues further, between the lake Michigan, the lake Huron, and the lake Superior, which are all three navigable. The greateft part of the trade which ufed to be carried on there with the natives, was transferred to the Streight, where it continued.

Befide the forts already mentioned, there were fome of lefs note, built in different parts of the country, either upon rivers, or at the openings between the mountains; for the firft fentiment which intereft infpires is that of miftruft, and its firft impulfe is that of attack or defence. Each of thefe forts was provided with a garrifon, which defended the French who were fettled in the neighbourhood. There were in all eight thoufand fouls, who inhabited the upper country.

Few of the colonifts had fuch manners as it could Manners of have been wifhed they had had. Thofe whom rural the French Canadians. labours fixed in the country, allowed only a few moments to the care of their flocks, and to other indifpenfable occupations, during the winter. The reft of the time was paffed in idlenefs, at public houfes, or in running along the fnow in fledges, in imitation of the moft diftinguifhed citizens. When the return of the fpring called them out to the neceffary labours of the field, they ploughed the ground fuperficially without

B O O K ever manuring it, fowed it carelefsly, and then return-
XVI. ed to their former indolent manner of life till harveft-
time. In a country where the people were too proud
or too lazy to work by the day, every family was obliged to gather in their own crops ; and nothing was to
be feen of that fprightly joy, which on a fine fummer's
day enlivens the reapers, while they are gathering in
their rich harveft.

This amazing negligence might be owing to feveral
caufes. The exceffive cold in winter, which froze up
the rivers, totally put a ftop to the exertions of the
inhabitants. They contracted fuch a habit of idlenefs
during the continuance of the fevere weather for eight
months fucceffively, that labour appeared infupport-
able to them even in the fineft weather. The numerous feftivals prefcribed by their religion, which owed
its increafe to their eftablifhment, prevented the firft
exertion, as well as they interrupted the progrefs of
induftry. Men are ready enough to comply with that
fpecies of devotion that flatters their indolence. Laftly, a paffion for war, which had been purpofely encouraged among thefe bold and courageous men, made
them averfe from the labours of hufbandry. Their
minds were fo entirely captivated with military glory,
that they thought only of war, though they engaged
in it without pay.

The inhabitants of the cities, efpecially of the capital, fpent the winter, as well as the fummer, in a conftant fcene of diffipation. They were alike infenfible
to the beauties of nature and to he pleafures of imagination ; they had no tafte for arts or fciences, for
reading or inftruction. Their only paffion was amufe-
ment ; and perfons of all ages were fond of dancing
at affemblies. This manner of life confiderably increafed the influence of the women, who were poffeffed of every attraction, except thofe foft emotions of
the foul, which aloue conftitute the merit and the
charm of beauty. Lively, gay, and addicted to co-
quetry and gallantry, th y were more fond of infpiring than feeing the tender paffions. There appeared

in both fexes a greater degree of devotion than virtue, more religion than probity, a higher fenfe of honour than real honefty. Superftition took place of morality, which will always be the cafe, wherever men are taught to believe that ceremonies will compenfate for good works, and that crimes are expiated by prayers.

Idlenefs, prejudice, and levity, would never have gained fuch an afcendant in Canada, had the government been careful to turn the attention of the people to lafting and ufeful objects. But all the colonifts were required to pay an implicit obedience to a mere military authority. They were unacquainted with the flow and fure procefs of laws. The will of the chief, or of his delegates, was an oracle, which they were not even at liberty to interpret; an awful decree, which they were to fubmit to without examination. Delays and reprefentations were fo many crimes in the eyes of a defpotic ruler, who had ufurped a power of punifhing or abfolving merely by his word. He had the authority of difpenfing all favours and penalties, rewards and punifhments; the right of imprifoning without the fhadow of a crime, and the ftill more formidable right of enforcing a reverence for his decrees as fo many acts of juftice, though they were but the irregular fallies of his own caprice.

In early times, this unlimited power was not exercifed in matters of military difcipline and political adminiftration only, but extended even to civil jurifdiction. The governor decided abfolutely, and without appeal, all differences arifing between the colonifts. Thefe contefts were fortunately very rare, in a country where all things might almoft be faid to be in common. This dangerous authority fubfifted till 1663, at which period a tribunal was erected in the capital for the definitive trial of all caufes depending throughout the colony. The cuftom of Paris, modified in conformity to local circumftances, formed the code of their laws.

This code was not mutilated or disfigured by a mixture of revenue laws. The adminiftration of the

Marginal notes: BOOK XVI.

Form of government eftablifhed in Canada. Impediments which cultivation, induftry, and fifhing, experienced from it.

B O O K finances in Canada only required a few fines of aliena-
    XVI.   tion, a trifling contribution from the inhabitants of
Quebec and Montreal towards maintaining the fortifications, and some duties upon all goods imported
and exported. Thefe feveral articles united brought
no more than 260,200 livres [10,841l. 13s. 4d.] into
the treafury, in the moft flourifhing times of the colony.

The lands were not taxed by government, but were
burdened with other charges. At the firft eftablifhment of the colony, the king rewarded his officers, civil and military, and others of his fubjects, whom he
wifhed to remunerate or to enrich, with grants of land,
from two to fix leagues fquare. Thefe great proprietors, who were men of moderate fortunes, and unfkill-
ed in agriculture, were unable to manage fuch vaft
eftates, and were therefore under a neceffity of making over their lands to veteran foldiers, or to the colonifts, for a perpetual annuity.

Each of thefe vaffals was commonly allowed ninety
acres of land, and engaged to pay annually to the
lord of the manor one or two fols [a halfpenny or a
penny] per acre, and a meafure of corn for the entire
grant. He likewife engaged to work in the lord's
mill, and to cede to him, for the miller's fees, the
fourteenth part of the flour; he alfo engaged to pay
one twelfth for the fines of alienation, and remained
fubject to the lord's right of repurchafe.

There have been writers who have applauded, with
enthufiafm, a fyftem which appeared proper to confirm
order and fubordination. But was not this introducing
into America the image of the feudal government
which for fo long a time had occafioned the ruin of
Europe? Was it not giving fubfiftence to a great
number of idle perfons, at the expence of the only
clafs of citizens with which an infant ftate ought to be
peopled? The burden of an annuitant nobility was
ftill increafed to thefe ufeful colonifts, by the additional weight of the exactions of the clergy. This rapacious body obtained of the miniftry, in 1663, that they

fhould receive *the thirteenth part of all that the foil fhould* B O O K *produce by the labour of man, and of all that it fhould* XVI. *produce fpontaneoufly.* This intolerable vexation, in a country which was not yet well fettled, had lafted four years, when the fupreme council of Quebec took upon themfelves, in 1667, to reduce the tithes to a twenty-fixth; and an edict of 1769 confirmed this regulation, which was ftill too favourable to the priefts.

So many impediments previoufly oppofed to the progrefs of agriculture, difabled the colony from paying for the neceffaries that came from the mother-country. The French miniftry were at laft fo fully convinced of this truth, that, after having always obftinately oppofed the eftablifhment of manufactures in America, they thought it their intereft even to promote them in 1706. But thofe late encouragements had very little effect; and the united induftry of the colonifts could never produce more than a few coarfe linens, and fome very bad woollens.

The fifheries were not much more attended to than the manufactures. The only one that could become an object of exportation was that of the feal. This animal has been ranked in the clafs of fifh, though he be not dumb; he is always produced on land, and lives more on dry ground than in the water. His head is fomewhat like that of a maftiff. He has four paws, which are very fhort, efpecially the hinder ones, which ferve him rather to crawl than to walk upon. They are fhaped like fins, but the fore-feet have claws. His fkin is hard, and covered with fhort hair. He is at firft white, but turns fandy or black as he grows up. Sometimes he is of all thefe three different colours.

There are two different kinds of feals. The larger one fometimes weighs two thoufand pounds, and feems to have a fharper fnout than the others. The fmall ones, whofe fkin is commonly marbled, are active, and more dexterous in extricating themfelves out of the fnares that are laid for them. The Indians have

BOOK the art of taming them fo far as to make them follow
XVI. them.

They couple upon the rocks, and fometimes on the
ice ; and it is there alfo that the dams bring forth
their young. They commonly bear two ; and they
ufually fuckle them in the water, but more frequently
on land. When they want to teach them to fwim, it
is faid they carry them upon their backs, drop them
now and then into the water, then take them up a-
gain, and proceed in this manner till they are ftrong
enough to fwim of themfelves. Moft little birds flut-
ter about from fpray to fpray, before they venture to
fly abroad ; the eagle carries her young, to train them
up to encounter the boifterous winds ; it is not, therefore, furprifing that the feal, produced on land, fhould
ufe her little ones to live under water.

This amphibious animal is fifhed for only on the
Labrador coaft. The Canadians go to this frozen and
almoft uninhabitable coaft towards the middle of October, and remain there till the beginning of June.
They place their nets between the continent and a
few fmall iflands at a little diftance. The feals, who
commonly come in fhoals from the eaft, attempt to
pafs thofe kinds of ftraits, and are caught. When
they are conveyed to land, they remain frozen there
till the month of May. They are then thrown into
hot kettles, from whence their oil flows into another
veffel, where it cools. Seven or eight of thefe animals
yield a hogfhead of oil.

The fkin of the feal was formerly ufed for muffs,
but afterwards to cover trunks, and to make fhoes
and boots. When it is well tanned, the grain is not
unlike that of Morocco leather. If it be not quite fo
fine, it preferves, however, its colour longer.

The flefh of the feal is generally allowed to be good,
but it turns to better account when boiled down to
oil. This oil keeps clear for a long time, has no bad
fmell, and leaves no fediment. It is ufed for burning
and dreffing leather.

Five or fix fmall fhips were fitted out yearly from Canada for the feal fifhery, and one or two lefs for the Caribbee Iflands. It received from the iflands nine or ten veffels laden with rum, molaffes, coffee, and fugar; and from France about thirty fhips, the lading of which together might amount to nine thoufand tons.

In the interval between the two laft wars, which was the moft flourifhing period of the colony, the exports did not exceed 1,200,000 livres [50,000l.] in furs, 800,000 [33,333l. 6s. 8d.] in beaver, 250,000 [10,416l. 13s. 4d.] in feal oil, the fame in flour and peas, and 150,000 livres [6250l.] in wood of all kinds. Thefe feveral articles put together amounted only to 2,650,000 livres [110,416l. 13s. 4d.] a year; a fum fufficient to pay for the commodities fent from the mother-country. The government made up the deficiency.

When the French were firft in poffeffion of Canada, they had very little fpecie. The fmall quantity that was brought in from time to time by the new fettlers, did not continue in the country, becaufe the neceffitous ftate of the colony foon occafioned it to return. This was a great obftacle to the progrefs of commerce and agriculture. In 1670, the court of Verfailles coined a particular fort of money for the ufe of all the French fettlements in America, and fet a nominal value upon it, one-fourth above the current coin of the mother-country. But this expedient was not productive of the advantages that were expected, at leaft with regard to New France. They therefore contrived to fubftitute paper-currency inftead of metal, for the payment of the troops, and other expences of government. This fucceeded till the year 1713, when the engagements that had been made with the adminiftrators of the colony were not faithfully obferved. Their bills of exchange drawn upon the treafury of the mother-country were not honoured, and from that time fell into difcredit. They were at laft paid off in 1720, with the lofs of five-eighths.

This event occafioned the revival of the ufe of fpe-

B O O K cie in Canada : but this expedient lafted only two
XVI. years. The merchants found it troublefome, charge-
able, and hazardous to fend money to France, and fo
did all the colonifts who had any remittances to make ;
fo that they were the firft to folicit the re-eftablifh-
ment of paper-currency. This confifted of cards, on
which were ftamped the arms of France and Navarre,
and they were figned by the governor, the intendant,
and the comptroller. They were of twenty-four [1l.],
twelve [10s.], fix [5s.], and three livres [2s. 6d.] ; and
of thirty [1s. 3d.], fifteen [7$\frac{1}{4}$d.], and feven fols and a
half [3$\frac{3}{4}$d.]. The value of the whole number that was
made out, did not exceed a million of livres [41,666l.
13s. 4d.]. When this fum was not fufficient for the
public exigencies, the deficiency was made up by orders figned only by the intendant. This was the firft
abufe ; but one of ftill greater confequence was, that
their number was unlimited. The fmalleft were of
twenty fols [10d.], and the higheft of a hundred livres
[4l. 3s. 4d.]. Thefe different papers circulated in the
colony, and fupplied the want of fpecie till the month
of October. This was the lateft feafon for the fhips
to fail from Canada. Then all this paper-currency
was turned into bills of exchange, payable in France
by the government, which was fuppofed to have made
ufe of the value. But they were fo multiplied by the
year 1754, that the royal treafury could no longer anfwer fuch large demands, and was forced to protract
the payment. An unfortunate war that broke out
two years after, fo increafed their number, that at laft
they were prohibited. This prefently raifed the price
of all commodities to an immoderate degree ; and as,
on account of the enormous expences of the war, the
king was the chief confumer, he alone bore the lofs
arifing from the difcarded paper, and from the dearnefs of the goods. In 1759, the miniftry were obliged to ftop payment of the Canada bills, till their
origin and their real value could be traced. They
amounted to an alarming number.

The annual expences of government for Canada,

which in 1729 did not exceed 400,000 livres [16,666l.
13s. 4d.], and before 1749 never were greater than
1,700,000 [71,833l. 6s. 8d.], were immenfe after that
period. The year 1750 coft 2,100,000 [87,500l.];
the year 1751, 2,700,000 [112,500l.]; the year 1752,
4,090,000 [170,416l, 13s. 4d.]; the year 1753, 5,300,000
[220,833l. 6s. 8d.]; the year 1754, 4,450,000 [185,416l.
13s. 4d.]; the year 1755, 6,100,000 [254,166l. 13s.
4d.]; the year 1756, 11,300,000 [470,833l. 6s. 8d.];
the year 1757, 19,250,000 [802,083l. 6s. 8d.]; the
year 1758, 27,900,000 [1,162,500l.]; the year 1759,
26,000,000 [1,083,333l. 6s. 8d.]; the firft eight months
of the year 1760, 13,500,000 [562,500l.]. Of thefe
prodigious fums 80,000,000 [3,333,333l. 6s. 8d.] were
due at the peace.

This infamous debt was traced up to its origin. The
malverfations were horrid. Some perfons, who had become delinquents from the abufe of the unlimited
power which government had granted them, were degraded, banifhed, and ftripped of part of their plunder. Others, not lefs guilty, by diftributing their gold
with a lavifh hand, efcaped reftitution and infamy, and
infolently enjoyed the fortune they had acquired by
fuch criminal means. The bills of exchange were reduced to one half, and the orders to a fourth part of their
value. They were both paid in bonds bearing four
per cent. intereft, which fell into the greateft difcredit.

In the debt of eighty millions [3,333,333l. 6s. 8d.],
the Canadians were holders of thirty-four millions
[1,416,666l. 13s. 4d.] in orders, and feven millions
[291,666l. 13s. 4d.] in bills of exchange. Their paper was fubjected to the general regulation : but Great
Britain, whofe fubjects they were become, obtained
for them an indemnity of three millions [125,400l.]
in bonds, and fix hundred thoufand livres [250,000l.]
in fpecie; fo that they received fifty-five per cent.
upon their bills of exchange, and thirty-four per cent.
upon their orders.

If Canada did not deferve thefe facrifices from the
mother-country, it was the fault of the power that

B O O K
    XVI.
might have
derived
from Ca-
nada.
gave laws to it.   Nature had made this country proper for the production of all kinds of grain, which are
here of a superior quality, and liable to few accidents,
becaufe when fown in May, they are gathered before
the end of Auguft.   The wants of the American
iflands, and of part of Europe, fecure the fale of them
at an advantageous price.   Neveitheleſs, no more
wheat was ever cultivated than what was neceſſary for
the colonifts, who were even fometimes reduced to the
neceſſity of drawing their fubfiftence from foreign
markets.

    If hufbandry had been encouraged and extended,
the breed of cattle would have increaſed.   There is
fuch plenty of pafture-ground and of acorns, that the
colonies might eafily have bred oxen and hogs enough
to fupply the French iflands with beef and pork, without having recourfe to Irifh beef.   Poffibly, thefe cattle might in time have increaſed fufficiently to furnifh
the traders of the mother country.

    The fame advantages could not have been obtain-
ed from their fheep, even if the rigour of the climate had not fet an invincible obftacle to their multiplication.   Their fleece, which muft always be coarfe,
can only be ufefully employed in the colony itfelf, for
ftuffs of a more or lefs ordinary kind.

    The fame thing cannot be faid of the ginfeng.
This plant, which the Chinefe procure from the Co-
rea, or from Tartary, and which they buy at the
weight of gold, was found in 1720 by the Jefuit La-
fitau, in the forefts of Canada, where it grows very
common.   It was foon carried to Canton, where it
was much efteemed, and fold at an extravagant price.
The ginfeng, which at firft fold at Quebec for thirty
or forty fols [about 1s. 6d. on an average] a pound,
rofe to twenty-five livres [1l. 1od.].   In 1752, the
Canadians exported this plant to the value of 500,000
livres [20,833l. 6s. 8d.].   There was fuch a demand
for it, that they were induced to gather in May what
ought not to have been gathered till September, and
to dry in the oven what fhould have been dried gra-

dually in the shade. This spoilt the sale of the gin- seng of Canada, in the only country in the world where it could find a market; and the colonists were severely punished for their exceffive rapacioufnefs, by the total lofs of a branch of commerce, which, if rightly managed, might have proved a fource of opulence.

Another, and a furer plan for the encouragement of induftry, was the working of the iron mines which abound in thofe parts. Mr. Dantic hath laboured for a long time to difcover a certain method of clafling all the kinds of iron that are known. After a great number of experiments, the detail of which would be improper here, he hath found that the iron of Styria was the beft. The fecond beft is the iron of North America, of Danemara in Sweden, of Spain, of Bayonne, of Roufillon, of the country of Foix, of Berri, of Thierache, and of Sweden, the common iron of France, and laftly, that of Siberia. If this be really the cafe, what advantage might not the court of Verfailles have derived from the mine which was difcovered at the Trois Rivieres, which is exceedingly abundant, and near the furface of the earth? At firft it was only carelefsly and improperly worked; but thefe labours were increafed and improved by a blackfmith arrived from Europe in 1739. The colony made ufe of no other iron than this; fome fpecimens of it were even exported, but there the matter refted. This negligence was the more inexcufable, as at this period the refolution had been taken, after much hefitation, to form a naval fettlement in Canada.

The firft Europeans who landed on that vaft region, found it entirely covered with forefts. The principal trees were oaks of prodigious height, and pines of all fizes. Thefe woods, when felled, might have been conveyed with eafe down the river St. Lawrence, and the numberlefs rivers that fall into it. By an unaccountable fatality, all thefe treafures were overlooked or defpifed. At length the attention of the court of Verfailles was turned towards them; and fome docks were conftructed by their orders at Quebec, for build-

B O O K ing men of war : but this bufinefs was, unfortunately,
XVI. trufted to agents, who had nothing in view but their
own private intereft.

The timber fhould have been felled upon the hills,
where the cold air hardens the wood by contracting
its fibres : whereas it was conftantly taken from marfhy
grounds, and from the banks of the rivers, where the
moifture gives it a loofer and a richer texture. Inftead
of conveying it in barges, they floated it down on
rafts to the place of its deftination, where, being forgotten and left in the water, it gathered a kind of
mofs that rotted it. Inftead of being put under fheds
when it was landed, it was left expofed to the fun in
fummer, to the fnow in winter, and to the rains in
fpring and autumn. It was then conveyed into the
dock-yards, where it again fuftained the inclemency
of the feafons for two or three years. Negligence or
difhonefty enhanced the price of every thing to fuch
a degree, that fails, ropes, pitch and tar, were imported from Europe into a country, which, with a little
induftry, might have fupplied the whole kingdom of
France with all thefe materials. This bad management had brought the wood of Canada entirely into
difrepute, and effectually ruined the refources which
that country afforded for the navy.

The colony furnifhed the manufactures of the mother-country with a branch of trade that might almoft
be called an exclufive one, which was the preparation
of the beaver. This commodity at firft was fubjected
to the oppreffive reftraints of monopoly. The India
Company could not but make an ill ufe of their privilege, and really did fo. What they bought of the
Indians was chiefly paid for in Englifh fcarlet cloths,
which thofe people were very fond of wearing. But
as they could make twenty-five or thirty per cent.
more of their commodities in the Englifh fettlements
than the Company chofe to give, they carried thither
all they could conceal from the fearch of the Company's agents, and exchanged their beaver for Englifh cloth and India callico. Thus did France, by

the abuse of an inftitution which fhe was by no means
obliged to maintain, deprive herfelf of the double advantage of furnifhing materials to fome of her own
manufactures, and of fecuring a market for the produce of others. She was equally ignorant of the facility of eftablifhing a whale fifhery in Canada.

The chief fources of this fifhery are Davis's Straits
and Greenland. Fifty fhips come every year into the
former of thefe latitudes, and a hundred and fifty into the latter. The Dutch are concerned in more
than three-fourths of them. The reft are fitted out
from Bremen, Hamburgh, and England. It is computed that the whole expence of fitting out 200 fhips
of 350 tons burden, upon an average, muft amount to
10,000,000 of livres [416,666l. 13s. 4d.]. The ufual
produce of each is rated at 80,000 livres [3333l. 6s.
8d.], and confequently the whole amount of the fifhery cannot be lefs than 3,200,000 livres [1,333,333l.
6s. 8d.]. If we deduct from this the profits of the
feamen who are employed in thefe hard and dangerous voyages, very little remains for the merchants concerned in this trade.

Thefe circumftances have by degrees difgufted the
Bifcayans of a trade, in which they were the firft adventurers. Other Frenchmen have not been induced
to take it up, infomuch that the whale fifhery has been
totally abandoned by that nation, which of all others
confumed the greateft quantity of blubber, whale-bone,
and fpermaceti.

It was an eafy matter to take it up again in the
gulf of St. Lawrence, and even at the mouth of the
Saguenay, which is clofe to the excellent port of Ta-
douffac. It is even affirmed, that it hath been tried
on the firft arrival of the French in Canada, and that
it hath been interrupted for no other reafon than becaufe the profits of the fur-trade were more eafy and
more rapid. It is, however, certain, that the fifhery
in the river St. Lawrence would have been attended
with lefs danger and lefs expence, than at Davis's
Straits or Greenland. It hath ever been the fate of

B O O K this colony, that the beft fchemes with regard to it
XVI. have not been purfued with perfeverance; and that
in particular the government have never done any
thing for the encouragement of the whale fifhery,
which might have proved an excellent nurfery for
feamen, and given to France a new branch of commerce.

The fame indifference hath been carried ftill further.
The cod fifh frequent particularly the river St. Lawrence, as high up as at the diftance of fourfcore leagues
from the fea. They may be caught as they pafs over
this vaft fpace. It would, however, be advantageous
to eftablifh a fettled fifhery at the harbour of Mont
Louis, fituated at the mouth of a pleafant river, which
can receive veffels of one hundred tons burden, and
which fhelters them from every kind of danger. The
fifh is more plentiful there than any where elfe. Every
convenience required for drying the fifh.is found upon the fhores; and the neighbouring lands are very
proper for pafture-grounds or culture. Every circumftance induces us to believe that a colony would profper in that fituation. This was the opinion in 1697;
and an affociation was formed at this period to begin ·
this undertaking, by the attention of Riverin, an active and intelligent man. Numberlefs obftacles occafioned the failure of this projeⅽt, which hath been
fince refumed, but very carelefsly executed. This was
a great misfortune for Canada, which, had it been remarkable for any fuccefs of this kind, would thereby
have greatly extended its connections with Europe and
with the Weft Indies.

Every circumftance, therefore, confpired to promote the profperity of the fettlements in Canada, if
they had been affifted by the men who feemed to be
moft interefted in them. But whence could proceed
that inconceivable want of induftry, which fuffered
them to remain in the fame wretched ftate they were
in at firft?

Difficul-
ties which   It muft be confeffed, that the nature of the climate
France had prefented fome obftacles to the efforts of policy. The

river St. Lawrence is frozen up for fix months in the year. At other times it is not navigable by night, on account of thick fogs, rapid currents, fand-banks, and concealed rocks, which make it even dangerous by day-light. From Quebec to Montreal, the river is only practicable for veffels of three hundred tons burden, and even thefe are frequently impeded by terrible winds, which detain them a fortnight or three weeks in this fhort paffage. From Montreal to the Lake Ontario, traders meet with no lefs than fix water-falls, which oblige them to unload their canoes, and to convey them and their lading a confiderable way by land.

B O O K
XVI.

to overcome, in order to derive advantages from Canada.

Far from encouraging men to furmount the difficulties of nature, a mifinformed government planned none but ruinous fchemes. To gain the advantage over the Englifh in the fur-trade, they erected three and thirty forts, at a great diftance from each other. The building and victualling of them diverted the Canadians from the only labours that ought to have engroffed their attention. This error engaged them in an arduous and perilous track.

It was not without fome uneafinefs that the Indians faw the formation of thefe fettlements, which might endanger their liberty. Their fufpicions induced them to take up arms, fo that the colony was feldom free from war. Neceffity made all the Canadians foldiers. Their manly and military education rendered them hardy from their youth, and fearlefs of danger. Before they had arrived to the age of manhood, they would traverfe a vaft continent in the fummer-time in canoes, and in winter on foot, through ice and fnow. Having nothing but their gun to procure fubfiftence with, they were in continual danger of ftarving; but they were under no apprehenfion, not even of falling into the hands of the favages, who had exerted all the efforts of their imagination in inventing tortures for their enemies, far worfe than death.

The fedentary arts of peace, and the conftant labours of agriculture, could have no attraction for men

B O O K accuftomed to an active but wandering life. The
XVI. court, which form no idea of the fweets or the utility
of rural life, increafed the averfion which the Canadians had conceived for it, by beftowing all their favours and honours upon military exploits alone. The
diftinction that was chiefly lavifhed was that of nobility, which was attended with the moft fatal confequences. It not only plunged the Canadians in idlenefs, but alfo infpired them with an unconquerable
paffion for every thing that was fplendid. Profits
which ought to have been kept facred for the improvement of the lands were laid out in ornament, and a
real poverty was concealed under the trappings of deftructive luxury.

Origin of Such was the ftate of the colony in 1747, when La
the wars
between Galiffoniere was appointed governor. He was a man
the Englifh poffeffed of very extenfive knowledge, active and refo-
and the
French in lute, and of a courage the more fteady, as it was the
Canada. effect of reafon. The Englifh wanted to extend the
limits of Nova Scotia, or Acadia, as far as the fouth
fide of the river St. Lawrence. He thought this an
unjuft claim, and was determined to confine them
within the peninfula, which he apprehended to be the
boundary fettled even by treaties. Their ambition of
encroaching on the inland parts, particularly towards
the Ohio, or Fair River, he likewife thought unreafonable. He was of opinion that the Apalachian
mountains ought to be the limits of their poffeffions,
and was fully determined they fhould not pafs them.
His fucceffor, who was appointed while he was preparing the means of accomplifhing this vaft defign, entered into his views with all the warmth they deferved.
Numbers of forts were immediately erected on all fides,
to fupport the fyftem which the court had adopted,
perhaps without forefeeing, or, at leaft, without fufficiently attending to the confequences.

At this period began thofe hoftilities between the
Englifh and the French in North America, which
were rather countenanced than openly avowed by the
refpective mother-countries. This clandeftine mode

of carrying on the war was perfectly agreeable to the B O O K miniftry at Verfailles, as it afforded an opportunity of XVI. recovering by degrees, and without expofing their weaknefs, what they had loft by treaties, at a time when the enemy had impofed their own terms. Thefe repeated checks at laft opened the eyes of Great Britain, and difclofed the political defigns of her rival. George II. thought that a clandeftine war was inconfiftent with the fuperiority of his maritime forces. His fhips were ordered to attack thofe of the French in all parts of the world. The Englifh accordingly took or difperfed all the French fhips they met with, and in 1758 fteered towards Cape-Breton.

This ifland, the key of Canada, had already been Conqueft of attacked in 1745; and the event is of fo fingular a Cape-Breton by the nature, that it deferves a particular detail. The plan Englifh. of this firft invafion was laid at Bofton, and New England bore the expence of it. A merchant, named Pepperel, who had excited, encouraged, and directed the enthufiafm of the colony, was intrufted with the command of an army of 6000 men, which had been levied for this expedition.

Though thefe forces, convoyed by a fquadron from Jamaica, brought the firft news to Cape-Breton of the danger that threatened it; though the advantage of a furprife would have fecured the landing without oppofition; though they had but 600 regular troops to encounter, and 800 inhabitants haftily armed, the fuccefs of the undertaking was ftill precarious. What great exploits, indeed, could be expected from a militia fuddenly affembled, who had never feen a fiege or faced an enemy, and were to act under the direction of fea-officers only? Thefe unexperienced troops ftood in need of the affiftance of fome fortunate incident, which they were indeed favoured with in a fingular manner.

The conftruction and repairs of the fortifications had always been left to the care of the garrifon of Louifbourg. The foldiers were eager of being employed in thefe works, which they confidered as con-

B O O K ducive to their fafety, and as the means of procuring
   XVI. them a comfortable fubfiftence. When they found
that thofe who were to have paid them appropriated
to themfelves the profit of their labours, they demanded juftice. It was denied them; and they determined
to affert their right. As thefe depredations had been
fhared between the chief perfons of the colony and
the fubaltern officers, the foldiers could obtain no redrefs. Their indignation againft thefe rapacious ex-
tortioners rofe to fuch a height, that they defpifed all
authority. They had lived in open rebellion for fix
months, when the Englifh appeared before the place.

This was the time to conciliate the minds of both
parties, and to unite in the common caufe. The foldiers made the firft advances; but their commanders
miftrufted a generofity of which they themfelves were
incapable. Had thefe mean oppreffors conceived it
poffible that the foldiers could have entertained fuch
elevated notions as to facrifice their own refentment
to the good of their country, they would have taken
advantage of this difpofition, and have fallen upon the
enemy while they were forming their camp, and beginning to open their trenches. Befiegers, unacquainted with the principles of the art of war, would have
been difconcerted by regular and vigorous attacks.
The firft checks might have been fufficient to difcourage them, and to make them relinquifh the undertaking. But it was firmly believed that the foldiers
were only defirous of fallying out, that they might
have an opportunity of deferting; and their own officers kept them in a manner prifoners, till a defence fo
ill managed had reduced them to the neceffity of ca-
pitulating. The whole ifland fhared the fate of Louifbourg, its only bulwark.

This valuable poffeffion, reftored to France by the
treaty of Aix la Chapelle, was again attacked by the
Englifh in 1753. On the 2d of June, a fleet of twenty-
three fhips of the line and eighteen frigates, carrying
16,000 well-difciplined troops, anchored in Gabarus
bay, within half a league of Louifbourg. As it was

evident' that it would be to no purpofe to land at a greater diftance, becaufe it would be impoffible to bring up the artillery and other neceffaries for a confiderable fiege, it had been attempted to render the landing impracticable near the town. In the prudent precautions that had been taken, the befiegers faw the dangers and difficulties they had to expect; but far from being deterred by them, they had recourfe to ftratagem; and while by extending their line they threatened and commanded the whole coaft, they landed by force of arms at the creek of Cormoran.

This place was naturally weak. The French had fortified it with a good parapet planted with cannon. Behind this rampart they had pofted 2000 excellent foldiers, and fome Indians. In front they had made fuch a clofe hedge with branches of trees, that would have been very difficult to penetrate, even if it had not been defended. This kind of pallifade, which concealed all the preparations for defence, appeared at a diftance to be nothing more than a verdant plain.

This would have preferved the colony, had the affailants been fuffered to complete their landing, and to advance, with the confidence that they had but few obftacles to furmount. Had this been the cafe, overpowered at once by the fire of the artillery and the fmall arms, they would infallibly have perifhed on the fhore, or in the hurry of embarking, efpecially as the fea was juft then very rough. This unexpected lofs might have interrupted the whole project.

But all the prudent precautions that had been taken, were rendered abortive by the impetuofity of the French. The Englifh had fcarce begun to move towards the fhore, when their enemies haftened to difcover the fnare they had laid for them. By the brifk and hafty fire that was aimed at their boats, and ftill more by the premature removal of the boughs that mafked the forces, which it was fo much the intereft of the French to conceal, they gueffed at the danger they were going to rufh into. They immediately turned back, and faw no other place to effect their landing

B O O K upon but a rock, which had been always deemed in-
XVI.   acceffible. General Wolfe, though much taken up
in reimbarking his troops, and fending off the boats,
gave the fignal to Major Scot to repair thither.

The officer immediately removed to the fpot with
his men. His own boat coming up firft, and finking
at the very inftant he was ftepping out, he climbed up
the rock alone. He was in hopes of meeting with a
hundred of his men, who had been fent thither fome
hours before. He found only ten. With thefe few,
however, he gained the fummit of the rock. Ten Indians and fixty Frenchmen killed two of his men, and
mortally wounded three. In fpite of his weaknefs, he
ftood his ground under cover of a thicket, till his brave
countrymen, regardlefs of the boifterous waves and
the fire of the cannon, came up to him, and put him
in full poffeffion of that important poft, the only one
that could fecure their landing.

The French, as foon as they faw that the enemy
had got a firm footing on land, betook themfelves to
the only remaining refuge, and fhut themfelves up in
Louifbourg. The fortifications were in a bad condition, becaufe the fea-fand, which they had been obliged to ufe, is by no means fit for works of mafonry.
The revetements of the feveral curtains were entirely
crumbled away. There was only one cafement, and
a fmall magazine, that were bomb-proof. The garrifon which was to defend the place confifted only of
2900 men.

Notwithftanding all thefe difadvantages, the befieged were determined to make an obftinate refiftance. While they were employed in defending themfelves with fo much firmnefs, the fuccours they expected from Canada might poffibly arrive. At all
events, this refiftance might be the means of preferving that great colony from all further invafion for the
remainder of the campaign. It is fcarce credible that
the French were confirmed in their refolution by the
courage of a woman. Madame de Drucourt was continually upon the ramparts, with her purfe in her

hand; and firing herself three guns every day, seemed to difpute with the governor, her hufband, the glory of his office. The befieged were not difmayed at the ill fuccefs of their feveral fallies, or the mafterly operations concerted by Admiral Bofcawen and General Amherft. It was but at the eve of an affault, which it was impoffible to fuftain, that they talked of furrendering. They made an honourable capitulation; and the conqueror fhowed more refpect for his enemy and for himfelf, than to fully his glory by any act of barbarity or avarice.

The conqueft of Cape-Breton opened the way into Canada. The very next year the feat of war was removed thither, or rather the fcenes of bloodfhed which had long been acted over that immenfe country were multiplied. The caufe of thefe proceedings was this:

The French, fettled in thofe parts, had carried their ambitious views towards the north, where the fineft furs were to be had, and in the greateft plenty. When this vein of wealth was exhaufted, or yielded lefs than it did at firft, their trade turned fouthward, where they difcovered the Ohio, to which they gave the name of the Fair River. It laid open the natural communication between Canada and Louifiana. For though the fhips that fail up the river St. Lawrence go no further than Quebec, the navigation is carried on in barges to lake Ontario, which is only parted from lake Erie by a neck of land, where the French, upon their firft fettling, built Fort Niagara. It is on this fpot, in the neighbourhood of lake Erie, that the fource of the river Ohio is found, which waters the fineft country in the world, and being increafed by the many rivers that fall into it, difcharges itfelf into the Miffiffippi.

The French, however, made no ufe of this magnificent canal. The trifling intercourfe that fubfifted between the two colonies was always carried on by the northern regions. The new way, which was much fhorter and eafier than the old, firft began to be frequented by a body of troops that were fent over to Canada in 1739, to affift the colony of Louifiana, then

B O O K engaged in an open war with the Indians,   After this
XVI.   expedition, the fouthern road was again forgotten, and
was never thought of till the year 1753.   At that period, feveral fmall forts were erected along the Ohio,
the courfe of which had been traced for four years paft.
The moft confiderable of thefe forts took its name from
the governor Duquefne who had built it.

The Englifh colonies could not fee without concern
French fettlements raifed behind them, which joined
to the old ones, and feemed to furround them.   They
were apprehenfive, left the Apalachian mountains,
which were to form the natural boundaries between
both nations, fhould not prove a fufficient barrier
againft the attempts of a reftlefs and warlike neighbour.   Urged by this motive, they themfelves paffed
thefe famous mountains, to difpute the poffeffion of
the Ohio with the rival nation.   This firft ftep proved
unfuccefsful.   The feveral parties that were fucceffively fent out were routed, and the forts were demolifhed
as faft as they were built.

To put an end to thefe national affronts, and revenge the difgrace they reflected on the mother-country, a large body of troops was fent over, under the
command of General Braddock.   In the fummer of
1755, as this general was marching to attack Fort
Duquefne with 36 pieces of cannon and 6000 men, he
was furprifed, within four leagues of the place, by 250
Frenchmen and 650 Indians, and all his army cut to
pieces.   This unaccountable difafter put a ftop to the
march of three numerous bodies that were advancing
to fall upon Canada.   The terror occafioned by this
accident made them haften back to their quarters; and
in the next campaign all their motions were guided by
the moft timorous caution.

The French were emboldened by this perplexity,
and though very much inferior to the Englifh, ventured to appear before Ofwego in Auguft 1756.   It was
originally a fortified magazine at the mouth of the river Onondago on the lake Ontario.   It ftood nearly in
the centre of Canada, in fo advantageous a fituation,

that many works had from time to time been erected there, which had rendered it one of the moſt capital poſts in thoſe parts. It was garriſoned by 1800 men, with 121 pieces of cannon, and great plenty of ſtores of all kinds. Though ſo well provided, it ſurrendered in a few days to the impetuous and bold attacks of 3000 men who were laying ſiege to it.

In Auguſt 1757, 5500 French and 1800 Indians marched up to Fort George, ſituated on lake Sacrament, which was juſtly conſidered as the bulwark of the Engliſh ſettlements, and the rendezvous of all the forces deſtined againſt Canada. Nature and art had conſpired to block up the roads leading to that place, and to make all acceſs impracticable. Theſe advantages were further ſtrengthened by ſeveral bodies of troops, placed at proper diſtances in the beſt poſitions. Yet theſe obſtacles were ſurmounted with ſuch prudence and intrepidity, as would have been memorable in hiſtory, had the ſcene of action lain in a more diſtinguiſhed ſpot. The French, after killing or diſperſing all the ſmall parties they met with, arrived before the place, and forced the garriſon, conſiſting of 2264 men, to capitulate.

This freſh diſaſter rouſed the Engliſh. Their generals applied themſelves during the winter to the training up of their men, and bringing the ſeveral troops under a proper diſcipline. They made them exerciſe in the woods, in fighting after the Indian manner. In the ſpring the army, conſiſting of 6300 regulars, and 13,000 militia belonging to the colonies, aſſembled on the ruins of Fort George. They embarked on lake Sacrament, which parted the colonies of both nations, and marched up to Carillon, which was only at the diſtance of one league.

That fort, which had been but lately erected on the breaking out of the war, to cover Canada, was not of ſufficient extent to withſtand the forces that were marching againſt it. Intrenchments were formed haſtily under the cannon of the fort, with ſtems of trees heaped up one upon another; and large trees

B O O K were laid in front, the branches of which being cut
XVI. and fharpened, anfwered the purpofe of chevaux-de-
frife. The colours were planted on the top of the*
ramparts, behind which lay 3500 men.

The Englifh were not difmayed at thefe formidable
appearances, being fully determined to remove the
difgrace of their former mifcarriages in a country
where the profperity of their trade depended on the
fuccefs of their arms. On the 8th of July 1758, they
rufhed upon thefe pallifades with the moft extravagant
fury. Neither were they difconcerted by the French
firing upon them from the top of the parapet, while
they were unable to defend themfelves. They fell
upon the fharp fpikes, and were entangled among the
ftumps and boughs through which their eagernefs had
made them rufh. All thefe loffes ferved but to increafe
their impetuous rage, which continued upwards of four
hours, and coft them above four thoufand of their brave
men before they would give up this rafh and defperate
undertaking.

They were equally unfuccefsful in fmaller actions.
They did not attack one poft without meeting with a
repulfe. Every party they fent out was beaten, and
every convoy intercepted. The feverity of the winter might have been fuppofed to fecure them; but
even in this rigorous feafon the Indians and Canadians
carried fire and fword to the frontiers and into the
very centre of the Englifh colonies.

All thefe difafters were owing to a falfe principle of
government. The court of London had always entertained a notion that the fuperiority of their navy was
alone fufficient to affert their dominion in America, as
it afforded a ready conveyance for fuccours, and could
eafily intercept the enemy's forces.

Though experience had fhown the fallacy of this
idea, the miniftry did not even endeavour, by a proper choice of generals, to rectify the fatal effects it had
produced. Almoft all thofe who were employed in
this fervice were deficient in point of abilities and activity.

The armies were not likely to make amends for the defects of their commanders. The troops, indeed, were not wanting in that daring spirit and invincible courage which is the characteristic of the English soldiers, arising from the climate, and still more from the nature of their government ; but these national qualities were counterbalanced or extinguished by the hardships they underwent, in a country destitute of all the conveniencies that Europe affords. As to the militia of the colonies, it was composed of peaceable husbandmen, who were not, like most of the French colonists, inured to slaughter by a habit of hunting, and by military ardour.

To these disadvantages, arising from the nature of things, were added others altogether owing to misconduct. The posts erected for the safety of the several English settlements were not so contrived as to support and assist each other. The provinces having all separate interests, and not being united under the authority of one head, did not concur in those joint efforts for the good of the whole, and that unanimity of sentiments, which alone can insure the success of their measures. The season of action was wasted in vain altercations between the governors and the colonists. Every plan of operation that met with opposition from any set of men was dropped. If any one was agreed upon, it was certainly made public before the execution, and by that means rendered abortive. To this may be added, the irreconcileable hatred subsisting between them and the Indians.

These nations had always shown a visible partiality for the French, in return for their kindness in sending them missionaries, whom they considered rather as ambassadors from the prince, than as sent from God. These missionaries, by studying the language of the savages, conforming to their temper and inclinations, and putting in practice every attention to gain their confidence, had acquired an absolute dominion over their minds. The French colonists, far from communicating to them the European manners, had adopted

BOOK those of the favages they lived with : their indolence
XVI. in time of peace, their activity in war, and their conftant fondnefs for a wandering life. Several officers
of diftinction had even been incorporated with them.
The hatred and jealoufy of the Englifh has traduced
them on this account ; and they have not fcrupled to
affert, that thefe generous men had given money for
the fkulls of their enemies ; that they joined in the
horrid dances that accompany the execution of their
prifoners, imitated their cruelties, and partook of their
barbarous feftivals. But thefe enormities would be
better adapted to people who have fubftituted national to religious fanaticifm, and are more inclined to
hate other nations, than to love their own government.

The ftrong attachment of the Indians to the French
was productive of the moft inveterate hatred againft
the Englifh. Of all the European favages, thefe were,
in their opinion, the hardeft to tame. Their averfion
foon rofe to madnefs ; and they even thirfted for Englifh blood, when they found that a reward was offered for their deftruction, and that they were to be expelled their native land by foreign affaffins. The fame
hands which had enriched the Englifh colony with
their furs, now took up the hatchet to deftroy it. The
Indians purfued the Englifh with as much eagernefs as
they did the wild beafts. Glory was no longer their
aim in battle, their only object was flaughter. They
deftroyed armies which the French only wifhed to fub-
due. Their fury rofe to fuch a height, that an Englifh
prifoner having been conducted into a lonely habitation, the woman immediately cut off his arm, and
made her family drink the blood that ran from it. A
Jefuit miffionary reproaching her with the atrociouf-
nefs of the action, her anfwer was, *My children muft be
warriors, and therefore muft be fed with the blood of their
enemies.*

Taking of   Such was the fituation of affairs, when an Englifh
Quebec by fleet, confifting of three hundred fail, and commanded
the Englifh.
The con- by admiral Saunders, entered the river St. Lawrence

at the end of June 1759. On a dark night, and with
a very favourable wind, eight fire-fhips were fent out
to deftroy it. Not a fhip nor a man could have e-
fcaped, if the operation had been carried on with that
degree of fkill, coolnefs, and courage, which it required. But thofe who had undertaken it were perhaps
deficient in every one of thefe qualities, or at leaft did
not unite them all. Impatient to fecure their return
to land, they fet fire to the fhips under their management a great deal too foon, and the enemy being warned by this of the danger that threatened them, efcaped
it by their activity and boldnefs, at the expence only
of two fmall veffels.

B O O K
XVI.

queft of
this capital
brings on
in time the
furrender of
the whole
colony.

While the naval forces had fo fortunately efcaped
being deftroyed, the army, confifting of ten thoufand
men, was attacking Levy Point, drove away the French
troops which were intrenched there, erected their own
batteries, and bombarded Quebec with the greateft
fuccefs. This town, though fituated on the oppofite
fhore of the river, was neverthelefs at no greater diftance from it than fix hundred toifes.

But thefe difadvantages did not lead to the defign
which the Englifh had in view. Their intention was
to become mafters of the capital of the colony; and
the coaft by which they muft have reached it was fo
well defended by redoubts, batteries, and troops, that
it feemed inacceffible. The enemy were more and
more confirmed in this opinion after they had attempted the fall of Montmorency, where they loft fifteen
hundred men, and where they might eafily have loft
all the men they had imprudently landed there.

In the mean time the feafon was advancing. General Amherft, who was to have caufed a diverfion towards the lake, did not make his appearance; and
every hope was even given up of forcing the French
in their pofts. A general difcouragement was beginning to prevail, when Mr. Murray propofed to go
with the army and part of the fleet two miles above
the town, and to feize upon the heights of Abraham,
which the French had neglected to guard, becaufe

B O O K they thought them fufficiently defended by the very
XVI. fteep rocks which furrounded them. This brilliant
and fortunate idea was eagerly adopted. On the 13th
of December, five thoufand Englifh landed at the foot
of the heights before day-break, and without being
perceived. They clambered up without lofing any
time, and formed the line of battle on the top of them,
when at nine o'clock they were attacked by two thoufand foldiers, five thoufand Canadians, and five hundred favages. The action began and proved favourable to the Englifh, who at the beginning of it had
loft the intrepid Wolfe, their general, but did not lofe
their confidence and refolution.

This was gaining a confiderable advantage, but it
might not have been decifive. The troops that were
pofted within a few leagues of the field of battle might
have been collected in twelve hours, to join the vanquifhed army, and march up to the conqueror with
a fuperior force. This was the opinion of General
Montcalm, who being mortally wounded in the retreat, had time enough before he expired to confult
the fafety of his men, and to encourage them to repair
their difafter. This generous motion was over-ruled
by the council of war. The army removed ten leagues
off. The chevalier de Levy, who had haftened from
his poft to fucceed Montcalm, cenfured this want of
courage. The French were afhamed of it, wifhed to
recal it, and make another attempt for victory, but it
was too late. Quebec, though three parts deftroyed,
had capitulated too precipitately on the 17th.

All Europe thought that the taking of this place
had put an end to the great conteft in North America. They never imagined that a handful of Frenchmen, in want of every thing, who feemed to be in a
defperate condition, would dare to think of protract-
ing their inevitable fate. They did not know what
thefe people were capable of doing. They haftily
completed fome intrenchments that had been begun
ten leagues above Quebec. There they left troops
fufficient to ftop the progrefs of the enemy; and pro-

ceeded to Montreal, to concert meafures to retrieve their difgrace.

It was there agreed, that in the fpring they fhould march with an armed force againft Quebec, to retake it by furprife, or, if that fhould fail, to befiege it in form. They had nothing in readinefs for that purpofe ; but the plan was fo concerted, that they fhould enter upon the undertaking juft at the inftant when the fuccours expected from France muft neceffarily arrive.

Though the colony had long been in want of every thing, the preparations were already made, when the ice, which covered the whole river, began to give way towards the middle, and opened a fmall canal. They dragged fome boats over the ice, and put them into the water. The army, confifting of citizens and foldiers, who made but one body, and were animated with one foul, fell down this ftream, with inconceivable ardour, as early as the 20th of April 1760. The Englifh thought they ftill lay quiet in their winter quarters. The army, already landed, came up with an advanced guard of 1500 men, pofted three leagues from Quebec. This party was juft upon the point of being cut to pieces, had it not been for one of thofe unaccountable incidents which no human prudence can forefee.

A gunner, attempting to ftep out of his boat, had fallen into the water. He caught hold of a flake of ice, climbed up upon it, and was carried down the ftream. As he paffed by Quebec, clofe to the fhore, he was feen by a centinel, who, obferving a man in diftrefs, called out for help. The Englifh flew to his affiftance, and found him motionlefs. They knew him by his uniform to be a French foldier, and carried him to the governor's houfe, where, by the help of fpirituous liquors, they recalled him to life for a moment. He juft recovered his fpeech enough to tell them that an army of 10,000 French was at the gates, and expired. The governor immediately difpatched orders to the advanced guard to retire within the walls with

B O O K all expedition. Notwithſtanding their precipitate re-
XVI. treat, the French had time to attack their rear. A
few moments later, they would have been defeated,
and the city retaken.

The aſſailants, however, marched on with an intrepidity which indicated that they expected every thing
from their valour, and thought no more of a ſurpriſe.
They were within a league of the town, when they
were met by a body of 4000 men, who were ſent out
to intercept them. The onſet was ſharp, and the reſiſtance obſtinate. The Engliſh were driven back
within their walls, leaving 1800 of their braveſt men
upon the ſpot, and their artillery in the enemy's hands.

The trenches were immediately opened before Quebec ; but as the French had none but field-pieces, as
no ſuccours came from France, and as a ſtrong Engliſh
ſquadron was coming up the river, they were obliged
to raiſe the ſiege on the 16th of May, and to retreat
from poſt to poſt till they arrived at Montreal. Theſe
troops, which were not very numerous at firſt, were
now exceedingly reduced by frequent ſkirmiſhes and
continual fatigues, were in want both of proviſions
and warlike ſtores, and found themſelves encloſed in
an open place ; being ſurrounded by three formidable
armies, one of which was come down, and another up
the river, while the third had paſſed over lake Champlain. Theſe miſerable remains of a body of ſeven
thouſand men, who had never been recruited, and had
ſo much ſignalized themſelves with the help of a few
militia and Indians, were at laſt forced to capitulate
for the whole colony. The conqueſt was confirmed
by the treaty of peace, when this country was added
to the poſſeſſions of the Engliſh in North America.

Hath the   How confined are the views of politics ! The En-
acquiſition   gliſh conſidered this acquiſition as the ultimate period of
of Canada
been advan- their grandeur, and the French miniſtry were not more
tageous or   enlightened than the Britiſh council. On one hand
prejudicial
to England? every thing was thought to be won by this conqueſt ;
on the other, every thing was thought to be loſt by
a ſacrifice which was to bring on the ruin of an irre-

concileable enemy.   Such is the neceſſary concatena- BOOK
tion of the events which inceſſantly change the in- XVI.
tereſts of empires, that it hath often happened, and
will frequently happen hereafter, that the moſt profound ſpeculations, and the meaſures apparently the
moſt prudent, have been, and will ſtill be erroneous.
The advantage of the moment is the only thing conſidered, in circumſtances where nothing is ſo common
as to ſee good ſpring from evil, and evil ariſe from
good.   If it be true of ſome individuals, that they
have for a long time wiſhed for what has proved their
misfortune ; it is ſtill more true of ſovereigns.   The
caprices of fortune, which are ſo apt to ſport with the
prudence of man, are never taken into the calculation,
and indeed there is no occaſion for it, when ſome unfortunate caſualty is concealed in a diſtant and ob-
ſcure futurity ; when it is almoſt devoid of probability, and when, ſuppoſing it ſhould happen, total ruin
will not be the conſequence.   But the people will be
governed by a mad miniſtry, when, without conſidering the tranquillity and the ſafety of the ſtate, they
ſhall think of nothing but its aggrandizement : when,
without conſidering whether a miſerable little iſland
will not occaſion cares and expences which cannot be
compenſated by any advantage, they will ſuffer themſelves to be dazzled with the frivolous glory of having added it to the national dominion : when, by re-
fuſing to make reſtitutions that were agreed upon,
they ſhall cement between the uſurping power and
that which is injured, a hatred which will, ſooner or
later, be followed by the effuſion of blood, upon the
ſea and upon the continent : when, for the preſervation of a few places, it ſhall be neceſſary to keep a
number of ſoldiers ſhut up, who will grow degenerate
by a long continuance in idleneſs : when laſting jealouſies ſhall be excited, or pretenſions encouraged,
which are ever ready to be renewed, and to engage
two nations in war with each other : when it ſhall be
forgotten, that a nation ſettled between one empire
and another, is ſometimes the beſt barrier that can be

B O O K interpofed betwen them; and that it is imprudent and
  XVI. dangerous to acquire, by the extinction of the intermediate nation, an ambitious, turbulent, warlike, and
powerful neighbour : when it fhall be forgotten, that
every domain, feparated from a ftate by a vaft interval,
is precarious, expenfive, ill-defended, and ill-govern-
ed ; that it will be, beyond any kind of doubt, a
real misfortune for two nations to have any poffeffion
on one fide and on the other of a river which ferves
as their boundary : that to renounce a country claimed by feveral powers, is commonly to fpare fuperfluous expences, alarms, and contefts ; and that to cede
it to one of thofe who were defirous of obtaining it,
is the only way to throw the fame calamities upon
them : in a word, when it fhall be forgotten that a fovereign, who is really a man of genius, will perhaps
difplay it lefs in availing himfelf of the real advantages of his country, than in giving up to rival nations
deceitful advantages, the fatal confequences of which
they can only be fenfible of in procefs of time ; this
is a kind of fnare which the rage of extending their
dominions will ever conceal from them.

BOOK XVII.

Englifh Colonies fettled at Hudfon's Bay, Canada, the
Ifland of St. John, Newfoundland, Nova-Scotia, New-
England, New-York, and New-Jerfey.

B O O K   THE defire of penetrating into futurity hath been
  XVII.   the paffion of all ages. The entrails of animals, and
Firft expe- the blood of victims, hath appeared to fome people an
ditions of   infallible mode of difcovering the deftiny of empires.
the Englifh
in North   Others have placed the fcience of divination in dreams,
America.   which they have chofen to confider as the moft certain interpreters of the will of Heaven. Whole nations have pretended to compel fate to reveal itfelf by
the flight of birds, and other prefages equally frivolous.
But, the confulting of the ftars hath been the moft fa-

vourite of thefe modes of auguration. Men have thought, that in thefe they beheld, marked out in cha-racters not to be effaced, the revolutions, more or lefs im-portant, which were to agitate the globe. Thefe reve-ries had not fubdued the minds of the vulgar only, they acquired an equal afcendant over men of the firft genius.

Since found philofophy hath deftroyed thefe chi-meras, mankind have fplit upon another rock. A fpi-rit of prefumption, too prevalent, hath induced men to believe, that nothing was more feafible than to de-termine, by combinations fettled without much diffi-culty, what was to happen in politics. Undoubtedly, it was poffible for perfons of attention and reflection to forefee fome events ; but how many miftakes will not happen to one fortunate conjecture !

The Britifh iflands have been drenched in blood. Numberlefs factions and fects have deftroyed each other there, with a degree of obftinacy, the fatal ex-ample of which hath rarely been difplayed in the de-plorable annals of the world. Who could have con-jectured, that the profperity of North America would have arifen from fo many calamities?

England was only known in America by her pi-racies, which were often fuccefsful, and always bold, when Sir Walter Raleigh conceived the project to procure his nation a fhare of the prodigious riches, which, for near a century paft, had flowed from that hemifphere into ours. This great man, who was born for bold undertakings, caft his eye on the eaftern coaft of North America. The talent he had, of bringing men over to his opinion, by reprefenting all his pro-pofals in a ftriking light, foon procured him affociates, both at court and among the merchants. The com-pany that was formed in confequence of his magnifi-cent promifes, obtained of government, in 1584, the abfolute difpofal of all the difcoveries that fhould be made ; and without any further encouragement, they fitted out two fhips in April following, that anchored in Roanoak bay, which now makes a part of Carolina. Their commanders, worthy of the truft repofed in them, behaved with remarkable affability in a country where they wanted to settle their nation, and left the savages at liberty to make their own terms in the trade they propofed to open with them.

The reports made by thefe fuccefsful navigators, on their return to Europe, concerning the temperature of the climate, the fertility of the foil, and the difpofition of the inhabitants, encouraged the fociety to proceed. They accordingly fent feven fhips the following fpring, which landed a hundred and eight free men at Roanoak, for the purpofe of commencing a fettlement. Part of them were murdered by the favages, whom they had infulted, and the reft, having been fo improvident as to neglect the culture of the land, were perifhing with mifery and hunger, when a deliverer came to their relief.

This was Sir Francis Drake, fo famous among feamen for being the next after Magellan who failed round the globe. The abilities he had fhown in that great expedition, induced Queen Elizabeth to make choice of him to humble Philip II. in that part of his extenfive dominions, where he ufed to difturb the peace of other nations. Few orders were ever more punctually executed. The Englifh fleet feized upon St. Jago, Carthagena, St. Domingo, and feveral other important places, and took a great many rich fhips. His inftructions were, after thefe operations, to proceed and offer his affiftance to the colony at Roanoak. The wretched few who furvived the numberlefs calamities that had befallen them, were in fuch defpair, that they refufed all affiftance, and only begged he would convey them to their native country. The admiral complied with their requeft; and thus the expences that had been hitherto beftowed on the fettlement were entirely thrown away.

The affociates were not difcouraged by this unforefeen event. From time to time they fent over a few colonifts, who, in the year 1589, amounted to a hundred and fifteen perfons of both fexes, under a regular government, and fully provided with all they wanted for their defence, and for the purposes of agriculture and commerce. These beginnings raised some expectations, but they were frustrated by the disgrace of Raleigh, who fell a victim to the caprices of his own wild imagination. The colony, having lost its founder, was totally forgotten.

It had been thus neglected for twelve years, when Gosnold, one of the first associates, resolved to visit it in 1602. His experience in navigation made him suspect that the right tract had not been found out, and that in steering by the Canary and Caribbee Islands, the voyage had been made longer than it need have been by above a thousand leagues. These conjectures induced him to steer away from the south and to turn more westward. The attempt succeeded; but when he reached the American coast, he found himself further north than any navigators who had gone before. The country where he landed, which now makes a a part of New-England, afforded him plenty of beautiful furs, with which he sailed back to England.

The rapidity and success of this undertaking made a strong impression upon the English merchants. Several of them joined in 1606 to form a settlement in the country that Gosnold had discovered. Their example revived in others the memory of the Roanoak; and this gave rise to two charter companies. As the continent where they were to carry on their monopoly was then known in Egland only by the general name of Virginia, the one was called the South-Virginia, and the other the North-Virginia Company.

The zeal that had been shown at first soon abated, and there appeared to be more jealousy than emulation between the two Companies. Though they had been favoured with the first lottery that ever was drawn in England, their progress was so slow, that in 1614 there were not above four hundred persons in both settlements. That sort of competency which was answerable to the simplicity of the manners of the times, was then so general in England, that no one was tempted to go abroad in quest of a fortune.

It is a fenfe of misfortune that gives men a diflike to their native country, ftill more than the defire of acquiring riches. Nothing lefs than fome extraordinary commotion could then have fent inhabitants even into an excellent country. This emigration was at length occafioned by fuperftition, which had given rife to commotions from the collifion of religious opinions.

The firft priefts of the Britons were the Druids, fo famous in the annals of Gaul, To throw a myfterious veil upon the ceremonies of a favage worfhip, their rites were never performed but in dark receffes, and generally in gloomy groves, where fear creates fpectres and apparitions. Only a few perfons were initiated into thefe myfteries, and intrufted with the facred doctrines; and even thefe were not allowed to commit any thing to writing upon this important fubject, left their fecrets fhould fall into the hands of the profane vulgar. The altars of a formidable deity were ftained with the blood of human victims, and enriched with the moft precious fpoils of war. Though the dread of the vengeance of Heaven was the only guard of thefe treafures, yet they were always deemed facred, becaufe the Druids had artfully repreffed a thirft after riches, by inculcating the fundamental doctrine of the endlefs tranfmigration of the foul. The chief authority of government was vefted in the minifters of that terrible religion; becaufe men are more powerfully and more conftantly fwayed by opinion than by any other motive. They were intrufted with the education of youth, and they maintained through life the afcendency they acquired in that early age. They took cognizance of all civil and criminal caufes, and were as abfolute in their decifions on ftate affairs as on the private differences between individuals. Whoever dared to refift their decrees, was not only excluded from all participation in the divine myfteries, but even from the fociety of men. It was accounted a crime and a reproach to hold any intercourfe with him; he was· irrevocably deprived of the protection of the laws, and nothing but death could put an end to his

miferies. The hiftory of human fuperftition's affords B o o K
no inftance of any one fo tyrannical as that of the XVII.
Druids. It was the only one that provoked the Romans to ufe feverity; with fo much violence did the
Druids oppofe the power of thofe conquerors.

That religion, however, had loft much of its influence, when it was totally abolifhed by Chriftianity in
the feventh century. The northern nations, that had
fucceffively invaded the fouthern provinces of Europe,
had found there the feeds of that new religion, amidft
the ruins of an empire that was fhaking on all fides.
Their indifference for their diftant gods, or that credulity which is ever the companion of ignorance, induced them readily to embrace a form of worfhip which,
from the multiplicity of its ceremonies, could not but
attract the notice of rude and favage men. The Sax-
ons, who afterwards invaded England, followed their
example, and adopted without difficulty a religion that
juftified their conquefts, expiated the criminality of
them, and enfured their permanency by abolifhing the
ancient forms of worfhip.

The effects were fuch as might be expected from a
religion, the original fimplicity of which was at that
time fo much disfigured. Idle contemplations were
foon fubftituted in lieu of active and focial virtues, and
a ftupid veneration for unknown faints took place of
the worfhip of the Supreme Being. Miracles dazzled
the eyes of men, and diverted them from attending to
natural caufes. They were taught to believe that
prayers and offerings would atone for the moft heinous
crimes. Every fentiment of reafon was perverted, and
every principle of morality corrupted.

Thofe who had been the promoters of this confufion knew how to avail themfelves of it. The priefts
obtained that refpect which was denied to kings, and
their perfons became facred. The magiftrate had no
power of infpecting into their conduct, and they even
evaded the watchfulnefs of the civil law. Their tribunal eluded, and even fuperfeded, all others. They
found means to introduce religion into every queftion

B O O K of law, and into all ftate affairs; and made themfelves
XVII. umpires or judges in every caufe. When faith fpoke,
every one liftened in filent attention to its inexplicable
oracles. Such was the infatuation of thofe dark ages,
that the fcandalous exceffes of the clergy did not diminifh their authority.

This authority was maintained by the immenfe
riches the clergy had already acquired. As foon as
they had taught that religion was preferved principally by facrifices, and required firft of all that of fortune
and earthly poffeffions, the nobility, who were fole
proprietors of all eftates, employed their flaves to build
churches, and allotted their lands to the endowment
of thofe foundations. Kings gave to the church all
that they had extorted from the people; and ftripped
themfelves to fuch a degree, as even not to leave a
fufficiency for the payment of the army, or for de-
fraying the other charges of government. Thefe de-
ficiencies were never made up by thofe who were the
caufe of them. They were not concerned in any of
the public expences. The payment of taxes with the
revenues of the church would have been a facrilege,
and a proftitution of holy things to profane purpofes.
Such was the declaration of the clergy, and the laity
believed them. The poffeffion of the third part of the
feudal tenures in the kingdom, the free-will offerings
of a deluded people, and the large fees required for
all prieftly offices, did not fatisfy the enormous avidity
of the clergy, ever attentive to their own intereft.
They found in the Old Teftament, that, by divine ap-
pointment, they had an undoubted right to the tithes
of the produce of the land. This claim was fo readily
admitted, that they extended it to the tithe of induftry, of the profits on trade, of the wages of labourers,
of the pay of foldiers, and fometimes of the falaries of
placemen.

Rome, which at firft was a filent fpectator of thefe
proceedings, and proudly enjoyed the fuccefs that attended the rich and haughty minifters of a Saviour
born in obfcurity, and condemned to an ignominious

death, foon coveted a fhare in the fpoils of England. B O O K
The firft ftep fhe took was to open a trade for relics, XVII.
which were always ufhered in with fome ftriking mi-
racle, and fold in proportion to the credulity of the
purchafers. The great men, and even monarchs, were
invited to go in pilgrimage to the capital of the world,
to purchafe a place in heaven fuitable to the rank they
held on earth. The popes by degrees affumed the
prefentation to church preferments, which at firft they
gave away, but afterwards fold. By thefe means their
tribunal took cognizance of all ecclefiaftical caufes;
and in time they claimed a tenth of the revenues of
the clergy, who themfelves levied the tenth of all the
fubftance of the realm.

When thefe pious extortions were carried as far as
they poffibly could be in England, Rome afpired to
the fupreme authority over it. Her ambitious deceit
was covered with a facred veil. She fapped the foundations of liberty, by employing the influence of opinion only. This was fetting men at variance with
themfelves, and availing herfelf of their prejudices, in
order to acquire an abfolute dominion over them. She
ufurped the power of a defpotic arbitrator between the
altar and the throne, between the prince and his fubjects, between one potentate and another. She kindled the flames of war with her fpiritual thunders. But
fhe wanted emiffaries to fpread the terror of her arms,
and made choice of the monks for that purpofe. The
fecular clergy, notwithftanding their celibacy, which
kept them from forming connections in the world,
were ftill attached to it by the ties of intereft, often
ftronger than thofe of blood. A fet of men, fecluded
from fociety by fingular inftitutions, which muft in-
cline them to fanaticifm, and by a blind fubmiffion to
the dictates of a foreign pontiff, were beft adapted to
fecond the views of fuch a fovereign. Thefe vile and
abject tools of fuperftition executed their fatal employment fuccefsfully. By their intrigues, affifted with the
concurrence of favourable circumftances, England,
which had fo long withftood the conquering arms of

B o o k the ancient Roman empire, became tributary to mo-
XVII. dern Rome.

At length the paffions and violent caprices of Henry VIII. broke the fcandalous dependence. The abufe
of fo infamous a power had already opened the eyes
of the nation. This prince ventured at once to fhake
off the authority of the pope, abolifh monafteries, and
affume the fupremacy over his own church.

This open fchifm was followed by other alterations
in the reign of Edward, fon and fucceffor to Henry.
The religious opinions, which were then changing the
face of Europe, were openly difcuffed. Something
was taken from every one; many doctrines and rites
of the old form of worfhip were retained; and from
thefe feveral fyftems or tenets arofe a new communion,
diftinguifhed by the name of the Church of England.

Elizabeth, who completed this important work,
found theory alone too fubtle, and thought it moft
expedient to captivate the fenfes, by the addition of
fome ceremonies. Her natural tafte for grandeur, and
the defire of putting a ftop to the difputes about points
of doctrine, by entertaining the eye with the external
parade of worfhip, inclined her to adopt a greater
number of religious rites. But fhe was reftrained by
political confiderations, and was obliged to facrifice
fomething to the prejudices of a party that had raifed
her to the throne, and was able to maintain her upon
it.

Far from fufpecting that James I. would execute
what Elizabeth had not even dared to attempt, it
might be expected that he would rather have been inclined to reftrain ecclefiaftical rites and ceremonies;
that prince having been trained up in the principles of
the Prefbyterians, a fect which, with much fpiritual
pride, affected great fimplicity of drefs, gravity of manners, and aufterity of doctrine, which loved to fpeak
in fcripture phrafes, and gave none but fcripture names
to their children. One would have fuppofed that fuch
an education muft have prejudiced the king againft
the outward pomp of the Catholic worfhip, and every

thing that bore any affinity to it. But the spirit of system prevailed over the principles of education. Stricken with the Episcopal jurisdiction which he found established in England, and which he thought conformable to his own notions of civil government, he abandoned, from conviction, the early impressions he had received, and grew passionately fond of a hierarchy modelled upon the political economy of a well-constituted empire. Instigated by his enthusiasm, he wanted to introduce this wonderful system into Scotland, his native country, and to engage a great many of the English, who still dissented, to embrace it. He even intended to add the pomp of the most awful ceremonies to the majestic plan, if he could have carried his grand projects into execution. But the opposition he met with at first setting out would not permit him to advance any further in his system of reformation. He contented himself with recommending to his son to resume his views, whenever the times should furnish a favourable opportunity; and represented the Presbyterians to him as alike dangerous to religion and to the throne.

Charles readily followed his advice, which was but too conformable to the principles of despotism he had imbibed from Buckingham, his favourite, the most corrupt of men, and the corrupter of the courtiers. To pave the way to the revolution he was meditating, he promoted several bishops to the highest dignities in the government, and conferred on them most of the offices that imparted a great share of influence in all public measures. These ambitious prelates, now become the masters of a prince who had been weak enough to be guided by the instigations of others, betrayed that spirit so frequent among the clergy, of exalting ecclesiastical jurisdiction under the shadow of the royal prerogative. They multiplied the church ceremonies without end, under pretence of their being of apostolical institution; and to enforce their observance, had recourse to acts of arbitrary power exercised by the king. It was evident that there was a settled

B O O K design of reftoring, in all its fplendour, what the Pro-
XVII. teftants called Romifh idolatry, though the moft violent means fhould be neceffary to compafs it.   This
project gave the more umbrage, as it was fupported
by the prejudices and intrigues of a prefumptuous
queen, who had brought from France an immoderate
paffion for popery and arbitrary power.

It can fcarcely be imagined what acrimony thefe
alarming fufpicions had raifed in the minds of the people.   Common prudence would have allowed time for
the ferment to fubfide.   But the fpirit of fanaticifm
endeavoured, even in thefe troublefome times, to reftore every thing to the unity of the church of England, which was become more odious to the diffenters,
fince fo many cuftoms had been introduced into it
which they confidered as fuperftitious.   An order was
iffued, that both kingdoms fhould conform to the worfhip and difcipline of the Epifcopal church.   This law
included the Prefbyterians, who then began to be
called Puritans, becaufe they profeffed to take the
pure and fimple word of God for the rule of their faith
and practice.   It was extended likewife to all the foreign Calvinifts that were in the kingdom, whatever
difference there might be in their opinions.   This hie-
rarchal worfhip was enjoined to the regiments and
trading companies difperfed in the feveral countries of
Europe.   The Englifh ambaffadors were alfo required
to feparate from all communion with the foreign Proteftants, fo that England loft all the influence fhe had
acquired abroad, as the head and fupport of the Reformation.

In this fatal crifis, moft of the Puritans were divided between fubmiffion and oppofition.   Thofe who
would neither ftoop to yield, nor take the pains to refift, turned their views towards North America, in
fearch of that civil and religious liberty which their
ungrateful country denied them.   Their enemies, in
order to have an opportunity of perfecuting them more
at leifure, attempted to preclude thefe devout fugitives from this afylum, where they wanted to worfhip

God in their own way in a defert land. Eight fhips B O O K that lay at anchor in the Thames, ready to fail, were XVII. ftopped; and Cromwell is faid to have been detained there by that very king whom he afterwards brought to the fcaffold. Enthufiafm, however, ftronger than the rage of perfecution, furmounted every obftacle; and that part of America was foon filled with Prefby-terians. The fatisfaction they enjoyed in their retreat gradually induced all thofe of their party to follow them, who were not fo evil-minded as to delight in the view of thofe dreadful fcenes which foon after made England a fcene of blood and horror. Many were af-terwards induced to remove thither in more peaceable times, with a view of advancing their fortunes. In a word, all Europe contributed greatly to increafe their population. Thoufands of unhappy men, oppreffed by the tyranny or intolerant fpirit of their fovereigns, took refuge in that hemifphere; concerning which we fhall now purfue our inquiries, and endeavour, before we quit the fpot, to gain fome information refpecting it.

It is furprifing that fo little fhould have been known Parallel be-of the New World, for fo long a time after it was dif- tween the covered. Barbarous foldiers and rapacious merchants the New were not proper perfons to give us juft and clear no- World. tions of this hemifphere. It was the province of phi-lofophy alone to avail itfelf of the informations fcatter-ed in the accounts of voyages and miffionaries, in or-der to fee America fuch as nature hath made it, and to find out its analogy to the reft of the globe.

It is now pretty certain, that the new continent has not half the extent of furface that the old has. At the fame time, the form of both is fo fingularly alike, that we might eafily be inclined to draw confequences from this particular, if it were not always neceffary to be upon our guard againft the fpirit of fyftem which often ftops us in our refearches after truth, and hinders us from attaining it.

The two continents feem to form, as it were, two broad tracks of land, that begin from the Arctic pole,

B O O K and terminate at the tropic of Capricorn, divided on
  XVII.   the eaſt and weſt by the ocean that ſurrounds them.
Whatever may be the ſtructure of theſe two continents, and the quality or ſymmetry of their form, it is
evident that their equilibrium does not depend upon
their poſition. It is the inconſtancy of the ſea that
conſtitutes the ſolid form of the earth. To fix the
globe upon its baſis, it ſeemed neceſſary to have an
element which, floating inceſſantly round our planet,
might by its weight counterbalance all other ſubſtances, and by its fluidity reſtore that equilibrium
which the conflict of the other elements might have
diſturbed. Water, by its natural fluctuation and
weight, is the moſt proper element to preſerve the
connection and balance of the ſeveral parts of the
globe round its centre. If our hemiſphere has a very
wide extent of continent to the north, a maſs of water
of equal weight at the oppoſite part will certainly produce an equilibrium. If under the tropics we have a
rich country covered with men and animals, under
the ſame latitude America will have a ſea filled with
fiſh. While foreſts full of trees, bending with the
largeſt fruits, quadrupeds of the greateſt ſize, the moſt
populous nations, elephants and men, are a load upon
the ſurface of the earth, and ſeem to abſorb all its fertility throughout the torrid zone; at both poles are
found whales, with innumerable multitudes of cods
and herrings, clouds of inſects, and all the infinite and
prodigious tribes that inhabit the ſeas, as it were, to
ſupport the axis of the earth, and prevent its inclining
or deviating to either ſide: if, indeed, elephants,
whales, or men, can be ſaid to have any weight on a
globe, where all living creatures are but a tranſient
modification of the earth that compoſes it. In a word,
the ocean rolls over this globe to faſhion it, in conformity to the general laws of gravity. Sometimes it
covers a hemiſphere, a pole, or a zone, which at other
times it leaves bare; but in general it ſeems to affect
the equator, more eſpecially as the cold of the poles
in ſome meaſure contracts that fluidity which is eſſen-

tial to it, and from which it receives all its power of
motion.　It is chiefly between the tropics that the fea
extends itfelf, and is agitated ; and that it undergoes
the greateft change, both in its regular and periodical
motions, as well as in thofe violent agitations occafionally excited in it by tempeftuous winds.　The attraction of the fun, and the fermentations occafioned by
its continual heat in the torrid zone, muft have a very
remarkable influence upon the ocean.　The motion of
the moon adds a new force to this, influence ; and the
fea, to conform itfelf to this double impulfe. muft, it
would feem, flow towards the equator.　Nothing but
the flatnefs of the globe at the p)les can poffibly account for that immenfe extent of water that has hitherto concealed from us the lands near the South
pole.　The fea cannot eafily pafs the boundaries of
the tropics, if the temperate and frozen zones be not
nearer to the centre of the earth than the torrid zone.
It is the fea, therefore, that maintains an equilibrium
with the land, and difpofes the arrangement of the
materials that compofe it.　One proof that the analo-
gous portions of land, which the two continents of the
globe prefent at firft view, are not effentially neceffary
to its conformation, is, that the New Hemifphere has
remained covered with the waters of the fea a much
longer time than the Old.　Befides, if there be an evident fimilarity between the two hemifpheres, there are
alfo differences between them, which will perhaps deftroy that harmony we think we obferve.

　　When we confider the map of the world, and fee
the local correfpondence between the ifthmus of Suez
and that of Panama, between the Cape of Good Hope
and Cape Horn, between the Archipelago of the Eaft
Indies and that of the Caribbee Iflands, and between
the mountains of Chili and thofe of Monomotapa, we
are ftricken with the fimilarity of the feveral forms this
picture prefents.　Land feems on all fides to be oppofed to land, water to water, iflands and peninfulas
fcattered by the hand of nature to ferve as a counter-
poife, and the fea, by its fluctuation, conftantly main-

taining the balance of the whole. But if, on the other hand, we compare the great extent of the Pacific Ocean, which feparates the Eaft and Weft Indies, with the fmall fpace which the ocean occupies between the coaft of Guinea and that of Brazil; the vaft quantity of inhabited land to the north, with the little we know towards the fouth; the direction of the mountains of Tartary and Europe, which is from eaft to weft, with that of the Cordeleirias, which run from north to fouth; the mind is in fufpenfe, and we have the mortification to fee the order and fymmetry vanifh, with which we had embellifhed our fyftem of the earth. The obferver is ftill more difpleafed with his conjectures, when he confiders the immenfe height of the mountains of Peru. He is then aftonifhed to fee a continent fo recent, and yet fo elevated; the fea fo much below the tops of thefe mountains, and yet fo recently come down from the lands that feemed to be effectually defended from its attacks by thofe tremendous bulwarks. It is, however, an undeniable fact, that both continents of the New Hemifphere have been covered with the fea. The air and the land confirm this truth.

The rivers, which in America are wider and of greater extent; the immenfe forefts to the fouth; the fpacious lakes and vaft moraffes to the north; the almoft eternal fnows between the tropics; few of thofe pure fands that feem to be the remains of an exhaufted ground; no men entirely black; very fair people under the line; a cool and mild air in the fame latitude as the fultry and uninhabitable parts of Africa; a frozen and fevere climate under the fame parallel as our temperate climates; and laftly, a difference of ten or twelve degrees in the temperature of the Old and New Hemifpheres; thefe are fo many tokens of a world that is ftill in its infancy.

Why fhould the continent of America be much warmer and much colder in proportion than that of Europe, if it were not for the moifture the ocean has left behind, in quitting it long after our continent was

peopled? Nothing but the fea can poffibly have prevented Mexico from being inhabited as early as Afia.
If the waters that ftill moiften the bowels of the earth
in the New Hemifphere had not covered its furface,
the woods would very eafily have been cut down, the
fens drained, a foft and watery foil would have been
made firm, by ftirring it up, and expofing it to the
rays of the fun, a free paffage would have been open
to the winds, and dykes would have been raifed along
the rivers; in a word, the climate would have been
totally altered by this time. But a rude and unpeo-
pled hemifphere denotes a recent world; when the
fea about its coafts ftill flows obfcurely in its channels.
A lefs fcorching fun, more plentiful rains, and thicker
vapours, more difpofed to ftagnate, are evident marks
of the decay or the infancy of nature.

The difference of climate, arifing from the waters
having lain fo long on the ground in America, could
not but have a great influence on men and animals.
From this diverfity of caufes muft neceffarily arife a
very great diverfity of effects. Accordingly, we fee
more fpecies of animals, by two-thirds, in the old continent than the new; animals of the fame kind confiderably larger; monfters that are become more favage
and fierce, as the countries have become more inhabited. On the other hand, nature feems to have ftrange-
ly neglected the New World. The men have lefs
ftrength and lefs courage; no beard and no hair; they
have lefs appearances of manhood; and are but little
fufceptible of the lively and powerful fentiment of
love, which is the principle of every attachment, the
firft inftinct, the firft band of fociety, without which
all other artificial ties have neither energy nor duration. The women, who are ftill more weak, are neither favourably treated by nature nor by the men,
who have but little love for them, and confider them
merely as fubfervient to their will: they rather facrifice them to their indolence, than confecrate them to
their pleafures. This indolence is the great delight
and fupreme felicity of the Americans, of which the

BOOK
XVII.
women are the victims, from the continual labours
impofed upon them. It muft, however, be confeffed,
that in America, as in all other parts, the men, when
they have fentenced the women to work, have been
fo equitable as to take upon themfelves the perils of
war, together with the toils of hunting and fifhing.
But their indifference for the fex, which nature has
intrufted with the care of multiplying the fpecies, implies an imperfection in their organs, a fort of ftate of
childhood in the people of America, fimilar to that of
the people in our continent, who are not yet arrived
to the age of puberty. This feems to be a natural
defect prevailing in the continent of America, which
is an indication of its being a new country.

But if the Americans be a new people, are they a
race of men originally diftinct from thofe who cover
the face of the Old World? This is a queftion which
ought not to be too haftily decided. The origin of
the population of America is involved in inextricable
difficulties. If we affert that the Greenlanders firft
came from Norway, and then went over to the coaft
of Labrador, others will tell us, it is more natural to
fuppofe that the Greenlanders are fprung from the
Efquimaux, to whom they bear a greater refemblance
than to the Europeans. If we fhould fuppofe that
California was peopled from Kamtfchatka, it may be
afked, what motive or what chance could have led
the Tartars to the north-weft of America? Yet it is
imagined to be from Greenland or from Kamtfchatka
that the inhabitants of the Old World muft have gone
over to the New, as it is by thofe two countries that
the two continents are connected, or at leaft approach
neareft to one another. Befides, how can we conceive
that in America the torrid zone can have been peopled
from one of the frozen zones? Population will indeed
fpread from north to fouth, but it muft naturally have
begun under the equator, where life is cherifhed by
warmth. If the people of America could not come
from our continent, and yet appear to be a new race,
we muft have recourfe to the flood, which is the fource

and the folution of all difficulties in the hiftory of nations.

Let us fuppofe that the fea having overflowed the
other hemifphere, its old inhabitants took refuge upon
the Apalachian mountains, and the Cordeleirias, which
are far higher than our Mount Ararat. But how could
they have lived upon thofe heights, covered with fnow,
and furrounded with waters? How is it poffible that
men, who had breathed in a pure and delightful climate, could have furvived the miferies of want, the
inclemency of a tainted atmofphere, and thofe numberlefs calamities which muft be the unavoidable confequences of a deluge? How will the race have been
preferved and propagated in thofe times of general
calamity, and in the miferable ages that muft have
fucceeded? Notwithftanding all thefe objections. we
muft allow that America has been peopled from thefe
wretched remains of the great devaftation. Every
thing exhibits the veftiges of a malady, of which the
human race ftill feels the effects. The ruin of that
world is ftill imprinted on its inhabitants. They are
a fpecies of men degraded and degenerated in their
natural conftitution, in their ftature, in their way of
life, and in their underftanding which is but little advanced in all the arts of civilization. A damper air,
and a more marfhy ground, muft neceffarily have infected the firft principles of the fubfiftence and increafe
of mankind. It muft have required fome ages to reftore population, and ftill a greater number before the
ground could be fettled and dried, fo as to be fit for
tillage, and for the foundation of buildings. The air
muft neceffarily be purified before the fky could clear,
and the fky muft neceffarily be clear before the earth
could be rendered habitable. The imperfection, therefore, of nature in America is not fo much a proof of
its recent origin, as of its regeneration. It was probably peopled at the fame time as the other hemifphere,
but may have been overflowed later. The large foffil
bones that are found under ground in America, fhow
that it had formerly elephants, rhinoceros, and other

BOOK
XVII

enormous quadrupeds, which have since disappeared in those regions. The gold and silver mines that are found just below the surface of the earth, are signs of a very ancient revolution of the globe, but later than those that have overturned our hemisphere.

Suppose America had, by some means or other, been repeopled by our roving hordes, that period would have been so remote, that it would still give great antiquity to the inhabitants of that hemisphere. Three or four centuries will not then be sufficient to allow for the foundation of the empire of Mexico and Peru; for, though we find no trace in these countries of our arts, or of the opinions and customs that prevail in other parts of the globe, yet we have found a police and a society established, inventions and practices which, though they did not show any marks of times anterior to the deluge, yet they implied a long series of ages subsequent to this catastrophe. For, though in Mexico, as in Egypt, a country surrounded with waters, mountains, and other invincible obstacles, must have forced the men enclosed in it to unite after a time, notwithstanding they might at first have destroyed each other in continual and bloody wars, yet it was only in process of time that they could invent and establish a form of worship and a legislation, which they could not possibly have borrowed from remote times or countries. It required a greater number of ages to render familiar the single art of speech, and that of writing, though but in hieroglyphics, to a whole nation unconnected with any other, and which must itself have created both these arts, than it would take up days to perfect a child in them. Ages bear not the same proportion to the whole race as years do to individuals. The whole race is to occupy a vast field, both as to space and duration, while the individuals have only some moments or instants of time to fill up, or rather to run over. The likeness or uniformity observable in the features and manners of the American nations, plainly show that they are not so ancient as those of our continent, which differ so much from

each other; but at the fame time, this circumftance B O O K
feems to confirm that they did not proceed from any XVII.
foreign hemifphere, with which they have no kind of
affinity that can indicate an immediate defcent.

Whatever may be the cafe with regard to their ori- Compari-
gin or their antiquity, which are both uncertain, it is ſon be-
perhaps more interefting to inquire whether thofe un- lized peo-
tutored nations are more or lefs happy than our civi- ple and
lized people.   Let us, therefore, examine whether the ſavages.
condition of rude man, left to mere animal inftinct,
who paffes every day of his life in hunting, feeding,
producing his fpecies, and repofing himfelf, is better
or worfe than the condition of that wonderful being,
who makes his bed of down, fpins and weaves the
thread of the filk-worm to clothe himfelf, hath exchanged the cave, his original abode, for a palace, and
hath varied his indulgences and his wants in a thoufand different ways.

It is in the nature of man that we muft look for his
means of happinefs. What does he want to be as happy as he can be? Prefent fubfiftence; and, if he fhould
think of futurity, the hopes and certainty of enjoying
that bleffing. The favage, who has not been driven
into and confined within the frigid zones by civilized
focieties, is not in want of this firft of neceffaries. If
he fhould lay in no ftores, it is becaufe the earth and
the fea are refervoirs always open to fupply his wants.
Fifh and game are to be had all the year, and will
fupply the want of fertility in the dead feafons. The
favage has no houfe, well fecured from the accefs of
the external air, or commodious fire-places; but his
furs anfwer all the purpofes of the roof, the garment,
and the ftove. He works but for his own benefit,
fleeps when he is weary, and is a ftranger to watchings
and reftlefs nights. War is a matter of choice to him.
Danger, like labour, is a condition of his nature, not a
profeffion annexed to his birth; a national duty, not
a domeftic fervitude. The favage is ferious, but not
melancholy; and his countenance feldom bears the
impreffion of thofe paffions and diforders that leave

such shocking and fatal marks on ours. He cannot feel the want of what he does not desire, nor can he desire what he is ignorant of. Most of the conveniencies of life are remedies for evils he does not feel. Pleasure is the mode of satisfying appetites which his senses are unacquainted with. He seldom experiences any of that weariness that arises from unsatisfied desires, or that emptiness and uneasiness of mind that is the offspring of prejudice and vanity. In a word, the savage is subject to none but natural evils.

But what greater happiness than this does the civilized man enjoy? His food is more wholesome and delicate than that of the savage. He has softer clothes, and a habitation better secured against the inclemencies of the weather. But the common people, who are to be the support and basis of civil society, those numbers of men who in all states bear the burden of hard labour, cannot be said to live happy, either in those empires where the consequences of war and the imperfection of the police have reduced them to a state of slavery, or in those governments where the progress of luxury and police has reduced them to a state of servitude. The mixed governments seem to present some prospects of happiness under the protection of liberty; but this happiness is purchased by the most sanguinary exertions, which repel tyranny for a time only, that it may fall the heavier upon the devoted nation, sooner or later doomed to oppression. Observe how Caligula and Nero revenged the expulsion of the Tarquins, and the death of Cæsar.

Tyranny, we are told, is the work of the people, and not of kings. But if so, why do they suffer it? Why do they not repel the encroachments of despotism; and, while it employs violence and artifice to enslave all the faculties of men, why do they not oppose it with all their powers? But is it lawful to murmur and complain under the rod of the oppressor? Will it not exasperate and provoke him to pursue the victim to death? The complaints of slaves he calls rebellion; and they are to be stifled in a dungeon, and sometimes put an end to on a scaffold. The man who should assert the rights of man would perish in neglect and infamy. Tyranny, therefore, must be endured, under the name of authority.

If so, to what outrages is not the civilized man exposed! If he be possessed of any property, he knows not how far he may call it his own, when he must divide he produce between the courtier who may attack his estate, the lawyer who must be paid for teaching him how to preserve it, the soldier who may lay it waste, and the collector who comes to levy unlimited taxes. If he should have no property, how can he be assured of a permanent subsistence? What species of industry is secured against the vicissitudes of fortune, and the encroachments of government?

In the forests of America, if there be a scarcity in the north, the savages bend their course to the south. The wind or the sun will drive a wandering clan to more temperate climates. But if in our civilized states, confined within gates, and restrained within certain limits, famine, war, or pestilence should consume an empire, it is a prison where all must expect to perish in misery, or in the horrors of slaughter. The man who is unfortunately born there, is compelled to endure all extortions, all the severities that the inclemency of the seasons and the injustice of government may bring upon him.

In our provinces, the vassal, or free mercenary, digs and ploughs, the whole year round, lands that are not his own, and the produce of which does not belong to him; and he is even happy if his labour can procure him a share of the crops he has sown and reaped. Observed and harassed by a hard and restless landlord, who grudges him even the straw on which he rests his weary limbs, the wretch is daily exposed to diseases, which, joined to his poverty, make him wish for death, rather than for an expensive cure, followed by infirmities and toil. Whether tenant or subject, he is doubly a slave; if he should possess a few acres, his lord comes and gathers upon them what he has not sown; if he

B O O K be worth but a yoke of oxen or a pair of horfes, he
  XVII.   muft employ them in the public fervice ; if he fhould
have nothing but his perfon, the prince takes him for
a foldier. Every where he meets with mafters, and always with oppreffion.

In our cities, the workmen and the artift who have
no manufacture of their own are at the mercy of greedy and idle mafters, who, by the privilege of monopoly, have purchafed of government a power of making
induftry work for nothing, and of felling its labours
at a very high price. The lower clafs have no more
than the fight of that luxury of which they are doubly the victims, by the watchings and. fatigues it occafions them, and by the infolence of the pomp that
humiliates and oppreffes them.

Even fuppofing that the dangerous labours of our
quarries, mines, and forges, with all the arts that are
performed by fire, and that the perils which navigation and commerce expofe us to, were lefs pernicious
than the roving life of the favages, who live upon
hunting and fifhing ; fuppofe that men, who are ever
lamenting the forrows and affronts that arife merely
from opinion, are lefs unhappy than the favages, who
never fhed a tear in the moft excruciating tortures ;
there would ftill remain a wide difference between the
fate of the civilized man and the wild Indian, a difference entirely to the difadvantage of focial life. This
is the injuftice that prevails in the partial diftribution
of fortunes and ftations ; an inequality which is at
once the effect and the caufe of oppreffion.

In vain does cuftom, prejudice, ignorance, and hard
labour ftupify the lower clafs of mankind, fo as to
render them infenfible of their degradation ; neither
religion nor morality can hinder them from feeing
and feeling the injuftice of the arrangements of policy
in the diftribution of good and evil. How often have
we heard the poor man expoftulating with Heaven,
and afking what he had done, that he fhould deferve
to be born in an indigent and dependent ftation?
Even if great conflicts were infeparable from the more

exalted ftations, which might be fufficient to balance all the advantages and all the fuperiority that the fo- cial ftate claims over the ftate of nature, ftill the ob- fcure man, who is unacquainted with thofe conflicts, fees nothing in a high rank, but that affluence which is the caufe of his own poverty. He envies the rich man thofe pleafures to which he is fo accuftomed, that he has loft all relifh for them. What domeftic can have a real affection for his mafter, or what is the at- tachment of a fervant? Was ever prince truly belov- ed by his courtiers, even when he was hated by his fubjects? If we prefer our condition to that of the fa- vages, it is becaufe civil life has made us incapable of bearing fome natural hardfhips which the favage is more expofed to than we are, and becaufe we are at- tached to fome indulgences that cuftom has made ne- ceffary to us. Even in the vigour of life, a civilized man may accuftom himfelf to live among favages and return to the ftate of nature. We have an inftance of this in that Scotchman who was caft away on the ifland of Fernandez, where he lived alone, and was happy as foon as he was fo taken up with fupplying his wants, as to forget his own country, his language, his name, and even the articulation of words. After four years, he felt himfelf eafed of the burden of focial life, when he had loft all reflection or thought of the paft, and all anxiety for the future.

Laftly, the confcioufnefs of independence being one of the firft inftincts in man, he who enjoys this primi- tive right, with a moral certainty of a competent fub- fiftence, is incomparably happier than the rich man, reftrained by laws, mafters, prejudices, and fafhions, which inceffantly remind him of the lofs of his liber- ty. To compare the ftate of the favages to that of children, is to decide at once the queftion that has been fo warmly debated by philofophers, concerning the advantages of the ftate of nature above thofe of focial life. Children, notwithftanding the reftraints of education, are in the happieft age of human life. Their habitual cheerfulnefs, when they are not under the

B O O K fchoolmafter's rod, is the fureft indication of the hap-
XVII.   pinefs they feel. After all, a fingle word may determine this great queftion. Let us afk the civilized man
whether he be happy, and the favage whether he be
unhappy. If they both anfwer in the negative, the
difpute is at an end.

Ye civilized nations, this parallel muft certainly be
mortifying to you! but you cannot too ftrongly feel
the weight of the calamities under which you are oppreffed. The more painful the fenfation is, the more
will it awaken your attention to the true caufes of
your fufferings. You may at laft be convinced that
they proceed from the confufion of your opinions, from
the defects of your political conftitutions, and from
capricious laws, which are in continual oppofition to
the laws of nature.

After this inquiry into the moral ftate of the Americans, let us return to the natural ftate of their country. Let us fee what it was before the arrival of the
Englifh, and what it is become under their dominion.

The ftate   The firft Englifhmen who went over to America to
in which   fettle colonies, found immenfe forefts. The vaft trees
the Englifh
found   that grew up to the clouds, were fo furrounded with
North A-   creeping plants, that they could not be approached.
merica and
what they   The wild beafts made thefe woods ftill more inaccef-
have done   fible. A few favages only were met with, clothed
there.   with the fkins of thofe monfters. The human race,
thinly fcattered, fled from each other, or purfued only
with intent to deftroy. The earth feemed ufelefs to
man, and its powers were not exerted fo much for his
fupport, as in the breeding of animals, more obedient
to the laws of nature. It produced fpontaneoufly
without affiftance and without direction; it yielded all
its bounties with uncontrouled profufion for the benefit of all, not for the pleafures or conveniencies of
one fpecies of beings. The rivers in one place glided
freely through the forefts, in another, fcattered their
unruffled waters in a wide morafs, from whence iffuing
in various ftreams they formed a multitude of iflands,

encompaſſed with their channels. Spring was renewed from the decay of autumn. The withered leaves,
rotting at the foot of the trees, ſupplied them with
freſh ſap to enable them to ſhoot out new bloſſoms.
The hollow trunks of trees afforded a retreat to prodigious numbers of birds. The ſea, daſhing againſt the
coaſts, and indenting the gulfs, threw up ſhoals of amphibious monſters, enormous whales, crabs, and turtles,
that ſported uncontrouled on the deſert ſhores. There
nature exerted her plaſtic power, inceſſantly producing
the gigantic inhabitants of the ocean, and aſſerting the
freedom of the earth and the ſea.

But man appeared, and immediately changed the
face of North America. He introduced ſymmetry by
the aſſiſtance of all the inſtruments of art. The impenetrable woods were inſtantly cleared, and made
room for commodious dwellings. The wild beaſts
were driven away, and flocks of domeſtic animals ſupplied their place; while thorns and briars made way
for rich harveſts. The waters forſook part of their domain, and were drained off into the interior parts of the
land, or into the ſea by deep canals. The coaſts were
covered with towns, and the bays with ſhips; and thus
the New World, like the Old, became ſubject to man.
What powerful engines have raiſed that wonderful
ſtructure of European induſtry and policy? Let us re-
ſume the conſideration of the particulars. In the re-
moteſt part ſtands a ſolitary ſpot, diſtinct from the
whole, and which is called Hudſon's Bay.

This ſtrait, of about ten degrees in depth, is formed by the ocean in the diſtant and northern parts of
America. The breadth of the entrance is ſix leagues,
but it is only to be attempted from the beginning of
July to the end of September, and is even then rather
dangerous. This danger ariſes from mountains of ice,
ſome of which are ſaid to be from 15 to 18 hundred
feet thick, and which having been produced by winters of five or ſix years duration in little gulfs conſtantly filled with ſnow, are forced out of them by
north-weſt winds, or by ſome other extraordinary cauſe.

Climate of Hudſon's Bay, and cuſtoms of its inhabi- tants. Trade car- ried on there.

The beſt way of avoiding them is to keep as near as poſſible to the northern coaſt, which muſt neceſſarily be leſs obſtructed and moſt free by the natural direction of both winds and currents.

The north-weſt wind, which blows almoſt conſtantly in winter, and very often in ſummer, frequently raiſes violent ſtorms within the bay itſelf, which is rendered ſtill more dangerous by the number of ſhoals that are found there. Happily, however, ſmall groups of iſlands are met with at different diſtances, which are of a ſufficient height to afford a ſhelter from the ſtorm. Beſide theſe ſmall Archipelagoes, there are in many places large piles of bare rock. Except the Alga Marina, the bay produces as few vegetables as the other northern ſeas.

Throughout all the countries ſurrounding this bay, the ſun never riſes or ſets without forming a great cone of light; this phenomenon is ſucceed by the Aurora Borealis, which tinges the hemiſphere with coloured rays of ſuch brilliancy, that the ſplendour of them is not effaced even by that of the full moon. Notwithſtanding this, there is ſeldom a bright ſky. In ſpring and autumn, the air is always filled with thick fogs, and in winter, with an infinite number of ſmall icicles. Though the heats in the ſummer be rather conſiderable for ſix weeks or two months, there is ſeldom any thunder or lightning, owing, no doubt to the great diſperſion of the ſulphureous exhalations, which, however, are ſometimes ſet on fire by the Aurora Borealis; and this light flame conſumes the barks of the trees, but leaves their trunks untouched.

One of the effects of the extreme cold or ſnow that prevails in this climate, is that of turning thoſe animals white in winter, which are naturally brown or grey. Nature has beſtowed upon them all, ſoft, long, and thick furs, the hair of which falls off as the weather grows milder. In moſt of theſe quadrupeds, the feet, the tail, the ears, and generally ſpeaking all thoſe parts in which the circulation is ſlower, becauſe they are the moſt remote from the heart, are extremely fhort. Wherever they happen to be fomething long- er, they are proportionably well covered. Under this gloomy fky, all liquors become folid by freezing, and break the veffels they are in. Even fpirit of wine lofes its fluidity. It is not uncommon to fee fragments of large rocks loofened and detached from the great mafs, by the force of the froft. All thefe phenomena, common enough during the whole winter, are much more terrible at the new and full moon, which in thefe regions has an influence upon the weather, the caufes of which are not known.

In this frozen zone, iron, lead, copper, marble, and a fubftance refembling fea-coal, have been difcovered. In other refpects, the foil is extremely barren. Except the coafts, which are for the moft part marfhy, and produce a little grafs and fome foft wood; the reft of the country affords nothing but very high mofs, and a few weak fhrubs very thinly fcattered.

This deficiency in nature extends itfelf to every thing. The human race are few in number, and there are fcarce any perfons above four feet high. Their heads bear the fame enormous proportion to the reft of their bodies, as thofe of children do. The fmallnefs of their feet makes them awkward and tottering in their gait. Small hands and a round mouth, which in Europe are reckoned a beauty, feem almoft a deformity in thefe people, becaufe we fee nothing here but the effects of a weak organization, and of a cold climate, that contracts and reftrains the principles of growth, and is fatal to the progrefs of animal as well as of vegetable life. All the men, even the youngeft of them, though they have neither hair nor beard, have the appearance of being old. This is partly occafioned from the formation of their lower lip, which is thick, flefhy, and projecting beyond the upper. Such are the Efquimaux, who inhabit not only the coaft of Labrador, from whence they have taken their name, but likewife all that tract of country which extends from the point of Belleifle to the moft northern parts of America.

The inhabitants of Hudſon's Bay have, like the
Greenlanders, a flat face, with ſhort but not flattened
noſes, the pupil yellow, and the iris black.   Their
women have marks of deformity peculiar to their ſex,
among others very long and flabby breaſts.   This defect, which is not natural, ariſes from their cuſtom of
giving ſuck to their children till they are five or ſix
years old.   As they often carry them at their backs,
the children pull their mothers breaſts forcibly, and
almoſt ſupport themſelves by them.

It is not true that there are hordes of the Eſquimaux entirely black, as has been ſuppoſed, and then
accounted for ; nor that they live under ground. How
ſhould they dig into a ſoil, which the cold renders
harder than ſtone?   How is it poſſible they ſhould
live in caverns where they would be infallibly drowned by the firſt melting of the ſnows?

It is, however, certain, that they ſpend the winter
under huts haſtily built with flints joined together
with cements of ice, where they live without any
other fire but that of a lamp hung in the middle of
the ſhed, for the purpoſe of dreſſing their game and
the fiſh they feed upon.   The heat of their blood,
and of their breath, added to the vapour ariſing from
this ſmall flame, is ſufficient to make their huts as hot
as ſtoves.

The Eſquimaux dwell conſtantly in the neighbourhood of the ſea, which ſupplies them with all their
proviſions.   Both their conſtitution and complexion
partake of the quality of their aliment.   The fleſh of
the ſeal is their food, and the oil of the whale is their
drink, which produces in them all an olive complexion,
a ſtrong ſmell of fiſh, an oily and tenacious ſweat, and
ſometimes a ſort of ſcaly leproſy.   This is, probably,
the reaſon why the mothers have the ſame cuſtom as
the bears, of licking their young ones.

Theſe people, weak and degraded by nature, are
notwithſtanding moſt intrepid upon a ſea that is conſtantly dangerous.   In boats made and ſewed together like ſo many Borachios, but at the ſame time

fo well clofed that it is impoffible for the water to pe- B O O K
netrate them, they follow the fhoals of herrings through XVII.
the whole of their polar emigrations, and attack the
whales and feals at the peril of their lives. One ftroke
of the whale's tail is fufficient to drown a hundred of
them, and the feal is armed with teeth to devour thofe
he cannot drown; but the hunger of the Efquimaux
is fuperior to the rage of thefe monfters. They have
an inordinate defire for the whale's oil, which is neceffary to preferve the heat in their ftomachs, and defend them from the feverity of the cold. Indeed,
whales, men, birds, and all the quadrupeds and fifh
of the north are fupplied by nature with a quantity
of fat which prevents the mufcles from freezing, and
the blood from coagulating. Every thing in thefe
arctic regions is either oily or gummy, and even the
trees are refinous.

The Efquimaux are, notwithftanding, fubject to two
fatal diforders, the fcurvy and the lofs of fight. The
continuation of the fnows on the ground, joined to
the reverberation of the rays of the fun on the ice,
dazzle their eyes in fuch a manner, that they are almoft conftantly obliged to wear fhades made of very
thin wood, through which fmall apertures for the light
are bored with fifh-bones. Doomed to a fix-months
night, they never fee the fun but obliquely, and then
it feems rather to blind them than to give them light.
Sight, the moft delightful bleffing of nature, is a fatal
gift to them, and they are generally deprived of it
when young.

A ftill more cruel evil, which is the fcurvy, confumes
them by flow degrees. It infinuates itfelf into their
blood, changes, thickens, and impoverifhes the whole
mafs. The fogs of the fea, which they infpire, the
denfe and inelaftic air they breathe in their huts, which
exclude all communication with the external air, the
continued and tedious inactivity of their long winters,
a mode of life alternately roving and fedentary; in a
word, every circumftance ferves to increafe this dreadful illnefs; which in a little time becomes contagious,

and fpreading itfelf throughout their habitations, is alfo probably entailed upon their pofterity.

Notwithftanding thefe inconveniences, the Efquimaux is fo paffionately fond of his country, that no inhabitant of the moft favoured fpot under heaven quits it with more reluctance than he does his frozen deferts. One of the reafons of this may be, that he finds it difficult to breathe in a fofter and more temperate climate. The fky of Amfterdam, Copenhagen, and London, though conftantly obfcured by thick and fetid vapours, is too clear for an Efquimaux. Perhaps too, there may be fomething in the change of life and manners ftill more unfavourable to the health of favages than the climate. It is not impoffible but that the delights of an European may be poifon to the Efquimaux.

Such were the inhabitants of the country difcovered in 1607 by Henry Hudfon, who had employed himfelf in fearching for a north-weft paffage to enter into the South Sea. This intrepid and able navigator, in 1611, was going through, for the third time, thefe ftraits, which were before unknown, when his bafe and treacherous crew placed him, with feven of the failors who were animated with the fame fpirit, in a very flight boat, and left him, without either arms or provifions, expofed to all the dangers both of fea and land. The barbarians, who refufed him the neceffaries of life, could not, however, rob him of the honour of the difcovery; and the bay which he firft found out will ever be called by his name.

The miferies of the civil war which followed foon after, had, however, made the Englifh forget this diftant country, which had nothing to attract them. A fucceffion of more quiet times had not yet induced them to attend to it, when Grofeillers and Radiffon, two French Canadians, having met with fome difcontent at home, informed the Englifh, who were engaged in repairing the mifchiefs of difcord by trade, of the profits arifing from furs, and of their claim to the country that furnifhed them. Thofe who propoſed this undertaking ſhowed ſo much ability, that they were intruſted with the execution of it; and the firſt eſtabliſhment they formed ſucceeded ſo well, that it ſurpaſſed their own hopes as well as their promiſes.

BOOK XVII.

This ſucceſs alarmed the French, who were afraid, and with reaſon, that moſt of the fine furs which they got from the northern parts of Canada, would be carried to Hudſon's Bay. Their alarms were confirmed by the unanimous teſtimony of their *Coureurs de Bois*, who, ſince 1656, had been four times as far as the borders of the ſtrait. It would have been an eligible thing to have gone by the ſame road to attack the new colony; but the diſtance being thought too conſiderable, notwithſtanding the convenience of the rivers, it was at length determined that the expedition ſhould be made by ſea. The fate of it was truſted to Groſeillers and Radiſſon, who had been eaſily prevailed upon to renew their attachment to their country.

Theſe two bold and turbulent men ſailed from Quebec in 1682, in two veſſels ill equipped; and on their arrival, finding themſelves not ſtrong enough to attack the enemy, they were contented with erecting a fort in the neighbourhood of that they deſigned to have taken. From this time there began a rivalſhip between the two companies, one ſettled at Canada, the other in England, for the excluſive trade of the bay, which was conſtantly kept up by the diſputes it occaſioned, till at laſt, after each of their ſettlements had been frequently taken and recovered, all hoſtilities were terminated by the treaty of Utrecht, by which the whole was ceded to Great Britain.

Hudſon's Bay, properly ſpeaking, is only a mart for trade. The ſeverity of the climate having deſtroyed all the corn ſown there at different times, has fruſtrated every hope of agriculture, and conſequently of population. Throughout the whole of this extenſive coaſt, there are not more than ninety or a hundred ſoldiers, or factors, who live in four bad forts, of which York fort is the principal. Their buſineſs is to receive

the furs brought by the neighbouring favages in exchange for merchandife, of which they have been
taught the value and ufe.

Though thefe fkins be much more valuable than
thofe which are found in countries not fo far north,
yet they are cheaper. The favages give ten beaver
fkins for a gun, two for a pound of powder, one for
four pounds of lead, one for a hatchet, one for fix
knives, two for a pound of glafs beads, fix for a cloth
coat, five for a petticoat, and one for a pound of
fnuff. Combs, looking-glaffes, kettles, and brandy,
fell in proportion. As the beaver is the common meafure of exchange, by another regulation as fraudulent
as the firft, two otter fkins and three martins are required inftead of one beaver. Befide this oppreffion,
which is authorifed, there is another which is at leaft
tolerated, by which the favages are conftantly defrauded in the quality, quantity, and meafure of what is
given them, and by which they lofe about one third of
the value.

From this regulated fyftem of impofition, it is eafy
to guefs that the commerce of Hudfon's Bay is a monopoly. The capital of the Company that is in poffeffion of it was originally no more than 241,500 livres
[10,062l. 10s.], and has been fucceffively increafed to
2,380,500 [99,187l. 10s.]. This capital brings them
in an annual return of forty or fifty thoufand fkins of
beavers or other animals, upon which they make fo
exorbitant a profit, that it excites the jealoufy and clamours of the nation. Two thirds of thefe beautiful
furs are either confumed in kind in the three kingdoms,
or made ufe of in the national manufactures. The reft
are carried into Germany, where the nature of the climate makes them a valuable commodity.

Whether
there be a
paffage
from Hud-
fon's Bay to
the Eaft In-
dies.
But it is neither the acquifition of thefe favage
riches, nor the ftill greater emoluments that might be
drawn from this trade, if it were made free, which
have alone fixed the attention of England, as well as
that of all Europe, upon this frozen continent. Hudfon's Bay always has been, and is ftill looked upon as

the neareſt road from Europe to the Eaſt Indies, and B O O K
to the richeſt parts of Aſia. XVII.

Cabot was the firſt who entertained an idea of a
north-weſt paſſage to the South Seas; but his diſco-
veries ended at Newfoundland. After him followed
a multitude of Engliſh navigators, many of whom had
the glory of giving their names to ſavage coaſts which
no mortal had ever viſited before. Theſe bold and
memorable expeditions were more ſtriking than really
uſeful. The moſt fortunate of them did not furniſh a
ſingle idea relative to the objeƈt of purſuit. The
Dutch, leſs frequent in their attempts, and who purſued them with leſs ardour, were of courſe not more
ſuccefsful; and the whole began to be treated as a
chimera, when the diſcovery of Hudſon's Bay rekindled all the hopes that were nearly extinguiſhed.

From this time the attempts were renewed with
freſh ardour. Thoſe that had been made before in
vain by the mother-country, whoſe attention was engroſſed by her own inteſtine commotions, were purſued by New England, whoſe ſituation was more favourable to the enterpriſe. Still, however, for ſome
time there were more voyages undertaken than diſco-
veries made. The nation was a long time kept in ſuf-
penſe by the contradiƈtory accounts received from the
adventurers. While ſome maintained the poſſibility,
ſome the probability, and others aſſerted the certainty
of the paſſage; the accounts they gave, inſteaḍ of
clearing up the point, involved it in ſtill greater darkneſs. Indeed, theſe accounts are ſo full of obſcurity
and confuſion, they are ſilent upon ſo many important circumſtances, and they diſplay ſuch viſible marks
of ignorance and want of veracity, that, however impatient we may be of determining the queſtion, it is
impoſſible to build any thing like a ſolid judgment upon teſtimonies ſo ſuſpicious. At length, the famous
expedition of 1746 threw ſome kind of light upon a
point which had remained enveloped in darkneſs for
two centuries paſt. But upon what grounds have the
later navigators entertained better hopes? What are

the experiments on which they found their conjectures?

Let us proceed to give an account of their arguments. There are three facts in natural hiftory, which
henceforward muft be taken for granted. The firft is,
that the tides come from the ocean, and that they extend more or lefs into the other feas, in proportion as
their channels communicate with the great refervoir
by larger or fmaller openings; from whence it follows, that this periodical motion either doth not exift,
or is fcarce perceptible in the Mediterranean, in the
Baltic, and other gulfs of the fame nature. A fecond
matter of fact is, that the tides are much later and
much weaker in places more remote from the ocean,
than in thofe which are nearer to it. The third fact
is, that violent winds, which blow in a direction with
the tides, make them rife above their ordinary boundaries; and that thofe which blow in a contrary direction retard their motion, at the fame time that they
diminifh their fwell.

From thefe principles it is moft certain, that if Hudfon's Bay were no more than a gulf enclofed between
two continents, and had no communication but with
the Atlantic, the tides in it would be very inconfiderable; they would be weaker in proportion as they
were further removed from the fource, and would be
much lefs ftrong wherever they ran in a contrary direction to the wind. But it is proved by obfervations
made with the greateft fkill and precifion, that the
tides are very high throughout the whole bay. It is
certain that they are higher towards the bottom of the
bay than even in the ftrait itfelf, or at leaft in the
neighbourhood of it. It is proved, that even this
height increafes whenever the wind blows from a corner oppofite to the ftrait; it is therefore certain, that
Hudfon's Bay has a communication with the ocean,
befide that which has been already found out.

Thofe who have endeavoured to explain thefe very
ftriking facts, by fuppofing a communication of Hudfon's with Baffin's Bay, or with Davis's Straits, are evi-

dently in an error. They would not fcruple to reject this opinion, for which; indeed, there is no real foundation, if they only confidered that the tides are much lower in Davis's Straits and in Baffin's Bay, than in Hudfon's.

But if the tides in Hudfon's Bay can come neither from the Atlantic ocean, nor from any other northern fea, in which they are conftantly much weaker, it follows that they muft have their origin in the South Sea. And this is ftill further apparent from another leading fact, which is, that the higheft tides ever obferved upon thefe coafts are always occafioned by the northweft winds, which blow directly againft the mouth of the ftrait.

Having thus determined, as much as the nature of the fubject will permit, the exiftence of this paffage, fo long and fo vainly wifhed for, the next point is, to find out in what part of the bay it is to be expected. From confidering every circumftance, we are induced to think that the attempts, which have been hitherto made without either choice or method, ought to be directed towards Welcome Bay, on the weftern coaft. Firft, the bottom of the fea is to be feen there at the depth of about eleven fathom, which is an evident fign that the water comes from fome ocean, as fuch a tranfparency could not exift in waters difcharged from rivers, or in melted fnow or rain. Secondly, the currents keep this place always free from ice, while all the reft of the bay is covered with it; and their violence cannot be accounted for, but by fuppofing them to come from fome weftern fea. Laftly, the whales, which towards the latter end of autumn always go in fearch of the warmeft climates, are found in great abundance in thefe parts towards the end of the fummer, which would feem to indicate that there is an outlet for them from thence to the South Seas, not to the northern ocean.

It is probable that the paffage is very fhort. All the rivers that empty themfelves on the weftern coaft of Hudſon's Bay are ſmall and ſlow, which ſeems to prove that they do not come from any diſtance, and that conſequently the lands which ſeparate the two ſeas are of a ſmall extent. This argument is ſtrength-ened by the height and regularity of the tides. Where-ver there is no other difference between the times of the ebb and flow, but that which is occaſioned by the retarded progreſſion of the moon in her return to the meridian, it is a certain ſign that the ocean from whence thoſe tides come is very near. If the paſſage be ſhort, and not very far to the north, as every thing ſeems to promiſe, we may alſo preſume that it is not very difficult. The rapidity of the currents obſervable in theſe latitudes, which prevents any flakes of ice from continuing there, cannot but give ſome weïght to this conjecture.

The diſcovery that ſtill remains to be made is of ſo much importance and utility, that it would be folly to neglect the purſuit of it. It is conſiſtent with the in-tereſt, as well as the dignity of Great Britain, that theſe attempts ſhould be purſued, either till they ſuc-ceed, or till the impoſſibility of ſucceeding ſhall be demonſtrated. The reſolution which they have taken in 1745, of promiſing a conſiderable reward to the na-vigators who ſhould ſucceed in this great project, diſ-plays their wiſdom even in their generoſity, but is not ſtill ſufficient to attain the end that is propoſed. The miniſtry of England muſt know, that the efforts of in-dividuals will not ſucceed, till the trade of Hudſon's Bay be entirely laid open. It ought to be made free on every account, and particularly, becauſe the term of the grant given by Charles II. has been expired for a long time, and hath never been legally prolonged. The Company in whoſe hands the trade is, ſince the year 1670, not ſatisfied with neglecting the object of their inſtitution, by taking no ſteps towards the diſco-very of a north-weſt paſſage, have even exerted their utmoſt efforts to thwart the deſigns of thoſe who, either from love of glory or from other motives, have been impelled to this undertaking. Nothing can alter that spirit of iniquity which conftitutes the effence of monopoly.

Perhaps we fhould, however, confine ourfelves chiefly to the northern feas, in order to difcover this long-wifhed-for paffage. About two centuries ago, a report was fpread that there exifted one fomewhere elfe, which was fometimes defcribed under the name of Anian. The Spaniards, who were not yet acquainted with the paffage from Cape Horn to the South Seas, and who got there only by the Straits of Magellan, which were dreaded on account of the frequent fhipwrecks that happened there, eagerly laid hold of this popular opinion. They fitted out five expeditions, as expenfive as they were ufelefs; and the refult of which was, that Europe was undeceived with refpect to this fabulous account, which the Spaniards themfelves were accufed of having propagated, in order to divert other nations from the defign of feeking a paffage towards the north.

This ftate of inaction did not, it is faid, laft long. The court of Madrid being informed that New England was preparing, in 1636, a new expedition, to difcover a paffage through the Frozen Sea, likewife ordered one to be fitted out at Peru, in order to meet thefe navigators. Admiral Fuentes, who was intrufted with this expedition, fet out from Callao, with four fhips, towards the middle of the year 1640. He rapidly overcame all the obftacles which nature oppofed to his operations, and arrived himfelf in Hudfon's Bay, while his lieutenants penetrated into Davis's Straits, and into the fea of Tartary, at the extremity of Afia. After the difcovery of thefe three paffages, the fmall fleet very happily regained the South Sea, from whence it had fet out. It hath been pretended, that the council in India had myfterioufly concealed the knowledge of this event from the nations, and that they had fuppreffed, with the greateft care, all the accounts which might one day revive the memory of it. The Spaniards, in their turn, affirm, that the expedition of Fuentes and the difcovery are both equally chimerical;

B O O K and there can be no doubt but that they are entirely
XVII. in the right.

It is very poffible that the writings recently publifhed upon this fubject have excited a laudable curiofity.
The government of Mexico, animated with the fame
fpirit which begins to ftimulate the mother-country,
difpatched, on the 13th of June 1773, a frigate, deftined to reconnoitre America at the higheft degree of
latitude poffible. The perfons on board this fhip perceived the coaft at 40, 49, and even at 55 degrees 43
minutes; precifely at the fame place where Captain
Tichivikow had difcovered it upon his firft expedition
from Kamtfchatka. The fhip entered into the port of
Saint Blas, to take in frefh provifions, and then recommenced its cruifes. It can fcarce be doubted, but
that the defire of gaining information with refpect to
the North-weft Paffage was the principal defign of all
thefe labours.

After fo many fruitlefs attempts, if fome navigator
fhould appear, whofe ftrong mind rifes fuperior to every fenfe of danger; who fears not to encounter the
greateft and moft various hardfhips, and whofe patience cannot be exhaufted by the duration of them:
if fuch a one fhould be animated with the fenfe of glory, the only principle which makes men regardlefs of
life, and excites them to great undertakings: if he
fhould be a well-informed man, fo as to underftand
what he fees, and a man of veracity, fo as to relate nothing but what he hath feen; his refearches will, perhaps, be crowned with better fuccefs.

This extraordinary man hath appeared in the perfon of Captain Cook: that navigator, who is fo much
beyond all his competitors, is gone for Otaheite. From
thence he is to proceed to the north of California, there
to feek for the north-weft paffage. He will have, for
the purpofe of effecting this difcovery, many advantages denied to thofe navigators who have gone by the
way of Hudfon's Bay, or of the neighbouring latitudes.
If this celebrated paffage fhould ftill remain concealed,
though it be fought for with all his refolution and fkill,

it muſt be concluded, either that it doth not exiſt, or
that it is not given to man to diſcover it.

But how inconceivable is the viciſſitude of all human affairs; how perpetual the ſway of deſtiny, which
thwarts or favours, retards or accelerates, ſtops or ſuſpends our enterpriſes! Cook, whom nature had endowed with the genius and intrepidity neceſſary for
extraordinary actions; whom a generous and enlightened nation had provided with all the means that can
enſure ſucceſs; whoſe ſhip, a young monarch, convinced undoubtedly that virtue attends upon the progreſs
of knowledge, had given orders to reſpect, and to aſ-
ſiſt during the courſe of hoſtilities, as in time of full
peace; Cook, who had ſailed over an immenſe extent
of ſpace, and whoſe labours were now drawing near
to an end, loſes his life by the hands of a ſavage. The
man whoſe remains ſhould have been depoſited by the
ſide of kings, is buried at the foot of a tree, in an iſland
almoſt unknown.

Should his ſucceſſor Captain Clerke, who purſues
his projects, at length diſcover this paſſage, which hath
been ſo obſtinately ſought for, and ſhould it prove eaſy
to ſail through it, the connections between Europe and
the Eaſt and Weſt Indies will become more animated,
more conſtant, and more conſiderable. Both the
Straits of Magellan and Cape Horn will be entirely
deſerted, and the Cape of Good Hope much leſs frequented.

Theſe revolutions, which may affect Hudſon's Bay
in ſo palpable a manner, will never change the deſtiny
of Canada, conquered from France in 1760.

This colony was divided, during the ſpace of four
years, into three military governments. Civil and criminal cauſes were tried at Quebec and at Trois Rivieres, by the officers of the army; while at Montreal,
theſe nice and important functions were intruſted to
the citizens. They were both equally ignorant of the
laws: and the commandant of each diſtrict, to whom
an appeal lay from their ſentences, was not better informed.

State of Ca-
nada ſince
it hath been
under the
dominion
of Great
Britain.

B O O K   A new fyftem was eftablifhed in the year 1764.
XVII.   Canada was difmembered of the coaft of Labrador,
which was united to Newfoundland ; of lake Champlain, and of all the fpace to the fouth of the forty-
fifth degree of latitude, which was added to New
York ; and of the immenfe territory to the weft of
Fort Golette, and of the lake Niffiping, which was
put under no government. The remainder, under the
title of the province of Quebec, was fubjeƈt to one governor.

At the fame period the colony was put under the
laws of the admiralty of England ; but this innovation
was hardly perceived, becaufe it fcarce interefted any
but the conquerors, who were in poffeffion of all the
maritime trade.

Greater attention was paid to the eftablifhment of
the code of criminal laws adopted in England. This
was one of the moft valuable prefents Canada could
poffibly receive.

Before that time, a culprit, whether guilty or only
fufpeƈted, was immediately feized, thrown into prifon,
and queftioned, without being made acquainted either
with his crime or with his accufer, and without being
allowed the liberty of feeing either his relations or
friends, or of applying to council. He was made to
fwear that he would tell the truth, that is to fay, ac-
cufe himfelf ; and to complete thefe abfurdities, his
teftimony was difregarded.

Attempts were then made to embarrafs him with
captious queftions, which an impudent and guilty perfon could more readily anfwer, than an innocent man
in confufion. One might have faid, that the funƈtion
of a judge was nothing more than the fubtle art of
finding out culprits. The prifoner was not confront-
ed with thofe who depofed againft him, till the inftant
before the judge pronounced either his releafe, or a
delay of paffing fentence, for the purpofe of obtaining
more ample information, or the punifhment of torture
or death. In cafe of releafe, the innocent man obtained no indemnity ; while, on the other hand, the fen-

tence of death was always followed by confifcation: B O O K
for fuch, in abridgment, is the mode of criminal pro- XVII.
cefs in France. The Canadians foon underftood, and
fenfibly felt, the value of a legiflation which removed
all thefe evils.

The civil code of Great Britain did not give equal
fatisfaction. Its ftatutes were complicated, obfcure,
and numerous ; they were written in a language which
was not then familiar to the conquered people. Independent of thefe confiderations, the Canadians had lived one hundred and fifty years under another kind of
adminiftration, which they were attached to by birth,
by education, by cuftom, and perhaps alfo by a kind
of national pride. They could not, therefore, but experience great uneafinefs at feeing a change in the rule
of their duties, and in the bafis of their property. If
difcontent was not carried fo far as to difturb public
tranquillity, it was becaufe the inhabitants of this region had not yet loft that fpirit of blind obedience
which had fo long directed all their actions ; it is becaufe the adminiftrators and magiftrates who had been
given to them, were conftantly deviating from their
inftructions, in order to come as near as poffible to the
cuftoms and maxims which they found eftablifhed.

The parliament was aware that this arrangement
could not be lafting. They fettled, that, on the firft
of May 1775, Canada fhould recover its firft limits :
that it fhould be governed by its former jurifprudence,
and by the criminal and maritime laws of England :
that the free exercife of the Catholic religion fhould
be allowed ; and that this kind of worfhip fhould never be an obftacle to any of the rights of the citizen :
that ecclefiaftical tithes, and the feudal obligations,
which had been fo fortunately difufed fince the time
of the conqueft, fhould recover their former influence.
A council, appointed by the king, might annul thefe
arrangements, and exercife every kind of power, except that of levying taxes. This council was to confift of twenty-three perfons, promifcuoufly chofen from

B O O K among the two nations, and fubjected only to take at
XVII. oath of allegiance.

This ariftocracy, which was very variable, and entirely of a new caft, was generally difliked. The ancient fubjects of Great Britain lately fettled in this
new poffeffion, were exceedingly diffatisfied at having
part of their rights taken from them. The Canadians,
who began to know the value of liberty, and who had
been flattered with the hopes of being under the Englifh government, found themfelves, with grief, deceived in their expectations. It is probable that the
court of London itfelf had not a more favourable opinion of this meafure. This kind of arrangement had
been fuggefted to the government by the difcontent
which was already known to prevail in moft of their
provinces of the New World. It may be prefumed
that they will retract when circumftances and policy
will admit of it.

But yet what became of Canada during the courfe
of thofe too rapid revolutions that have happened in
the government?

Its population, which the events of war had feverely decreafed, hath arifen to one hundred and thirty
thoufand fouls, in the fpace of fixteen years. The
province hath not been indebted to new colonifts for
this increafe. There has fcarce arrived a fufficient
number of Englifhmen, to replace one thoufand or
twelve hundred Frenchmen who had quitted it at the
conqueft. This fortunate event hath alone been produced by peace, by eafy circumftances, and by a multiplication of ufeful labours.

The firft years of tranquillity have ferved to extri-
cate the colony from that kind of chaos into which it
had been plunged by a deftructive and unfortunate
war. Thefe events have foon been fucceeded by improvements.

Stockings, lace, coarfe linens, and common ftuffs,
had for a long time been manufactured at Canada.
Thefe manufactures have been extended but not im-

proved. The two latter muft remain in this ftate of B O O K
degradation till they are taken out of the hands of XVII.
women, who are alone employed in them, as well as
in others more fuitable to their fex.

The beaver and fur trade hath not diminifhed, as it
was apprehended. It hath even rather increafed, becaufe the Canadians, more active than their neighbours, and better fkilled in treating with the favages,
have fucceeded in reftraining the intercourfe between
Hudfon's Bay and New York. Befides, the value of
the furs is doubled in Europe, while the price of the
articles which are given in exchange is but a little enhanced.

Though the feas in the neighbourhood of Canada
abound in fifh, the Canadians have feldom frequented
them. The natural obftacles which render them averfe
from navigation, alfo difguft them of fifhing. The
cod fifhery, however, formerly attempted at Gafpé
and at Mont Louis; that of the falmon and of the
feal, eftablifhed upon the coaft of Labrador, have made
fome progrefs fince the conqueft. The whale fifhery
hath even been attempted, but not with fufficient fuccefs to be continued. It will undoubtedly be revived,
when an increafe of failors and of knowledge, and perhaps when gratuities, properly beftowed, fhall have levelled every difficulty.

The cattle have increafed, and yet there is no meat
falted, except for the internal confumption, and for the
exterior navigation of the colony. Some of thefe falt
provifions will foon be fent to the Weft Indies, in the
fame manner as horfes now are; which, though fmall,
are indefatigable.

The culture of flax, hemp, and tobacco, hath vifibly increafed. That of corn hath particularly engaged
the attention of the colony. In 1770, it began to furnifh flour to the Weft Indies, and feeds to Italy, to
Portugal, to Spain, and even to England; and this
exportation increafes continually.

In 1769, the productions fold to foreigners amounted to 4,077,602 livres 7 fols 8 deniers [about 169,900l.

2s. 4d.]. They were carried off by about feventy veffels from Old or New England, feveral of which came
with their ballaft only. The others brought to the
colony rum, molaffes, coffee, and fugar, from the Weft
Indies; falt, oil, wine, and brandy, from Spain, Italy,
and Portugal; and ftuffs, linens, and houfehold furniture, from the mother-country. Canada is properly
in poffeffion of no other fhips except thofe which are
neceffary for the internal confumption; a dozen of
fmall veffels, which are employed in the feal fifhery;
and five or fix, which are fent to the Antilles. The
conftruction of veffels, far from having been more frequent, hath diminifhed fince the conqueft; and it is
to the dearnefs of labour, in which more hands are
employed, that this change, which it was not natural
to expect, muft be attributed.

This inconvenience hath not prevented the colony
from becoming richer than it was under another dominion. Its debts have been entirely paid fince the
year 1772, and it hath no paper currency. Its fpecies
increafes daily, both by the multiplication of its commodities, and by the expences of government. Befides
what Great Britain hath expended for the troops, the
civil adminiftration of Canada cofts the country annually 625,000 livres [26,041l. 13s. 4d.], while it receives only 225,000 livres [9375l.] from the duties
which it hath impofed, in 1765, 1772, and 1773, on
the wines, brandy, rum, molaffes, glafs, and colours.

The extent of Canada, the fertility of its foil, the
falubrity of its climate, fhould feem to invite it to a
great degree of profperity; but this is impeded by
powerful obftacles. This region hath only one river
for its exports and imports, and even this is blocked
up by ice, fo as not to be navigable during fix months,
while heavy fogs render the navigation of it flow and
difficult throughout the reft of the year. Hence it
will happen, that the other northern colonies which
have the fame productions as this colony, and have
not fimilar obftacles to furmount, will always have a
decided advantage over it, for the large fifheries, and

for the navigation to the Weft Indies and to Europe. In this refpect the ifland of St. John is more fortunately circumftanced.

When the Englifh took poffeffion of the ifland of St. John, fituated on the Gulf of St. Lawrence, they had the bad policy to expel from thence more than three thoufand Frenchmen, who had lately formed fettlements there. No fooner had the property of the ifland been enfured to the conqueror by treaties, than the Earl of Egmont was defirous of becoming mafter of it. He engaged to furnifh twelve hundred armed men for the defence of the colony, provided he were permitted to cede, on the fame conditions, and in mefne fee, fome confiderable portions of his territory. Thefe offers were agreeable to the court of London; but by a law which was made at the memorable period of the reftoration of Charles II. the granting of the domains of the crown upon the ftipulation of a military fervice, or of a feudal homage, had been forbidden. The lawyers determined that this ftatute affected the New as well as the Old World, and this decifion fuggefted other ideas to government.

The long and cruel ftorm by which the globe had been agitated was appeafed. Moft of the officers who had fealed the triumphs of England with their blood, were unemployed, and without fubfiftence. It was imagined to divide the foil of St. John among them, upon condition that, after ten years of free enjoyment, they fhould annually pay to the treafury, as they do in moft of the provinces of the continent of America, 2 livres 10 fols 7 deniers and a half [about 2s. $1\frac{1}{4}$d.] for every hundred acres they fhould poffefs. Very few of thefe new proprietors intended to fettle in thefe diftant regions; very few of them were able to furnifh the fums neceffary for clearing a portion of land of any extent. Moft of them ceded their rights, for a greater or lefs time, and for a rent more or lefs moderate, to fome Irifhmen, and efpecially to fome Scotch Highlanders. The number of colonifts doth not yet

B O O K amount to twelve hundred ; who are employed in the
XVII. cod fifhery, and in cultures of different kinds. They
have no intercourfe with Europe, but trade only with
Quebec and with Halifax.

Till 1772, St. John depended upon Nova Scotia.
At this period it formed a feparate ftate. It obtained
a governor, a council, an affembly, a cuftom-houfe,
and an admiralty. Port la Joie, which is now called
Charlotte Town, is the capital of the colony.

An ifland of fo fmall an extent fcarce appeared
worthy of the importance it acquired by favours which
we cannot account for. In order to give a kind of
reality to this fettlement, the iflands of Magdalen, inhabited by a few perfons employed in the cod fifhery,
and in catching fea-cows, were annexed to it ; as was
alfo Cape Breton, which was formerly famous, but
which hath loft its importance by its change of government. Louifbourg, the terror of Englifh America
not twenty years ago, is now no more than a heap of
ruins. The four thoufand Frenchmen who had been
difperfed after the conqueft, by an unjuft and ill-
judged miftruft, have only been replaced by five or
fix hundred men, who are more engaged in fmuggling
than in fifhing. Even the coal mines have no longer
been attended to.

Thefe mines are very abundant at Cape-Breton, are
eafily worked, and are in fome meafure inexhauftible.
Under the former poffeffors a great confufion prevailed in them, which the new government have wifhed
to prevent, by referving the property to themfelves,
in order to cede it only to thofe who fhould have fufficient means to render it ufeful. Thofe who will engage in this undertaking, with the funds requifite, will
find an advantageous mart in all the weftern iflands of
America, and even upon the coafts, and in the ports
of the northern continent, where the dearnefs of wood
is already experienced, and where it will be ftill more
fenfibly felt every day. This fpecies of induftry would
form a trade to the colony, which would be ever in-

creafing ; and it would even extend to fifheries, but not to that degree as ever to render them equal to thofe of Newfoundland.

This ifland, fituated between 46 and 52 degrees of north latitude, is feparated from the coaft of Labrador only by a channel of moderate breadth, known by the name of Belleifle Straits. It is of a triangular form, and fomething more than three hundred leagues in circumference. We can only fpeak by conjecture of the inland parts of it, on account of the difficulty of penetrating far into it, and the apparent inutility of fucceeding in the attempt. The little that is known of it is, that it is full of very fteep rocks, mountains covered with bad wood, and fome very narrow and fandy valleys. Thefe inacceffible places are ftocked with deer, which multiply with the greater eafe on ac- count of the fecurity of their fituation. No favages have ever been feen there except fome Efquimaux, who come over from the continent in the hunting feafon. The coaft abounds with creeks, roads, and harbours ; is fometimes covered with mofs, but more commonly with fmall pebbles, which feem as if they had been placed there by defign, for the purpofe of drying the fifh caught in the neighbourhood. In all the open places, where the flat ftones reflect the fun's rays, the heat is exceffive. The reft of the country is entirely cold ; lefs fo, however, from its fituation, than from the heights, the forefts, the winds, and above all, the vaft mountains of ice which come out of the north- ern feas, and fix on thefe coafts. The fky towards the northern and weftern parts is conftantly ferene, but is much lefs fo towards the eaft and fouth, both of thefe points being too near the great bank, which is enve- loped in a perpetual fog.

Newfoundland was difcovered in 1497, by John Cabot, a Venetian ; but this difcovery was not pur- fued. At the return of this great navigator, England was too much taken up with its difputes with Scot- land, to give any ferious attention to fuch diftant in- terefts.

Thirty years afterwards, Henry VIII. fent two fhips
to take a more particular furvey of the ifland, which
had as yet been only perceived.   One of thefe fhips
was loft upon thofe favage coafts, and the other returned to England without having acquired any information.

Another voyage, undertaken in 1536, was more
fuccefsful.   The adventurers, who had undertaken it
with the affiftance of government, informed their country that a great quantity of cod-fifh might be caught
at Newfoundland.   This information was not entirely
ufelefs : and foon after, fome fmall veffels were fent
from England in the fpring, which returned in autumn
with their whole freight of fifh, both falt and dried.

At firft, the territory which was requifite to prepare
the cod-fifh belonged to the firft perfon who feized
upon it.   This cuftom proved a perpetual fource of
difcord.   Sir Thomas Hampfhire, who was fent by
Queen Elizabeth, in 1582, into thefe latitudes with
five fhips, was authorifed to fecure to every fifherman
the property of that portion of the coaft which he
chofe.

This new arrangement multiplied the expeditions
to Newfoundland to fuch a degree, that, in 1615, two
hundred and fifty Englifh veffels were feen upon thofe
coafts, the lading of which amounted in all to fifteen
thoufand tons.   All thefe veffels had failed from Europe.   It was not till fome years after that fixed habitations were formed there, which gradually occupied,
on the eaftern coaft, the fpace that extends from Conception Bay to Cape Ras.   Thofe who were concerned in the fifhery being forced, both from the nature
of their employment and that of the foil, to live at a
diftance from each other, opened paths of communication through the woods.   Their general rendezvous
was at St. John's, where, in an excellent harbour,
formed between two mountains at a very fmall diftance from each other, they met with privateers from
the mother-country, who fupplied them with every

neceffary article, in exchange for the produce of their fifhery.

The French had turned their views towards New-foundland before this profperity of the Englifh trade. They pretend even that they have frequented the coafts of this ifland fince the beginning of the fixteenth century. This period may be too remote; but it is certain that they frequented them before the year 1634, when they obtained, according to the account of their rivals, from Charles I. the liberty of fifhing in thefe latitudes, on the condition of paying him a duty of five per cent. But this tribute, which was equally burdenfome and humiliating, was foon after taken off.

However this fact may be, the truth of which is not afcertained by any record, it is proved, that, towards the middle of the feventeenth century, the French went annually to Newfoundland. They did not, it is true, fifh on the weftern coaft of the ifland, though, as it made part of the Gulf of St. Lawrence, it was un-derftood to belong to them; but they frequented in great numbers the northern part, which they had call-ed *Le Petit Nord*. Some of them had even fixed upon the fouthern part, where they had formed a kind of town upon the Bay of Placentia, which united all the conveniencies that could be wifhed for to obtain a fuccefsful fifhery.

Among all the fettlements with which the Euro-peans have covered the New World, there is none of the nature of that of Newfoundland. The others have generally been the deftruction of the firft colonifts they have received, and of a great number of their fuccef-fors; this climate, of itfelf, hath not deftroyed one fingle perfon; it hath even reftored ftrength to fome of thofe whofe health had been affected by lefs whole-fome climates. The other colonies have exhibited a feries of injuftice, oppreffion, and carnage, which will for ever be holden in deteftation. Newfoundland a-lone hath not offended againft humanity, nor injured the rights of any people. The other fettlements have yielded productions, only by receiving an equal value

BOOK in exchange. Newfoundland alone hath drawn from
XVII. the depths of the waters riches formed by nature a-
lone, and which furnifh fubfiftence to feveral countries
of both hemifpheres.

How much time hath elapfed before this parallel
hath been made ! Of what importance did fifh appear,
when compared to the money which men went in
fearch of in the New World ? It was long before it
was underftood, if even it be yet underftood, that the
reprefentation of the thing is not of greater value than
the thing itfelf ; and that a fhip filled with cod, and a
galleon, are veffels equally laden with gold. There is
even this remarkable difference, that mines can be exhaufted, and that the fifheries never are. Gold is not
reproduced, but the fifh are fo inceffantly.

The wealth of the fifheries of Newfoundland had
made fuch a fmall impreffion upon the court of Verfailles in particular, that they had not even thought
of thofe latitudes before 1660 ; and that even then,
they took no further notice of it, than to deftroy the
good which had been done there by their fubjects
without their fanction. They gave up the property
of Placentia Bay to a private man named Gargot ; but
this rapacious man was driven away by the fifhermen,
whom he had been allowed to fpoil. The miniftry did
not perfift in fupporting the injuftice of which they
had been guilty ; and neverthelefs the oppreffion of
the colony was not diminifhed. The laborious men,
whom neceffity had united upon this barren and favage land, being now drawn out of that fortunate
oblivion in which they had remained, were perfecuted
without intermiffion by the commanders who fucceeded each other in a fort which had been conftructed.
This tyranny, by which the colonifts were prevented
from acquiring that degree of competency that was
neceffary to enable them to purfue their labours with
fuccefs, muft alfo hinder them from increafing their
numbers. The French fifhery, therefore, could never
profper fo well as that of the Englifh.

Notwithftanding this, Great Britain, at the treaty

of Utrecht, did not forget that her enterprifing neigh- bours, fupported by the Canadians, accuſtomed to ſudden attacks, and to the fatigues of the chafe, had ſeveral times, during the two laſt wars, carried devaſtation into her ſettlements. This was ſufficient to induce her to demand the entire poſſeſſion of the iſland ; and France, exhauſted by her misfortunes, refolved to make this facrifice ; not, however, without referving to themfelves not only the right of fiſhing on one part of the iſland, but alfo on the Great Bank, which was confidered as belonging to it.

The fiſh for which theſe latiutdes are ſo famous is the cod. The length of this fiſh does not exceed three feet, and is often leſs ; but the fea does not produce any with mouths as large in proportion to their ſize, or who are ſo voracious. Broken pieces of earthen ware, iron, and glaſs, are often found in their bellies. The ſtomach, indeed, does not, as has been imagined, digeſt theſe hard fubſtances, but by a certain power of inverting itſelf, like a pocket, diſcharges whatever loads it. This fiſh would have been leſs voracious, if its ſtomach had not been capable of being inverted. Its organization makes it indifferent with reſpect to the nature of the fuſtenance it feeds upon. The conformation of the organs is the principle of appetite in all the living fubſtances in the three natural kingdoms.

It is the cod fiſh alone which renders Newfoundland of importance. Preſent ſtate of this fiſhery, divided into wandering and ſtationary fiſhery.

The cod fiſh is found in the northern feas of Europe. The fiſhery is carried on there by thirty Engliſh, ſixty French, and 150 Dutch veſſels, which, taken together, carry from 80 to 100 tons burden. Their competitors are the Iriſh, and above all, the Norwegians. The latter are employed, before the fiſhing feafon, in collecting upon the coaſt, the eggs of the cod, which is the uſual bait for pilchards. They fell, *communibus annis*, from twenty to twenty-two thouſand tons of this fiſh, at nine livres [7s. 6d.] per ton. If markets could be found for it, it might be taken in greater quantity : for an able naturaliſt, who has had the patience to count the eggs of one

B O O K ſingle cod, has found 9 344,000 of them.   This boun-
XVII.   ty of nature muſt be ſtill more conſiderable at Newfoundland, where the cod fiſh is found in infinitely
greater plenty.

The fiſh of Newfoundland is alſo more delicate,
though not ſo white ; but it is not an object of trade
when freſh, and only ſerves for the food of thoſe who
are employed in the fiſhery.   When it is ſalted and
dried, or only ſalted, it becomes a uſeful article to a
great part of Europe and America.   That which is
only ſalted is called green cod, and is caught upon the
great bank.

This bank is one of thoſe mountains that are formed under water by the earth which the ſea is continually waſhing away from the continent.   Both its
extremities terminate ſo much in a point, that it is
difficult to aſſign the preciſe extent of it, but it is generally reckoned to be 160 leagues long, and 90 broad.
Towards the middle of it, on the European ſide, is
a kind of bay, which has been called the Ditch.
Throughout all this ſpace, the depth of water is very
different ; in ſome places there are only five, in others
above ſixty fathom.   The ſun ſcarce ever ſhows itſelf
there, and the ſky is generally covered with a thick
cold fog.   The waves are always agitated, and the
winds always high about this ſpot, which muſt be owing to this circumſtance, that the ſea being irregular-
ly driven forward by currents, bearing ſometimes on
one ſide, and ſometimes on the other, ſtrikes with im-
petuoſity againſt the borders, which are every where
perpendicular, and is repelled from them with equal
violence.   This is moſt likely to be the true reaſon,
becauſe on the bank itſelf, at a little diſtance from
the borders, the ſituation is as tranquil as in a harbour,
except when a violent wind, which comes from a
greater diſtance, happens to blow there.

From the middle of July to the latter end of Auguſt, there is no cod found either upon the Great
Bank, or any of the ſmall ones near it, but all the
reſt of the year the fiſhery is carried on.

Previous to their beginning the fishery, they build
a gallery on the outside of the ship, which reaches
from the main-mast to the stern, and sometimes the
whole length of the vessel. This gallery is furnished
with barrels, with the tops beaten out. The fishermen place themselves within these, and are sheltered
from the weather by a pitched covering fastened to
the barrels. As soon as they catch a cod they cut
out its tongue, and give the fish to one of the boys,
to carry it to a person appointed for the purpose, who
immediately strikes off the head, plucks out the liver
and entrails, and then lets it fall through a small
hatchway between the decks; when another man takes
it and draws out the bone as far as the navel, and then
lets it sink through another hatchway into the hold,
where it is salted and ranged in piles. The person
who salts it takes care to leave salt enough between
each row of fish, but not more than is sufficient to
prevent their touching each other, for either of these
circumstances neglected would spoil the cod.

But it is a well-attested phenomenon, that the cod
fishery is scarcely begun before the sea becomes oily,
grows calm, and the barks are seen floating upon the
surface of the waters as upon a polished mirror. The
same effect is produced by the oil which runs from a
whale when it is cut to pieces. A ship newly tarred
appeases the sea under it and round the vessels which
are near it. In 1756, Dr. Franklin, going to Louisbourg with a great fleet, observed that the way of two
ships was remarkably smooth, while that of the others
was agitated; upon asking the captain the reason of
this, he was told that this difference was occasioned
by the washing of the kitchen utensils. Dr. Franklin was not satisfied with this reason, but soon found
out the truth of it by a series of experiments, by
which he discovered that a few drops of oil, the whole
of which, united together, would scarce have filled a
spoon, quieted the waves at more than a hundred toises
distance, with a celerity of expansion as marvellous as
its division.

BOOK
XVII.

It appears that vegetable oil is more efficacious than animal oil. The calm which is produced by this is reckoned to laſt two hours out at ſea, where this effect requires the effuſion of a conſiderable quantity of oil. The ſacrifice of a few barrels of this fluid hath ſaved ſome great veſſels from ſhipwreck, with which they were threatened by the moſt dreadful tempeſt.

Notwithſtanding an infinite number of authentic facts, it is as yet doubtful whether oil, or in general all fat ſubſtances, whether fluid or ſeparated, have the property of lowering the height of the waves. They appear to have no effect but againſt the breakers.

It is ſaid that the ſea breaks when it riſes very high in foaming, and in forming as it were columns of water which fall down again with great violence. When the ſea is high, the waves aſcend, but follow each other regularly, and the ſhips give way without danger to this motion, which ſeems to carry them up to the ſkies or down to the infernal regions. But when the waves are violently agitated by winds which blow in contrary directions, or from ſome other cauſe, this is not the caſe. Two ſhips cloſe enough to ſpeak, are ſuddenly hid from each other's ſight. A mountain of water riſes between them, which when it comes to break and fall upon them, is ſufficient to daſh them to pieces. This ſtate of the ſea is not a common one. One may ſail a long time without being expoſed to it. But if the uſe of oil ſhould preſerve but one ſingle veſſel among the multitude of thoſe which cover the ocean in a great number of years, the importance of this eaſy ſuccour would ſtill be very conſiderable.

The fiſhermen of Liſbon, and thoſe of the Bermudas, reſtore calm and tranſparency to the ſea with a little oil, which immediately puts a ſtop to the irregularity of the rays of light, and enables them to perceive the fiſh. The modern divers, who go in ſearch of pearls in the bottom of the ſea, accuſtom themſelves, in imitation of the ancients, to fill their mouths with oil, which they throw out drop by drop, in proportion as the darkneſs conceals their prey from them. Some of them guefs at the prefence of the fhark, or at the abundance of the herring, in thofe places where the fea offers them a calm not to be found in the neigh- bouring latitudes. Some perfons attribute this to the oil which makes its efcape from the body of the her- ring; others fay that it is preffed out of the herring by the teeth of the fhark while he is devouring that fifh. The fame method is ufed fometimes to difcover the points of rocks concealed by the agitation of the waves, fometimes to reach land with lefs danger. For this purpofe fome fufpend behind their boats a parcel of inteftines filled with the fat of the Fulmar or Petrel, a bird which throws up in its natural ftate the oil of the fifh upon which it feeds. Others, inftead of this ufe a jar turned upfide down, from which the oil drops gradually through an opening made in the cork. The terrible element, therefore, which hath feparated con- tinents from each other; which deluges whole coun- tries; which drives animals and men before it, and which will one day encroach upon their dwellings, may be appeafed in its wrath, if a feather dipped in oil be paffed over its furface. Who knows what may be the confequence of this difcovery, if we may give that name to a piece of information, the knowledge of which cannot be difputed with Ariftotle or Pliny? If a feather dipped in oil can fmooth the waves, what will not be the effect of long wings conftantly moift- ened with this fluid, and mechanically adapted to our fhips?

This idea will not fail of exciting the ridicule of our fuperficial-minded men; but it is not for fuch that I write. We treat popular opinions with too much contempt. We decide with too much hafte on the poffibility or impoffibility of things. In our opi- nion of Pliny the naturalift, we have paffed from one extreme to the other. Our anceftors have granted too much to Ariftotle, while we perhaps have denied him more than it became men, the moft informed among whom hath not fufficient knowledge either to approve or contradict his book on Animals. This dif-

B O O K dain might perhaps be excufed in a Buffon, a Dau-
XVII. benton, or a Linnæus; but it always excites our indignation when we meet with it in him, who, depart-
ing from his own fphere, and neglecting fame which
offers itfelf to him, in order to run after that which
flies from him, fhall venture to decide upon the merit
of thefe men of genius, with peremptorinefs which
would difguft us, if even it were fupported by the moft
ftriking and leaft conteftible claims.

According to natural right, the fifhery upon the
Great Bank ought to have been common to all mankind; notwithftanding which the two powers that had
formed colonies in North America, have made very
little difficulty of appropriating it to themfelves. Spain,
who alone could have any claim to it, and who, from
the number of her monks, might have pleaded the
neceffity of afferting it, entirely gave up the matter at
the laft peace, fince which time the Englifh and French
are the only nations that frequent thefe latitudes.

In 1773, France fent there five veffels, which formed nine thoufand three hundred and feventy-five tons,
and the crews of which confifted of fixteen hundred
and eighty-eight men. Two millions one hundred
and forty-one thoufand cod fifh were caught, which
produced one hundred and twenty-two hogfheads of
oil; the entire produce was fold for 1,421,615 livres
[59,233l. 19s. 2d.].

The fifheries of the rival nation were much more confiderable. Few of thofe who were employed in it had
come from Europe. Moft of them came from New-
England, Nova-Scotia, and from the ifland of Newfoundland itfelf. Their veffels were fmall, eafily managed, rifing little above the furface of the water, and
not liable to be ftrongly affected by the winds or the
agitation of the waves. Thefe veffels were manned
with failors more inured to fatigue, more accuftomed to bear cold, and more ufed to ftrict difcipline.
They carried with them a bait infinitely fuperior to
that which was found upon the fpot. Their fifhery
was therefore infinitely fuperior to that of the French;

but as they had lefs opportunities of getting rid of the green cod than the latter, the greater part of the fifh which they caught was carried to the neighbouring coafts, where it was converted into dried cod.

This branch of trade is carried on in two different ways. That which is called the wandering fifhery belongs to veffels which fail every year from Europe to Newfoundland, at the end of March, or in April. As they approach the ifland, they frequently meet with a quantity of ice, driven by the northern currents towards the fouth, which is broken to pieces by repeated fhocks, and melts fooner or later at the return of the heats. Thefe portions of ice are frequently a league in circumference; they are as high as the loftieft mountains, and extend above fixty or eighty fathom under water. When joined to fmaller pieces, they fometimes occupy a fpace of a hundred leagues in length, and twenty-five or thirty in breadth. Intereft, which obliges the mariners to come to their landings as foon as poffible, that they may have their choice of the harbours moft favourable to the fifhery, makes them brave the rigour of the feafons and of the elements, which are all in confpiracy againft human induftry. The moft formidable rampart erected by military art, the dreadful cannonade of a befieged town, the terrors of the moft fkilful and obftinate feafight, require lefs intrepidity and experience to encounter them, than thefe enormous floating bulwarks, which the fea oppofes to thefe fmall fleets of fifhermen. But the moft infatiable of all paffions, the thirft of gold, furmounts every obftacle, and carries the mariner acrofs thefe mountains of ice to the fpot where the fhips are to take in their lading.

The firft thing to be done after landing is to cut wood, and erect or repair fcaffolds. All hands are employed in this work. When it is finifhed, the company divide; one half of the crew ftays afhore to cure the fifh, and the other goes on board in fmall boats. The boats defigned for the fifhery of the caplain carry four men, and thofe for the cod three. Thefe laft

boats, of which there is the greateſt number, ſail before
it is light, generally at the diſtance of three, four, or
five leagues from the coaſt, and return in the evening
to the ſcaffolds near the ſea-ſide, where they depoſit
the produce of the day.

When one man has taken off the cod's head, and
gutted it, he gives it to another, who ſlices it, and puts
it in ſalt, where it remains eight or ten days. After
it has been well waſhed, it is laid on gravel, where it
is left till it is quite dry. It is then piled up in heaps,
and left for ſome days to drain. It is then again laid
on the ſtrand, where it continues drying, and takes the
colour we ſee it have in Europe.

There are no fatigues whatever to be compared
with the labours of this fiſhery, which hardly leaves
thoſe who work at it four hours reſt in the night. Happily, the ſalubrity of the climate preſerves the health
of the people under ſuch ſevere trials; and theſe labours would be thought nothing of, if they were better rewarded by the produce.

But there are ſome harbours where the ſtrand is at
ſo great a diſtance from the ſea, that a great deal of
time is loſt in getting to it; and others, in which the
bottom is of ſolid rock, and without varec, ſo that the
fiſh do not frequent them. There are others again,
where the fiſh grow yellow, from a mixture of freſh
water with the ſalt; and ſome, in which it is ſcorched
by the reverberation of the ſun's rays reflected from
the mountains.

Even in the moſt favourable harbours, the people
are not always ſure of a ſucceſsful fiſhery. The fiſh
cannot abound equally in all parts: it is ſometimes
found to the north, ſometimes to the ſouth, and at
other times in the middle of the coaſt, according as it
is driven by the winds, or attracted by the caplain.
The fiſhermen who happen to fix at a diſtance from
the places which the fiſh frequent, are very unfortunate, for their expences are all thrown away becauſe
it is impoſſible for them to follow the fiſh with all
their neceſſary apparatus.

The fifhery ends about the beginning of September, becaufe at that time the fun has not power enough to dry the fifh; but when it has been fuccefsful, the managers give over before that time, and make the beft of their way either to the Caribbee Iflands, or to the Roman Catholic ftates in Europe, that they may not be deprived of the advantages of the firft markets, which might be loft by an over-ftock.

In 1773, one hundred and four veffels, which compofed fifteen thoufand fix hundred and twenty-one tons, and which were manned by feven thoufand two hundred and fixty-three failors, were fent from the ports of France for this fifhery. Their labours were rewarded by a hundred and ninety thoufand one hundred and fixty quintals of fifh, and two thoufand eight hundred and twenty-five hogfheads of oil. Thefe two articles united produced 3,816,580 livres [159,024l. 3s. 4d.].

But how hath it happened, that an empire, the population of which is immenfe, and its coafts very extenfive; that a government which has fuch confiderable demands, both for its provinces in Europe, and for its colonies in the New World: how hath it happened, that the moft important of its fifheries hath been reduced to fuch a trifle? This event hath been brought on by internal and external caufes.

The cod fifh was for a long time overloaded with duties on its entrance into the kingdom, and other taxes were put upon its confumption. It was hoped in 1764, that thefe grievances were going to ceafe. Unfortunately the council was divided; fome of its members objeéted to the taking off of the duties from the falt fifh, becaufe other members had declared themfelves againft the exportation of the brandies made from cyder and perry. Reafon at length prevailed over thefe objeétions. The treafury confented, in 1773, to facrifice half of the duties which had till then been required of this branch of induftry; and two years after they entirely gave up this inconfiderable refource.

B O O K   Salt is a very principal article in the cod-fishery.
XVII.   This production of the sea and of the sun had arisen
to an exceffive price in France. In 1768 and 1770,
fifhermen were allowed for a year only, and in 1774,
for an unlimited time, to purchafe their falt from foreigners. This indulgence hath fince been refufed to
them, but it will be reftored. The miniftry will com-
prehend that its navigators will never employ, without
extreme neceffity, the falt of Spain and Portugal pre-
ferably to that of Poitou and Brittany, which is fo
much fuperior.

When the cod arrives from the north of America,
there remains between its feveral layers a confiderable
quantity of undiffolved falt. The farmers of the crown
made for a long time an abufe of the afcendant which
they had affumed in the public refolutions, in order to
have this falt prohibited as ufelefs, and even dangerous. A century hath been wafted in folicitations, and
in giving proofs of its utility, before the government
would allow it to be employed, as it is with great advantage, in the fifheries of the dried cod.

Moft of the obftacles, therefore, which a power, not
fufficiently acquainted with its own interefts, oppofed
to its own profperity, are at length removed. Let us
fee what idea muft be formed of thofe which an odious
fpirit of rivalfhip hath given rife to.

Newfoundland had formerly two mafters. By the
peace of Utrecht, the property of this ifland was confirmed to Great Britain, and the fubjects of the court
of Verfailles preferved only the right of fifhing from
the Cape of Bonavifta, turning towards the north as
far as Point Rich. But this laft line of demarkation
was not found in any of the charts which had preceded the treaty. The Englifh geographer Herman Moll
was the firft who noticed it in 1715, and he placed it
at Cape Raye.

It was generally believed that it muft be fo, when,
in 1764, the Britifh miniftry pretended, upon the faith
of a letter from Prior, who had fettled the bufinefs of
the limits, and of a petition prefented to parliament,

in 1716, by the Englifh fifhermen, that it was at fifty degrees thirty minutes of latitude that Point Rich ought to be fixed. The council of Louis XIV. immediately agreed with an authority which they might have contefted : but having themfelves difcovered in their archives a manufcript chart, which had ferved in the negotiation, and which placed Point Rich in forty-nine degrees of latitude, upon the border, and to the north of the bay of the Three Iflands, they demanded for thefe claims the fame deference as they had fhown for thofe which had been prefented to them. This was reafonable and juft; and yet the French, who ventured to frequent the contefted fpace, experienced the difgrace and the lofs of having their boats confifcated. Such was the ftate of things, when hoftilities were again renewed between the two nations. It is to be hoped, that, at the enfuing peace, the court of Verfailles will obtain a redrefs of this firft grievance.

They will alfo undoubtedly attend to another, of much greater importance. By the treaties of Utrecht and of Paris, their fubjects were to enjoy the fpace which extends between the Capes of Bonavifta and St. John. Three thoufand Englifhmen have formed fixed fettlements there at feveral periods, and have thus neceffarily kept off the navigators who arrived annually from Europe. France hath remonftrated againft thefe ufurpations, and hath obtained, that the Britifh miniftry fhould order their fifhermen to carry their activity elfewhere. This order hath not been carried into execution; nor could it be. Therefore, the court of Verfailles have demanded, as an equivalent, the liberty of fifhing from Point Rich to the iflands of St. Peter and Miquelon. This conciliatory plan appeared likely to fucceed; but the difturbances that have happened have thrown every thing into confufion; fo that this is alfo an arrangement to be expected at the approaching peace.

That peace will likewife enfure to the French navigators the exclufive fifhery of that part of Newfoundland which they are allowed to frequent. This right

B O O K had not been contefted before the year 1763: the En-
XVII. glifh had till then contented themfelves with going
there in the winter, in order to fifh for feal; they had
always finifhed their bufinefs, and quitted the diftrict,
before the fpring. At the above period, they began
to frequent the fame harbours which were formerly
occupied by their competitors alone. The court of
Verfailles muft have been reduced to the humiliation
of giving up the coafts of Labrador, Gafpé, St. John,
and Cape Breton, which abounded in fifh, before a
nation, too proud of its triumphs, could have ventured
to form this new pretenfion. Its admirals carried even
the infolence of victory fo far, as to forbid the French
fifhermen to fifh for cod on a Sunday, upon a pretence
that the Englifh fifhermen abftained from catching
any on that day. We are authorifed to believe, that
the council of St. James's did not approve of thefe enterprifes, fo palpably contrary to the fpirit of the treaties. They were fenfible that the right which France
had referved to herfelf in ceding the property of Newfoundland, became elufive, if her fifhermen could find
the places abounding in fifh occupied by rivals, who,
being fettled upon the neighbouring coaft, were always fure to arrive there firft. Neverthelefs, they determined to fupport, that the enjoyment, in the ftricteft fenfe, ought to be common to the two people.
They ought to have had more power and more courage than they were poffeffed of, to bid defiance to
the clamours of oppofition, and to the complaints
which fuch a fyftem of equity muft neceffarily excite.
But they depended upon the weaknefs of Louis XV.,
and were not deceived. The circumftances of the
times, and the character of his fucceffor, are totally
different; this grievance will be redreffed, as well as
many others. It is not even impoffible, but that the
ftationary fifheries of this crown may receive fome augmentation.

By ftationary fifhery, we are to underftand, that
which is carried on by the Europeans who have fettlements on thofe coafts of America where the cod is moft

plentiful. It is infinitely more profitable than the wandering fifhery, becaufe it is attended with much lefs
expence, and may be continued much longer. Thefe
advantages the French enjoyed, before the errors committed by their government made them lofe the vaft
territories they had in thofe regions. All the fixed
eftablifhments left them by the peace of 1763, are reduced to the ifland of St. Peter, and to two iflands of
Miquelon, which they are not even allowed to fortify.

It is fimple and natural, that a conqueror fhould appropriate his conquefts to himfelf as much as he can,
and that he fhould weaken his enemy, while he ag-
grandizes himfelf; but he fhould never leave fubfifting
permanent fubjects of humiliation, which are of no
avail to him, and which inftil hatred into the hearts of
thofe over whom he hath triumphed. The regret we
feel on any lofs diminifhes and goes off with time.
The fenfe of fhame becomes daily more poignant, and
never ceafes. If an opportunity fhould offer of mani-
fefting itfelf, it then breaks out, with a degree of fury
fo much the greater, as it hath been the longer concealed. Powers of the earth, therefore, be modeft
with refpect to the terms which you impofe upon the
conquered people, in the monuments by which you
mean to perpetuate the memory of your fuccefs. It is
impoffible to fubfcribe with fincerity to an humiliating compact. There are already too many falfe pre-
tences and unjuft motives for the infringement of treaties, without adding to them one fo legitimate and fo
urgent as that of fhaking off ignominy. Exact only
in profperity, fuch facrifices as you would fubmit to
without fhame in adverfity. A public monument of
infult, and upon which an enemy who is croffing your
capital cannot turn his eyes without experiencing a
deep emotion of indignation, is a perpetual ftimulus to
revenge. If it were ever poffible, that one of the infulted nations, in that public fquare called *La Place
des Victoires*, where they are all bafely loaded with
chains, by the moft abject and moft impudent of all
flatteries, fhould enter victorious into Paris, there is

B O O K no doubt but that the ſtatue of the proud monarch
XVII. who approved of this indiſcreet homage would in an
inſtant be pulled to pieces; perhaps even a ſpirit of
reſentment, for a long time ſtifled, would reduce to
aſhes the proud city that exhibits ſuch a monument.
You may appear crowned with victory, but you ſhould
not ſuffer that your foot ſhould be put upon the head
of your enemy. If you have been ſucceſsful, conſider
that you may experience a reverſe of fortune; and
that theie is more diſgrace in being one's-ſelf obliged
to deſtroy a monument, than glory in having erected
it. The Engliſh would, perhaps, have withdrawn their
inſpector from one of the ports of France, had they
known with what impatience he was ſuffered there;
and how often the French have ſaid to themſelves,
Are we to ſubmit to this humiliation much longer?

St. Peter hath twenty-five leagues in circumference;
it hath a harbour where thirty ſmall veſſels find a ſafe
aſylum, a road which is capable of containing about
forty ſhips of all ſizes, and coaſts well adapted for the
drying of a quantity of cod. In 1773, it contained ſix
hundred and four fixed inhabitants, and nearly an
equal number of ſailors paſſed their time there in the
intervals of the fiſheries.

The two Miquelons, leſs important in every reſpect,
had not more than ſix hundred and forty-nine inhabitants; and only one hundred and twenty-ſeven foreign
fiſhermen remained there during the winter.

The labours of theſe iſlanders, joined to thoſe of
four hundred and fifty men, arrived from Europe upon thirty-five veſſels, produced only thirty-ſix thouſand ſix hundred and ſeventy quintals of cod-fiſh, and
two hundred and fifty-three hogſheads of oil, which
were ſold for 805,490 livres [33,562l. 1s. 8d.].

This profit, added to 1,421,615 livres [59,233l. 19s.
2d.], which were got by the green cod caught on the
Great Bank, and to 3,816,580 livres [159,024l. 3s. 4d.]
produced by the cod dried at Newfoundland itſelf,
made the French fiſhery amount, in 1773, to the ſum
of 6,033,685 livres [251,403l. 10s. 10d.].

Of thefe three products, there were only that of St. B O O K
Peter, and of Miquelon, which received any increafe XVII.
in the following years.

Thefe iflands are only three leagues diftant from the
fouthern part of Newfoundland. By the treaties, the
pofleffion of the coaft is included in this extent. This
fpace fhould therefore have been in common, or divided between the Englifh and French fifhermen, who
had an equal right to it; but force, which feldom attends to the fuggeftions of equity, took every thing to
itfelf. Reafon, or policy, at length gave rife to more
moderate fentiments; and, in 1776, an equal diftribution of the canal was agreed to. This alteration enabled St. Peter and the Miquelons to catch, the enfuing year, feventy thoufand one hundred and four
quintals of dried cod, and feventy-fix thoufand feven
hundred and ninety-four of green cod.

But this increafe did not enable France to fupply
the foreign markets, as it did twenty years before. Its
fifhery was fcarce fufficient for the confumption of the
kingdom. Nothing, or fcarce any thing, remained for
its colonies, the wants of which were fo extenfive.

This important branch of commerce had paffed entirely into the hands of its rivals, fince victory had
given to them the North of America. They fupplied
the South of Europe, the Weft Indies, and even the
French iflands, with cod, notwithftanding the tax of
four livres [3s. 4d.] per quintal, with which it had been
loaded, in order to prevent its entry; and notwithftanding a gratuity of thirty-five fols [1s. 5¼d.] per
hundred weight, granted to the national fifhery. Great
Britain beheld, with great fatisfaction, that, befides the
confumptions in its feveral fettlements, this branch of
induftry yielded annually to its fubjects of the Old
and of the New World, a confiderable quantity of
fpecie, and a great plenty of commodities. This object of exportation would have become ftill more confiderable, if at the time of the conqueft the court of
London had not had the inhumanity to expel from the
iflands of Cape Breton and St. John the Frenchmen

who were fettled there, who have never yet been re-placed, and poffibly never will be. The fame bad po-licy had formerly been followed in Nova Scotia; for it is the property of the jealoufy of ambition to de-ftroy, in order to poffefs.

Nova Scotia, by which at prefent is underftood all the coafts, of three hundred leagues in length, includ-ed between the limits of New England and the fouth coaft of the river St. Lawrence, feemed at firft to have comprehended only the great triangular peninfula fi-tuated about the middle of this vaft fpace. This pe-ninfula, which the French called Acadia, is extremely well fituated to ferve as an afylum to the fhips coming from the Caribbee Iflands. It difplays to them, at a diftance, a great number of excellent ports, where fhips may enter and go out with all winds. There is a great quantity of cod upon this coaft, and ftill more upon fmall banks at the diftance of a few leagues. The neighbouring continent attracts attention by a few furs. Its arid coafts afford gravel for drying the fifh upon, and the goodnefs of the inland grounds invites to every fpecies of culture. Its woods are fit for ma-ny purpofes. Though this climate be in the tempe-rate zone, the winters are long and fevere, and follow-ed by fudden and exceffive heats, to which generally fucceed very thick fogs, that laft a long time. Thefe circumftances make this rather a difagreeable country, though it cannot be reckoned an unwholefome one.

It was in 1604, that the French fettled in Acadia, four years before they had built the fmalleft hut in Canada. Inftead of fixing towards the eaft of the pe-ninfula, where they would have had larger feas, an eafy navigation, and plenty of cod, they chofe a fmall bay, afterwards called French Bay, which had none of thefe advantages. It has been faid, that they were invited by the beauty of Port Royal, where a thoufand fhips may ride in fafety from every wind, where there is an excellent bottom, and at all times four or five fa-thom of water, and eighteen at the entrance. It is more probable that the founders of this colony were

led to choofe this fituation from its vicinity to the
countries abounding in furs, of which the exclufive
trade had been granted to them.   This conjecture is
confirmed by the following circumftance : that both
the firft monopolizers, and thofe who fucceeded them,
took the utmoft pains to divert the attention of their
countrymen, whom an unfettled difpofition, or neceffity, brought into thefe regions, from the clearing of
the woods, the breeding of cattle, fifhing, and every
kind of culture, choofing rather to engage the induftry of thefe adventurers in hunting or in trading with
the favages.

The mifchiefs arifing from a falfe fyftem of adminiftration, at length difcovered the fatal effects of exclufive charters.   It would be inconfiftent with truth
and the dignity of hiftory to fay, that this happened
in France, from any attention to the common rights
of the nation, at a time when thofe rights were moft
openly violated.   Thefe facred rights, which only can
enfure the fafety of the people, while they give a fanction to the power of kings, were never known in
France.   But in the moft abfolute governments, a fpirit of ambition fometimes effects, what in equitable and
moderate ones is done from principles of juftice.   The
minifters of Louis XIV. who wifhed, by making their
mafter refpectable, to reflect fome honour on themfelves, perceived that they fhould not fucceed without
the fupport of riches ; and that a people to whom nature has not given any mines, cannot acquire wealth
but by agriculture and commerce.   Both thefe refources had been hitherto precluded in the colonies
by the univerfal reftraints that are always impofed,
when the government interferes improperly in every
minute concern.   Thefe impediments were at laft removed ; but Acadia either knew not how, or was not
able, to make ufe of this liberty.

This colony was yet in its infancy, when the fettlement, which has fince become fo famous under the
name of New-England, was firft eftablifhed in its
neighbourhood.   The rapid fuccefs of the plantations

B O O K in this new colony did not much attract the notice of
XVII. the French. This kind of profperity did not excite
any jealoufy between the two nations. But when
they began to fufpect that there was likely to be a
competition for the beaver trade and furs, they endeavoured to fecure to themfelves the fole property of
it, and were unfortunate enough to fucceed.

At their firft arrival in Acadia, they had found the
peninfula, as well as the forefts of the neighbouring
continent, peopled with fmall favage nations, who
went under the general name of Abenakies. Though
equally fond of war as other favage nations, they
were more fociable in their manners. The miffionaries eafily infinuating themfelves among them, had fo
far inculcated their tenets, as to make enthufiafts of
them. At the fame time that they taught them their
religion, they infpired them with that hatred which
they themfelves entertained for the Englifh name.
This fundamental article of their new worfhip, being
that which made the ftrongeft impreffion on their
fenfes, and the only one that favoured their paffion
for war, they adopted it with all the rage that was
natural to them. They not only refufed to make
any kind of exchange with the Englifh, but alfo frequently difturbed and ravaged the frontiers of that
nation. Their attacks became more frequent, more
obftinate, and more regular, after they had chofen St.
Cafteins, formerly captain of the regiment of Carig-
nań, for their commander, who was fettled among
them, had married one of their women, and conform-
ed in every refpect to their mode of life.

When the Englifh faw that all efforts, either to reconcile the favages, or to deftroy them in their forefts,
were ineffectual, they fell upon Acadia, which they
looked upon, with reafon, as the only caufe of all
thefe calamities. Whenever the leaft hoftility took
place between the two mother-countries, the peninfula was attacked. Unable to procure any affiftance
from Canada, on account of its diftance, and having
but a feeble defence in Port Royal, which was only

furrounded by a few pallifades, it was conftantly ta- B O O K
ken. It undoubtedly afforded fome fatisfaction to the XVII.
New-Englanders to ravage this colony, and to retard
its progrefs ; but ftill this was not fufficient to remove
the fufpicions excited by a nation always more formidable by what fhe is able to do, than by what fhe
really does. Obliged as they were, however unwill-
ingly, to reftore their conqueft at each treaty of peace,
they waited with impatience till Great Britain fhould
acquire fuch a fuperiority as would enable her to difpenfe with this reftitution. The events of the war
on account of the Spanifh fucceffion brought on the
decifive moment ; and the court of Verfailles was for
ever deprived of a poffeffion of which it had never
known the importance.

The ardour which the Englifh had fhown for the France is
poffeffion of this territory did not manifeft itfelf after- compelled
wards in the care they took to maintain or to improve va Scotia to
it. Having built a very flight fortification at Port England.
Royal, which they called Annapolis, in honour of Queen
Anne, they contented themfelves with putting a very
fmall garrifon in it. The indifference fhown by the
government was adopted by the nation, a circumftance
not ufual in a free country. Not more than five or
fix Englifh families went over to Acadia, which flill
remained inhabited by the firft colonifts, who were
only perfuaded to ftay upon a promife made them of
never being compelled to bear arms againft their ancient country. Such was the attachment which the
French then had for the honour of their country.
Cherifhed by the government, refpected by foreign
nations, and attached to their king by a feries of pro-
fperities which had rendered their name illuftrious,
and aggrandized their power, they poffeffed that pa-
triotic fpirit which is the effect of fuccefs. They e-
fteemed it an honour to bear the name of Frenchmen, and could not think of foregoing the title. The
Acadians therefore, who, in fubmitting to a new yoke,
had fworn never to bear arms againft their former ftandards, were called the French neutrals.

What a powerful inducement is this example of attachment, as well as a multitude of others which have
preceded and followed it, to the fovereign of France,
to exert himfelf inceffantly for the happinefs of fuch
a nation; of a nation fo mild, fo proud, and fo generous? Treafon hath been fometimes the crime of an
individual, or of a particular fociety, but it was never
that of the fubjects in general. The French are the
people who know how to fuffer with infinite patience
the longeft and moft cruel vexations, and who demon-
ftrate the moft fincere, the moft ftriking tranfports
of gratitude, at the leaft token of the clemency of
their fovereign. They love and cherifh him; and
it depends upon him only to be adored by them. The
fovereign whom they fhould defpife would be the moft
contemptible of men; he whom they fhould hate
would be the worft of fovereigns. Notwithstanding
all the efforts that have been made, during a feries of
ages, to ftifle in our hearts the fentiment of patriotifm,
it exifts not, perhaps, among any people in a more
lively and energetic manner. Witnefs our mirth at
thofe glorious events, which, however, will not re-
lieve our mifery. What fhould we not be, if public
felicity were to fucceed to the glory of our arms?

There were twelve or thirteen hundred Acadians
fettled in the capital; the reft were difperfed in the
neighbouring country. No magiftrate was ever appointed to rule over them; and they were never acquainted with the laws of England. No rents or
taxes of any kind were ever exacted from them. Their
new fovereign feemed to have forgotten them; and
they were equally ftrangers to him.

Manners of
the French
who re-
mained fub-
ject to the
Englifh
govern-
ment in No-
va Scotia.
Hunting, which had formerly been the delight of
the colony, and might ftill have fupplied it with fubfiftence, had no further attraction for a fimple and
quiet people, and gave way to agriculture. It had
been begun in the marfhes and the low lands, by re-
pelling the fea, and rivers, which covered thefe plains,
with dykes. Thefe grounds yielded fifty times as much
as before, and afterwards fifteen or twenty times as

much at leaſt. Wheat and oats ſucceeded beſt in B O O K
them, but they likewiſe produced rye, barley, and XVII.
maize. There were alſo potatoes in great plenty, the
uſe of which was become common.

At the ſame time the immenſe meadows were covered with numerous flocks. Sixty thouſand head of
horned cattle were computed there ; and moſt of the
families had ſeveral horſes, though the tillage was carried on by oxen.

The habitations, built entirely with wood, were extremely convenient, and furniſhed as neatly as a ſub-
ſtantial farmer's houſe in Europe. The people bred
a great deal of poultry of all kinds, which made a
variety in their food, which was in general wholeſome
and plentiful. Their common drink was beer and
cyder, to which they ſometimes added rum.

Their uſual clothing was in general the produce of
their own flax and hemp, or the fleeces of their own
ſheep. With theſe they made common linens and
coarſe cloths. If any of them had any inclination
for articles of greater luxury, they procured them from
Annapolis or Louiſbourg, and gave in exchange, corn,
cattle, or furs.

The neutral French had no other articles to diſpoſe
of among their neighbours, and made ſtill fewer exchanges among themſelves, becauſe each ſeparate family was able, and had been uſed to provide for its
wants. They, therefore, knew nothing of paper currency, which was ſo common throughout the reſt of
North America. Even the ſmall quantity of ſpecie,
which had ſtolen into the colony did not promote that
circulation, which is the greateſt advantage that can
be derived from it.

Their manners were of courſe extremely ſimple.
There never was a cauſe, either civil or criminal, of
importance enough to be carried before the court of
judicature eſtabliſhed at Annapolis. Whatever little
differences aroſe from time to time among them, were
amicably adjuſted by their elders. All their public

B O O K acts were drawn by their paſtors, who had likewiſe
XVII. the keeping of their wills, for which, and their religious ſervices, the inhabitants voluntarily gave them
a twenty-ſeventh part of their harveſts.

Theſe were plentiful enough to ſupply more than a
ſufficiency to fulfil every act of liberality. Real miſery was entirely unknown, and benevolence prevented the demands of poverty. Every misfortune was re-
lieved, as it were, before it could be felt; and good
was univerſally diſpenſed, without oſtentation on the
part of the giver, and without humiliating the perſon
who received. Theſe people were, in a word, a ſociety of brethren, every individual of which was equally ready to give and to receive what he thought the
common right of mankind.

So perfect a harmony naturally prevented all thoſe
connections of gallantry which are ſo often fatal to
the peace of families. There never was an inſtance
in this ſociety of an unlawful commerce between the
two ſexes. This evil was prevented by early mar-
riages; for no one paſſed his youth in a ſtate of celibacy. As ſoon as a young man came to the proper
age the community built him a houſe, broke up the
lands about it, ſowed them, and ſupplied him with all
the neceſſaries of life for a twelvemonth. Here he
received the partner whom he had choſen, and who
brought him her portion in flocks. This new family
grew and proſpered like the others. They all together amounted to eighteen thouſand ſouls.

Who will not be affected with the innocent manners, and the tranquillity of this fortunate colony?
Who will not wiſh for the duration of its happineſs?
Who will not conſtruct, in imagination, an impenetrable wall, that may ſeparate theſe coloniſts from
their unjuſt and turbulent neighbours? The calamities
of the people have no period; but, on the contrary,
the end of their felicity is always at hand. A long
ſeries of favourable events is neceſſary to raiſe them
from miſery, while one inſtant is ſufficient to plunge

them into it. May the Acadians be excepted from B O O K this general curſe. But, alas! it is to be feared that XVII. they will not.

Great Britain perceived, in 1749, of what conſe-quence the poſſeſſion of Acadia might be to her com-merce. The peace, which neceſſarily left a great number of men without employment, furniſhed an op-portunity, by the diſbanding of the troops, for peo-pling and cultivating a vaſt and fertile territory. The Britiſh miniſtry offered particular advantages to all per-ſons who choſe to go over and ſettle in Acadia. Eve-ry ſoldier, ſailor, and workman, was to have fifty acres of land for himſelf, and ten for every perſon he car-ried over in his family. All non-commiſſioned officers were allowed eighty for themſelves, and 15 for their wives and children; enſigns 200; lieutenants 300; captains 400; and all officers of a higher rank 600; together with thirty for each of their dependents. The land was to be tax free for the firſt ten years, and never to pay above on livre two ſols ſix deniers [about 1s.] for fifty acres. Beſide this, the government en-gaged to advance or reimburſe the expences of paſ-ſage, to build houſes, to furniſh all the neceſſary in-ſtruments for fiſhery or agriculture, and to defray the expences of ſubſiſtence for the firſt year. Theſe en-couragements determined three thouſand ſeven hun-dred and fifty perſons, in the month of May 1749, to go to America, rather than run the riſk of ſtarving in Europe.

It was intended that theſe new inhabitants ſhould form a ſettlement to the ſouth-eaſt of Acadia, in a place which the ſavages formerly called Chebucto, and the Engliſh, Halifax. This ſituation was prefer-red to ſeveral others where the ſoil was better, for the ſake of eſtabliſhing in its neighbourhood an excellent cod fiſhery, and fortifying one of the fineſt harbours in America. But as it was the part of the country moſt favourable for the chaſe, the Engliſh were obli-ged to diſpute it with the Micmac Indians, by whom it was moſt frequented. Theſe ſavages defended with

B O O K obſtinacy a territory they held from nature; and it
XVII. was not without very great loſſes that the Engliſh
drove them from their poſſeſſions.

This war was not entirely finiſhed, when ſome diſturbances began to break out among the neutral French. Theſe people, whoſe manners were ſo ſimple, and who enjoyed ſuch liberty, had already perceived that their independence muſt neceſſarily ſuffer ſome encroachments from any power that ſhould turn its views to the countries they inhabited. To this apprehenſion was added that of ſeeing their religion in danger. Their prieſts, either heated by their own enthuſiaſm, or ſecretly inſtigated by the governors of Canada, made them believe all they choſe to ſay againſt the Engliſh, whom they called heretics. This word, which has ſo powerful an influence on deluded minds, determined this happy American colony to quit their habitations and remove to New France, where lands were offered them. This reſolution many of them executed immediately, without conſidering the conſequences of it; the reſt were preparing to follow as ſoon as they had provided for their ſafety. The Engliſh government, either from policy or caprice, determined to prevent them by an act of treachery, always baſe and cruel in thoſe whoſe power gives them an opportunity of purſuing milder methods. Under a pretence of exacting a renewal of the oath which they had taken at the time of their becoming Engliſh ſubjects, they called together all the remaining inhabitants, and put them on board of ſhip. They were conveyed to the other Engliſh colonies, where the greater part of them died of grief and vexation rather than want.

Such are the effects of national jealouſies, and of the rapaciouſneſs of government, to which men, as well as their property, become a prey. What our enemies loſe is reckoned an advantage, what they gain is looked upon as a loſs. When a town cannot be taken, it is ſtarved; when it cannot be kept, it is burnt to aſhes, or its foundations razed. A ſhip or a fortified town is

blown up, rather than the failors or the garrifon will
furrender. A defpotic government feparates its enemies from its flaves by immenfe deferts, to prevent the
irruptions of the one and the emigrations of the other.
Thus it is that Spain has rather chofen to make a wil-
dernefs of her own country, and a grave of America,
than to divide its riches with any other of the European nations. The Dutch have been guilty of every
public and private crime to deprive other commercial
nations of the fpice trade. They have frequently
thrown whole cargoes into the fea rather than they
would fell them at a low price. France rather chofe
to give up Louifiana to the Spaniards, than to let it
fall into the hands of the Englifh; and England deftroyed the neutral French inhabitants of Acadia, to
prevent their returning to France. Can it be faid after this, that policy and fociety were inftituted for the
happinefs of mankind? Yes, they were inftituted to
fcreen the wicked, and to fecure the powerful.

Since the emigration of a people who owed their
happinefs to their virtuous obfcurity, Nova Scotia remained in a languid ftate. Envy, which had depopulated this country, feemed to have fhed its baneful influence over it. The punifhment of injuftice fell at
leaft upon the authors of it. At laft a few unfortunate people were driven there by the various calamities they experienced in Europe. They amounted in
1769 to twenty-fix thoufand; moft of them were difperfed, and were only collected in any number at Halifax, Annapolis, and Lunenbourg. This laft colony,
formed by Germans, was the moft flourifhing. It owed
its improvements to that fondnefs for labour, to that
well-regulated economy, which are the diftinguifhing
characteriftics of a wife and warlike nation, who, con-
tenting themfelves with defending their own country,
feldom leave it, except to go and cultivate diftricts
which they are not ambitious of conquering.

In the year 1769, the colony fent out fourteen veffels and one hundred and forty-eight boats, which to-

BOOK
XVII.

Prefent
ftate of No-
va Scotia.

gether amounted to feven thoufand three hundred and
twenty-four tons, and received twenty-two veffels and
one hundred and twenty boats, which together made
up feven thoufand and fix tons. They conftructed
three floops, which did not exceed one hundred and
ten tons burden.

Their exportation for Great Britain, and for the
other parts of the globe, did not amount to more than
729,850 livres 12 fols 9 deniers [about 30,410l. 8s.
10d.].

Notwithftanding thefe encouragements, which the
mother-country had inceffantly beftowed upon this
colony, in order to accelerate its cultures, it had itfelf
borrowed 450,000 livres [18,750l.], for which it paid
an intereft of fix per cent. It had not then any paper
currency, and hath not ufed any fince.

The troubles which at prefent agitate North America have not extended to Nova Scotia. It hath even
drawn fome advantages from them. Its population
hath arifen to forty thoufand fouls, by the arrival of
fome cautious or pufillanimous citizens who fled from
the horrors of war. The neceffity of fupplying the
wants of the Britifh armies and fleets hath occafioned
a great increafe of provifions. An immenfe quantity
of fpecie, circulated by the troops, hath given life to
every thing, and communicated a rapid motion to men
and things.

Should the other colonies at length detach themfelves from the mother-country, and fhould it retain
Nova Scotia, this province, which was very infignificant, will become very important. It is fupplied with
every advantage that may enfure its profperity. · Its
paftures are proper for the breeding of cattle, and its
lands for the cultivation of corn, and efpecially for
the growing of flax and hemp. There are few coafts
known to be fo favourable for large fifheries ; and its
boats can with eafe perform feven voyages to the great
bank of Newfoundland, while thofe of New England
can only perform five, and with a great deal of diffi-

culty. The Englifh iflands will furnifh it with a cer- B O O K tain, eafy, and almoſt excluſive mart for its merchan- XVII. diſe.

There can be no fear of any invaſion, becauſe Halifax, which was formely defended only by a few batteries properly or improperly placed, is at preſent ſurrounded by good fortifications, which may ſtill be increaſed.

New-England, like the mother-country, has ſigna-   Foundation lized itſelf by many acts of violence, and has been ac-   of New- England. tuated by the ſame turbulent ſpirit. It took its riſe in troubleſome times, and its infant ſtate was diſturbed with many dreadful commotions. It was diſcovered in the beginning of the laſt century, and called North-Virginia ; but no Europeans ſettled there till the year 1608. The firſt colony, which was weak and ill-directed, did not ſucceed ; and for ſome time after, there were only a few adventurers who came over at times in the ſummer, built themſelves temporary huts, for the ſake of trading with the ſavages, and, like them, diſappeared again for the reſt of the year. Fanaticiſm, which had depopulated America to the ſouth, was deſtined to repeople it in the north. Some Englifh Preſbyterians, who had been driven from their own country, and had taken refuge in Holland, that univerſal aſylum of liberty, reſolved to found a church for their ſect in the new hemiſphere. They therefore purchaſed, in 1621, the charter of the Englifh North-Virginia Company ; for they were not reduced to ſuch a ſtate of poverty, as to be obliged to wait till proſperity became the reward of their virtues.

On the 6th of September 1621, they embarked at Plymouth, to the number of 120 perſons, under the guidance of enthuſiaſm, which, whether founded upon error or truth, is always productive of great actions. They landed at the beginning of a very hard winter, and found a country entirely covered with wood, which offered a very melancholy proſpect to men already exhauſted with the fatigues of their voyage. Near one half periſhed either by cold, the ſcurvy, or distress; the rest were kept alive, by that strength of character which they had acquired under the persecution of episcopal tyranny. But their courage was beginning to droop, when it was revived by the arrival of sixty savage warriors, who came to them in the spring, headed by their chief. Freedom seemed to exult that she had thus brought together, from the extremities of the world, two such different colonies; who immediately entered into a reciprocal alliance of friendship and protection. The old inhabitants assigned for ever to the new ones all the lands in the neighbourhood of the settlement they had formed under the name of New-Plymouth; and one of the savages, who understood a little English, staid to teach them how to cultivate the maize, and instruct them in the manner of fishing upon their coast.

This humanity enabled the colony to wait for the companions they expected from Europe, with seeds, with domestic animals, and with every assistance they wanted. At first the settlement advanced but slowly, since, in 1629, it contained no more than three hundred persons: but the persecution of the Puritans, which increased daily in England, hastened the augmentation of their number in America. Such multitudes of them arrived the following year, that it became necessary to disperse them. The colonies which they established formed the province of Massachuset's Bay. The colonies of New Hampshire, Connecticut, and of Rhode Island, soon sprang up from this settlement; and these were so many separate states, each of which obtained from the court of London a distinct charter.

The blood of martyrs hath ever been, in all places, and at all times, a source of proselytism. A few ecclesiastics only, deprived of their benefices on account of their opinions, had at first passed into America, and a few obscure sectaries, whose new tenets attracted numbers from among the people. The emigrations became gradually more common amongst other classes of citizens; and in process of time, men of the first rank, who had been drawn into Puritanifm by ambi- tion, humour, or confcience, thought of fecuring to themfelves an afylum in thofe diftant climates. They had caufed houfes to be built, and lands to be cleared, with a view of retiring there, if their endeavours in the caufe of civil and religious liberty fhould prove abortive. The fame fanatical fpirit that had introduced anarchy into the mother-country, kept the colony in a ftate of fubordination, or rather a feverity of manners, had the fame effect as laws in a favage country.

The inhabitants of New England lived peaceably Form of government eftablifhed at New-England. for fome time without thinking of fettling their felicity upon a firm bafis. Not that their charter had not authorifed them to eftablifh any mode of government they might choofe, but thefe enthufiafts did not think of it ; and government did not pay a fufficient attention to them to urge them to fecure their own tranquillity. At length they grew fenfible of the neceffity of giving fome confiftency to their colony. At this period it was agreed, that there fhould be an affembly holden every year, the deputies of which fhould be chofen by the people, in which none but thofe who were members of the eftablifhed church could have a feat, and over which a chief was to prefide, without any diftinct authority. Two remarkable regulations were at the fame time made : the firft ftated the price of corn, and by the fecond the favages were deprived of all the lands which they fhould not cultivate ; and all Europeans were prohibited, under a heavy penalty, to fell them any ftrong liquors or warlike ftores.

The national council were charged with the regulation of public affairs. They were alfo obliged to determine upon all fuits, but by the lights of reafon alone, and without the affiftance or embarraffments of any code.

Neither were any criminal laws inftituted ; but thofe of the Jews were adopted. Witchcraft, blafphemy, adultery, and falfe teftimony, were punifhed with death. Children, who were fo unnatural as to ftrike or to curfe the authors of their being, drew upon themfelves

B O O K   the fame punifhment.   All perfons who were detected
XVII.   either in lying, drunkennefs, or dancing, were ordered
to be publicly whipped ; and amufements were forbidden equally with vices and crimes.   Swearing, and
the violation of the Sabbath, were expiated by a heavy
fine.   Another indulgence allowed was, to atone by
a fine for a neglect of prayer, or for uttering a rafh
oath.

It is alfo known, that government forbade, on pain
of death, the Puritans to worfhip images ; and that
the fame punifhment was decreed againft Roman Catholic priefts, who fhould return into the colony after
having been banifhed.

Fanaticifm   The unfortunate members of the colony, who, lefs
occafions   violent than their brethren, ventured to deny the co-
great cala- ercive power of the magiftrate in matters of religion,
mities in
New-Eng-   were the objects of perfecution.   This was confidered
land.   as blafphemy by thofe very divines who had rather
chofen to quit their country than to fhow any deference to epifcopal authority.   By that natural propenfity of the human heart, which leads men from the
love of independence to that of tyranny, they had
changed their opinions as they changed the climate;
and only feemed to arrogate freedom of thought to
themfelves, in order to deny it to others.   This fyftem
of intoleration was fupported by the fervices of the
law, which attempted to put a ftop to every difference
in opinion, by inflicting capital punifhment on all who
diffented.   Thofe who were either convicted, or even
fufpected, of entertaining fentiments of toleration, were
expofed to fuch cruel oppreffions, that they were forced to fly from their firft afylum, and feek refuge in
another lefs expofed to difturbances.

This intemperate religious zeal extended itfelf to
matters in themfelves of the greateft indifference.   A
proof of this is found in the following public declaration, tranfcribed from the regifters of the colony :

" It is a circumftance univerfally acknowledged,
" that the cuftom of wearing long hair, after the
" manner of immoral perfons and of the favage In-

" dians, can only have been introduced into England, B o o K
" but in facrilegious contempt of the exprefs command ︸XVII︸
" of God, who declares, that it is a fhameful practice
" for any man who has the leaft care for his foul to
" wear long hair. As this abomination excites the
" indignation of all pious perfons, we, the magiftrates,
" in our zeal for the purity of the faith, do exprefsly
" and authentically declare, that we condemn the
" impious cuftom of letting the hair grow; a cuftom
" which we look upon to be very indecent and dif-
" honeft, which horribly difguifes men, and is offen-
" five to modeft and fober perfons, in as much as it
" corrupts good manners. We, therefore, being juft-
" ly incenfed againft this fcandalous cuftom, do de-
" fire, advife, and earneftly requeft all the elders of
" our continent, zealoufly to fhow their averfion from
" this odious practice, to exert all their power to put
" a ftop to it, and efpecially to take care that the
" members of their churches be not infected with it;
" in order that thofe perfons, who, notwithftanding
" thefe rigorous prohibitions, and the means of cor-
" rection, that fhall be ufed on this account, fhall ftill
" perfift in this cuftom, may have both God and man
" at the fame time againft them."

This feverity, which a man exercifes againft himfelf,
or againft his fellow-creatures, and which makes him
firft the victim, then the oppreffor, foon exerted itfelf
againft the Quakers. They were whipped, banifhed,
and imprifoned. The proud fimplicity of thefe new
enthufiafts, who in the midft of tortures and ignominy
praifed God, and called for bleffings upon men, infpired a reverence for their perfons and opinions, and
gained them a number of profelytes. This circumftance exafperated their profecutors, and hurried them
on to the moft atrocious acts of violence. They caufed five of them, who had returned clandeftinely from
banifhment, to be hanged. It feemed as if the Englifh
had come to America to exercife upon their own countrymen the fame cruelties the Spaniards had ufed a-
gainft the Indians; whether it was that the change of

B O O K climate had rendered the Europeans more ferocious,
XVII. or that the fury of religious zeal can only be extinguifhed in the deftruction of its apoftles and its martyrs. This fpirit of perfecution was, however, at laft
fupprefled by the interpofition of the mother-country,
from whence it had been brought.

A people, whofe character was naturally difpofed to
melancholy, were become gloomy and ftern. The
blood of their monarch was ftill before them. Some
of them lamented in fecret this great affaffination,
others would willingly have celebrated it as a feftival.
The nation was divided between two violent parties.
On one hand revenge was meditated ; on the other, it
was endeavoured to prevent it by informations, which
were always followed by exile, imprifonment, or capital punifhment. Reciprocal miftruft prevailed between
fathers and children, and between friends. The fufpicious tyrant was furrounded by fufpicious courtiers,
who kept up his apprehenfions, either to raife themfelves to the high pofts of the ftate, or to expel their
enemies or their rivals from them. The axe was fuf-
pended over every head. The frequency of rebellions
occafioned a frequency of executions, and thefe repeated executions of illuftrious as well as of obfcure
citizens, perpetually maintained the popular terror.
At length Cromwell difappeared. Enthufiafm, hypo-
crify, and fanaticifm, which compofed his character ;
factions, rebellions, and profcriptions, were all buried
with him ; and England began to have the profpect
of calmer days. Charles the Second, at his reftoration, introduced among his fubjects a focial turn, a
tafte for convivial pleafures and diverfions, and for all
thofe amufements he had been engaged in while he
was travelling from one court to another in Europe,
to endeavour to regain the crown which his father had
loft upon a fcaffold. The propagators of his principles
were a multitude of women of gallantry, of corrupt
favourites, and licentious men of wit. In a fhort time
he brought on a general change of manners ; and nothing but fuch a revolution could poffibly have fecur-

---

ed the tranquillity of his government upon a throne BOOK XVII. stained with blood. He was one of those voluptuaries, whom the love of sensual pleasures sometimes excites to sentiments of compassion and humanity. Moved with the sufferings of the Quakers, he put a stop to them by a proclamation in 1661; but he was never able totally to extinguish the spirit of persecution that prevailed in America.

The colony had placed at their head Henry Vane, the son of that Sir Henry Vane who had such a remarkable share in the disturbances of his country. This obstinate and enthusiastic young man, in every thing resembling his father, unable either to live peaceably himself, or to suffer others to remain quiet, had contrived to revive the obscure and obsolete questions of grace and free will. The disputes upon these points ran very high, and would probably have plunged the colony into a civil war, if several of the savage nations united had not happened at that very time to fall upon the plantations of the disputants, and to massacre great numbers of them. The colonists, heated with their theological contests, paid at first very little attention to this considerable loss. But the danger at length became so urgent and so general, that all took up arms. As soon as the enemy was repulsed, the colony resumed its former dissensions; and this frenzy manifested itself in 1692, by such atrocious acts of violence, as were scarce ever recorded in history.

There lived in a town of New England, called Salem, two young women, who were subject to convulsions, accompanied with extraordinary symptoms. Their father, minister of the church, thought that they were bewitched; and having in consequence cast his suspicions upon an Indian girl who lived in his house, he compelled her by harsh treatment to confess that she was a witch. Other women, upon hearing this, seduced by the pleasure of exciting the public attention, immediately believed that the convulsions which proceeded only from the nature of their sex, were owing to the same cause. Three citizens, casual-

ly named, were immediately thrown into prifon, accufed of witchcraft, hanged, and their bodies left expofed to wild beafts and birds of prey. A few days
after, fixteen other perfons, together with a counfel-
lor, who, becaufe he refufed to plead againft them,
was fuppofed to fhare in their guilt, fuffered in the
fame manner. From this inftant, the imagination of
the multitude was inflamed with thefe horrid and gloomy fcenes. The innocence of youth, the infirmities
of age, virgin modefty, fortune, honour, virtue, and
the moft dignified employments of the ftate, were no
fecurity againft the fufpicions of a people infatuated
with vifionary fuperftition. Children of ten years of
age were put to death; young girls were ftripped naked, and the marks of witchcraft fearched for upon
their bodies with the moft indecent curiofity : thofe
fpots of the fcurvy which age impreffes upon the bodies of old men, were taken for evident figns of the
infernal power. Fanaticifm, wickednefs, and vengeance united, felected their victims at pleafure. In de-
fault of witneffes, torments were employed to extort
confeffions dictated by the executioners themfelves.
If the magiftrates, tired with executions, refufed to punifh, they were themfelves accufed of the crimes they
tolerated; the very minifters of religion raifed falfe
witneffes againft them, who made them forfeit with
their lives the tardy remorfe excited in them by humanity. Dreams, apparitions, terror, and confternation of every kind, increafed thefe prodigies of folly
and horror. The prifons were filled, the gibbets left
ftanding, and all the citizens involved in gloomy apprehenfions. The moft prudent quitted a country
ftained with the blood of its inhabitants; and thofe
that remained wifhed only for peace in the grave. In
a word, nothing lefs than the total and immediate fubverfion of the colony was expected; when on a fudden, in the height of the ftorm, the waves fubfided,
and a calm enfued. All eyes were opened at once,
and the excefs of the evil awakened the minds which
it had at firft ftupified. Bitter and painful remorfe was

the immediate confequence; the mercy of God was B O O K
implored by a general faft, and public prayers were XVII.
offered up to afk forgivenefs for the prefumption of
having fuppofed that Heaven could have been pleafed
with facrifices with which it could only have been offended.

Pofterity will, probably, never know exactly what
was the caufe or remedy of this dreadful diforder. It
had, perhaps, its firft origin in the melancholy which
thefe perfecuted enthufiafts had brought with them
from their own country, which had increafed with the
fcurvy they had contracted at fea, and had gathered
frefh ftrength from the vapours and exhalations of a
foil newly broken up, as well as from the inconveniences and hardfhips infeparable from a change of climate and manner of living. The contagion, however,
ceafed like all other epidemical diftempers, exhaufted
by its very communication; as all the diforders of the
imagination are .expelled in the tranfports of a deli-
rium. A perfect calm fucceeded this agitation; and
the Puritans of New England have never fince been
feized with fo gloomy a fit of enthufiafm.

But though the colony has renounced the perfecuting fpirit which hath ftained all religious fects with
blood, it has preferved fome ftrong marks of that fanaticifm and ferocioufnefs which had fignalized the
melancholy days in which it took its rife.

The fmall-pox, which is lefs frequent, but more deftructive, in America, than it is in Europe, occafioned,
in 1721, inexpreffible ravages in the province of Maffachufet's Bay. This calamity fuggefted the idea of
inoculation. In order to prove the efficacy of this fortunate prefervative, a fkilful and courageous phyfician
inoculated his wife, his children, his fervants, and himfelf. He was immediately infulted, confidered as an
infernal monfter, and threatened with affaffination.
Thefe outrages not having been able to prevent a very promifing young man from having recourfe to this
falutary practice, a wicked, fuperftitious perfon got up

B O O K to his window in the night-time, and threw a grenade
  XVII. into his room, filled with combuftible materials.

The moft reafonable among the citizens were not
difgufted with thefe atrocious acts; and their indignation was exerted rather againft thofe bold fpirits who
were accufed of preferring the fkill of man to the care
of Providence. The people were confirmed by thefe
extravagant doctrines, in the refolution of rejecting a
novelty, which was to draw down upon the whole
ftate the infallible and terrible effects of the divine
wrath. The magiftrates, who were apprehenfive of
an infurrection, ordered the phyficians to affemble;
and they, either from conviction, pufillanimity, or policy, declared inoculation dangerous. It was prohibited by a bill, which was received with unparalleled
applaufe.

Europeans, you feel your hair rifing on your heads;
you fhudder with horror; and you have forgotten the
obftacles which this falutary practice met with among
yourfelves; and you do not confider, that two hundred years ago you would have committed the fame
outrages. Acknowledge, therefore, the important fervices you have received from the progrefs of fcience;
and entertain that refpect and gratitude for the promoters of it, which you owe to ufeful men, who have
preferved you from fo many crimes, which ignorance
and fuperftition would otherwife have made you commit.

A few years after, a new fcene was exhibited, ftill
more atrocious. For a long time paft an odious reward had been granted in thefe provinces to fuch of
the colonifts as fhould put an Indian to death. This
reward was increafed in 1724 to 2250 livres [93l. 15s.].
John Lovewell, encouraged by fo confiderable a pre-
mium, formed a confpiracy of men as ferocious as himfelf, to go in queft of the favages. One day he difcovered ten of them quietly fleeping round a large fire.
He murdered them, carried their fcalps to Bofton, and
received the promifed reward. After this, have you,

ye Anglo-Americans, any reproaches to make to the Spaniards? Have they ever done, or could they possibly ever do, any thing more inhuman? And yet you were men, civilized men; and you boasted of being Christians. No, you were rather monsters, fit to be exterminated; you were monsters, against whom a league that might have been formed would have been less criminal than the one that Lovewell formed against the savages.

[The author here introduces the story of Polly Baker, who was brought before the magistrates, and convicted the fifth time of having had a bastard child. He gives the speech she is said to have made on this occasion at full length. But as this speech is in the hands of every English reader, the translator has judged it unnecessary to swell his translation with it. The author's reasoning upon it is as follows:]

This speech produced an affecting change in the minds of all the audience. She was not only acquitted of either penalty or corporal punishment, but her triumph was so complete, that one of her judges married her. So superior is the voice of reason to all the powers of studied eloquence. But popular prejudice has resumed its influence; whether it be, that the representations of nature alone are often stifled by an attention to political advantages, or to the benefit of society; or that, under the English government, where celibacy is not enjoined by religion, there is less excuse for an illicit commerce between the sexes, than in those countries where the clergy, the nobility, luxury, poverty, and the scandalous example given by the court and the church, all concur in degrading and corrupting the married state, in rendering it burdensome.

New England has some remedy against bad laws in the constitution of its mother-country, where the people, who have the legislative power in their own hands, are at liberty to correct abuses; and it has others derived from its situation, which open a vast field to industry and population.

B O O K
XVII.

Extent, na-
tural histo-
ry, fisheries,
population,
cultures,
manufac-
tures, and
exporta-
tions of
New Eng-
land.

This colony, bounded on the north by Canada, on the weft by New York, and on the eaft and fouth by Nova Scotia and the ocean, extends full three hundred miles along the fea coafts, and upwards of fifty miles in the inland parts.

The clearing of the lands is not directed by chance, as in the other provinces. This matter, from the firft, was fubjected to laws which are ftill religioufly obferved. No citizen whatever has the liberty of fettling even upon unoccupied land. The government, defirous of preferving all its members from the inroads of the favages, and of placing them in a condition to fhare in the protection of a well-regulated fociety, hath ordered that whole villages fhould be farmed at once. As foon as fixty families offer to build a church, maintain a clergyman, and pay a fchoolmafter, the general affembly allot them a fituation, and permit them to have two reprefentatives in the legiflative body of the colony. The diftrict affigned them always borders upon the land already cleared, and generally contains fix thoufand fquare acres. Thefe new people choofe the fituation moft convenient for their habitation, which is ufually of a fquare figure. The church is placed in the centre; the colonifts divide the land among themfelves, and each enclofes his property with a hedge. Some woods are referved for a common. It is thus that New England is conftantly enlarging its territory, though it ftill continues to make one complete and well-conftituted province.

Though the colony be fituated in the midft of the temperate zone, yet the climate is not fo mild as that of fome European provinces, which are under the fame parallel of latitude. The winters are longer and colder, the fummers fhorter and hotter. The fky is commonly clear, and the rains more plentiful than lafting. The air has grown purer fince its circulation has been made free by cutting down the woods; and malignant vapours, which at firft carried off fome of the inhabitants, are no longer complained of.

The country is divided into four provinces, which

at firft had no connection with one another. The ne-
ceffity of maintaining an armed force againft the fa-
vages, obliged them to form a confederacy in 1643,
when they took the name of the United Colonies. In
confequence of this league, two deputies from each
eftablifhment ufed to meet in a ftated place, to delibe-
rate upon the common affairs of New England, ac-
cording to the inftructions they had received from the
affembly by which they were fent. This affociation
was not in any manner repugnant to the right which
each of its members had, to act in every refpect as he
chofe.

They were almoft as much independent of the mo-
ther-country. When the fettlement was allowed to
be made, it had been agreed that their code of laws
fhould not contradict, in any refpect, the legiflation of
the mother-country; that the judging of any capital
crime committed upon their territory, fhould be re-
ferved for it; and that their whole trade fhould be
centered in its ports. None of thefe engagements
were fulfilled; and other obligations, of lefs impor-
tance, were equally neglected. The fpirit of republi-
canifm had already acquired fo great an influence, as
to prevent thefe arrangements from being confidered
as binding. The colonifts limited their fubmiffion to
the acknowledging, in a vague manner, the king of
England to be their fovereign.

Maffachufet, the moft flourifhing of the four pro-
vinces, indulged itfelf in greater liberties than the
others, and did it openly. This haughty behaviour
drew the refentment of Charles II. upon them. In
1684 this monarch took away the charter which had
been granted to them by his father. He eftablifhed
an almoft arbitrary government, and ventured to le-
vy taxes for his own ufe. Defpotifm did not decreafe
under his fucceffor. Accordingly, on the firft intel-
ligence of his being dethroned, his deputy was arreft-
ed, put in irons, and fent back to Europe.

William III. though very well fatisfied with this ar-
dent zeal, did not reftore to the Maffachufets their

B O O K ancient privileges, according to their defires, and, per-
XVII. haps, to their wifhes. It is true that he reftored them
a charter, but a charter which was in nothing refembling the firft.

By the new charter, the governor appointed by the
court, was to be in poffeffion of the exclufive right of
convening, proroguing, or diffolving the national affembly. It was he alone who could give a fanction
to the laws that were decreed, and to the taxes impofed by the affembly. The nomination of every
military employment belonged to this commandant.
It was he, affifted by the council, who appointed the
magiftrates. The other lefs important places could
not be difpofed of without his confent. The public
treafury was never opened but by his order, confirmed by the concurrence of the council. His authority
was likewife extended to fome other matters, which put
a great reftraint upon liberty. Connecticut and Rhode
Ifland, by a timely fubmiffion, prevented the punifhment the province of Maffachufet's Bay had incur-
red, and retained their original charter. That of New
Hampfhire had been always regulated by the fame
mode of adminiftration as the province of Maffachufet's Bay. The fame governor prefided over the four
provinces; but with regulations adapted to the conftitution of each colony.

According to an account publifhed by the general
congrefs of the Englifh American continent, there are
four hundred thoufand inhabitants at Maffachufet's
Bay; one. hundred and ninety-two thoufand at Connecticut; one hundred and fifty thoufand at New
Hampfhire; and fifty-nine thoufand fix hundred and
feventy-eight at Rhode Ifland; which forms, in this
fettlement alone, a population of eighty-one thoufand fix hundred and feventy-eight fouls.

This great multiplication of men fhould feem to
arife from an excellent foil; but this is not the cafe.
All the countries, except fome parts of Connecticut,
were originally covered with pine trees; and, confequently, are either entirely barren, or not very fertile.

None of the European feeds thrive there ; and their produce hath never been fufficient for the nourifhment of its inhabitants. They have always been obliged to live upon maize, or to draw part of their fubfiftence from elfewhere. Accordingly though the country be generally very fit for the culture of fruit and of vegetables, and for the breeding of cattle, yet the country places are not the moft interefting part of thofe regions. It is upon coafts furrounded with rocks, but which are favourable to fifhing, that the population hath augmented, activity hath increafed, and eafy circumftances are become general.

This infufficiency of the harvefts ought to have excited induftry in New England fooner, and more particularly, than in the reft of the continent. Several fhips were even conftructed there for foreign navigators, the materals for which, at prefent fo fcarce and fo expenfive, were, for a long time, common and cheap. The facility of procuring beaver fkins, occafioned the eftablifhing of a confiderable hat manufactory. Cloths were alfo made of flax and hemp ; and with the fleeces of their flocks, the colony fabricated ftuffs, which are coarfe but ftrong.

To thefe manufactures, which may be called national, another branch of induftry was added, fupported by foreign materials. Sugar yields a refiduum known by the name of fyrup, or molaffes. The people of New England went to fetch it from the Weft Indies, and ufed it at firft juft as it was, for various purpofes. At length the idea of diftilling it fuggefted itfelf to them. They fold a prodigious quantity of this rum to the neighbouring favages ; to the men employed in the cod-fifhery, and to all the northern provinces ; they even carried it to the coafts of Africa, where they difpofed of it with confiderable advantage to the Englifh employed in the purchafe of flaves.

This branch of trade, and other circumftances, enabled the inhabitants of New England to appropriate to themfelves part of the commodities, both of South

B O O K and of North America. The exchanges between thefe
XVII. two regions, which are fo neceffary to them both, paffed through their hands ; and they became, in fome
meafure, brokers, as the Hollanders, of the New
World.

The greateft refource of thofe provinces, however,
always was the fifhery ; which was very confiderable,
even upon their own coafts. A prodigious quantity
of boats is feen in every river, bay, or port, which
are employed in catching falmon, fturgeon, cod, and
other kinds of fifh, which are all fold to advantage.

Mackerel is caught principally at the mouth of the
Pentagouet, which empties itfelf in Fundy, or French
Bay, at the extremity of the colony. In fpring and
in autumn, fourteen or fifteen hundred boats, and two
thoufand five hundred men are employed in this fifhery.

The cod fifhery is ftill more advantageous to New
England. Its numerous ports fend out annually five
hundred veffels, of fifty tons burden, the crews of
which amount to four thoufand men. They catch
at leaft two hundred and fifty thoufand quintals of
cod.

Thefe colonies employ themfelves likewife in the
whale fifhery. Before the year 1763, New England
carried on this fifhery in the Gulf of Florida, in March,
April, and May; and to the eaft of the Great Bank of
Newfoundland, in June, July, and Auguft. There
were no more than one hundred and twenty floops,
each of feventy tons burden, and fixteen hundred failors, fent out for this purpofe at that time. In 1767,
this fifhery employed feven thoufand two hundred and
ninety failors. Let us inveftigate the caufes of this
confiderable increafe.

Great Britain was for a long time agitated with the
defire of fharing the whale fifhery with the Dutch.
In order to fucceed in this, towards the latter end of
the reign of Charles II. the inhabitants of that kingdom were difcharged from paying any duty to the
cuftom-houfe, upon the produce arifing from the fifh
which they fhould obtain from the Northern Sea : but

this indulgence was not extended to the colonies, who were obliged to pay a duty of 56 livres 5 fols [2l. 6s. 10½d.] for every ton of oil and of whalebone, at their entrance into the mother-country; this duty was only diminished by one half, when these articles were imported on English bottoms.

To this tax, which was already too burdenfome, another was added in 1699, of 5 fols 7 deniers [about 2¾d.] for every pound weight of whalebone; which bore equally upon America and upon Europe. This new tax produced fuch fatal consequences, that it was found neceffary to fupprefs it in 1723; but it was only taken off for the whales caught in Greenland, in Davis's Straits, or in the adjoining feas. The fifhery on the Northern continent ftill remained fubject to the new as well as the old duty.

The miniftry, perceiving that the exemption of the duty was not fufficient to excite the emulation of the Englifh, had recourfe to encouragements. In 1732, a gratuity of 22 livres 10 fols [18s. 9d.] was given; and fixteen years after, another of 45 livres [1l. 17s. 6d.] for every ton conveyed by the fhips employed in this important fifhery. This generofity of government produced part of the good effects which were expected from it. Great Britain, however, far from being able to vie with their rivals in foreign markets, was ftill obliged to purchafe annually to the value of three or four hundred thoufand livres [from 12,500l. to 16,666l. 13s. 4d.] of train oil and whalebone.

Such was the ftate of things, when the feas of North America, which belonged to the French, became an Englifh poffeffion at the laft peace. Immediately the New-Englanders went there in numbers to catch whales, which are very plenty. They were exonerated by parliament from the duties which oppreffed them; and their induftry became ftill more active. It muft naturally be communicated to the neighbouring colonies; and it is probable that the United Provinces will, in procefs of time, be deprived of this important branch of their trade.

The whale fifhery is carried on in the Gulf of St. Lawrence, and in the adjacent latitudes, upon feas lefs tempeftuous, and lefs embarraffed with ice, than thofe of Greenland. Accordingly, it begins fooner, and ends later. Fewer fatal accidents happen there. The fhips employed for the purpofe are fmaller, and have lefs numerous crews. Thefe reafons muft give to the American continent advantages, which the economy of the Dutch will never be able to balance. The Englifh of Europe themfelves hoped to fhare this fuperiority with their colonifts, becaufe they expected to add to the profits accruing from the fifhery, that which they were to collect from the fale of their cargoes; a refource which was not allowed to the navigators who frequented Davis's Straits or the Greenland feas.

The vendible productions of New England are cod, train-oil, whales, tallow, cyder, falt meats, maize, hogs and oxen, pot-afh, pulfe, mafts for merchantmen and men of war, and all kinds of woods. The Azore Iflands, Madeira, the Canaries, Portugal, Spain, Italy, Great Britain, and principally the Weft Indies, hitherto confumed thefe articles. In 1769, the united exports of the four provinces amounted to 13,844,430 livres 19 fols 5 deniers [about 576,851l. 5s. 9¼d.]. But this colony received habitually more than it fent out, fince it was conftantly indebted twenty-four or twenty-five millions of livres [from 1,000,000l. to 1,041,666l. 13s. 4d.] to the mother-country.

Some fhips are difpatched from every one of the extremely numerous ports that are on thefe coafts. The principal voyages, however, from Connecticut, are undertaken at Newhaven; thofe to Rhode Ifland, at Newport; thofe to Hampfhire, at Portfmouth; and thofe to Maffachufet's Bay, at Bofton.

This laft city, which may be confidered as the capital of New England, is fituated on a peninfula, four miles in length, at the bottom of the fine bay of Maffachufet, which reaches about eight miles within land. The opening of the bay is fheltered from the impetuofity of the waves by a number of rocks which rife above the water, and by twelve fmall iflands, moft of which are inhabited. Thefe dykes and natural ramparts will not allow more than three fhips to come in together. At the end of the laft century, a regular citadel, named Fort William, was erected in one of the iflands upon this narrow channel. It is defended by a hundred pieces of cannon of the largeft fize, and very well placed. A league further on, is a very high light-houfe, the fignals from which may be perceived and repeated by the fortrefs along the whole coaft, at the fame time that Bofton has her own light-houfes, which fpread the alarm to all the inland country. Except when a very thick fog happens to prevail, which fome fhips might take advantage of to flip into the iflands, the town has always five or fix hours to prepare for the reception of an enemy, and to affemble ten thoufand militia, which can be collected in four-and-twenty hours. If a fleet fhould ever be able to pafs the artillery of Fort William, it would infallibly be ftopped by a couple of batteries, which being erected to the north and fouth of the place, command the whole bay, and would give time for all the veffels and commercial ftores to be fheltered from cannon fhot in the river Charles.

The harbour of Bofton is fo fpacious, that fix hundred veffels may anchor in it fafely and commodioufly. There is a magnificent pier conftructed, projecting fufficiently into the fea to allow the fhips to unload their goods without the affiftance of a lighter, and to depofit them into the warehoufes which are ranged on the north fide. At the extremity of the pier, the town appears built upon an uneven territory, in form of a crefcent round the harbour. Before the difturbances, it contained about thirty-five or forty thoufand inhabitants, of various fects. The houfes, furniture, drefs, food, converfation, cuftoms and manners, were fo exactly fimilar to the mode of living in London, that it was fcarce poffible to find any other difference, but that which arifes from the greater numbers of people there are in large capitals.

BOOK XVII.

The Dutch found the colony of New Belgia, afterwards called New York.

New England, which refembles the mother-country in fo many refpects, is contiguous to New York. The latter, bounded on the eaft by this principal colony, and on the weft by New Jerfey, occupies at firft a very narrow fpace of twenty miles along the fea-fhore, and infenfibly enlarging, extends to the north above a hundred and fifty miles up the country.

This country was difcovered towards the beginning of the feventeenth century, by Henry Hudfon, a famous Englifh navigator, at that time in the Dutch fervice. He entered into a confiderable river, to which he gave his name, and after flightly reconnoitering the coaft, returned to Amfterdam, from whence he had failed. A fecond voyage, undertaken by this adventurer, gave fome better idea of this favage country.

According to the European fyftem, which never pays any attention to the people of the New World, this country fhould have belonged to the United Provinces. It was difcovered by a man in their fervice, who took poffeffion of it in their name, and gave up to them any perfonal right he might have in it. His being an Englifhman did not in the leaft invalidate thefe uncontrovertible titles. It muft therefore have occafioned great furprife, when James I. afferted his pretenfions to it, upon the principle that Hudfon was born his fubject; as if any man's country was not that in which he earns his fubfiftence; and indeed the king laid but a flight ftrefs upon a pretenfion for which there was fo little foundation.

The republic, who faw nothing in this property, which was no longer contefted with them, except a fettlement for the trade of the beaver and other peltries, ceded it to the Weft India Company. This fociety directed all its attention towards thefe favage riches; and in order to get as near them as poffible, they caufed Fort Orange, fince called Albany, to be erected upon the borders of Hudfon's River, at the diftance of one hundred and fifty miles from the fea. It was there that the furs were brought to their agents who gave in exchange to the Iroquois, fire-arms and

warlike ftores, to enable them to refift the French, B O O K
who were lately arrived in Canada.

At that time New Belgia was nothing more than a
factory. The city of Amfterdam became fenfible that
it would be a judicious thing to eftablifh a colony in
that part of the New World, and eafily obtained the
ceffion of it, by giving 700,000 livres [29,1661. 13s.
4d.] to the proprietors.

Thefe more extenfive views required other arrangements. The poft placed in the neighbourhood of the
Five Nations was left ftanding; but it appeared neceffary to eftablifh a more confiderable one at the
mouth of the river, in the ifland of Manahatan; and
accordingly, New Amfterdam was built there. Neither the town, its territories, nor the reft of the province, were ever difturbed by the neighbouring favages, fome of whom were too weak to make any attempts, and the others were perpetually at war with
the French. This poffeffion, therefore, was making
a rapid progrefs, when it was vifited by an unexpected
ftorm.

England, which had not at that time thofe intimate
connections with Holland, which the ambition and
fucceffes of Lewis XIV. have fince given rife to between the two powers, beheld, with a jealous eye a
fmall ftate, but lately formed in its neighbourhood, extending its flourifhing trade to all parts of the world.
She was inwardly incenfed at the idea of not being
able to attain to an equality with a power which ought
not even to have entered into a competition with her.
Thefe rivals in commerce, as in navigation, by their
vigilance and economy, ruined her in all the great
markets of the univerfe, and obliged her to act only
a fecondary part. Every effort fhe made to eftablifh
a competition ended either to her difadvantage or difcredit, while univerfal commerce was evidently con-
centrating itfelf in the moraffes of the republic. At
length the nation was roufed by the difgrace of their
merchants, and refolved to fecure to them by force
what they could not obtain by their induftry. Charles

At what period, and in what manner the Englifh make them-felves ma-fters of New Bel-gia.

II. notwithftanding his averfion for bufinefs, and his
immoderate love of pleafure, eagerly adopted a plan
which gave him a profpect of acquiring the riches of
thofe diftant regions, together with the maritime empire of Europe. His brother, more active and more
enterprifing than himfelf, encouraged him in thefe
difpofitions ; and with one confent, they ordered that
the fettlements and fhips of the Dutch fhould be attacked, without any previous declaration of war.

Hoftilities begun in this manner are both cowardly
and perfidious. They are the act of a horde of favages,
and not of a civilized nation ; of a dark affaffin, and
not of a warlike prince. No perfon who puts any
confidence in his ftrength, and who hath any elevation of foul, will furprife a fleeping adverfary. If any
one may be allowed to take advantage of my fecurity,
may I not alfo avail myfelf of his? Such conduct
compels both parties to be inceffantly in arms ; the
ftate of war becomes permanent, and peace is no more
than a word devoid of meaning. There is either a
juft reafon for attacking an enemy, or there is none.
If there be none, the party that begins the attack is
nothing more than a dangerous robber, againft whom
all ought to unite, and whom they have a right to exterminate. If, on the contrary, there be a reafon for
commencing hoftilities, it ought to be notified. Nothing can authorife the feizure of poffeffions, except
the refufal to repair an injury, or to reftore any thing
that is ufurped. Before you become the aggreffor, let
the world be convinced of the injuftice that is done to
you. The only thing that can be allowed, is to make
fecret preparations for revenge ; to diffemble your projects, if they caufe any alarm ; and to leave no interval between the refufal of juftice and the beginning of
hoftilities. If you fhould be weaker than your adverfary, you muft entreat and fuffer with patience. Muft
you be a traitor, becaufe another perfon is an ufurper?
Defpife the common maxim ; and do not fupply either
the ftrength you may be deficient in, or the courage
which might expofe you, by treachery. Let the opi-

nion of your cotemporaries, and that of posterity, be
always present to your mind.

In the month of August 1664, an English squadron
anchored on the coasts of New Belgia, the capital of
which surrendered upon the first summons, and the rest
of the colony made no greater resistance. This conquest was ensured to the English by the treaty of Bre-
da. But they were deprived of it again by the republic in 1673, when the intrigues of France had set these
two maritime powers at variance, which, for their mutual interests, ought ever to be united. A second treaty again restored to the English, in the following year,
a province which hath since remained attached to their
dominion, but as the property of the king's brother,
who gave his name to it.

New York was governed by the deputies of this
prince with sufficient address to prevent the indignation of the colonists from being excited against their
persons. The public hatred was fixed upon their master, who had kept all the power in his own hands.
This political slavery equally disgusted both the Dutch,
who had preferred their plantations to their country,
and the English, who had joined them. The people,
accustomed to liberty, became impatient under the
yoke. Every thing seemed tending either to an insurrection, or to an emigration. The commotion was
put a stop to only in 1683, when the colony was invited to choose representatives, who might regulate in
assemblies what would be proper for its interests.

The colony
is ceded to
the Duke
of York.
Principles
upon which
he founded
its admini-
stration.

Colonel Duncan, who was intrusted with this business, was a man of a bold and extensive mind. He
did not confine himself, like those who had hitherto
governed the province, to the ceding of lands to every person who offered to clear them; he also extended
his care to the Five Nations, which had been too
much neglected by his predecessors. The French were
for ever endeavouring to disunite these savages, in
hopes of enslaving them: and they had advanced this
great undertaking by means of the converts made by

their miffionaries. It was the bufinefs of England to difconcert this plan ; but the Duke of York, who had views of intereft diftinct from that of his country, was defirous that his deputy fhould favour the execution of it. Duncan, though a Catholic, conftantly deviated from the plan that was traced out for him, and exerted his utmoft efforts to thwart a fyftem which appeared to him to be founded rather upon policy than religion. He even annoyed, by every poffible meafure, the nation that was the rival of his ; and the memoirs of the times atteft,' that he greatly retarded their progrefs.

The conduct of this able chief was different in the interior part of the colony. He encouraged, both from inclination, and in obedience to orders, the eftablifhment of the families of his own and of his prince's religion. This protection was accompanied with a kind of myftery ; but as foon as James II. had afcended the throne, the collector of the public revenues, the principal officers, and a great number of citizens, declared themfelves partifans of the church of Rome.

This occafioned a great ferment in the minds of the people. The Proteftant caufe was thought to be in danger; and prudent men were apprehenfive of an infurrection. Duncan fucceeded in keeping the malecontents in order; but the revolution obliged him to make a voluntary refignation of his poft. He fubmitted, like a good Englifhman, to the new government; and by a haughtinefs of character peculiar to his nation, he fent over to the dethroned monarch all the riches he had acquired in a long and profperous adminiftration.

This fingular man had fcarce quitted America, before the inhabitants of New England expelled their governor, Edmund Andrews, one of the moft active promoters of the arbitrary views of King James. Some militia of New York, feduced by this example, endeavoured to treat Nicholfon, who was temporarily intrufted with the government, in the fame manner;

but he fucceeded in forming a party in his favour, and the colony became the prey of two armed factions, till the arrival of Colonel Slaughter.

This commander, who was fent by King William, convoked the members of the ftate, on the 9th of April 1691. This affembly annulled every thing which had been previoufly decreed contrary to the Britifh conftitution, and enacted laws which have ever fince been the rule of the colony. At this period, the executive power was placed in the hands of the governor appointed by the crown, which gave him twelve counfellors, without whofe concurrence he could not fign any act. The commons were reprefented by thirty deputies, chofen by the inhabitants; and thefe feveral bodies conftituted the general affembly, in which every power was vefted. The duration of this affembly, originally unlimited, was afterwards fixed at three years; and it now continues feven, like the Britifh parliament, the revolutions of which it hath followed.

It was time that an invariable order fhould be eftablifhed in the colony. It was obliged to fuftain, againft the French in Canada, a brifk and obftinate war, which had been kindled by the dethroning of James II. Thefe hoftilities, terminated by the treaty of Ryfwick, began again on account of the Spanifh fucceffion. The provinces adjacent to New York took fome part in thefe divifions; but it was this province which gave or fuftained the greateft ftrokes, which paid the troops, and which was drawn into the moft confiderable expences.

Unfortunately, the contributions of the citizens, which were ordered by the general affembly, were collected in a cheft, that was entirely at the difpofal of the governor. It often happened, that rapacious or extravagant commanders converted to their own ufe the funds deftined for the public fervice. This became a perpetual fource of diffenfion. Queen Anne decreed, in 1705, that the fame authority by which the taxes were impofed, fhould determine the ufe they were to be applied to, and might require an account to be

B O O K given of the manner in which they had been em-
XVII. ployed.

Though the malverfations were ftopped by this arrangement, yet the duties paid by the province were
not adequate to the expences which the continuation
of the war required. This embarraffment occafioned,
for the firft time, in 1709, the creation of bills of credit, which were afterwards much more multiplied than
either the wants of the colony required, or than was
confiftent with its advantage.

Burnet, a fon of the famous bifhop of that name
who had fo much contributed to the placing of the
houfe of Orange upon the throne, was appointed governor of the colony in 1720. But though he did not
fucceed in putting a ftop to this diforder, yet he formed another plan for the profperity of the colony. The
French inhabitants of Canada wanted, for the purpofe
of their exchange with the favages, feveral articles
which were not furnifhed by their mother-country :
thefe they drew from New York. The general affembly of that province, by the advice of their governor,
prohibited this communication. But as it was not fufficient to have embarraffed the meafures of an active
rival, it was determined to fupply their place.

A great part of the furs which were carried to Montreal paffed over the weftern fhores of the lake Ontario. Burnet obtained the confent of the Iroquois, in
1722, to build there the fort Ofwego, where thefe favage riches might be eafily intercepted. As foon as
this fettlement was formed, the merchants of Albany
fent their merchandife to Chenectady, where they were
embarked upon the Mohawks, which conveyed them
to Ofwego. The navigation of this river is very difficult, and yet the Englifh fucceeded beyond their expectations. Thefe exchanges would even have been
increafed, had they not been thwarted by every kind
of difficulty.

In 1726, the French conftructed a fort at Niagara,
where the furs, which, without this fettlement, muft

have been carried to Ofwego, were detained. The B o o κ
Englifh merchandife, which could no more be openly XVII.
received, was fraudulently conveyed till the year 1729,
a remarkable period in which the interefts of individuals caufed the law which forbade this commerce to
be revoked. England too, at length, laid heavier taxes
upon the fur trade than were paid by the French.

While thefe various impediments diminifhed the
connections which it was hoped would have been
formed with the favages, the cultures were carried on
with great fpirit and fuccefs throughout the whole extent of the province. They had languifhed for fome
time, indeed, in thefe countries where James II. had
granted immenfe territories to fome men too highly
favoured; but thefe countries had at length been peopled. as well as the others. Unfortunately, moft of
the inhabitants only occupied, as in Scotland, lands
transferable at the will of the ground landlord; and
ftill more unfortunately, this dependence gave the
great proprietors a very dangerous influence in the
public deliberations.

This defect in the government was particularly fatal in the two deftructive wars which the colony was
obliged to fuftain againft the French, in 1744 and in
1756. It experienced, during thefe misfortunes, calamities which it might at leaft partly have avoided, if
the efforts made to repulfe thefe enterprifing men, and
their ferocious allies, had been concerted in time, and
better planned. It was neceffary that Canada fhould
become a Britifh poffeffion at the peace of 1763, in
order to enable New York to attend conftantly, and
without embarraffment or anxiety, to the extenfion of
its trade with the favages, and to the clearing of its
plantations.

This province, the limits of which were not fettled Soil, popu-
till after the longeft, the moft violent, and the moft lation, and
obftinate contefts, with New England, New Jerfey, of the co-
and Pennfylvania, confifts at prefent of ten counties. lony.
It hath but a fmall extent towards the fea; but in
depth its territory reaches as far as lake George or St.

Sacrament, and as far as lake Ontario.   Hudfon's River ifiues from mountains fituated between thefe two lakes.   This can receive none but fmall canoes for the fpace of fixty-five miles ; and even that navigation is interrupted by two waterfalls, which oblige the perfons concerned in it fo carry their cargoes twice over land the length of about two hundred toifes each time.   But from Albany to the ocean, that is to fay, through a fpace of one hundred and fifty miles, veffels of forty or fifty tons burden are feen conftantly failing, day and night, with the tide, upon this magnificent canal, during all feafons, without the leaft rifk ; and which keep up a continual and rapid circulation in the colony.

Long Ifland, the part of this great fettlement which the navigators firft meet with, is feparated from the continent by a narrow channel.   It is one hundred and twenty miles long, and twelve broad, and is divided into three counties.   The favages who occupied this great fpace, either removed from it, or perifhed fucceffively.   Their oppreffors owed their firft profperity to the whale and the feal fifhery.   When thefe fifh, who delight in deferted coafts, difappeared, the breeding of cattle, efpecially of horfes, was attended to. Some cultures have fince been eftablifhed upon this too fandy foil.

The ground is more uneven upon the continent; but it becomes more even and more fertile in proportion as one approaches the lakes of Canada.   If the marfhes which ftill cover the extremity of this colony fhould be ever dried up, and if the rivers by which it is watered fhould be ever confined within their beds, this country will become the moft fruitful of the colony.

According to the laft accounts, the province contains two hundred and fifty thoufand inhabitants, of various nations and of different feds.   The rich peltries which they obtain from the favages, and fuch of their own produdions as they do not confume, are conveyed to the general mart.   This is a city of importance, at prefent known, as well as the reft of the colony, by the name of New York. It was formerly built by the Dutch, in the ifland of Manahatton, which is fourteen miles long, and one mile is its greateft breadth.

Trade hath collected in this city, the climate of which is very wholefome, eighteen or twenty thou-fand inhabitants, upon an extent of ground which is partly low and partly raifed. The ftreets are very ir-regular, but exceedingly neat. The houfes, built with brick, and covered with tiles, are more convenient than elegant. The provifions are abundant, of excel-lent quality, and cheap. Eafy circumftances prevail univerfally. The loweft clafs of people have a certain refource in oyfters, the fifhery of which alone employs two hundred boats.

The town, fituated two miles from the mouth of Hudfon's River, hath, properly fpeaking, neither har-bour nor bafon, but doth not ftand in need of either. Its port, which is open in all feafons, is acceffible to fhips of the largeft fizes, and being fheltered from all ftorms, is fufficient for it. From hence the numerous fhips come forth, which are difpatched to different la-titudes. The provifions or merchandife which were exported in 1769, amounted to 4,352,446 livres 7 fols 9 deniers [about 181,351l. 18s. 8d.]. Since this pe-riod, the productions of the colony have increafed vi-fibly; and this increafe muft be carried ftill further, fince no more than one half of the lands are cleared, and fince thofe grounds which are fo are not fo well cultivated as they will be when the population fhall become more confiderable.

The Dutch, who were the firft founders of the co-lony, eftablifhed in it that fpirit of order and economy which is the univerfal characteriftic of their nation. As they always conftituted the majority of the peo-ple, even after thefe had changed mafters, thofe whom conqueft had affociated to them generally adopted their manners. The Germans, compelled to take re-fuge in America by the religious perfecution which

B O O K drove them out of the Palatinate, or the other pro-
XVII. vinces of the empire, were naturally inclined to this
modeft behaviour; and the Englifh and French, who
were not accuftomed to fo much frugality, foon con-
formed, either from motives of wifdom or emulation,
to a mode of living lefs expenfive and more familiar
than that which is regulated by fafhion and parade.
From thence it followed, that the colonifts did not
contract any debts with the mother-country; that
they preferved an entire liberty in their fales and pur-
chafes, and have been enabled always to give the moft
advantageous turn to their affairs.

Such was the ftate of the colony till 1763. At this
period New York became the general abode of the
principal officers and of part of the troops which Great
Britain thought neceffary to maintain in North America, either to keep it in awe, or to defend it. This
multitude of unemployed or unmarried men, who
were conftantly endeavouring to deceive their own
idlenefs, and to ftrive againft the wearifomenefs of life,
difperfed themfelves among the citizens, to whom they
infpired a tafte for the luxuries of the table, and a turn
for play. By their affiduity with the women, their
converfation and their manners, they engaged them
in thofe frivolous purfuits, thofe gallantries, and thofe
amufements which had fo much allurement for them.
The two fexes foon led the fame kind of life. They
rofe with the fame projects, and went to bed with the
fame extravagant ideas. This pernicious fpirit communicated itfelf from one to another, and it ftill continues, unlefs the terrible fcenes which have fince
ftained thefe countries with blood have brought about
a happy revolution in the manners.

Revolu-   New Jerfey is fituated in the neighbourhood of
tions which New York, and was known at firft by the name of
have hap-
pened in   New Sweden. It was called thus by fome adventu-
New Jer-   rers of that nation, who landed upon thefe favage coafts
fey.   towards the year 1638. They formed three fettlements there, Chriftiana, Elzimbourg, and Gottenbourg.
This colony was of no importance when it was attack-

ed and conquered by the Dutch. Thofe of the inhabitants who had a greater regard for their mother-
country than for their plantations returned into Europe. The others fubmitted to the laws of the conqueror, and their territory was united to New Belgia.
When the Duke of York received the inveftiture of
the province to which he gave his name, he feparated
what had been added, and divided it between two of
his favourites, under the name of New Jerfey.

Carteret and Berkley, the firft of whom received
the eaftern, and the other the weftern part of the province, folicited this vaft territory, with no other view
but to put it up to fale. Several fpeculative perfons
purchafed from them large diftricts at a low price,
which they fold again in fmaller parcels. In the midft
of thefe fubdivifions, the colony remained divided into two diftinct provinces, each feparately governed by
the heirs of their original proprietors. The difficulties
which they experienced in their adminiftration difgufted them of this kind of fovereignty, which indeed was
ill adapted to the condition of a fubject. They gave
up their charter to the crown in 1702; and from that
time the two provinces became one, and, like the
greater part of the other Englifh colonies, were under
the direction of a governor, a council, and the deputies
of the commons.

This large country, before the revolution, contained
only fixteen thoufand inhabitants, the defcendants of
Swedes and Dutch, who were its firft cultivators;
fome Quakers, and fome Church of England men
with a great number of Scotch Prefbyterians, had joined the colonifts of the two nations. The defects of
government ftopped the progrefs, and occafioned the
indigence, of this fmall colony. It might therefore
have been expected, that the era of liberty fhould have
been that of the profperity of the colony; but almoft
all the Europeans who went to the New World, in
fearch either of an afylum or riches, preferred Pennfylvania or Carolina, which had acquired a greater
fhare of celebrity. At length, however, New Jerfey

B O O K
XVII.

Prefent
ftate of
New Jer-
fey, and
what it
may be-
come.
hath been peopled; and it reckons at prefent one
hundred and thirty thoufand inhabitants.

The colony is covered with flocks and with grain in
abundance. Hemp thrives better there than in any of
the neighbouring countries. An excellent copper
mine hath been worked with fuccefs in it. Its coafts
are acceffible, and the port of Amboix, its capital, is
tolerably good. It is in want of none of the means of
profperity proper for that part of the globe, and yet
it hath always remained in a profound obfcurity. Its
name is fcarcely known in the Old World, and not
much more in the New. But, perhaps, it is not on this
account the more unfortunate.

If we read over the hiftory of nations both ancient
and modern, it will be found, that there is fcarce any
one of them, the fplendour of which hath not been
acquired but at the expence of its felicity. People of
whom no mention fhall have been made in the melancholy annals of the world muft neither have been
aggreffors, nor expofed to attacks; they muft not
have interrupted the tranquillity of others, nor muft
theirs have been difturbed by diftant or neighbouring
enemies. They muft not have had heroes who had
returned to their country laden with the fpoils of the
enemy. They muft have had no hiftorian to relate
either their miferies or their crimes. There mankind
would never have fhuddered from one age to another,
at the fight of thofe monuments which call to mind,
in all parts, the effufion of blood, and the fhackles of
flavery impofed at a diftance, or broken at home.
They muft not have been torn to pieces by political
factions, nor intoxicated by abfurd opinions. The
oppreffion of tyranny muft never have drawn tears
from their eyes, nor excited them to revolt. They
muft never have delivered themfelves from a defpot
by affaffination, nor muft they ever have exterminated
nis fatellites; for fuch are the events which at all
times have given a celebrity to nations. On the contrary, in the midft of a long and profound tranquillity,
the fields would have been cultivated, fome traditional

hymns would have been fung in honour of the Deity, and the fame love fongs would have been handed down from one generation to the other. Wherefore muft this alluring picture of happinefs be chimerical? Becaufe it hath never exifted; and if it fhould exift, it could not poffibly be for a long time in the midft of turbulent and ambitious nations. Whatever may be the reafon of the obfcurity of New Jerfey, it is our duty to give them our advice upon their prefent and future fituation.

The poverty of this province not fuffering it at firft to open a direct trade with the diftant or foreign markets, it was obliged to fell its productions at Philadelphia, and more commonly at New York; it obtained from thefe cities, in exchange, fome merchandife of the mother-country, and a few of the productions of the iflands. Their richeft merchants even advanced money to the province, which kept it ftill more in a ftate of dependence. Notwithftanding the increafe of its cultures and of its productions, it hath not yet fhaken off this kind of fervitude. We have now before us, accounts of incontestable authority, which prove, that in 1762 New Jerfey did not fend any fhips to Europe; and that it fent only twenty-four boats to the Weft Indies, the value of whofe cargoes did not amount to more than 56,965 livres 19 fols 9 deniers [about 2373l. 11s. 8d.]. All the reft of its territorial riches were delivered to the neighbouring colonies who traded with them.

This fituation is both ruinous and degrading. New Jerfey muft itfelf conftruct fhips, all the materials for which nature hath given it. It muft fend them out into divers feas, fince it is no longer in want of men. It muft convey its productions to the people, who have hitherto only received them through the means of intermediatory agents. It muft provide itfelf with the produce of foreign induftry at firft hand, for which it hath hitherto paid too dear, on account of the ufelefs circuits it hath gone through. It may then form vaft projects, devote itfelf to great enterprifes, be raifed to

B O O K that rank to which its advantages feem to call it, and
XVII. be more upon a level with the provinces which have
too long deſtroyed it by their ſhadow, or eclipſed it
with their ſplendour.

May the views which I offer, and the counſels I
addreſs to New Jerſey, be realized! May I live long
enough to be a witneſs of them, and to rejoice at
them. The happineſs of my fellow creatures, at whatever diſtance they may exiſt from me, hath never been
indifferent to me: but I have felt myſelf moved with
warm concern, in favour of thoſe whom ſuperſtition or
tyranny have expelled from their native country. I
have commiſerated their ſufferings. When they have
embarked, I have turned my eyes up towards Heaven.
My voice hath been joined to the noiſe of the winds
and the waves which were carrying them beyond the
ſeas; and I have repeatedly exclaimed, Let them proſper! Let them find in the deſert and ſavage region
which they are going to inhabit, a felicity equal, or
even ſuperior, to ours; and if they ſhould found an
empire there, let them think of preſerving themſelves
and their poſterity from the calamities which they have
felt.

END OF THE FIFTH VOLUME.